A Commentary on Cicero, De Divinatione II

MICHIGAN CLASSICAL COMMENTARIES

Andrew R. Dyck
A Commentary on Cicero, *De Divinatione II*

Patrick Paul Hogan
A Student Commentary on Pausanius Book 1

Celia E. Schultz
A Commentary on Cicero, *De Divinatione I*

Erin K. Moodie
Plautus' *Poenulus*: A Student Commentary

Donka D. Markus
Reading Medieval Latin with the Legend of Barlaam and Josaphat

Patrick Paul Hogan
A Student Commentary on Pausanius Book 2

Charles Platter
A Student Commentary on Plato's *Euthyphro*

A Commentary on Cicero, *De Divinatione II*

Andrew R. Dyck

University of Michigan Press
Ann Arbor

Published in the United States of America by the
University of Michigan Press
Manufactured in the United States of America
Printed on acid-free paper
First published August 2020

A CIP catalog record for this book is available from the British Library.

Library of Congress Cataloging-in-Publication Data

Names: Cicero, Marcus Tullius. De divinatione. Liber 2. | Dyck, Andrew R. (Andrew Roy), 1947– Commentary on Cicero, De divinatione II.

Title: A commentary on Cicero, De divinatione II / Andrew R. Dyck.

Description: Ann Arbor : University of Michigan Press, 2020. | Series: Michigan classical commentaries | Contains the Latin text of Cicero's De divinatione, Liber 2 and commentary in English by Andrew R. Dyck. | Includes bibliographical references and indexes.

Identifiers: LCCN 2020006812 | ISBN 9780472074570 (hardcover) | ISBN 9780472054572 (paperback)

Subjects: LCSH: Cicero, Marcus Tullius. De divinatione. Liber 2. | Divination—Early works to 1800.

Classification: LCC PA6296 .D15 2020 | DDC 202/.3—dc23

LC record available at https://lccn.loc.gov/2020006812

For Janis

Preface

"What is wrong with Book 2?" was the (half-serious) response of a graduate student of F. Santangelo's upon hearing the news that a second commentary on Book 1 of *De divinatione* was being published within a decade of the previous one.[1] The subtext is that for an English commentary on Book 2 one still had to have recourse to a book written in the early '20s. I hope that this volume will supply what was missing and show that there is, in fact, nothing wrong with Book 2 but that, to the contrary, it is a vibrant and feisty text, filled with wry humor and goal-oriented argumentation on a subject of great interest both when it was written and today.

A word may be in order about the commentary from 1923 that has previously been the Anglophone student's chief tool for understanding this text. It was written by Arthur Stanley Pease (1881–1964), who once said of himself: "I will confess that I am by nature a collector, that I began with marbles and horse chestnuts, advanced to postage stamps, continued with botany and books, and at all times have gathered facts and occasional ideas."[2] His commentary on *De divinatione* was the first of several that he produced, the other two being devoted to Book 4 of the *Aeneid* (1935) and *De natura deorum* (1955–58). In all of them, his talent for collecting and organizing materials is on full display. Even in its day, however, Pease's technique of commentary, focused on individual words or phrases taken for the most part out of context, was retrograde, predecessors such as Richard Heinze on Lucretius 3 (1897) having shown how the author's train of thought can be reconstructed or Eduard Norden on *Aeneid* 6 having elucidated the structure of the text (1st edition 1903). What Pease does provide, however, is a resource of lasting value for understanding the text, and as a collection of parallels for its words and phrases, it will not be superseded by this or any other commentary.

As C. E. Schultz remarked (2014, vii), Pease's commentary "is not suited

1. Santangelo 2016b, 309.
2. Pease, "Twenty-Fifth Anniversary Class Report," quoted by Elder et al. 1965, ix.

to most readers who approach the text today." Of more recent commentaries, that of Timpanaro (1988) can be recommended for those who read Italian. This commentary aims to make the text more accessible to Anglophone students and other readers. The goal is not to produce a "potted Pease," but rather, using Pease's materials as well as more recent insights into the Latin language, Roman history, religion, and philosophy, to rethink the text, raise questions today's readers may find of interest, and offer references to enable them to follow up and form views of their own.

Unfortunately, Wynne 2019 came into my hands only after this book was already in press and so could not be taken into account in what follows. My confidence in my conclusion on Marcus' tentative Philonian/Metrodorian position on theology was strengthened, however, when I saw that he follows a similar approach (Wynne 2019, ch. 6; 27–29 below). However, his attempt to establish a different status for Marcus' arguments at §§148b ff. from the rest of Book 2 is unconvincing in view of the similar position taken at §41 and on superstition throughout (cf. on §148b). Wynne bases his argument on the phrase *ut vere loquamur* (§148b), which he takes to indicate that the author drops the mask of the dialogue speaker (Wynne 2019, 267). Though this, and the similar *(ut) vere dicam*, are formulas by which a speaker suggests that he is being candid, it does not have the effect of the speaker's dropping of the mask; cf. *De orat.* 2.15, *Leg.* 2.4, and *Brut.* 232. In any case, readers will be well advised to supplement this commentary with Wynne 2019, chs. 5 and 6.

I would like to thank Dr. Ellen Bauerle, acquiring editor for classics at University of Michigan Press, for her support and encouragement throughout, to the Press's anonymous readers for a number of helpful suggestions, and to John T. Ramsey for a critical review of the biographical section of the Introduction. I am responsible for remaining errors. My greatest debt is indicated in the dedication.

Contents

Abbreviations

Some works cited here are abbreviated as follows:

Adam	J. Adam. 1963. *The* Republic *of Plato, edited with critical notes, commentary, and appendices.* 2nd ed. 2 vols. Cambridge (repr. 1979–80).
Alesse	F. Alesse. 1997. *Panezio di Rodi: Testimonianze; Edizione, traduzione e commento.* Naples.
Astbury	R. Astbury. 1985. *M. Terentii Varronis Saturarum Menippearum fragmenta.* Leipzig.
Ax	W. Ax. 1938. *M. Tulli Ciceronis scripta quae manserunt omnia.* Vol. 46, *De divinatione, De fato, Timaeus.* Leipzig (repr. Stuttgart, 1965).
Barigazzi	A. Barigazzi. 1966. *Favorino di Arelate, Opere: Introduzione, testo critico e commento.* Florence.
Bl.	J. Blänsdorf. 2011. *Fragmenta poetarum Latinorum epicorum et lyricorum praeter Enni Annales et Ciceronis Germanicique Aratea post W. Morel et K. Büchner.* Berlin.
BNP	H. Cancik and H. Schneider. 2002–17. *Brill's New Pauly.* 30 vols. Leiden.
Breysig	A. Breysig. 1867. *Germanici Caesaris Aratea cum scholiis.* Berlin (repr. Hildesheim, 1967).
CA	I. U. Powell. 1925. *Collectanea Alexandrina.* Oxford.
CAG	*Commentaria in Aristotelem Graeca.* 1882–1909. 23 vols. Berlin.
CAH	*Cambridge Ancient History.* 1970–2005. 2nd ed. 14 vols. Cambridge.
CCAG	F. Cumont and F. Boll. 1898–1953. *Corpus codicum astrologorum Graecorum.* 12 vols. Brussels.
CGL	G. Goetz. 1888–1923. *Corpus glossariorum Latinorum.* 7 vols. Leipzig.
CSEL	*Corpus scriptorum ecclesiasticorum Latinorum.* 1864–. Vienna.

del Corno	D. del Corno. 1969. *Graecorum de re onirocritica scriptorum reliquiae*. Milan.
Courtney	E. Courtney. 2003. *The Fragmentary Latin Poets*. Oxford (paperback ed. with addenda; orig. 1993).
Cugusi	P. Cugusi. 1970. *Epistolographi Latini minores*. Vol. 1: *Aetatem anteciceronianum amplectens*. Turin.
D.–K.	H. Diels. 1964. *Die Fragmente der Vorsokratiker*. 3 vols. 11th ed. Ed. W. Kranz. Zurich.
E.–K.	L. Edelstein and I. G. Kidd. 1989. *Posidonius*. 2nd ed. Cambridge.
E.–M.	A. Ernout and A. Meillet. 1959. *Dictionnaire étymologique de la langue Latine*. 4th ed. Paris.
Falconer	*See* Falconer 1923a *in Bibliography*.
FGrH	F. Jacoby et al. 1923–. *Die Fragmente der Griechischen Historiker*. Berlin, Leiden.
Frassinetti	P. Frassinetti. 1955. *Fabularum atellanarum fragmenta*. Turin.
FRH	T. J. Cornell. 2013. *The Fragments of the Roman Historians*. 3 vols. Oxford.
FRL	S. M. Goldberg and G. Manuwald. 2018. *Fragmentary Republican Latin: Ennius*. Cambridge, MA.
G.	A. Grilli. 1962. *M. Tulli Ciceronis Hortensius*. Milan.
G–L	B. L. Gildersleeve and G. Lodge. 1895. *Gildersleeve's Latin Grammar*. 3rd ed. New York (repr. Wauconda, IL, 1989).
Garbarino	I. Garbarino. 1984. *M. Tulli Ciceronis fragmenta*. Turin.
H–S	J. B. Hofmann and A. Szantyr. 1965. *Lateinische Syntax und Stilistik*. Munich.
Huschke	P. E. Huschke. 1908. *Iurisprudentiae anteiustinianae reliquiae in usum maxime academicum compositae*. 6th ed. Ed. E. Seckel and B. Kuebler. Leipzig.
Iordan	H. Iordan. 1860. *M. Catonis praeter librum De re rustica quae extant*. Leipzig.
J.	H. D. Jocelyn. 1967. *The Tragedies of Ennius*. Cambridge.
K.	W. Krenkel. 1970. *Lucilius, Satiren: Lateinisch und Deutsch*. Berlin.
Kn.	R. Kannicht. 2004. *Euripides* (= *TGrF* 5). 2 vols. Göttingen.
Körte	A. Körte. 1959. *Menandri quae supersunt*. Pars altera. 2nd ed. Ed. A. Thierfelder. Leipzig.
K–S	R. Kühner and C. Stegmann. 1962. *Ausführliche Grammatik der lateinischen Sprache*. 2. Teil, *Satzlehre*. 4th ed. Ed. A. Thierfelder. 2 vols. Hannover.
L.	W. M. Lindsay. 1933. *Sexti Pompei Festi De verborum significatu quae supersunt cum Pauli epitome*. Leipzig.
Lasserre	F. Lasserre. 1966. *Eudoxos von Knidos: Die Fragmente*. Berlin.

LIMC	*Lexicon iconographicum mythologiae classicae*. 1981–99. 18 vols. Zurich.
LPPR	G. Rotondi. 1912. *Leges publicae populi Romani*. Milan.
L–S	A. A. Long and D. N. Sedley. 1987. *The Hellenistic Philosophers*. 2 vols. Cambridge.
LSJ	H. G. Liddell and R. Scott. 1940. *A Greek-English Lexicon*. 9th ed. Ed. H. S. Jones. Oxford.
LTUR	E. M. Steinby. 1993–2000. *Lexicon topographicum urbis Romae*. 6 vols. Rome.
Mette	H.-J. Mette. 1985. "Weitere Akademiker heute (Fortsetzung von Lustr. 26,7–94): Von Lakydes bis zu Kleitomachus." *Lustrum* 27: 39–148.
Mirhady	D. C. Mirhady. 2001. "Dicaearchus of Messana: The Sources, Text and Translation." In W. W. Fortenbaugh and E. Schütrumpf, eds., *Dicaearchus of Messana: Text, Translation, and Discussion*, 1–142. New Brunswick.
MRR	T. R. S. Broughton. 1951–86. *Magistrates of the Roman Republic*. 3 vols. New York, Atlanta.
NLS	E. C. Woodcock. 1959. *A New Latin Syntax*. Cambridge, MA.
OCD	S. Hornblower, A. Spawforth, and E. Eidinow. 2012. *The Oxford Classical Dictionary*. 4th ed. Oxford.
OLD	P. G. W. Glare. 1982. *Oxford Latin Dictionary*. Oxford.
Pease	A. S. Pease. 1920–23. *M. Tulli Ciceronis De divinatione libri duo*. Urbana (repr. Darmstadt, 1963).
PHI	Classical Latin Texts: A Resource Prepared by Packard Humanities Institute (http://latin.packhum.org/).
PL	J.-P. Migne. 1841–1902. *Patrologia Latina*. Paris.
R.[3]	O. Ribbeck. 1897. *Tragicorum Romanorum fragmenta*. 3rd ed. Leipzig.
RE	G. Wissowa, K. Mittelhaus, and K. Ziegler. 1893–1980. *Paulys Realencyclopädie der classischen Altertumswissenschaft*. 83 vols. Stuttgart.
Rose	V. Rose. 1886. *Aristotelis qui ferebantur librorum fragmenta*. Leipzig.
Roth	C. L. Roth. 1871. *C. Suetoni Tranquilli quae supersunt omnia*. Leipzig.
RRC	M. H. Crawford. 1974. *Roman Republican Coinage*. 2 vols. Cambridge.
Schäublin	C. Schäublin. 1991. *M. T. Cicero, Über die Wahrsagung*. Munich.
sch. Bob.	*See* Stangl.
SH	H. Lloyd-Jones and P. Parsons. 1983. *Supplementum Hellenisticum*. Berlin.

Sk. O. Skutsch. 1985. *The* Annals *of Q. Ennius*. Oxford.

Smith M. F. Smith. 1984. "Diogenes of Oenoanda, New Fragments 122–24." *Anatolian Studies* 34: 43–57.

SOD P. Stork, J. M. van Ophuijsen, and T. Dorandi. 2000. "Demetrius of Phalerum: The Sources, Text and Translation." In W. W. Fortenbaugh and E. Schütrumpf, eds., *Demetrius of Phalerum: Text, Translation and Discussion*, 1–310. New Brunswick.

Soubiran J. Soubiran. 1972. *Cicéron: Aratea, fragments poétiques*. Paris.

Stangl T. Stangl. 1912. *Ciceronis orationum scholiastae: Asconius, scholia Bobiensia, scholia Pseudasconii Sangallensia, scholia Cluniacensia et recentiora Ambrosiana ac Vaticana, scholia Lugdunensia sive Gronoviana et eorum excerpta Lugdunensia; Commentarii*. Leipzig (repr. Hildesheim, 1964).

Sudhaus S. Sudhaus. 1892–96. *Philodemi volumina rhetorica*. 2 vols. Leipzig.

SVF I. ab Arnim. 1903–24. *Stoicorum veterum fragmenta*. 4 vols. Leipzig.

TGrF B. Snell et al. 1971–2004. *Tragicorum Graecorum fragmenta*. 5 vols. in 6. Göttingen.

TLG *Thesaurus linguae Graecae*. University of California, Irvine (stephanus.tlg.uci.edu).

TLL *Thesaurus linguae Latinae*. 1900–. Leipzig.

TLRR M. C. Alexander. 1990. *Trials of the Late Roman Republic, 149 BC to 50 BC*. Toronto.

TRF G. Manuwald. 2012. *Tragicorum Romanorum fragmenta*. Vol. 2, *Ennius*. Göttingen.

Usener H. Usener. 1887. *Epicurea*. Leipzig.

Vitelli C. Vitelli. 1979. *M. Tulli Ciceronis Consolationis fragmenta*. Turin.

W(armington) E. H. Warmington. 1935. *Remains of Old Latin*. 4 vols. Cambridge, MA.

Wachsm. C. Wachsmuth. 1897. *Ioannis Laurenti Lydi Liber de ostentis et calendaria graeca omnia*. 2nd ed. Leipzig.

We F. Wehrli. 1967–74. *Die Schule des Aristoteles*. 10 vols. + 2 supplements. 2nd ed. Basel.

Concerning the Text

De divinatione is one of eight Ciceronian philosophical works transmitted in what is known as the "Leiden corpus," which is so named because three of its four principal codices are housed in the library of the University of Leiden. The two oldest are Voss. Lat. 84 (A) and Voss. Lat. F 86 (B), both written in the middle of the ninth century in northeastern France. A third Carolingian ms., Vienna 189 (V), was copied in the early ninth century, perhaps at Ferrières. The other notable ms., H, also kept in the library of the University of Leiden (Leiden B.P.L. 118), was written in Montecassino in the eleventh century. B forms its own branch of the family tree, whereas AVH occupy another at one remove from the archetype, as is shown on the slightly simplified diagram below:[1]

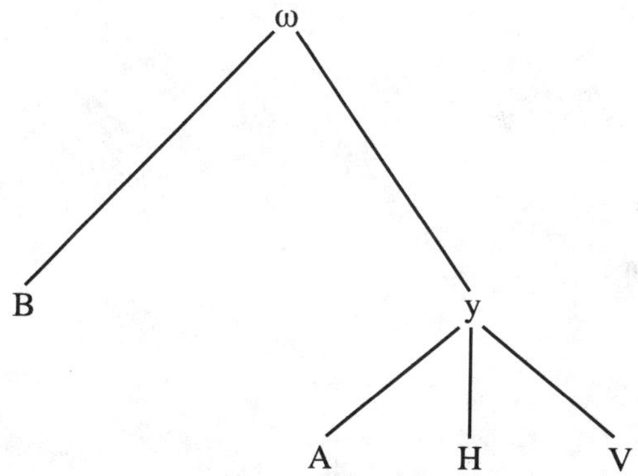

This text follows the edition of W. Ax (Leipzig, 1938), based upon preliminary studies by O. Plasberg. Students should note the preference here for *u* rather than *i* in open medial syllables before labials (e.g., *maxumus*, not *maximus*; cf. Adams 2016, 204–5) and a less thoroughgoing assimilation of verbal prefixes than is often found (e.g., *adfers*, not *affers*). The text printed

1. For the transmission, see further R. H. Rouse in Reynolds 1983, 124–28.

here shows some variations from Ax-Plasberg in punctuation, paragraphing, and spelling (e.g., Claudius, not Clodius [§§20 and 71], second declension genitives such as *negoti*, not *negotii* [§40]; cf. Leumann 1977, 424-25), as well as the following deviations. Since this book is meant for teaching, there is a bias toward printing an intelligible text (as opposed to enclosing corrupt matter within *cruces*):

Ax	Dyck
12 vatis	vates ($V^{corr.}$)
13 vatis	vates ($BV^{corr.}$)
15 ut vel aliter cadere atque evenire	ut vel <non cadere atque evenire vel> aliter cadere atque evenire ($V^{corr.}$)
17 facta	[facta] (secl. Timpanaro in adn.)
21 ‘Certe potuit’.	certe <non> potuit (Pearce)
22 in solitudine Aegyptiorum	in solitudine, <scelere> Aegyptiorum (Dyck)
33b dicuntur	dicunt ($A^{corr.}$)
36a tristissuma	[tristissuma] (secl. Hottinger)
37 ortus atque obitus (Davies)	interitus atque ortus (Davies)
39 dicis esse	esse dicis (textus traditus)
40 recte	recta (Dyck)
41 non est autem divinatio	<si est divinatio, sunt di;> non est autem divinatio (Dyck)
47 radicem	[radicem] (secl. Dyck)
<ex>cogitavit (Markland)	cogitavit (textus traditus)
48 set quadringentis (Plasberg)	sed quadringentis (Davies)
52b tramitteret	transmitteret (V^2)
54 ea di inmortales primum	di inmortales primum ea (Lambinus)
59 rosissent	rossent (textus traditus)
62a †cum	[cum] (om. Davies)
63 penetraret	†penetraret (susp. Timpanaro)
64 duro formavit tegmine saxi	†duro formavit† tegmine saxi (susp. Timpanaro)
vorsarier ($A^{corr.}$)	versarier (B)
68 subita	subito (Lambinus)
humano satu	divino satu (Schäublin)
72 inquit	[inquit] (susp. Christ)
77 nam ex acuminibus quidem, quod totum auspicium militare est, iam M. Marcellus ille quinquiens consul totum omisit, idem imperator idem augur optumus. ubi ergo avium divinatio? quae, quoniam ab iis qui auspicia nulla habent bella administrantur, ab urbanis retenta videtur, a bellicis esse sublata.	ubi ergo avium divinatio? quae, quoniam ab iis qui auspicia nulla habent bella administrantur, ad urbanas res [a.u.r. ci. Müller] retenta videtur, a bellicis esse sublata. nam ex acuminibus quidem, quod totum auspicium militare est, iam M. Marcellus ille quinquiens consul totum omisit, idem imperator idem augur optumus. (transpos. Madvig)
79 Trochamorum	Trocmorum (Brodaeus)
82 nominaverunt	<ita> nominaverunt (Timpanaro)
86 sit	sit<a est> (Marsus)
92b quicumque gignantur	quicumque <eodem tempore> gignantur (Schäublin)
nonne eius modi sunt	nonne eius modi <ea> sunt (Timpanaro)

Ax	Dyck
93 Troglodytas (ed. Veneta 1496)	Trogodytas (-itas textus traditus)
94 sint	sunt V$^{\text{corr.}}$
quod non certe pertinet	quod [non] certe pertinet (*non* om. Davies)
95 declarant	declarat (Davies)
106 nec si significent, non dare	nec si significent, non dant (in mg. Lambinus 1565)
108 existimandus sit	existimandus est (Dyck)
111 ex primis versus litteris	ex primis <cuiusque> versus litteris (Christ)
112 ex primo versu . . . litteris	<excerptis> ex primo versu . . . litteris (Dyck)
illius sententiae	[illius sententiae] (secl. Giomini)
115 obsides	obtines (Ursinus coll. Var. *L.* 7.17)
deferendae	deferenda (V$^{\text{corr.}}$)
116 aio	aiio (Timpanaro post Skutsch ad Enn. *An.* v. 167)
117 eduntur non modo	eduntur? <cur> non modo (Schäublin)
†tantum modo iam†	tam otiosa iacent (Schäublin)
123 gubernantibus	<gubernationem> gubernantibus (Dyck)
124 quoque	[quoque] (secl. Christ)
125 et horum neutrum	at horum neutrum (Ascensius 1521)
127b inscitius	insidiosius (Dyck)
129a somnio	somno (A^{1}; cf. 1.40, §§27, 126)
132 poëta nemo ne<mo>	poëta nemone <nemo> (Timpanaro)
133 Pacuianus	Pacuvianus (B$^{\text{corr.}}$)
137 'quod fuerat; plena sunt imaginum omnia.' ista igitur me imago Mari in campum Atinatem persequebatur?	'quod fuerat.' ista igitur me imago Mari in campum Atinatem persequebatur? 'Plena sunt imaginum omnia.' (transp. Christ)
143 opinio erroris	opinio [erroris] (secl. Dyck)
148b is libris	iis libris (A)

Introduction

Life of Cicero

Marcus Tullius Cicero was born on January 3, 106, to an equestrian family in the town (*municipium*) of Arpinum, some sixty miles southeast of Rome. Although citizens of Arpinum had enjoyed Roman citizenship as early as 188, the Social War (91–89) was a major cataclysm in Cicero's early life and brought issues of citizenship and identity to the fore (resulting in the general enfranchisement of Italians residing south of the Po River). His origin in a *municipium* was an important part of Cicero's identity, as he himself emphasized when he spoke of having "two homelands" (*duo patriae*: *Leg.* 2.5), though it was more frequently his adversaries who emphasized this fact in public.[1]

Cicero evidently showed early promise, since his father, also named Marcus Tullius Cicero, a studious man but burdened by chronic ill-health, devoted himself to overseeing the education of Marcus and his somewhat younger brother Quintus. Equipped with outstanding verbal skills, an excellent memory, and a competitive nature, Cicero seems to have been marked out for a career at the bar and in politics, being assigned at an early age to memorize Rome's first law code, the Twelve Tables (*Leg.* 2.59), and read speeches of the *novus homo* C. Flavius Fimbria (cos. 104: *Brut.* 129), a possible role model.[2] The elder Cicero moved to a house in Rome and arranged to have the boys taught by outstanding tutors in the home of L. Licinius Crassus (cos. 95; *De orat.* 2.1–2).

After he assumed the man's toga in a ceremony probably held on the Liberalia (March 17, 90) in Arpinum, Cicero was placed in the charge of Q. Mucius Scaevola the Augur (cos. 117) for the *tirocinium fori*, that is, he was allowed to be present when the great man gave responses to clients seeking legal advice and observe his activities in the Forum, the Roman way of learning

1. See further Carlà-Uhink 2017 with literature. All dates are BCE unless otherwise indicated. Here the annotation is kept to a minimum; for further references see Dyck (forthcoming). References to *Div.* are by book number for Book 1 and to chapter preceded by § for Book 2.

2. See van der Blom 2010, 158, 160, 183, 284.

the law.[3] It was in the circle of Scaevola that Cicero first made the acquaintance of another studious young equestrian, Titus Pomponius, later called Atticus, who would be his fast friend for life (*Amic.* 2). Cicero's legal apprenticeship was interrupted, however, probably in 89, by his being called to duty in the Social War that had recently flared between Rome and its Italian allies, seeking to assert independence.[4] By 88 Cicero was back in Rome and, besides continuing his legal training, was closely observing the assembly speeches (*contiones*) of the tribune of the plebs P. Sulpicius Rufus, who was a gifted orator, but not above inciting mob violence. Sulpicius was killed when Sulla marched on Rome later that year, and his head was placed on the Rostra as a bloody warning.[5]

Troubles between political factions, including a civil war culminating in Sulla's victory in November 82, continued to occupy Rome for much of the 80s. With forensic business suspended, Cicero was forced to postpone his debut at the bar to the end of the decade. But in fact, it was this period of enforced, intense study of rhetoric and philosophy with outstanding Greek teachers, above all Molon of Rhodes and Philo of Larissa, that set Cicero apart, or so he later hinted, from other orators (*Brut.* 322, a description of the deficiencies of his rivals). During this time he produced a rhetorical treatise, *De inventione*, and translations of philosophical works (Xenophon's *Oeconomicus*, Plato's *Protagoras*).

Realizing that in regard to his delivery an orator could profit from close observation of actors on the stage, Cicero cultivated an acquaintance with the leading actor of the day, Q. Roscius, and it was Roscius who brokered Cicero's participation in his first extant defense, that of P. Quinctius, Roscius' brother-in-law. As the *Pro Quinctio* of 81 shows, Cicero began his work at the bar as a polished advocate.[6] One pattern among Cicero's early clients is that they tend to be outsiders lacking access to powerful circles at Rome. Thus Quinctius had Marian connections, which he did not repudiate, even though, under Sulla, such ties were undesirable. Another early client was a woman from Arretium who was struggling to assert her right to Roman citizenship in the face of penalties imposed on her city by Sulla. Yet another, a defendant on charges of poisoning, was Titinia the wife of Cotta. Sextus Roscius from the Umbrian *municipium* of Ameria is a partial exception to the pattern: Cicero portrays him in 80 as the victim of a powerful *societas* in which Sulla's freedman Chrysogonus played a role, but Roscius did have support from the noble family of the Metelli (thanks to his father's connections). Another Umbrian client, but apparently without

3. *Amic.* 1; cf. J. Regner, *RE* 6A2:1450.25 (s.v. Tirocinium fori); Stroup 2010, 141–55; Scholz 2011, 264–91.

4. On the Social War, cf. Mouritsen 1998, ch. 3.2; for Cicero's service, Mitchell 1979, 9; in the course of that service, he witnessed the incident described at 1.72 and §65.

5. *Rhet. Her.* 4.31; Cic. *Brut.* 306; Vell. 2.19.1.

6. See also *Brut.* 311.

Sextus Roscius' ties to the nobility, was L. Varenus, an unsuccessful defense that Cicero nonetheless published.[7]

His early advocacy brought Cicero some successes, notably in Sextus Roscius' case (*Brut.* 312), and enabled him to contract a marriage with an upper-class woman, Terentia, so that he could establish a household and begin a family, their daughter Tullia being born probably on August 5, 79.[8] The early oratory did not, however, form the basis for a sustainable career, since Cicero was speaking with excessive vocal strain. In search of an improved technique, Cicero, accompanied by Quintus and others, embarked on a study-tour of Greece and Asia Minor, where he continued his training in rhetoric and philosophy (79–77).

When he returned from his extended trip "virtually transformed" (*prope mutatus*: *Brut.* 316), Cicero had to rebuild his forensic career virtually from the ground up. In addition, unlike most equites active at the bar, Cicero was also driven by ambition to seek public office, which he did in the year 76, canvassing for quaestor, the first rung on the career-ladder (*cursus honorum*) of the Roman politician. He was elected "among the first" of the candidates (*Pis.* 2) and assigned by lot to serve on the island of Sicily, a grain-rich province, in a time of scarcity (75). He took pride in his conscientious administration and that of his governor, Sextus Peducaeus[9] but later recalled his disappointment that achievements in the provinces scarcely registered at Rome (*Planc.* 64–65). This experience helped settle his Rome-centric orientation: he would decline to govern a province after his praetorship and consulship and accept such appointment only very reluctantly under pressure in 51.

For the remainder of the 70s Cicero participated, as a back-bencher, in meetings of the senate and handled low-profile cases before the bar, his clients determined by geographical and sociopolitical affinities, mostly from his ties to the equites and publicani. As he planned to canvass for aedile during the year 70, however, Cicero needed a way to distinguish himself from the pack.[10] He hit upon the idea of prosecuting C. Verres for extortion, Verres having recently returned from a three-year term as governor of Sicily (73–71). The move was not wholly risk-free, but one who read the political tea leaves as astutely as Cicero could see that the old order, in which the senatorial jurors took an indulgent view of senatorial defendants, was ripe for challenge and that such a challenge, carefully packaged as a protest against a corrupt system, could resonate with the electorate.

---

7. His publication practice would later become more discriminating, but at this early stage he needed to build a reputation and client-base; see further Melchior 2008.

8. Cf. Treggiari 2007, 28. On the birth of a son, Marcus jr., in 65, cf. *Att.* 1.2(11).1.

9. *Ver.* 2.3.182 (Cicero's own administration) and 2.2.56, 3.216, 4.142 (that of Peducaeus).

10. Cf. Steel 2012, 259 and 261.

Cicero and Verres were in some respects not dissimilar. Neither man was a member of the old nobility (though Verres' father was a member of the senate). They were thus both dependent on the favor of the nobles and on their ability to accumulate both literal and cultural capital. Verres played the game well, using his position as governor to assemble a large collection of artworks that he gave or lent out strategically to curry favor with the nobles. Cicero cannot suppress a certain envy at Verres' social success (*Ver.* 2.3.6–9).

Cicero claims that as governor Verres stated that his policy was to amass three fortunes, one for himself, one for his advocates, and the third for the jurors (*Ver.* 1.40). He was thus able to secure the services of Rome's leading advocate of the time, Q. Hortensius. Hortensius and Verres tried out various stratagems. They first put up Verres' former quaestor, Q. Caecilius Niger, as a collusive prosecutor. After Cicero had defeated Caecilius in a *divinatio* (a preliminary trial to choose the prosecutor), he faced a new maneuver: he requested and was granted 110 days for his onsite investigation of the Sicilians' complaints, but the next day, another prosecutor indicted a governor of Achaea for extortion and requested 108 days for his investigation (*Ver.* 2.1.30), thus placing his case ahead of Cicero's on the docket. In light of this apparently collusive move, it became clear that the defense strategy was to "run out the clock" of the current official year and force proceedings into the next one when, with a new constellation of magistrates, the prospects of the defense were likely to improve (*Ver.* 1.29–30). Cicero countered cleverly: instead of delivering a long set-speech in the first hearing of the case, he delivered a brief speech and then introduced, with devastating effect, a long parade of Sicilian witnesses against Verres (August 6–13). After the compulsory adjournment, Verres decided that the case was hopeless and departed for what must have been a comfortable exile. In the aftermath, Cicero published not only the delivered speeches (*Div. Caec.*, *Ver.* 1) but also five speeches he had prepared for the second session of the trial but had been unable to use.

The Verrine case and Cicero's portrayal of his handling of it were the making of his career at the bar, albeit the picture painted of Verres is very one-sided: it includes details that Cicero cannot have known from any source and must have made up out of whole cloth.[11] These speeches are the earliest examples he cites of his mature style (*Orat.* 103 and 131). Henceforth Cicero's *regnum* in the courts, not that of Hortensius, was destined to be the target of criticism (*Sul.* 21). The move also paid political dividends, since Cicero was elected to the aedileship with a greater vote-count than his colleague, in spite of the massive bribery deployed against him by Verres (*Ver.* 1.22–24; *Pis.* 2).

The aediles of Rome were in charge of various sorts of urban housekeeping,

---

11. Cf., e.g., Nisbet 1992; Freund 2013.

but the politically significant aspect of the post lay in the production of games for the entertainment of the populace, the point emphasized by Cicero as he anticipates entry into office (*Ver.* 2.5.36). A rich incumbent (or one willing to take on large debts) could leave a deep impression by mounting splendid entertainments (cf. *Off.* 2.57). Cicero, however, was in no position to compete at that level; he speaks, rather, of having offered aedilician entertainment in the year 69 "in line with my means" (*pro facultatibus*: *Off.* 2.58) and was helped by donations of goods brought to Rome for the purpose by the grateful Sicilians (Plut. *Cic.* 8.1–2).

During the early to mid-60s Cicero also continued to be active in the courts, choosing cases with an eye to his political advancement. Thus his defense of A. Caecina included another plea on behalf of the civil rights of Etruscan communities that had suffered discrimination under Sulla (*Caec.* 95–103). He appealed to influential groups of voters by his defense of the scribe Matrinius and his defense of members of electoral bribery clubs. Taking on Cluentius' case will have won him backing in Larinum and neighboring communities of Apulia and Samnium, where the defendant was popular (*Clu.* 197). In 67 he won election to the praetorship "at the top" of the list (*Pis.* 2) and went on to preside over the same (extortion) court where he had won his greatest forensic success (*MRR* 2:152). As praetor, he also delivered his first political speech at a *contio* in support of Manilius' bill placing Pompey in sole command of the war in Asia against Mithridates VI of Pontus, a relatively uncontroversial move. In 65 he burnished his *popularis* credentials with a defense of the tribune of the plebs C. Cornelius, accused of treason (*maiestas*) for ignoring the veto of a fellow-tribune (*TLRR* 209). Cicero also shrewdly avoided other defenses, such as that of Manilius, also accused of *maiestas*. By 64, in spite of being a *novus homo* without previous family members in government, Cicero was poised to mount a strong candidacy for the consulate.

L. Sergius Catilina (usually known in Anglophone literature as "Catiline") and C. Antonius, two figures with checkered pasts, formed an electoral alliance (*coitio*) and emerged as Cicero's chief rivals. Catiline began his career as a Sullan partisan during the civil war and went on to be a brutal henchman during the following proscriptions. He was thought to have seduced the Vestal Virgin Fabia, a cousin or stepsister of Cicero's wife Terentia (73) and in 65 was prosecuted for extortion and other abuses as governor of Africa, but managed to escape conviction (*TLRR* 212). C. Antonius was the son of M. Antonius, one of the leading orators of the generation prior to Cicero's, and the uncle of the later triumvir Mark Antony. Having enriched himself in the civil war and proscriptions, Gaius served as quaestor but was then expelled from the senate in the year 70 for excessive debts. However, he won election as praetor along with Cicero in 67. Bribery, a problem endemic to Roman elections was particularly rife in the year 64, with Rome's richest man, M. Licinius Crassus, providing lavish support to Cicero's opponents. When Cicero sought the aid of a tougher anti-corruption law, the measure was vetoed by the tribune Q. Mucius Orestinus (probably a relation of Catiline's wife Aurelia Orestilla). Orestinus argued, either in the senate or in a *contio*, that Cicero was unworthy to be consul and had recourse to anti-bribery legislation because he was otherwise unelectable. At a meeting of the senate the following day, dressed in the whitened garb of a candidate, Cicero delivered an impassioned speech denouncing Orestinus, Antonius, and above all Catiline (the so-called *Speech in a White Toga*). This speech, cataloguing Catiline's various (alleged) crimes, together with behind-the-scenes efforts by Cicero's friend Atticus to reassure his "noble friends" of the orator's trustworthiness, seems to have been decisive: when the votes were counted, Cicero carried all the centuries, and C. Antonius narrowly defeated Catiline.

As with most Roman politicians, the consular year was the highlight of Cicero's career. Soon after his election, he moved to win the cooperaton of his colleague-elect, Antonius, by an exchange of the provinces assigned for them to govern in their postconsular year. Cicero thus accepted Cisalpine Gaul (which he would later renounce altogether) and yielded the more lucrative province of Macedonia to the chronically impecunious Antonius. By neutralizing any opposition from Antonius, he created scope for exerting political leadership. In view of his previous political record, which had included some deviations from optimate policies (such as his backing of Pompey's command in Asia) and *popularis* gestures (the prosecution of Verres, including criticism of senatorial juries, and the defense of Cornelius), one might not have anticipated Cicero's taking such a decidedly optimate stand as he did as consul. Thus he defended the status quo against an ambitious land reform bill promoted by tribunes of the plebs led by P. Servilius Rullus, opposed lifting Sulla's ban on the holding of political office by the children of the proscribed, and supported a triumph for L. Lucullus' Asian victories, which had long been blocked. He proposed some reforms of his own, but relatively modest ones: the limitation of "free embassies" (*liberae legationes*)[12] to one year (a compromise; Cicero had wanted to abolish them altogether) and the stiffening of penalties for electoral malfeasance (the *lex Tullia de ambitu*). He also participated in several defenses this year, including that of C. Rabirius, who was accused for his part in mob action resulting in the murder of the tribune Saturninus in the year 100, and that of the consul-elect for the following year, L. Licinius Murena, on charges of electoral bribery (*TLRR* 221, 224).

12. On such embassies, senators traveled abroad for private purposes with approval of the senate, whereby the expenses were charged to the local populace; see further Dyck 2004b, 490–91.

What Cicero's consulship is most remembered for, however, is his opposition to Catiline, who, after failing a second time to gain election as consul, plotted to seize control of the government through armed revolt.[13] As a *novus homo* confronting a pedigreed member of the nobility, Cicero had to proceed cautiously, however, and his initial warnings were met with reserve or outright disbelief. But when credible reports arrived of an army gathered in Etruria, the senate was prepared to vote its emergency decree (*senatusconsultum ultimum* [*s.c.u.*]) on October 21.[14] After the conspirators mounted a failed attempt on his life, Cicero confronted Catiline in a speech in the senate on November 8 whereby the consul isolated him so completely that he saw no alternative but to withdraw from Rome and join his troops in Etruria (*Catil.* 1 and 2). In doing so, however, Catiline left behind some of his key followers to continue the plotting in the City. With the cooperation of the Allobroges, a Gallic tribe the conspirators were eager to enlist in order to supply their army with a cavalry arm, Cicero was able to secure incriminating documents, which he kept under seal and dramatically opened at a senate meeting on December 3. The conspirators present were taken by surprise and were either speechless or confessed outright. They were then taken into custody (*Catil.* 3). Since Rome had no system in place for long-term detention of prisoners, the fate of the conspirators was debated in the senate on December 5, with Cicero presiding, Caesar pleading for making ad hoc arrangements for long-term detention of the captives in Italian *municipia*, and Cato advocating the death penalty in view of the continued military threat (*Catil.* 4). When Cato's solution prevailed, Cicero supervised the execution of the five who were in custody.

The course adopted was, however, controversial, since it involved flouting the Sempronian law against putting a Roman citizen to death without allowing appeal to a popular assembly. As the consul in charge, Cicero faced criticism from the tribunes of the plebs L. Calpurnius Bestia and Q. Caecilius Metellus Nepos, who vetoed his valedictory speech upon laying down the office of consul on the ground that one who had denied Roman citizens the right to speak before the people should not be permitted to exercise such a right himself (Sal. *Cat.* 43.1; Plut. *Cic.* 23.1–2)—a harbinger of stormy weather ahead.

The following year brought the dénouement: the military defeat of Catiline's army and a series of trials of the surviving conspirators, in which Cicero played a major role as a witness against the accused, who were all convicted, with one exception, P. Sulla, a nephew of the dictator, whom Cicero defended. Since a previous conviction had removed Sulla from politics, the quid pro quo was

---

13. The following account reflects Cicero's point of view; we lack the evidence for a full account from Catiline's perspective (but cf. Catiline's letter quoted at Sal. *Cat.* 35); for an alternative reconstruction cf. Seager 1973.

14. Cf. Dyck 2008, 71.

a loan of two million sesterces, which enabled Cicero to purchase a splendid house on Rome's fashionable Palatine Hill, the visible symbol of the "arrival" of the "new man" from Arpinum in the highest ranks of Roman society. This year also provides our first evidence of Cicero's efforts to curate his legacy. This comes to light in the course of his defense of the poet Archias, who, Cicero claims, has "begun" (*incohavit*) a poem devoted to Cicero's achievements (§28), which, however, was never to be completed, if indeed it was begun at all.

In December of the year 62, a scandal broke that had far-reaching consequences for Roman politics in general and Cicero in particular. Publius Clodius, a young aristocrat, was detected in the house of the pontifex maximus, Julius Caesar, on the occasion of the annual sacrifice in honor of the Bona Dea, which was meant to be for women only. Clodius made his escape with the assistance of a maidservant. An affair with Caesar's wife Pompeia was thought to have been afoot. In the sequel, Caesar divorced his wife but refused to take action against Clodius.[15] Talk of Clodius' crime and trial for sacrilege (*incestum*) dominated Roman politics in early 61. Clodius sought to distract attention from himself and bring public opinion over to his side with attacks in *contiones* against Cicero as a tyrant who slew Roman citizens without a trial. Cicero, though at first disinclined to become involved in the matter, now struck back, attacking Clodius in other *contiones*. When the trial was held, Cicero appeared as a witness, destroying Clodius' alibi by testifying that he had met with him in Rome on the day of the crime. Clodius was nonetheless acquitted by the (surely bribed) jury. But the rancor between the two men lingered.

As Cicero grew increasingly dissatisfied with the current state of politics, marked by the rise of Clodius and the lack of leadership exerted by senior optimates (the "gentlemen of the fishponds" [*piscinarii*] as he calls them satirically in his letters to Atticus at this period), he drew closer to the senate's other prominent outsider, Pompey, now back from his campaigns in Asia. He also made provision again for his legacy, preparing in 60 a "consular corpus" of ten speeches plus two fragments, the concept modeled explicitly on Demosthenes' twelve-speech *Philippics* corpus (*Att.* 2.1[21].3). Having failed to secure a panegyric from Archias or any other poet, he essayed the task himself, producing *De consulatu suo*, in which he depicts the events of his consular year according to the conventions of epic, including participation by the gods. He also wrote and circulated a Greek draft on the events of his consulship.

With his focus on the past and commitment to optimate principle, Cicero was slow to appreciate the political realignment brought about by the coalition of Caesar, Pompey, and Crassus, and he let slip several opportunities at the end

15. *Att.* 1.12(2).3; Plut. *Caes.* 10 and *Cic.* 28; for Caesar's divorce, *Att.* 1.13(13).3; Suet. *Jul.* 74.2; for Caesar's possible recourse and the attitude he adopted, Moreau 1982, 26–50. On Clodius in general, cf. Tatum 1999; Fezzi 2008.

of the year 60 and in the first half of 59 to hold prestigious positions on the boards implementing the agrarian reform laws that Caesar pushed through as consul.[16] Not only that, but he offended Caesar. In the course of defending his former consular colleague C. Antonius, now back from governing Macedonia and facing charges of extortion, Cicero digressed, lamenting the current state of the commonwealth, in order to distract from Antonius' guilt. Word was immediately brought to Caesar, who arranged that very day for Clodius to be adopted by a plebeian so that he could stand for tribune of the plebs, an essential step in his plan to wreak vengeance on Cicero.

Clodius was, in fact, elected tribune for 58 and came forward with a program of legislation carefully designed to consolidate the backing of the plebs and junior senators and to isolate Cicero from his supporters in the senate. One of his measures provided exile for anyone who put a Roman citizen to death without a trial or supported such a measure in the senate (a sharpening of the Sempronian law intended to isolate Cicero). Cicero realized at once that he was the target of this proposal. Putting on mourning clothes, he appealed to the people, but the move was blocked by Clodius, whose mobs controlled the streets. Clodius had also bought the support of the consuls Piso and Gabinius by arranging for them to govern lucrative provinces the following year. Cicero appealed to Pompey, but he replied that nothing could be done without the backing of a high magistrate.[17] Completely isolated, Cicero followed the advice of those who urged him to go into voluntary exile. He departed on the very day when Clodius' plebiscite was enacted, probably in the third week of March, 58.

The next seventeen months were the most miserable of Cicero's life, documented in excruciating detail in his correspondence.[18] He at first hoped for a simple exile from Italy and so traveled south toward Sicily, where he still had many friends from his quaestorship and prosecution of Verres. But a second Clodian law was passed, condemning Cicero by name and relegating him to a distance of 400 (or 500) miles[19] from Rome. So he changed course and proceeded to Macedonia, where he took refuge at the headquarters of Cn. Plancius, who was serving as quaestor in Thessalonica.

The loss at one stroke of the public prestige in which he was so heavily invested was almost too much for Cicero, and his family and friends barely dissuaded him from suicide (*Att.* 3.3[47], 3.4[49]; *Q.fr.* 1.4[4].4). His first instinct was to seek scapegoats on whom to blame his plight, especially Hortensius and others who had advised him to go into exile and held out the prospect of a speedy recall. Only gradually did he come to take full responsibility

16. Cf. Rising 2015.
17. *Sest.* 41; *Pis.* 77.
18. Cf. detailed study by Garcea 2005.
19. Alternative readings at *Att.* 3.4(49).

for what had occurred. Moreover, a swift recall was not feasible, since Clodius' law forbade any discussion of the possibility in the senate, and Clodius and his fellow-tribune Aelius Ligus were prepared to enforce that prohibition with their vetoes. The two prerequisites for Cicero's recall were a new constellation of magistrates and a shift in the balance of power in Rome's streets. The latter was provided by T. Annius Milo, an ambitious young politician who bought a troop of gladiators and met Clodius' violence head-on. Once the streets were clear, there was a path for political action. To judge from Cicero's expressions of thanks, it was primarily P. Lentulus Spinther, who, as consul in 57, orchestrated Cicero's recall, acting in accord with a strategy formulated by Pompey, which drew upon Cicero's great popularity in the Italian *municipia* to counteract hostility among the urban plebs. The bill for Cicero's recall was passed in the Comitia Centuriata on August 4, 57—a rare use of that body for legislation in the late Republic—with Milo providing security.[20]

Upon his return, Cicero had to repair his public image, presenting his departure for exile as an act of self-sacrifice in order to avoid a bloodbath of Roman citizens.[21] The reality was, however, more complex, and Cicero had to struggle to reassert his standing, first obtaining (with the speech *De domo sua*) restoration of the site of his Palatine house (which had been destroyed by an angry mob at his departure and replaced by a temple of Libertas erected by Clodius), then funding from the senate for the rebuilding. In addition, he continued his work in the forum, where he enjoyed a string of successes, including two of his most brilliant defenses, *Pro Caelio* and *Pro Sestio*, both in the spring of 56, leading him to conclude that his standing in the courts was as it had been before the exile (*Q.fr.* 2.5[9].4). He also continued to follow optimate policies in the senate. But his influence was perceived by Crassus and Caesar as a threat to their position. Conferences held among members of the coalition at Ravenna and Luca in April 56 led Pompey to intervene strongly, pointedly reminding Cicero and his brother of promises made in connection with the former's recall from exile (i.e., that he would not oppose the coalition on major issues). Rather than face another exile, Cicero drew back from his previous political positions and joined a public alliance with the coalition, including defense of some of their favorites, such as Gabinius and Vatinius in 54 (both of whom he had criticized severely in the past), even while complaining privately of the state of the commonwealth. This can be considered Cicero's first period of "inner exile." The sole deviation from this public subservience was Cicero's

20. *LPPR* 400–402; security: Dio 39.8.3.
21. See further Dyck 2004a.

(unsuccessful) defense of Milo on April 5–8, 52,[22] for the murder of Clodius, a minor act of defiance in the face of Pompey's clear opposition to the defendant (*TLRR* 309).

Cicero's work on his public image also continued, but now in a subtler vein, in the theoretical writings of the 50s, comprising the dialogues *De oratore*, *De republica*, and *De legibus*. In the former two (the third was published posthumously), instead of depicting himself directly as in the *De consulatu suo* or the Greek commentary on his consulship, he expressed his views through fictive historical personae and merely threw out hints about his own position, for example, the possibility of an orator better than the distinguished L. Crassus or a "perfect orator" raised in *De orat.* (1.79, 95; 3.80). In *De legibus*, however, Cicero introduces himself for the first time as an interlocutor in a dialogue, apparently following a suggestion of his friend Sallustius (not the historian: *Q.fr.* 3.5.1–2), so that he could express views on current political problems. The two published dialogues, displaying a lofty conception of the role of the orator/statesman in the body politic and painting an idealized portrait of the Roman constitution, appear, in contrast to the *De consulatu suo*, to have enjoyed considerable success.[23]

In compliance with a law enacted by Pompey as consul in 52 mandating that consulars who had not previously governed a province should now do so (*LPPR* 411–12), Cicero reluctantly interrupted his forensic work and theoretical writing, departing for Cilicia in southeast Asia Minor in May 51. A feared invasion of the province by the Parthians was averted by a victory won over the invaders near Antioch in the neighboring province of Syria by C. Cassius Longinus, Caesar's later assassin. Cicero did, however, fight against rebels in the Amanus region, culminating in the capture of the town of Pindenissum after a siege of almost two months—an action forming the basis of his later claim to a triumph.[24] Cicero and his staff set a new tone by refusing to charge local communities for the expenses of their travel through the province. In addition, according to the account given in his letters, Cicero refused to charge communities for the nonbilleting of troops, investigated past cases of corruption and forced guilty officials to disgorge ill-gotten gains, and won approval of both tax-farmers and the locals by his fair adjudication of disputes. Cicero was, however, stymied by a loan made to the city of Salamis on Cyprus by M. Brutus requiring payment of interest at a rate of 48 percent. Since Brutus had obtained senatorial decrees requiring enforcement of the original terms,

22. For the date, see Ramsey (forthcoming) on Asc. 30C.

23. For *De oratore*, cf. Caesar *apud* Plin. *Nat.* 7.117; for *De republica*, Caelius, *Fam.* 8.1(77).4; for negative reaction to *Cons.*, cf. *Dom.* 92; *Pis.* 72–74; [Sal.] *Cic.* passim.

24. Cf. Wistrand 1979; Beard 2007, 187–97.

Cicero felt he could do nothing to protect the provincials and left the matter for his successor to resolve.

On his return to Italy at the end of the year 50, Cicero found civil war brewing, with Caesar demanding to be allowed to stand for consul in absentia while governing his Gallic provinces, whereas Pompey and a majority of the senate insisted upon Caesar's prior supersession. Cicero attempted to mediate, but in vain, and upon the senate's enactment of the *s.c.u.* on January 7, 49, the tribunes Mark Antony and Q. Cassius Longinus, who had been protecting Caesar's interests, withdrew to join Caesar, who crossed the Rubicon ca. January 10, 49.[25] Cicero now faced difficult choices, whether to join one side or the other or stay neutral, later whether to withdraw from Italy to join the Pompeians in Greece. In the second half of the 50s he had developed ties with Caesar, accepting his dedication of the treatise *On Analogy* as well as a substantial loan and seeing his brother serve as a legate with Caesar's army in Gaul (54–52). Cicero also had long-standing ties to Pompey. He condemned Caesar's invasion of Italy but also the intransigence of Pompey and senior senators that drove Caesar to take that measure. He had no confidence that a victory by either side would restore the republic. His correspondence of this period exhibits a complex weighing of factors at different levels. In the end, he decided to cast his lot with Pompey simply because he feared that, in view of his many services, Pompey would otherwise reproach him with ingratitude.

When he fetched up in Pompey's camp in Thessalonica, Cicero, the reluctant warrior, was the odd man out. The Pompeians' bloodthirsty talk grated on him.[26] His intelligence, cool objectivity, and wit, assets in civilian life, were now liabilities and made him unpopular.[27] He played little role, claiming that Pompey failed to assign him duties appropriate to his rank, and he missed the battle of Pharsalus (August 9, 48) because of illness.[28] In the aftermath, he was only too happy to abandon what had been, for him, a commitment to a man, not a cause. He erred, however, in returning to Italy prematurely, without receiving the necessary permission from Caesar, and had to spend a miserable year in Brundisium until he received clearance to move freely in Italy.

Upon his return to Rome in late 47, Cicero had to make a new beginning in several respects. In the first place, his long marriage to Terentia, from whom he had been separated, with a few months' exception, since May 51, unraveled, since he had lost trust in her, first as an administrator of his financial affairs and then comprehensively.[29] Then, too, with active participation in the senate

25. For the date cf. Gelzer 1968, 192 and n. 3; Ramsey and Raaflaub 2017, 188.
26. *Att.* 11.6(217).2 and 6; *Fam.* 7.3(153).2; cf. *Marc.* 16–18.
27. Cf. *Phil.* 2.39–40; the jokes: pp. 140–42 (nos. 45–50) Garbarino.
28. *Att.* 11.4(215); cf. Plut. *Cic.* 38.2; *Div.* 1.68; §114.
29. Cf. Scheuermann 2015, 85.

and courts now out of the question because of the massive power concentrated in Caesar's hands, he had to carve out a new role for himself. This would take, initially, two forms: (1) continuing his writing, aimed, in the first instance, at defining his place in the history of oratory, since he assumed that his oratorical corpus was now closed; (2) exerting behind-the-scenes influence on behalf of former Pompeian friends who were applying to be allowed to return from exile. From one point of view this was a natural result of his empathy for those in a position similar to the one he himself had occupied but a short time before. From another standpoint, it could be viewed as aiming to provide capable leaders for the state once the republican constitution had been restored.[30] In addition to those two roles, in the course of the year (46) it becomes clear that Cicero is also eyeing another possibility, a role for which traditional Roman society had no precedent or name but which we would call that of a "public intellectual."

During the 50s Cicero's oratory had encountered criticism for the first time (so far as we know) from a younger group of orators who complained of his overwrought and redundant style, use of rhythm, and sense of humor. They called themselves "Atticists" and claimed to be following the pure Attic (and spare) style of Lysias, as opposed to the overdone "Asianist" style they disapproved. The leader of this group was C. Licinius Macer Calvus, a friend of the poet Catullus, and he counted M. Brutus among his followers. Their disagreements had previously been vented in private correspondence, but in 46 Cicero moved to publish his own views on the matter in a dialogue on the history of oratory entitled *Brutus*,[31] fixing Calvus (the "alleged Atticist," who had died ca. 54), Hortensius (as an "Asianist"), and himself (the "true Atticist") in their respective places. The work also contains a pointed reminder to Brutus of the glorious tyrannicides in his ancestry.[32] The polemic continued in the *Orator*, composed later that year, at Brutus' request. This time the topic was the best *kind* of orator, defined with reference to the three styles (High, Middle, Low), and included detailed precepts on prose rhythm and citation of specific works and passages.

Other projects of this year were likewise dedicated to Brutus: the *Stoic Paradoxes*, a jeu d'esprit arguing for some of the Stoics' most counterintuitive doctrines in grand oratorical style, and an encomium of Brutus' uncle Cato Uticensis, whose suicide had been recently reported. This latter posed,

30. Explicitly expressed at *Fam.* 4.8(229).2 (to Marcellus): "if there is to be some form of commonwealth, you ought to be in it as one of its leaders" (trans. Shackleton Bailey).

31. The title can be taken both as a reference to the dedicatee and dialogue-participant, M. Brutus, and to his (alleged) ancestor L. Brutus, styled as the first orator of the free republic; cf. Martin 2014, 235.

32. Cf. Balsdon 1958, 91; Strasburger 1990, 30; Dugan 2012, esp. 125–26; Martin 2014, 233–35.

Cicero said, an "Archimedian problem," namely, how to praise Cato, who had committed suicide rather than beg for pardon from Caesar, without offending the Dictator (*Att.* 2.4[240].2). In the event, Caesar did not ban the work but wrote a reply (the *Anticato*) instead.

Cicero the candidate for "public intellectual," or at least senior advisor to Caesar, emerges from the so-called *On Behalf of Marcellus*, a speech delivered, not in court but in the senate, thanking Caesar for his grant of pardon to M. Claudius Marcellus (cos. 51), one of his principal opponents in the recent political controversies and in the civil war. After praising Caesar's disposition in the aftermath of victory, in the second half of the speech Cicero boldly comes forward with advice on next steps, urging the rebuilding of civil society as top priority—arguably one of the most creditable actions of Cicero's later career.[33]

At the end of 46 and beginning of 45 Cicero was busy writing another work unprecedented in Latin literature, the *Hortensius*, a protreptic, that is, a work exhorting readers to study philosophy. This, too, was a dialogue and placed Cicero in a circle of senior optimate leaders, including, besides the eponymous orator, Lucullus and Catulus (whose father had been a speaker in *De oratore*). Hortensius, who is presented in the dialogue as a bon vivant (as he was in real life), ridicules philosophy and thinks nature itself a sufficient guide to happiness, whereas "Cicero" undertakes to defend philosophy against the attack. The *Hortensius*, which exercised a profound influence on the youthful Augustine (*Conf.* 3.4.7–8, similarly *Vit. Beat.* 4 [*CSEL* 63.91.13–16]), does not survive; it is perhaps the most regretted of Cicero's lost works.

In February 45, the death of his beloved daughter Tullia—so like himself physically and mentally—from complications after bearing a child triggered a profound crisis for Cicero. This was a particularly vulnerable moment for him, lacking the support of Terentia, now divorced, and his recent marriage to a teenager named Publilia not yet having solidified. Indeed, this marriage was a casualty of the crisis, since the new wife, perhaps having envied Tullia's secure place in Cicero's affection, failed to show the expected grief. Cicero also had reason to be depressed over the state of the commonwealth, as there seemed no end in sight for Caesar's dictatorship, with gradual erosion of republican institutions.

In this crisis, Cicero found refuge in the house of his friend Atticus in Rome, and took to heart his advice to devote himself to writing as a cure. The first product of his pen was the *Consolation*, which as a self-consolation, was a work without literary precedent. In it he gathered together all the consolatory topoi and examples he could find in literature, though he later remarked that

33. To Cicero's disappointment, Marcellus never returned to Rome, being murdered at Athens en route (*Fam.* 4.12[253]).

he ignored Stoic precept in writing it when his grief was still in full spate (*Tusc.* 4.63; cf. 3.76). Insofar as we can reconstruct it, the work follows a trajectory from utter despair to reflections on the misery of human life in general, to larger issues of the fate of the soul in the afterlife, and concludes with questions of proper memorialization and the vow of a temple for Tullia, which he set out to fulfill with the assistance of Atticus (albeit the project was still pending at his death).

Cicero followed up the *Consolation* with a highly sophisticated work on epistemology in two dialogues, the *Catulus* and the *Lucullus*. Conceived as a sequel to the *Hortensius* and featuring the same cast of characters, these dialogues seem to have been completed by May 13 (*Att.* 12.44[285].4). But Atticus persuaded him to redraft the dialogue with different interlocutors, since the optimates depicted were by no means versed in such abstruse matters.[34] The upshot was a new edition now divided into four books (the *Academici libri*), with Varro, Atticus, and Cicero as the speakers. By mid-July it was in the hands of Varro, who was also the dedicatee (*Att.* 13.44[336].2).[35] In view of readers' reactions, Cicero formulated the plan of treating the whole of philosophy in a series of works with the goal of making it unnecessary for readers of Latin to have recourse to philosophical literature in Greek—an extraordinary act of cultural appropriation.[36] So arose the stately series of *philosophica* catalogued at §§1–3 of our text.

Meanwhile Cicero cautiously continued to work on his relations with the Dictator. Thus in May, at Atticus' suggestion, Cicero interrupted his philosophical writing to compose a carefully researched letter of advice to Caesar (*Att.* 13.26[286].2). In an abundance of caution, Cicero had Atticus submit his draft to his "friends," the Dictator's advisors Balbus and Oppius, for approval in advance. After several days a response arrived demanding a number of changes—so many, in fact, that Cicero decided to scrap the project altogether—another minor act of defiance. Toward the end of the year Cicero defended his old friend the Galatian king Deiotarus at a private hearing in Caesar's house—a foreshadowing of judicial procedure under the Empire.[37] He also entertained Caesar and some 2,000 of his veterans at the end of the year at one of his estates (probably the one at Puteoli) in Campania. They talked companionably about literature but skirted politics—a manifestation of the

34. For details on the change of plan, cf. Griffin 1997, 14–27.

35. Of the epistemological dialogues, only the *Lucullus* plus the beginning of Book 1 of the *Academici libri* survives; see detailed study by Cappello 2019 (but also the criticisms of Osorio 2019).

36. Cf. *Fin.* 1.2; *Tusc.* 2.6; Stok 1981, 21-28; Görler 2017.

37. For details on this and the pleading (in the Forum) of Ligarius' case (toward the end of 46), see Bringmann 1986.

"inner exile" to which Cicero was once again relegated.[38] He wished no return visit (*Att.* 13.52[353])!

Cicero appears to have been an eyewitness to Caesar's assassination on the Ides of March, 44 (§23). Though Cicero was not himself a participant in the conspiracy,[39] Brutus called out his name while still holding the bloody dagger, thus indicating that he was the inspiration for the deed (*Phil.* 2.30). But the conspirators had no follow-up plan, and Cicero criticized as too tepid the "Atticist"-style speech that Brutus delivered at a public meeting to justify the deed (*Att.* 15.1a[378].2). Moreover, the legions and the apparatus of government were in the hands of Caesarians, who soon brought in troops and established firm control of Rome. In this situation, the best that Cicero could achieve at a meeting of the senate on March 17 was a compromise by which the Liberators received amnesty and Caesar's acts, including proposals contained in his notebooks, were recognized as valid. At Caesar's public funeral, held ca. March 20, the speech of the consul Mark Antony inflamed the mob, which threatened to burn down the Liberators' houses. By early April they were virtually prisoners in their own homes. Thoroughly disgusted by the trend of events, Cicero departed Rome on April 7.[40]

Word of the assassination reached Caesar's great-nephew C. Octavius while he was undergoing military training at Apollonia near Dyrrachium on the Adriatic coast.[41] Wasting no time, he had arrived in Rome by April 11 (*Att.* 14.5[359].3) and by the eighteenth had come to the Bay of Naples. By that time he was already planning to accept Caesar's legacy, so a quarrel with Antony was anticipated (ibid. 14.10[364].3). On the twenty-second Cicero reports on a courtesy call Octavius paid to him at his estate at Puteoli. Though he found the young man agreeable enough, Cicero worried about his followers and their obvious hatred for Brutus and Cassius (ibid. 14.11[366].2). One suspects that it was the pressure of Octavian[42] and his claim to the allegiance of Caesar's veterans that caused Antony to distance himself from the compromise of March 17 and seek to secure his own position by means of a five-year Gallic command on the Caesarian model, which was enacted by plebiscite in early June.[43]

Upset by this development, Cicero planned to travel abroad to visit his son, who was studying philosophy in Athens, and await the new year and new constellation of magistrates before undertaking further political action. But

38. Cf. Herescu 1961, 143–46.

39. Cf. the letter to Cassius in which he wishes he had been a participant (*Fam.* 12.3[345].1).

40. *Att.* 14.1(355) and 14.5(359).2.

41. Cf. Suet. *Aug.* 5 and 8.2; Bleicken 2015, 33.

42. As he is called in Cicero's correspondence once he has accepted the legacy with entailed change of name to C. Iulius Caesar Octavianus.

43. Cf. Matijevič 2006, 125; Jordan 2017, 186–90.

forced back to harbor by contrary winds and hearing reports of criticism of his own absence and of L. Calpurnius Piso's lonely stand against Antony at the senate meeting of August 1, he resolved to return to Rome and join his voice to the opposition (*Att.* 16.7[415]; *Phil.* 1.7–10). Here is visible both Cicero's reluctance to pick a fight but also his unwillingness to be outdone in a contest over patriotism.

The opposition to Antony, a project undertaken in part with an eye to his legacy, unfolded in stages. Around this time Cicero repeatedly alludes to his advanced age (*Att.* 16.7[415].7; *Phil.* 1.38, 2.118); and he ultimately modeled and named a collection of speeches after Demosthenes' *Philippics*. It was originally planned as a corpus of twelve members against Antony as a distant enemy, just as Demosthenes' corpus had consisted of twelve speeches against Philip; at a later date, however, the first two speeches were added, bringing the total to fourteen.[44] In the first speech, delivered in the senate on September 2, Cicero ostensibly tenders advice to Antony as a friend, but the implications of his remarks are devastating.[45] Sensing danger to his position, particularly with Octavian now using lavish bribery to raise an army of Caesarian veterans, Antony struck back hard, delivering in the senate on September 19 a no-holds-barred attack on Cicero's character and career. Cicero replied to Antony's criticism and launched a devastating attack of his own in the *Second Philippic*, which was never delivered but probably circulated as a pamphlet.[46] Around the same time he also composed *De officiis*, a book with practical ethical precepts for his son, meant to replace the aborted visit to Athens, but also containing extensive and impassioned political commentary.

Cicero allowed himself to be persuaded by Octavian to return to Rome and upon his arrival began to organize the opposition, appealing to D. Brutus, one of the Liberators, who held Cisalpine Gaul, not to yield control of it to Antony but hold it in the name of the republic (*Fam.* 11.5[353] and 11.7[354]). Upon receiving D. Brutus' agreement, Cicero moved swiftly, using a meeting of the senate scheduled on December 20 to arrange security for the inaugural meeting of the new consuls on January 1 as an opportunity to seize the initiative and gain legitimization both of D. Brutus' action and Octavian's privately recruited army. His speech (*Phil.* 3) took those present completely by surprise, and his motion was passed.

By the beginning of 43, however, the Caesarians had prepared a counterstrategy, proposing dispatch of an embassy to negotiate with Antony, which, after four days' debate, was finally approved over the opposition of

44. Cf. Stroh 1983, with further support from Schäublin 1988; in general Manuwald 2007, 47–54 and 65–90.

45. Cf. Stevenson 2009 and Usher 2010.

46. Cf. Ott 2013, but also the reservations of Manuwald 2016.

Cicero, who wanted to move quickly to a war footing and relieve D. Brutus, who was now under siege at Mutina. The *Philippics* of this period, supplemented by Cicero's surviving correspondence, paint a vivid picture of the struggles in the senate in the early part of the year. The senior ranks of the senate were sadly depleted as a result of the civil war, and the survivors were, of course, in the main Caesarians. Q. Fufius Calenus (cos. 47), the father-in-law of the consul C. Vibius Pansa, was the first called upon for his opinion in these debates; hence this wily advocate of Antony's cause held a certain rhetorical advantage. There was also a natural reluctance to take the step Cicero was urging, viz., to declare Antony a public enemy (*hostis*) and thus accept that civil war was at hand. Meanwhile, Brutus and Cassius were active in the East recruiting armies of their own, which, no less than those of D. Brutus and Octavian, required legitimization by the senate. Through it all Cicero had to counter Antony's propaganda, which claimed that peace was possible, and try to keep together an unstable coalition of Caesarians and ex-Pompeians.

In the event, Antony was defeated in the battles of Forum Gallorum on April 14 and Mutina on April 21, but he managed to escape with three legions. The position of his followers in the senate was now untenable, and he was declared a *hostis*. However, both of the consuls died as a result of the fighting, with entailed administrative delays, and the coalition fell apart when Octavian refused to follow D. Brutus' order to follow up the victory at Mutina by pursuing Antony (*Fam.* 11.10[385].4). Instead, Antony was able to link up with M. Aemilius Lepidus, governor of Gallia Narbonensis and Nearer Spain, while D. Brutus joined forces with L. Munatius Plancus, the governor of Transalpine Gaul, who later went over to the side of Antony and Lepidus. Octavian held the balance of power, a fact that he used as leverage in negotiating with the senate for bounties for his troops and a suffect consulship for himself. Cicero now found he could no longer control the young man, since the prizes he wanted to offer (an *ovatio*, not a triumph, for the military success; a praetorship, not the suffect consulship) failed to satisfy him. In these circumstances, Octavian marched on Rome and forced the senate to grant his demands. He also reconciled with Antony and Lepidus and joined with them in a coalition with the goal of avenging Caesar's murder. A new set of proscriptions was inaugurated, with Cicero's name, at Antony's insistence, on the first list of victims. He died at the hands of Antony's henchman on December 7, 43, his head and hand(s)[47] displayed as another bloody warning on the Rostra.

Cicero put on various personae during the course of his life. He began as a young striver, first the eager student, then the young advocate building his

47. For the division of sources on this, cf. Homeyer 1964, 14; Wright 2001, 450n51; Butler 2002, 1–2.

career at the bar and later in politics. Once he attained the consulship, he was a senior statesman, guiding events during his consular year and as a significant voice in the senate's deliberations thereafter down to the beginning of Caesar's consulship in 59. That role was long interrupted, however, and only resumed at the very end of 44, through the first half of 43. In the meantime, Cicero suffered exile at the hands of P. Clodius and "inner exile," periods in which he publicly supported the "powers that be" but expressed his dissatisfaction in private correspondence with confidants and in encoded messages in some of his theoretical writings. For posterity, it was his writings, both the speeches he published to advertise his oratorical talents and especially his theoretical writings, that have established his reputation as the leading Roman intellectual, who, even while hallowing tradition in some respects, was able to free himself from its bonds in others.

The Impulse to Write

When late in the year 45 or early in 44 Cicero sat down to write his dialogue *De divinatione*, he saw this as a continuation of the "philosophical encyclopedia" he had begun ca. one year previously with the protreptic dialogue *Hortensius*. He portrays himself as having plenty of leisure for philosophy (1.11). During the course of the writing, Julius Caesar's assassination on the Ides of March turned Roman politics on its head. Cicero was caught offguard by this (§142) but was quick to take in the situation and reinvolve himself in affairs of state. He completed *Div.*, albeit hastily, adding references to the assassination, where he thought it appropriate, to the part already completed, as well as a preface to Book 2 surveying and justifying his philosophical writings to date and announcing that further work on this topic would be limited to time left over from politics (see below 88 and 92–93).

Since Cicero had just completed the three books *De natura deorum*, which, he claims, contain a complete treatment of that problem (*in quibus omnis eius loci quaestio continetur*: §3), it is not obvious that an additional work on divination was required. To judge from the matters highlighted in *Div.*, several divinatory predictions may have prompted the inquiry: (1) dreams that he and Quintus had experienced during his exile (58–57) that seemed to portend his restoration (1.58–59; §§136–41); (2) predictions astrologers made to all three of the so-called triumviri, Caesar, Pompey, and Crassus, that they would die peacefully and in honor at home, whereas none of them did (§99); (3) predictions connected with the recent civil war, including: (a) the prodigy of a mule's foaling shortly before its outbreak, taken by the haruspices as a dire omen (1.36, §49b); (b) the (apparently) favorable signs given to Deiotarus as he set out to join Pompey's (doomed) army (1.26–27; §§78–79); (c) favorable predictions given to Pompey (§53); (d) the Rhodian oarsman's (correct) prediction of catastrophe prior to Pharsalus but escape of the Rhodian fleet (1.68–69, §114); and (e) the fact that Caesar refused to follow the advice of an haruspex but in the sequel nonetheless celebrated a victory (§52). These varied experiences of divinatory predictions may have led Cicero to ponder whether a unified theory could be formulated to account for the phenomena and to study relevant works of Chrysippus (a Stoic) and Clitomachus (who recorded arguments of the Skeptic Carneades) in search of an answer.[48] In the dialogue itself, however, he creates a connection with *De natura deorum* by making the *causa efficiens* for the discussion Quintus' wish, upon reading *N.D.*, to revive the Stoic argument for the existence of the deity based upon the practice of divination (1.8–11).

The Subject and Approach

The dialogue has a particular orientation. Cicero begins the author's preface by postulating that Latin *divinatio* is the equivalent of Greek μαντική (*mantikē*).[49] There were, however, significant differences, μαντική being focused on prediction of future events, whereas *divinatio* as practiced by Romans of Cicero's day was used to obtain confirmation that a certain contemplated course of action was approved by the gods.[50] Cicero was interested in joining this dialogue to the Greek tradition of writing on μαντική and evidently had a personal interest in exploring predictions.[51] Hence this work is more focused on the possibility of accurate prediction of the future than one might have expected a work on *divinatio* to be.[52]

Another aspect sets this dialogue apart from Greek works on the subject, viz., its emphasis on examples drawn from high politics, historical figures, and the like.[53] Indeed, Quintus criticizes the Stoic philosophers Chrysippus and

48. Linderski 1982, 37–38 = 1995, 483–84, followed by Krostenko 2000, 384–85 n. 83 (similarly Blänsdorf 1991, 57–59), saw Cicero's attitude toward divination changed since *Leg.* and attributed this to political manipulation of the divinatory apparatus by Caesar and his allies, but cf. Wardle 2006, 12–13, who rightly points out that Skeptical reservations were explicitly sidelined at *Leg.* 1.39, but not in *Div.* Pavis d'Escurac (1981, 34–35) traces the difference to the different goals of the two dialogues (political vs. theoretical).

49. The equivalence is already asserted at *Leg.* 2.32.

50. Cf. North 1990, 57.

51. See above 19–20. Cicero claimed skill in making predictions based upon rational criteria; cf., e.g., *Sest.* 47, cited on §98 *fin.*; *Fam.* 6.6(234).3–4 (to Caecina); *Phil.* 2.24; Schneider 2004, 156–70.

52. There is a similar imperfect match of Greek and Latin terms when Cicero renders εἱμαρμένη as *fatum*; see further Weidemann 2019, 13.

53. On the importance of *exempla* in Roman culture for commemoration and education, cf.

Antipater for use of trivial examples (1.39), and Marcus praises the fact that Quintus chose distinguished Romans for many of his examples (§8), the point obviously being to engage the interest of upper-class Roman readers. Indeed, examples involving private individuals without some public dimension (such as those at 1.104 and §§134 and 144–45) are rare in this work.

Finally, the distinction between two types of divination, systematic, that is, based upon an acquired skill (τέχνη/*ars*), such as haruspicy, augury, or astrology, and "natural," that is, prophetic dreams or divine possession, a distinction already drawn by Plato[54] and invoked by Quintus as early as 1.12, is all-pervasive in *Div.* Though in Book 1 Quintus skips back and forth between one type and the other, in Book 2 this distinction provides the basic structure.[55] This way of organizing the material was not inevitable, however. Both types could be united as consisting of divine sign mediated via some randomizing device, such as the Pythia (the medium who delivered the oracles at Delphi) or the child who drew the lots at the temple of Fortuna at Praeneste (§86). It has also been suggested that the various diviners could be arrayed across a spectrum from the one requiring most inspiration (the Pythia) to the ones where the least inspiration is demanded (e.g., seers accompanying military commanders).[56] Finally, the distinction between the two is not airtight (see on §124).

Interpreting De divinatione

De divinatione deals with the interpretation of signs. In the course of it, Cicero has scattered various clues as to how the dialogue should be read. It is a two-person dialogue, a form that Cicero tended to favor after the *Brutus*, with different speakers assigned to argue pro and contra a particular thesis. Each speaker is usually allotted a separate book, as at *Fin.* 1–2 and 3–4 or *N.D.* 2–3, though the case pro and contra could be accommodated in a single book, as in *Luc.*, *Fin.* 5, or *N.D.* 1.[57] In our work, Quintus argues the case for divination in Book 1, to which Marcus replies in Book 2.

Cicero describes his general dialogic practice at this period as one in which the author holds the "leading position" (*principatus*) in the conversation (*Att.*

Roller 2018, introduction; Langlands 2018.

54. *Phaedrus* 244a–e; the distinction has even been found *in nuce* at Hom. *Od.* 20.100–101; see further Pease 1920–23, 70–71.

55. For the plans of the two books, see MacKendrick 1989,185–96.

56. So Flower 2008, 90, with reference to Greek divination, but applicable, mutatis mutandis, to Roman.

57. *Hort.*, in a single book, is a variant on this pattern in that the first speaker, Hortensius, offers a case contra (*sc.* philosophy), the second speaker, Cicero, the case pro.

13.19[326].4). Hence it is no surprise that the character "Cicero" figures in this dialogue as he has in all the nonhistorical dialogues.[58] Quintus' inclusion as a speaker is not a surprise either. The brothers had been close down to the battle of Pharsalus (48), Quintus having received the dedications of *De oratore* and *De re publica* and being featured as one of the three speakers in the unpublished *De legibus* (all written during the 50s). After Pharsalus, the brothers quarreled bitterly, Quintus hoping to obtain pardon from Caesar by blaming Marcus for their choice of Pompey's side in the civil war. After both brothers had been pardoned, they made up their quarrel, their first known meeting thereafter scheduled for November 30, 46 (*Att.* 12.1[248].3). Quintus makes a brief appearance in *De finibus* 5, written in the summer of 45, but our dialogue represents his first (and only) major speaking role in the 40s. It is an appropriate choice in view of the subject matter, since one of the topics of conversation will be dreams that both brothers had at the time of Marcus' exile. It may well also be, as Santangelo suggests, that the brothers grew up with a traditional belief in divination but that Marcus abandoned it in view of his training in Academic Skepticism, whereas Quintus retained (a version of) it, the contrasting views of Quintus and Marcus thus marking the length of the path Marcus has travelled on his intellectual journey.[59]

Cicero's dialogues can be viewed as dramas, and some hermeneutic clues will be apparent from Cicero's general practices in staging. Thus the scene is set at the home of a senior statesman, who takes the major role, in this case Cicero's Tusculan villa (1.8). This speaker is visited by another speaker or speakers, who are younger and/or less distinguished in rank; so here the consular Cicero is visited by his younger brother Quintus, who is of praetorian rank.[60] It is the

---

58. He appears in *N.D.*, but not in a major role; for a theory about this, cf. Levine 1957.

59. Cf. §§100–101; Santangelo 2013, 26. Perhaps Santangelo (ibid. 19–20) goes a bit too far, however, in thinking that Marcus Cicero may have meant to snub his brother with the kinds of refutation to which his views were exposed in *Div.* 2. It is true that, though the brothers are now reconciled, there would never again be quite the former closeness (e.g., the warm address of *Leg.* 3.25 *optime et dulcissime frater* is not repeated here; cf. also Shackleton Bailey 1971, 184–85). But no-holds-barred refutation was the business of Ciceronian dialogue, as Quintus must by now have known. Surely the historical Quintus had agreed to be represented in the dialogue and knew what was coming. In any case, in Book 2 Marcus often uses the second person plural to direct criticism to the Stoics in general instead of Quintus personally and at several points specifically substitutes the authors of the doctrines or Quintus' sources as his targets (cf. on §§35, 69,109, and 117); rather, he praises Quintus' accuracy in citing doctrines and fine memory in quoting verses (§§8 and 14) and graciously accepts his partial recantation at §100.

60. The claim of Beard 1986, 44, that the choice of Quintus was meant "to equalize as nearly as possible the weight of each side of the debate" seems dubious. The Romans were acutely sensitive to distinctions of age and rank (cf., e.g., Flower 2010, 161). Cicero could have selected a consular as his interlocutor if his goal had been the one indicated by Beard, or he could have had the interlocutors meet in a neutral place if he wanted to represent them as roughly equal in authority though different in status, as he has Cato and himself encounter by accident in the library of Lucullus in *Fin.* 3.

younger/less distinguished speaker who sets the topic for discussion, as Quintus does (1.8–11). The dogmatist states his thesis and usually also his case.[61] Toward the end of it, however, he may betray signs of weakness, as Velleius apologizes (unnecessarily) for prolixity at the end of his argument for Epicurean theology (*N.D.* 1.56) or at 1.132 Quintus disavows the ordinary run of diviners.[62]

In Book 2, Quintus makes important concessions about the ground rules: he accepts that this is a private discussion and so he will not appeal to public opinion or the like (§28), and he allows that the criterion should be what is acceptable to a natural philosopher (§§27, 33b, 37, 43b, 46, 58, 129a). Two-thirds of the way through Book 2 Quintus abandons his case for technical divination altogether (§100), even though this was, from the Roman point of view, the major part, and claims that he always regarded this as too superstitious (though he gave no hint of this in Book 1). After Marcus has refuted the general arguments of the Stoics and Cratippus and the defense of inspired prophecy and prophetic dreams in particular, Marcus and Quintus part, agreeing to continue such dialogues in future, but it is notable that Quintus does not promise to return to save his case for divination with better arguments (as Balbus in *N.D.* and Cato in *Fin.* undertake to do for their positions). On the face of it, it would appear that Quintus' case has collapsed under the assault of Marcus' "lethal" arguments.[63]

This is the way the dialogue has been read for centuries.[64] A reassessment of this interpretation was launched by several papers appearing in 1985–86 that still exert influence. In the first, Denyer (1985) claims that the argument in Book 2 is flawed in that it assumes that the Stoic theory of divination posits a cause-and-effect relation between the divinatory sign and the event it foretells, whereas the Stoics in fact posit what Grice called "non-natural meaning,"[65] that is, an arbitrary relation of sign and event, like the arbitrary relation between the signifiers of natural languages and the things they signify. Denyer illustrates with English word *rose*, which in one context may refer to a flower, in another may be the past tense of the verb *rise* (Denyer 1985, 7). Cicero's problem, according to Denyer, is that he treats Stoic divination as an attempt to do science when it was, in fact, "a branch of applied semiotics, concerned with understanding the utterances of the gods" (ibid. 9). He remarks that "science is one thing, and

61. The statement of the dogmatic case is elided, however, in *Tusc.* and *Fat.*

62. This makes him vulnerable to Marcus' argument at §§129–31.

63. Cf. Schofield 1986, 62: "the arguments of Book II are indeed lethal—they strike us that way, and they must have seemed so to Cicero and those for whom he wrote."

64. Cf., e.g., Voltaire 1968–2018, vol. 27, 24–26 ("Essai sur les moeurs et d'esprit des nations. Textes annexes"), a depiction of a Roman embassy to the Chinese court that threatens to end in disaster but is saved by the mention of *De divinatione*, which the emperor has translated and reads, subsequently becoming an admirer of republican Rome.

65. Grice 1957, 378–79, cited by Denyer 1985, 5 and 10n4.

divination another. Cicero simply misses this point" (ibid. 6). As a result, "Stoic divination . . . emerges unscathed from Cicero's criticisms" (ibid. 9).

Denyer compares the critique of divination in *Div.* 2 with the Stoic doctrine of divination at the stage of Chrysippus (throughout, Denyer takes the views expressed in *Div.* 2 to be those of Cicero the author).[66] Though Denyer is right to insist that *Div.* 2 has limited value as a critique of Stoicism, he tends to take Book 2 out of the context of the dialogue as a whole. The task of the speaker of Book 2 (whom I will call "Marcus" for clarity) is not to refute the Stoic doctrine per se, much less Stoic doctrine at the stage of Chrysippus, but rather the case for divination argued by Quintus in Book 1, which makes use of both Peripatetic and Stoic theory, with special emphasis given to the later Stoic theory of Posidonius (1.64, 125). In light of that, it is much less clear that "Cicero . . . misses the point." For in naming "nature" alongside god and fate as one of the causes of divination and emphasizing the sympathetic connections between all the parts of the universe (1.125, 2.33b–35), Posidonius blurred the distinction between cause and sign, as Denyer himself acknowledges.[67] Moreover, if Denyer had scrutinized Book 1 with the same thoroughness as Book 2, he would have seen that in various passages of that book Quintus also blurs the distinction between sign and cause.[68] It might also be relevant that at *Fat.* 14 Cicero, evidently on his own, imports a *naturalis causa* (unfittingly) into a context concerned with divinatory predictions.[69] It is thus likely that "causes" do not function in the dialogue to negatively characterize Marcus or "equalize" his arguments with those of Quintus,[70] but are there because Cicero as author did not observe a firm distinction. In addition, Cicero includes astrology within the ambit of divination, and the astrologers regularly spoke of the planetary configurations they used in their predictions as the causes of earthly phenomena.[71]

Marcus' argumentation in Book 2 may sometimes be wide of the mark, but it is not so completely wrongheaded as is suggested by Denyer, who sometimes forecloses argument in such a way as to leave out important points in Marcus'

66. His picture of Chrysippean doctrine on this point has in the meantime been elaborated and refined by Bobzien 1998, 159–75; cf. also Allen 2001, 161–70.

67. Denyer 1985, 10n2, citing 1.13 and §47 apropos of attempts by Boethus and Posidonius "to offer meteorological explanations of the reliability of certain omens." Cf. also Kany-Turpin 2004, 55–57.

68. Cf. 1.109: *quae potest esse sine motu atque inpulsu deorum, cum quid ex quoque eveniat et quid quamque rem significet crebra animadversione perspectum est?*; 1.126: *ita fit ut et observatione notari possit quae res quamque causam plerumque consequatur*; 1.131: *quid est igitur . . . cur ii quid ex quoque eveniat et quid quamque rem significet perspicere non possint?*

69. Cf. Bobzien 1998, 171 and n. 72.

70. Cf. Schofield 1986, 62-63, using Denyer's claims to such effect.

71. Cf. Bobzien 1998, 165–66 and n. 56.

case. Take, for instance, the problem of free will in a fated universe. Denyer proposes to "sidestep" this problem and claims that "Cicero does not press this difficulty" (2–3), but in fact he does, precisely at §20 (*si omnia fato, quid mihi divinatio prodest . . . ?* etc.). What about "natural divination," that is, inspired prophecy and prophetic dreams, to which both Quintus and Marcus devote considerable attention? Does Denyer find Marcus' arguments on this topic persuasive? Here Denyer is curiously noncommittal, quoting the doctrine and saying merely "Maybe so" before quickly moving on to technical divination (4), which is evidently Denyer's main interest (even though, in the economy of the dialogue, it is discarded, by mutual agreement of the interlocutors, at §100).

Denyer's chief point, however, is that "science is one thing, divination another" (6). Cicero's taking divination as a (would-be) art or science may seem odd at first sight, but it is not peculiar to Cicero and is in line with the Stoics' own definition of science (*technē*).[72] The Greek and Latin terms suggested this classification, the Greek μαντική (*mantikē*), belonging to the series of feminine adjectives designating disciplines (with τέχνη [*technē* = art, science] to be supplied). Thus Zeno, the founder of Stoicism, treated divination as an art (*technē*) as did Chrysippus (*SVF* 1:174, 2:1191). Carneades' criticism of divination, followed by Marcus, viz., that it was masquerading as an art (§9), implies a general view that it was an art. This categorization is further assisted by the fact that *astronomia* and *astrologia*, one a fact-based science, the other an occult science, were not clearly distinguished in Greek or Latin, and by the Latin designation of haruspicy as the *disciplina Etrusca*. Denyer (1985, 9) constructs a dichotomy between "natural science" on the one side and divination as "applied semiotics, concerned with understanding the utterances of the gods," on the other. But if we use Quintus' own analogy of the diviner interpreting a sign to a grammarian interpreting a poetic text (1.34 and 116), grammar (*grammatikē*) is also one of the feminines implicitly depending on *technē*,[73] so Marcus' treatment of divination as a technical discipline is, in the ancient context, not unreasonable; he should not be convicted of a category error simply for failing to use modern categories.[74]

What, in Denyer's view, would be required in order to refute the Stoic theory of divination? He opines that "if it is to be attacked successfully it must . . . be

72. The treatment of divination as a *technē* goes back to Plato; cf. Hankinson 1988, 128 and n. 28; cf. *SVF* 1:73 for Zeno's definition of a *technē* as an "assemblage of perceptions exercised toward a goal useful for life."

73. Cf. also the argument of Ptolemy the Peripatetic (otherwise unknown) *apud* S.E. *M.* 1.60–62 that *grammatikē* should be considered a *technē*; see further Blank 1998, 130–32.

74. Cf. Hankinson 1988, 146–48, who suggests that divination should be classed as a stochastic *technē*, like medicine. But ancient divination of historical times for which we have evidence does not appear to be seeking to test theory against outcomes, as a physician of the Empirical school would do. Marcus, in any case, rejects the analogy (§§12, 13, 142, 145).

attacked on theological grounds" (9). But the Stoics' theological premises are precisely the target of Marcus' attack at §§104–6.[75] Denyer goes on to claim (10) that "the successful attack" on Stoic divination was made by Christians and cites Tertullian (*Apology* 22, on fallen angels or demons as the source of pagan divination). What he fails to note, however, is that Tertullian does not reject divination per se (he believes in Christian prophecy) but merely pagan divination, that is, rather than provide a refutation of divination, he simply substitutes one belief system for another.[76]

In a well-intended attempt to save Cicero himself from Denyer's strictures, Beard (1986) and others have developed the theory that *Div.* stages a debate between two opponents whose arguments are meant to carry equal weight without Cicero's taking a position as author. Her interpretation is based upon: (1) "literary theory [that] has called into question the notion of any easy relationship between the author and his text" (34); (2) the structure of the dialogue in two "halves" with no conclusion and a statement at the end (§150b) leaving it to readers to make up their own minds; (3) the assumption that "no weight is added to the arguments against divination merely because they are spoken in the dialogue by the character of Marcus himself" (35); and (4) "the apparent shift in the opinions of the character of Marcus between *De Natura Deorum* and *De Divinatione*," seen as evidence of "the lack of a clear authorial voice" (ibid.).

Much of Beard's argument pertains to the relation of Cicero the author to Marcus the dialogue-speaker. The first time Cicero contemplated introducing himself as a speaker in a philosophical dialogue was when he was at work on *De republica* in the fall of 54. Then his friend Sallustius (not the historian) suggested that instead of Scipio Cicero should take the leading part himself, on the ground that in view of his consular rank, his views would have greater *auctoritas* than those of a transparently fictitious character (*Q.fr.* 3.5[25].1).[77] Though in the end Cicero rejected this advice, it did cause him to engage in some serious rethinking about the plan of the dialogue. So his own attributes, transferable to a dialogue-character, were clearly a factor in his thinking.

Cicero's attitude toward the personae of his dialogues appears most clearly, however, in his correspondence with Atticus about the revision of his epistemological dialogues. In this case, Atticus persuaded Cicero to remove Lucullus, Catulus, and Hortensius from the cast of characters since they had essentially no knowledge of epistemology; as revised, the conversation

75. Cf. Kany-Turpin 2004, 65, arguing for the cogency of the attack.

76. Cf. Timpanaro 1994, 255, a paper containing a detailed critique of Denyer 1985 still too little known and cited in Anglophone scholarship. On Denyer's detailed criticism of Marcus' argumentation, see the Appendix to this Introduction.

77. For considerations of relative *auctoritas* in the choice of a dialogue-speaker, cf. also *Sen.* 3.

was conducted by Varro, Atticus, and Cicero. In this, Cicero shows concern to match the speaker to the subject matter, Varro being suitable to represent Antiochus' position, Cicero himself to take the Skeptical line.[78] Furthermore, Schofield (2008, 80–83) has called attention to Cicero's subsequent references to the *Academici libri*, where the Skeptical case was assigned to "Cicero," as a kind of manifesto of Cicero's own philosophical position (*N.D.* 1.11; §1) as well as to the fact that when challenged by his interlocutor at *Tusc.* 5.32 about apparently contradictory views expressed by the character "Cicero" in Book 4 of *Fin.*, he does not attempt to deny the relevance by distinguishing between author and character (as he might have done if he regarded them as distinct). Cicero, then, clearly took careful thought for which parts he assigned himself and others in his philosophical dialogues and regarded his own qualities as adhering to his dialogue-character.[79] Moreover, to judge from Augustine, hardly an unintelligent reader, ancient readers took the views of "Marcus" in *Div.* to be those of the author (*Civ.* 4.30 and 5.9).

As to a change in opinions of the character "Cicero" between *N.D.* and *Div.*, this is more apparent than real: at *N.D.* 3.95 "Marcus" gives carefully hedged approval to Balbus' (Stoic) position; at §148 "Marcus" clarifies what part of Stoicism he accepts, that is, "natural religion" based upon the observation of regularities in the universe, even while rejecting divination; see further ad loc.

As to the structure of the dialogue in two "halves" and the final statement that judgment is left up to the reader, this is the usual Academic procedure of *in utramque partem disputare*, but it does not imply that the author has no opinion of his own on the matter or made no attempt to show which view is preferable.[80] Beard contrasts Cicero's works on theology with those on political or ethical themes, for which, she acknowledges, "Cicero uses dialogue to direct the argument to a conclusion which the reader tends to equate with the position of the writer" (1986, 44). This is right for the ethico-political works but is surely also the case for the works on theology, where Cicero states his own views

78. See above 15 and n. 34.

79. The one instance where there is a clear divergence of the view of Cicero the author and "Marcus" the dialogue-character is in the *Brutus*, and that for a special reason: Marcus is being disingenuous in claiming Crassus and Antonius as the greatest orators (to avoid self-praise); the real position (viz., that Cicero is the model orator) is disclosed by the character Atticus; see further Dyck (forthcoming).

80. Indeed, the Skeptical speaker Marcus calls himself "a great holder of opinions" (*magnus quidam . . . opinator*) at *Luc.* 66. Cf. Brittain 2016, 17, citing *Fin.* 1.12 to show that Cicero "does not claim—in his authorial voice—to be neutral between" the philosophical views he presents. Cicero is rightly categorized as a "Philonian/Metrodorian" Skeptic, i.e., he retains *akatalepsia* (the view that nothing can be known for certain) but abandons *epochē* (abstention from holding opinions); cf. Brittain 2001, 275–76 n. 42 (albeit in the meantime Brittain 2016 sees Cicero as a thoroughgoing Carneadean Skeptic); Görler 1997, 52–54.

clearly enough at *N.D.* 3.95 and §148.[81] The general framework also needs to be considered. In the latter passage (§148, not addressed by Beard), the character Marcus who passionately denounces superstition and wants to root it out for the benefit of his fellow citizens is surely the same as the author who speaks of offering public benefits by his writing on philosophy at §§1 and 7, just as the dialogue-speaker Cicero who cautiously approaches the subject of divination at §8 is surely the same as the similarly cautious author Cicero at 1.7.[82]

Finally, Beard proposes to offer "a broader approach than is usually adopted in this subject" but brackets out consideration of the third member of Cicero's theological trilogy, *De fato* (1986, 36). In fact, it is widely agreed among scholars that *Fat.* undertakes a refutation of Stoic determinism.[83] At 1.127 Cicero implies that he intends to treat fate by the same method of *in utramque partem disputare* that he has used for the gods and divination; but he was hindered by a certain event (*casus*) and therefore presented only the case *contra* (*Fat.* 1b).[84] This suggests that the point of all three works was the Skeptical case and that Cicero was prepared to forego the positive case if necessary.[85]

Schofield 1986 is sometimes lumped together with Beard 1986 (cf. Schultz 2014, 1), but, though also influenced by Denyer, his position is subtler. Thus

---

81. See also above 23 on the ways in which Quintus' case is undercut.

82. Against the attempt to see our dialogue as an example of *in utramque partem disputare* with no authorial commitment to either side, see also Repici 1995; Kany-Turpin 2004, 51, describing *Div.* as "pseudo-aporetic" ("faussement aporétique"). Schultz (2014, 13) describes her approach, placing the two books of *Div.* "on a par," as "more integrative" (*sc.* than the traditional interpretation). In fact, however, in treating the two books as autonomous, the approach is less integrative in that it fails to take account of the author's signals about the dialogue's overall trajectory (see above 22–23).

83. Cf. *Fat.* 38 *fin.*; Cicero's attitude is ultimately connected with his concern for educating Rome's young people (§4b) and his conviction that determinism destroys the basis for morality (*Fat.* 40). Cf. Sharples 1991, 22–23; Schallenberg 2008, 301–5; Woolf 2015, 86–92; Weidemann 2019, 24–25.

84. I take it that Quintus' promise at 1.127 *init.* that an all-controlling fate would be demonstrated *alio loco* was drafted when Cicero was still planning to present *De fato* by the *in utramque partem disputare* method, which he later abandoned. Surely the motivating event (*casus*: *Fat.* 1b) was Caesar's assassination and Cicero's consequent reinvolvement in politics, with a concomitant reduction of time available for philosophical writing; cf. §7; Weidemann 2019, 166–67.

85. See also Santangelo 2013, 17: "The scholars who maintain that the *De divinatione* is not an attack on divination because it is argued *in utramque partem* . . . do not account for Cicero's change of strategy in the work that he wrote immediately afterwards, and do not explain how this may fit within the framework of the trilogy." Beard's arguments are followed in essentials by Schultz (2009; 2014, 1–2 and 12–13). In claiming that there is no requirement for the dialogue-character to reflect the actual views of the historical namesake, Schultz notes that a Peripatetic position is assigned to Quintus at *Fin.* 5.96, whereas he states the Stoic case for divination in *Div.* 1 (2014, 12). But both examples involve evidence from the dialogues; it cannot be claimed as historical fact in one case but fiction in the other; and in one case, ethics is at issue, in the other, divination. In any event, the dialogue-character Quintus explains his greater attachment (on the topic of divination) to the Peripatetic position at §100.

he finds that "at the end of Book II Cicero unites the voice of the spokesman for scepticism with what appears to be his authorial voice" and that "Cicero identifies himself with the sceptical case against the Stoic" (57). He then veers toward Beard's position, however, in claiming that "there is no such thing as *the* voice of Cicero in *Div.*" and in dismissing §§148–49 as "a rhetorical flourish" (59). In fact, however, the rejection of superstition at §§148–49 is not an eccentric Epicurean argument pasted on to the otherwise Skeptical content of *Div.* 2, as Schofield suggests (59–60), but rather the theme of the entire work, which has, throughout, been targeting superstition. That superstition is to be avoided was the premise enunciated by Cicero the author at 1.7 and reaffirmed by Quintus at 1.132 and §100b. Marcus repeatedly denounces superstitition in Book 2, sometimes using a coded reference to what an "old woman/old women" would or would not believe: §§19, 36a, 76, 81, 83a–b, 118, 125, 129a, 136b, 141a.[86] Marcus would, like Cotta in *N.D.* (3.5), retain the elements of state religion *rei publicae causa* (§28); this is what is "eccentric" in Book 2, but this sociopolitically obligatory exception,[87] once made, is ignored in the subsequent discussion; it is not treated as disabling Marcus' other arguments.[88] As to the rhetoric of §§148–49, *Div.* 2 is replete with rhetorical flourishes. As we are coming to understand, Cicero's way of doing philosophy is to offer a highly rhetorical presentation of philosophical arguments.[89] And as noted above, Schofield later (2008) shows that full weight should be attached to the fact that Cicero assigns the role of Skeptical speaker to himself.[90]

86. Rejection of superstition is uncontroversial among the speakers in Cicero's dialogues; besides the positions of Marcus and Quintus in our work, cf. *N.D.* 1.45 and 55 (Velleius), 77a, 117 (Cotta), 2.63, 70, 71–72 (Balbus), 3.52 and 92 (Cotta again).

87. As Lehoux 2012, 37, argues, this should be taken seriously as "a genuine attempt to ground a desperately faltering but—as Cicero sees it—a very honorable and worthy political system."

88. Schofield 1986, 60, puts the emphasis the other way around, trying to discount §§148–49 because they conflict with §28 (and with Cotta's position in *N.D.*; but see n. 86 above).

89. Cf., e.g., Inwood 1990; Krostenko 2000, 370–73; Sauer 2007, 250–51.

90. Krostenko 2000 also claims an equivalence of the arguments of Marcus and Quintus, but on a different basis. He criticizes Marcus for supplying the kinds of assumptions about the gods and their behavior that elite Roman readers might have been expected to make (356–61)—an effective rhetorical move and hardly problematic within the context of the culture. But Krostenko points (374) to Marcus' dismissal of Romulus' belief in augury with the words *errabat . . . multis in rebus antiquitas* (§70) and comments that Marcus "protects Roman identity at the expense of Roman history." This is, however, in line with the attitude toward Romulean legend at *Leg.* 1.3–4 and merely shows that Cicero (and presumably others of his educational level and class) did not take such things seriously; cf. also the reference to *commenticia exempla* at §27 and the stipulation at §28 that this is a private dialogue. One doubts that Cicero's intended readers would have found a problem here. Promoting a political interpretation of the dialogue as a reaction to Caesar's flouting of omens and civil war victory, Krostenko extrapolates from *Div.* a *via media* between the positions of Quintus and Marcus that is never articulated in the text; similarly Fox 2007, 224, thinks that we must "look outside the dialogue for a resolution of the two positions."

In sum, in light of the debate of the last thirty or so years, the pendulum may now be swinging back to the earlier interpretation, but now buttressed by a better understanding of Cicero's goals and procedures.[91]

Composition

Cicero's final years were tumultuous, bringing many surprising twists and turns. He thus found himself sometimes adjusting the flow of his writing to take account of new developments. A case in point is his dialogue on the history of oratory, the *Brutus*, composed in the first half of 46. During the composition, with the civil war still ongoing, the battle of Thapsus was fought, and the results were reported at Rome. Of the republican commanders involved, Cicero mentions Scipio as living (§21) but later inserts an obituary of L. Manlius Torquatus, who died in the immediate aftermath (§265). *Div.* presents a similar situation. It was begun when Cicero had abundant leisure (1.11; cf. §142), but before it was completed, Caesar was assassinated on the Ides of March, an event that Cicero mentions several times (and which entailed his reinvolvement in politics: §7). These allusions were probably worked into an already completed text. Thus, 1.119 can be removed en bloc without damage to the train of thought.[92] Similarly, at §23 it looks as though the example of Caesar, who was a risk taker who had scant regard for omens, has been forced into a context predetermined by other examples (see ad loc.). At §99, the topic of horoscopes could have concluded with the observation *cotidie refelluntur* and then have been followed immediately by §100 (*Restant duo divinandi genera* . . .), with the examples of Pompey, Crassus, and Caesar added later. The

91. Yet another approach is that of Altman 2008, who wants to collapse the distinction between speakers and make Marcus into a Platonic dogmatist instead of a Skeptic (cf. 113: "despite his skeptical pose . . . Cicero himself underwrites the dualism of body and soul defended by Quintus"). This conclusion perhaps results from considering *Div.* too narrowly within the prism of its reaction to Plato; in fact, adoption of dogmatic positions for purposes of refutation was a Skeptical strategy used already by Carneades; cf. Striker 1980, 81–83.

92. Cf. Durand 1903, who still offers the most convincing contextualization. Contrast Falconer 1923b, 321 (followed by Timpanaro 1988, LXVI–LXXIV), who thinks that the text prior to 1.119 was written before the Ides and 1.119 to the end of the dialogue after that date. For another view, see Boes 1981, who sees the work as subsequent to the meeting with Brutus, Cassius, and their relatives recorded at *Att.* 15.11(389), which he dates to June 8. But this ignores that *Div.* was published by the fictive date of *Fat.* (*Fat.* 1b), which was during Cicero's rhetorical exercises with Hirtius at Puteoli, roughly mid-April through mid-May (first attested *Att.* 14.12[366].2, April 22; last letter from Puteoli ibid. 15.1[377], May 17). The citation from Accius' *Brutus* at 1.44–45 (= vv. 651–74 Dangel) is rightly connected by Boes with M. Brutus; but the idea of a Brutus introducing a new, positive age for Rome fits the immediate aftermath of Caesar's assassination and so should be reckoned to the passages subsequently added, as Pease 1920–23, 170, saw. There is no need to connect it with the games Brutus was scheduled to produce in July, as Boes thinks (Cicero was well familiar with the play, having previously quoted from it at *Sest.* 123 = v. 674 Dangel).

complaint of not having been warned by a dream *tantis praesertim de rebus* (§142) may be an oblique allusion to Caesar's assassination (cf. ad loc.), but these words, too, could have been added later. Certainly the rest of this passage, with its description of the interruption of forensic work, greater time taken for sleep, and the impression of unreality when Cicero visits the senate or the Forum, looks like a description of his alienation under Caesar's dictatorship, not the reinvolvement with politics heralded at §7.[93] After the Ides of March, Cicero will have added not only the references to the assassination but also the proem to Book 2 and hastened to bring the text to completion. If that is so, it is understandable that *Div.*, though published by Cicero (*Fat.* 1b), nonetheless bears traces of hasty composition.[94]

Language and Style

Cicero's dialogues are among his most attractive literary creations. Modeled in their relaxed manner, and in some cases their setting, on Plato's dialogues, they present a picture of gentlemen of the Roman upper class using their leisure to explore topics from philosophy or rhetoric. There is no comprehensive study of the style of Cicero's *philosophica*;[95] here only a brief survey of salient features of *Div.* (with emphasis on Book 2) can be offered.

Cicero deploys the *sermo cotidianus* as the diction appropriate to the characters and setting. One thus encounters such features as adjectives and adverbs in *per-*, as opposed to the fussy comparative and superlative forms, or pronouncements introduced with *equidem* ("I for one").[96] The diction is lively, with an infusion of colloquial words, phrases, or usages that Cicero avoids in his oratory: *nihil* for *non* (§§12, 81), *nullo modo* (§§24, 71, 79, 94, 108), *omnibus modis* (§140), *mihi crede* (§36a), *verba facere* (§46), *di immortales* (§§53, 76b), *belle* (§66), *valde* (§81), *nulla res* for *nihil* (§96), *ain tandem?* (§146). Colloquial speech also includes drastic expressions, such as *monstra* used in sharp invective (§87b). An upper-class speaker may allow himself an archaism, such as *reor* (§§5, 35) or *propter* for *prope* (§85). There is also the occasional surprise, such as *flexiloquus*, which looks like a poetic compound but is not attested previously (§115). Diminutives, also characteristic of informal speech but avoided in oratory or historiography, are deployed for purposes of distancing and/or ridicule (§§33b, 34, 52b).

93. Cf. Guillaumont 2006, 26–33, esp. 31; for a different view cf. Timpanaro 1988, LXX.

94. Cf. the false cross-reference at 1.87 as well as phenomena discussed by Schultz 2014, 57, 162, 192; and see below on §§50b, 53, 77, and 122a.

95. Some good points are made, however, by von Albrecht 2003, 27–45, 49, 85–92, and 114–16. Von Albrecht 1989, 102–11, offers stylistic analysis of a sample passage (*Rep.* 6.25–26 = 29–30 P.).

96. Cf. *permulta* (§§48, 120), *permirum* (§99); *equidem* (§75).

A special difficulty Cicero faced in writing in Latin on philosophical topics previously broached only in Greek was how to express some of the specialized terminology.[97] He judged that certain words had by now been sufficiently "naturalized" in Latin that no translation was required, as in the case of *amphibolia* and *aenigma* (§§116 and 132) or *astrologus* (1.12 etc.) and *astrologia* (§§87, 88). The word *sorites* ("accumulator" but traditionally "heap" in English[98]) was evidently on the borderline: Cicero first offers a Latin rendering but then decides it is unnecessary (§11). Of astronomical terms, ζωδιακός ("zodiac") is allowed to stand untranslated, whereas ὁρίζοντες ("horizons") prompts the Latin *orbes finientes* (§§89, 92). He had no confidence, however, that dialectical terminology would be intelligible to his readers, offering *sumptio* and *adsumptio* for "premise" and "additional" or "minor premise" (= λῆμμα, πρόσληψις: §§108–9). When he speaks of an acrostic, he cites but immediately explains the Greek ἀκροστιχίς, its first attestation in any Greek or Latin text (§111). On occasion, Cicero evidently felt that a single Latin word would not suffice; thus ἔργον becomes *officium et munus* (§107); and he tries out a congeries of synonyms in an effort to render the Stoic concept of συμπάθεια (*sympatheia*: §§33b, 34) before finally accepting the Greek word as a technical term (§143). Cicero's pioneering use of *flecto* = "turn a bend" may have been modeled on the similar Greek usage of κάμπτω (§94).

Though philosophical discourse counts per se as an *aequabile et temperatum orationis genus* (*Off.* 1.3), Cicero likes to enliven it with rhetorical gestures and turn up the heat with invective language, here directed not so much at Quintus as the Stoic philosophers from whom he derived his arguments. Thus he applies the epithet *ineptus* (§§118, 121), speaks of their *stultitia*, *deliratio*, or *dementia* (§§56, 90, 94) and of their views as *aniles* or to be disbelieved even by *aniculae* or *sagae* (§§19, 36a, 125, 129a).

In the *philosophica*, as in his other writings, Cicero deploys various types of stylistic ornament to assist the argument. One is the quotation of various illustrative passages from the poets. Ennius was a special favorite and is well represented here,[99] but Pacuvius' *Antiopa* provides helpful examples of riddling language (§133), and even Atellan farce is invoked (§25).[100] Unlike his practice in the letters to Atticus, where the Greek poets are cited in Greek, here they appear in Cicero's own poetic versions.[101] And passages from Cicero's own

97. See further Powell 1995a; Glucker 2012; on the fact that works on philosophy of religion contain the most Greek borrowings of Cicero's prose writings, cf. Oksala 1953, 145 and 146.

98. Cf. Burnyeat 1982, 316 and n. 3.

99. 1.40–42, 88, 107–8, 132; §§57, 82, 104, 111, 116, 127.

100. Quintus cites other passages from the poets; cf. 1.24, 42, 44, 65–67, 80, 114, and 131, with Schultz ad locos. On the different uses to which Marcus and Quintus put their poetic citations, cf. Krostenko 2000, 365–70.

101. Cf., e.g., on §12, where Cicero quotes his rendering of a verse that he cites in the original

earlier poetry, both the *Prognostica* rendered from Aratus and the *De consulatu suo*, are quoted back to him by Quintus in an effort to establish common ground in favor of divination.[102] Other ornaments include such figures of speech as personification, simile, and metaphor. Thus he uses military metaphors to describe the planned course of the argument, beginning with a sortie of light-armed troops and advancing to an attempt to roll up the flanks of the enemy army (§26a). Again, when he complains that the gods send messages that are difficult or impossible to decipher, he compares the situation that would obtain if ambassadors of the Carthaginians or Spaniards were to attempt to address the Roman senate in their native languages (§131b). Finally, he makes the problem of finding a role for divination more vivid by personifying it as if it were a magistrate in search of a portfolio (§12).

Other types of ornament involve the arrangement of words for effect and include marshaling points in a tricolon (§§50b, 54, 125), a formal syllogism (§§25, 41, 61, 102, 103–4), or a chiastic pattern (§§16, 38, 39, 55a, 56, 63.5 and 8, 92b, 94, 115, 119, 122a, 136b). Hyperbaton (separation of related words) may be used to create emphasis (§§1, 42, 54, 100b, 122a). Cicero may also drive his point home through an incongruous juxtaposition (§39: *duce* deo servus *deducitur*; §56: *hoc . . . per* gallinas Iuppiter *tantae civitati signum dabat?*). Other unexpected placements include the verb in initial position to emphasize vigorous or drastic actions (§§79, 134, 149). Sound devices include alliteration and assonance (§§21, 83b, 143) and deployment at the ends of sentences or clauses of particular rhythms based on variation between heavy and light syllables (marked below respectively as — and ˘ with x a syllable that is anceps, i.e., may be either), Cicero's favorites being the following:

1 — ˘ — — x (cretic + trochee)
2 — — — — ˘ x (molossus + cretic).
3 — ˘ — — ˘ x (double cretic)
4 — — — — ˘ — x (molossus + double trochee)
5 — ˘ — — ˘ — x (cretic + double trochee)
6 — ˘ — ˘ x (cretic + iamb)
7 — ˘ ˘ ˘ — x (first paeon + trochee).[103]

Greek in a letter to Atticus (*Att.* 7.13[136].4). Particularly notable the rendering of *Il.* 2.299–330 at §§63–64; see ad loc.

102. 1.13–15 and 17–22 respectively. Krostenko 2000, 380–85, thinks that Cicero's poetry is quoted by way of self-criticism (in view of Caesar's acceptance of quasi-divine symbolic attributes); thus he interprets §46 as a "refusal to defend his poetic . . . productions" (385). But what is at issue there is not the poetry per se but Quintus' attempt to derive from it a justification for divination; cf. Atticus' overliteral interpretation of the *Marius* at *Leg.* 1.1–5.

103. The clausulae of *Div.* have been studied in detail by Bornecque 1907, 296–304. Wilkinson 1963, 156, summarizes Cicero's preferences. For some notable examples, see on §§62a, 94, 105, 122a.

Several syntactic features contribute to the effectiveness of the argument. One is the syntactic non sequitur known as anacoluthon that Cicero uses to help create a conversational atmosphere but also to ensure that key points are clearly highlighted (cf. on §135b). In early Latin the present participle, including its verbal properties, was underexploited. Particularly in his later work, Cicero changes this, perhaps inspired by the Greek authors he read, so that the present participle comes into its own as a compact and powerful instrument capable of replacing a relative clause;[104] cf., e.g., §112: *hoc* [i.e., use of acrostics] *scriptoris est, non furentis, adhibentis diligentiam, non insani*, where the substantivized participle *furentis* is parallel with the substantivized adjective *insani* but offers an advantage in precision over *furiosi* in denoting a temporary state, whereas the second participle with object (*adhibentis diligentiam*) replaces a descriptive relative clause. Again, in §126, Cicero repeatedly takes advantage of the opposed substantivized participles *somniantes—vigilantes* to describe persons in a sleeping or waking state. He likewise finds the present participle very useful in describing the actions of figures depicted in art (*Romulus lactens*: §47; *Iovis pueri, qui lactens . . . in gremio sedens, mammam adpetens*: §85) or in general whenever actions are the key point (e.g., §59: *quasi vero quicquam intersit mures* diem noctemque aliquid rodentes *scuta an cribra corroserint*).[105]

As a skilled practitioner of persuasive rhetoric, Cicero gets his point across in various ways, including rhetorical questions, often of the "railroading" type in which a particle such as *num*, *nonne*, or *non* guides the reader in the desired direction. Sometimes such a question even substitutes for an argument.[106] Cicero admired Socrates as a great ironist (*Off.* 1.108) and follows in his footsteps here.[107] He also loves to play with the Latin language itself, and this tendency, too, is on full display in *Div.*[108]

De divinatione, then, gives proof of Cicero's ability to see and set out the main lines of philosophical arguments and counter them with great rhetorical skill.[109]

Key Moments of Reception

De divinatione has essentially two faces, Book 1 comprising a collection of anecdotes pertaining to divination, Book 2 an extended philosophical

104. Cf. §§9, 10, 51, 58, 71a, 92b, 144.

105. Cf. Laughton 1964, 45.

106. Rhetorical question: §20; "railroading" questions: §§42, 51, 71, 92; for a question replacing an argument, cf. on §§138–39.

107. Cf. on §§31, 35–36a, 44–45a, and 92.

108. Cf. on §§28, 37, 79, 108, 115.

109. Cf. Görler 1989, 257.

argument against divination as traditionally understood. By the time he wrote *De fato*, probably in May/June 44, Cicero had already published *Div.* (*Fat.* 1b). But any hope he may have cherished that the work would stimulate a lively debate among educated Romans about the status of divination was not to be realized. Writers did, however, appropriate its content for their own purposes. Lexicographers ransacked it in search of rare words and etymologies.[110] Valerius Maximus exploited the work for the collection of *Memorable Deeds and Sayings* he assembled in the principate of Tiberius, especially the religiously themed first eight chapters of Book 1.[111] Other learned compilers followed suit, such as the Elder Pliny under the Flavian dynasty and Aulus Gellius in the next century.[112]

It is no surprise that, with his interest in omens, Plutarch mined *Div.* to provide colorful anecdotes for his biographies. Thus Tiberius Gracchus' appearance in a dream to his brother Gaius, prophesying that he would die the same death as he had, is reported early in Gaius' biography and sets the tone for the following narrative (*C. Gracchus* 1 ~ 1.56). Similarly, the omen contained in Tertia's lament over the death of a pet named Persa on the day of Aemilius Paulus' appointment to lead the expedition against Perseus, king of Macedon, duly features in the commander's biography (*Aem. Paul.* 10 [also in *Apophth. reg. et imp.* Aem. 2 = *mor.* 197f–198a] ~ 1.103).

Traces of an acquaintance with *Div.* are also perceptible in several ancient Christian authors. Imitating Ciceronian philosophical dialogue in his *Octavius*, Minucius Felix (*fl.* third century, first half) has the pagan speaker Caecilius present himself, in Ciceronian fashion, caught between the dangers of *anilis . . . superstitio* and laying waste to all religion (13.5 ~ 1.7 *fin.*). Lactantius also alludes to our work several times in his *Divinae institutiones*.[113] Augustine seems not to have known *Div.* until he set to work on his large-scale apologetic

110. Verrius Flaccus did so under Augustus: cf. Fest. pp. 302 and 498 L. (s.vv. *praesagitio* ~ 1.65; *tripudium* ~ 2.72); later (early fourth century?) Nonius Marcellus p. 279 L. ~ 1.69; p. 406 L. ~ 2.5.

111. V. Max. 1.1.1b ~ *Div.* 1.92; 1.1.3 ~ 2.74; 1.1 ext. 9 ~ 1.81; 1.4 praef. ~ Ennius in 1.107–8; 1.4.1 ~ 1.32; 1.4.3 ~ 1.29 etc.; 1.4.4 ~ 2.71; 1.4 ext. 2 ~ 1.26 and 2.20; 1.5.3 ~ 1.103 and 2.83; 1.5.4 ~ 1.104 and 2.83; 1.6.3 ~ 1.100; 1.6.5. ~ 1.72 and 2.65; 1.6.13 ~ 1.119 and 2.36–37; 1.6 ext. 2 ~ 1.78 and 2.66; 1.6 ext. 3 ~ 1.78 and 2.66; 1.7.4 ~ 1.55 and 2.136; 1.7.5 ~ 1.59 and 2.136–37; 1.7.6 ~ 1.56; 1.7 ext. 1 ~ 1.49; 1.7 ext. 3 ~ 1.56 and 2.135; 1.7 ext. 7 ~ 1.39; 1.7 ext. 8 ~ 1.50; 1.7 ext. 9 ~ 2.143; 1.7 ext. 10 ~ 1.57; 1.8.11 ~ 1.30 and 2.80; 1.8 ext. 10 ~ 1.47 and 63. For discussion, see Mueller 2002, 10–11 and index locorum under the passages.

112. Plin. *Nat.* 2.191 ~ 1.112; 11.186 ~ 1.119; on Pliny's use of Cicero, see in general Darab 1995. At 15.13.7, Gellius cites 1.53 and 87; at 4.11.3, he quotes at some length from 1.62.

113. At 3.17.14 three lines are quoted from *Cons.* via *Div.* 1.19 (F 10.36–38 Courtney); at 4.15.27 Cicero is cited for an allusion to the Erythraean Sibyl (~ 1.34); at 7.14.4 he quotes with reference to *Div.* 1 (*sc.* 36) the figure 470,000 years claimed for the duration of the Chaldaean astronomical observations.

work, the *City of God*.[114] He expressly cites *Div.* at *Civ.* 3.17 and 5.9 and alludes to it ibid. 2.16 and 10.13 (~1.96 apropos of Lycurgus) as well as 4.30 (~ §78).[115] *Civ.* 5.9 contains, in fact, an extensive discussion of free will and fate taking as its starting point a critical review of Cicero's position. Augustine aims to break down the Ciceronian dichotomy between the two with the argument that events Cicero assigns to chance have causes that are obscure to mortals but known to God and that human free will is taken into account by the divine will. He thus aims to vindicate divine foreknowledge and rehabilitate prophecy. While *Div.* is cited explicitly at *Civ.* 5.9 (alongside *N.D.*), Augustine's argument appears to be directed primarily at *De fato*, of which only some two-thirds is extant. So the engagement with *Div.* is less deep than might appear at first glance.[116]

The survival of *Div.* through the Middle Ages, with their prioritization of Christian texts and aversion to anything closely connected to pagan cult, was by no means assured. The dialogue did, however, have the good fortune to be transmitted as part of a corpus of Cicero's *philosophica*. This fact becomes visible to us in a florilegium (Cod. Vat. Regin. 1762) compiled by Hadoard, librarian of the abbey of Corbie in northern France, in the third quarter of the ninth century, an early indication of the existence of a group of eight philosophical works which has come to be known as the "Leiden corpus," since three of its four principal manuscripts make their home in that Dutch city.[117] One of those three manuscripts (Leiden B.P.L. 118 = H) was written in Montecassino in the second half of the eleventh century. Containing only *N.D.* and partial texts of *Leg.* and *Div.*, it is the first representative of the Leiden corpus to appear south of the Alps. A fourteenth-century codex, Trecensis (Troyes) 552, perhaps descended from a sister of H, was owned by Francesco Petrarch, the father of Italian humanism, and contains almost all of Cicero's extant rhetorical and philosophical works, including *Div.*[118] Petrarch's fondness for *Div.* is shown, for instance, by three nested citations in a letter to Boccaccio on the prophetic powers of persons who are dying.[119] With the publication of the *editio princeps* (Rome, 1471) the survival of the work was placed beyond doubt.

Habent sua fata libelli. Certain authors and works meet a particular need at a particular time. So it was with Cicero. If Christian readers valued him initially for his works on (especially practical) ethics, later, in the Renaissance, as a personality

114. Or he would surely have cited it in the *De divinatione daemonum*.

115. Cf. also on §145.

116. Hagendahl (1967, 525–35) claims that Augustine essentially misrepresents the argument of *De fato*; certainly he reads the treatise in the light of his own philosophical agenda; cf. Sharples 1991, 25.

117. For details, see above xv.

118. Cf. R. H. Rouse in Reynolds 1983, 121–28.

119. Cf. Fantham 2017, VII.5.28: Hector's prophecy of Achilles' death (~ 1.65), Calanus' prophecy of that of Alexander (~ 1.47), and the Rhodian's prophecy of the deaths of six of his contemporaries in the correct order (~ 1.64).

and stylistic model, it was left to the Enlightenment to probe his philosophical works more deeply. Among the promoters of deism in seventeenth-century England, John Wilkins (1614–72) esteemed Cicero as an ally in grounding his conception of "natural religion" based upon the consensus of all peoples and the design of the universe (cf. *N.D.* 1.43b, 2.4–5, *Div.* 2.148) as well as divine providence (cf. *N.D.* 2.133–67); he did, however, depart from Cicero in accepting miracles.[120] In the eighteenth century, however, a more critical view prevailed, distinguishing Cicero's own views from those of various other speakers in his dialogues. While making such distinctions, John Toland (1670–1722) remarks that at the end of *Div.* Cicero drops the mask and reveals his own opinions.[121] In addition, the more militant deism of Toland's time embraced the destructive side of Cicero's philosophical works as well. Thus Anthony Collins (1676–1729) quotes appreciatively Cato's anecdote about haruspices being unable to contain their laughter (§51) and declares that in *Div.* Cicero "destroy'd the whole reveal'd religion of the Greeks and Romans by showing the imposture of all their miracles and the weakness of the other reasons on which it was pretended to be founded."[122]

In the nineteenth century, Cicero's reputation as a philosopher suffered a steep decline. This was connected with a new interest in the Hellenistic period and the reconstruction of its literature, as well as the cult of originality that Romanticism introduced, Cicero being seen as merely reproducing the doctrines of Hellenistic predecessors. There was also, especially in Germany, a reaction against Cicero the man, based upon moral disapproval of the advocate's profession.[123] Only in recent decades have Ciceronian studies started to reorient toward what Cicero is actually aiming at and achieving in his philosophical writings (as opposed to focusing on "errors" foisted upon him by scholars supposing that his Greek sources said something different).[124]

Appendix: Denyer's Seven Criticisms of Marcus' Argument in Book 2

Once Denyer has pointed out the difference between causation and communication, he would appear to have shot his bolt, having little to add

120. Wilkins 1710 under the arguments for the existence of the deity (Book 1, chapter 4).

121. Toland 1726, 263–64, citing §§148–49: *nam ut vere loquamur . . . stirpes omnes eiciendae*, which Toland also chose as the motto of his *Adeisidaimon*; cf. Gawlick 1963, 664. The point about Cicero's persona was anticipated by Augustin. *Civ.* 5.9; cf. also Fox 2007, 294–95 and his ch. 10 in general on Toland and Cicero.

122. Collins 1713, 135–36. On Voltaire's high opinion of *Div.*, see above 23n64, as well as Zielinski 1929, 247 and 253; on Diderot, cf. on §80 *init.*

123. See further Fuhrmann 2000; Begemann 2015, who highlights the weaknesses of source-criticism of the late nineteenth century, based on the assumption that Cicero merely muddled what was crystal clear in his sources.

124. For a more detailed study of the reception of *Div.*, cf. Pease 1920–23, 29–37.

about the detailed argumentation of Book 2. He lists seven points in Marcus' argument and has essentially the same reply for each, namely, that one must look from the standpoint of communication, not causation:

(1) "The triviality of certain signs" (6), where he refers to the argument at §56 about the Theban victory being signaled by a cock crowing and remarks that trivial signs may herald grand events. Perhaps, but there is a deeper epistemological problem here to which Cicero points when he says that cocks always crow and implies that it is impossible, on the theory of divination, for the observer to distinguish between the normal behavior of poultry and a sign from the gods. Denyer leaves the point unaddressed.[125]

(2) "The sheer arbitrariness of the connexion between portents and what they portend" (6). Here Denyer cites Cicero apropos of marks on a liver portending financial gain (§34) or the number of sparrows killed by a serpent portending the number of years of the Trojan War (§65). We can grant Denyer that "there need be no such [inherent] connexion between future events and the statements that foretell them," but again, from the point of view of the recipient of the sign, how can any such connection be reliably inferred?

(3) "The unsystematic character of divination," whereby a thunderbolt on the left may have different meanings in different contexts (7, citing §§43 and 74). Here Denyer points to the analogy of natural languages and their unsystematic procedures and cites the example of the ambiguity of *rose*. Timpanaro (1994, 252), however, rightly objects that the Stoic divinity, which is the Logos interpenetrating the universe, ought to be able to create an unambiguous medium. Another problem unaddressed by Denyer is that the Roman system whereby thunder on the left is a favorable sign except for the holding of elections seems an arbitrary arrangement, perhaps, as Marcus suggests, influenced by political considerations. Why should the gods be thought to have adapted their signs to it? Here Stoic theory fits awkwardly with Roman practice,[126] but instead of shedding light Denyer ignores the problem.

(4) "National differences in the interpretation of omens" (7, with reference to §§28, 76, and 82). Denyer appeals again to natural language(s) and suggests that the gods will choose different ways of expressing their messages to different audiences. But would the Stoic deity, immanent in the universe

---

125. The point is made by Timpanaro 1994, 250–51. Denyer should also have considered this aspect when he raises "the possibility of a *one-off* communication" (1985, 5, his emphasis): how could it be recognized as such?

126. On the mismatch of Stoic theory and Roman practice, see further Kany-Turpin 2004, 57–61.

from all eternity, accommodate local conventions, that is, superstition?[127] Such differences are also a problem for the Stoics insofar as they appealed to "consensus of all" as an argument for divination (1.2–3, 11, 90–108). If divination is not in fact a unified system, then that particular argument dissolves (a point which Denyer does not address).[128]

(5) A "punlike . . . or symbolic" connection of sign and event (8), where Denyer again cites the cock crowing to portend victory (1.74). He makes the same point as on (1), and the same epistemological problem arises.[129]

(6) The attack on the ambiguity of omens (9, citing the dreams interpreted at §§144–45). Denyer, of course, invokes the ambiguity of natural language, but dreams are still more difficult to interpret than language. This is a particular problem if, as the Stoics claim, the signs are given by the gods in order to benefit human beings (cf. the apostrophe to the Stoic god at §133: *mea causa me mones quod non intellegam: quid me igitur mones?*).

(7) "Diviners make much of marvellous portents, yet their marvellous character is entirely subjective" (9), with following citation of §49: *causarum ignoratio in re nova mirationem facit*. Here Denyer seems not to follow (or not to want to engage with) Marcus' argument. Marcus' point is that a mule's foaling, which was taken as a portent, is a natural occurrence and is merely considered a portent because of its rarity and people's ignorance. In other words, Marcus is saying not that the miraculous character of claimed portents is subjective, but that it is nonexistent, since he aimed to draw a line between a rare event and a supernatural one. Denyer's argument that the gods need to send an "eye-catching" message in order to attract attention is beside the point.

127. Cf. Timpanaro 1994, 252.

128. Burnyeat *apud* Denyer 1985, 7–8, raised the problem that in a universe organized on Stoic principles, all signs should be correctly interpreted by the recipient without the need for a diviner. Denyer responds that the doctrine that the sage is the true diviner (cf. on §129b) means that the gods give true messages only to the sage and deceive others, but this too entails problems in a Stoically organized universe, and Denyer quickly abandons the topic as related to the problem of evil.

129. On Denyer's (inapposite) citation of Borges' story "The Garden of Forking Paths," see Timpanaro 1994, 253–54.

TEXT

M. Tulli Ciceronis *De Divinatione* Liber Secundus

1 Quaerenti mihi multumque et diu cogitanti quanam re possem prodesse quam plurimis, ne quando intermitterem consulere rei publicae, nulla maior occurrebat quam si optimarum artium vias traderem meis civibus; quod conpluribus iam libris me arbitror consecutum. nam et cohortati sumus ut maxime potuimus ad philosophiae studium eo libro qui est inscriptus Hortensius, et quod genus philosophandi minime adrogans maximeque et constans et elegans arbitraremur quattuor Academicis libris ostendimus. **2** cumque fundamentum esset philosophiae positum in finibus bonorum et malorum, perpurgatus est is locus a nobis quinque libris, ut quid a quoque et quid contra quemque philosophum diceretur intellegi posset. totidem subsecuti libri Tusculanarum disputationum res ad beate vivendum maxime necessarias aperuerunt: primus enim est de contemnenda morte, secundus de tolerando dolore, de aegritudine lenienda tertius, quartus de reliquis animi perturbationibus, quintus eum locum complexus est qui totam philosophiam maxime inlustrat, docet enim ad beate vivendum virtutem se ipsa esse contentam. **3** quibus rebus editis tres libri perfecti sunt de natura deorum, in quibus omnis eius loci quaestio continetur. quae ut plane esset cumulateque perfecta, de divinatione ingressi sumus his libris scribere; quibus, ut est in animo, de fato si adiunxerimus, erit abunde satis factum toti huic quaestioni. atque his libris adnumerandi sunt sex de re publica, quos tum scripsimus cum gubernacula rei publicae tenebamus, magnus locus philosophiaeque proprius a Platone, Aristotele, Theophrasto totaque Peripateticorum familia tractatus uberrime. nam quid ego de Consolatione dicam? quae mihi quidem ipsi sane aliquantum medetur; ceteris item multum illam profuturam puto. interiectus est etiam nuper liber is quem ad nostrum Atticum de senectute misimus. in primisque quoniam philosophia vir bonus efficitur et fortis, Cato noster in horum librorum numero ponendus est. **4a** cumque Aristoteles itemque Theophrastus, excellentes viri, cum subtilitate tum copia cum philosophia dicendi etiam praecepta coniunxerint, nostri quoque oratorii libri in eundem librorum numerum referendi videntur. ita tres erunt De oratore, quartus Brutus, quintus Orator.

4b Adhuc haec erant; ad reliqua alacri tendebamus animo, sic parati ut, nisi quae causa gravior obstitisset, nullum philosophiae locum esse pateremur qui non Latinis litteris inlustratus pateret. quod enim munus rei publicae adferre maius meliusve possumus quam si docemus atque erudimus iuventutem, his praesertim moribus atque temporibus, quibus ita prolapsa est ut omnium opibus refrenanda ac coercenda sit? **5** nec vero id effici posse confido, quod ne postulandum quidem est, ut omnes adulescentes se ad haec studia convertant: pauci utinam! quorum tamen in re publica late patere poterit industria. equidem ex iis etiam fructum capio laboris mei, qui iam aetate provecti in nostris libris adquiescunt; quorum studio legendi meum scribendi studium vehementius in dies incitatur; quos quidem plures quam rebar esse cognovi. magnificum illud etiam Romanisque hominibus gloriosum, ut Graecis de philosophia litteris non egeant; **6a** quod adsequar profecto, si instituta perfecero.

6b Ac mihi quidem explicandae philosophiae causam adtulit casus gravis civitatis, cum in armis civilibus nec tueri meo more rem publicam nec nihil agere poteram nec quid potius quod quidem me dignum esset agerem reperiebam. dabunt igitur mihi veniam mei cives, vel gratiam potius habebunt, quod cum esset in unius potestate res publica, neque ego me abdidi neque deserui neque adflixi neque ita gessi quasi homini aut temporibus iratus neque porro ita aut adulatus aut admiratus fortunam sum alterius ut me meae paeniteret. id enim ipsum a Platone philosophiaque didiceram, naturales esse quasdam conversiones rerum publicarum, ut eae tum a principibus tenerentur, tum a populis, aliquando a singulis. **7** quod cum accidisset nostrae rei publicae, tum pristinis orbati muneribus haec studia renovare coepimus ut et animus molestiis hac potissimum re levaretur et prodessemus civibus nostris qua re cumque possemus. in libris enim sententiam dicebamus, contionabamur, philosophiam nobis pro rei publicae procuratione substitutam putabamus. nunc quoniam de re publica consuli coepti sumus, tribuenda est opera rei publicae, vel omnis potius in ea cogitatio et cura ponenda; tantum huic studio relinquendum quantum vacabit a publico officio et munere. sed haec alias pluribus; nunc ad institutam disputationem revertamur.

8 Nam cum de divinatione Quintus frater ea disseruisset quae superiore libro scripta sunt satisque ambulatum videretur, tum in bibliotheca quae in Lycio est adsedimus. atque ego: Adcurate tu quidem, inquam, Quinte, et Stoice Stoicorum sententiam defendisti, quodque me maxime delectat, plurimis nostris exemplis usus es, et iis quidem claris et inlustribus. dicendum est mihi igitur ad ea quae sunt a te dicta, sed ita, nihil ut adfirmem, quaeram omnia dubitans plerumque et mihi ipse diffidens. si enim aliquid certi haberem quod dicerem, ego ipse divinarem, qui esse divinationem nego! **9** etenim me movet illud quod in primis Carneades quaerere solebat, quarumnam rerum divinatio esset: earumne quae sensibus perciperentur? at eas quidem cernimus, audimus, gustamus, olfacimus, tangimus. num quid ergo in his rebus est quod provisione aut permotione mentis magis quam natura ipsa sentiamus? aut num nescio qui ille divinus, si oculis captus sit, ut Tiresias fuit, possit quae alba sint, quae nigra dicere aut, si surdus sit, varietates vocum aut modos noscere? ad nullam igitur earum rerum quae sensu accipiuntur divinatio adhibetur. atqui ne in iis quidem rebus quae arte tractantur divinatione opus est. etenim ad aegros non vates aut hariolos sed medicos solemus adducere, nec vero qui fidibus aut tibiis uti volunt ab haruspicibus accipiunt earum tractationem, sed a musicis.

10 Eadem in litteris ratio est reliquisque rebus quarum est disciplina. num censes eos qui divinare dicuntur posse respondere sol maiorne quam terra sit an tantus quantus videatur, lunaque suo lumine an solis utatur; sol, luna quem motum habeat, quem quinque stellae quae errare dicuntur? nec haec qui divini habentur profitentur se esse dicturos nec eorum quae in geometria describuntur quae vera, quae falsa sint: sunt enim ea mathematicorum, non hariolorum. de illis vero rebus quae in philosophia versantur, num quid est quod quisquam divinorum aut respondere soleat aut consuli, quid bonum sit, quid malum, quid neutrum? sunt enim haec propria philosophorum. **11** quid, de officio num quis haruspicem consulit, quem ad modum sit cum parentibus, cum fratribus, cum amicis vivendum, quem ad modum utendum pecunia, quem ad modum honore, quem ad modum imperio? ad sapientes haec, non ad divinos referri solent. quid, quae a dialecticis aut physicis tractantur, num quid eorum divinari potest, unusne mundus sit an plures, quae sint initia rerum, ex quibus nascuntur omnia? physicorum est ista prudentia. quo modo autem 'mentientem,' quem ψευδόμενον vocant, dissolvas aut quem ad modum 'soriti' resistas (quem, si necesse sit, Latino verbo liceat 'acervalem' appellare; sed nihil opus est: ut enim ipsa 'philosophia' et multa verba Graecorum, sic 'sorites' satis Latino sermone tritus est), ergo haec quoque dialectici dicent, non divini. quid, cum quaeritur qui sit optimus rei publicae status, quae leges, qui mores aut utiles aut inutiles, haruspicesne ex Etruria arcessentur an principes statuent et delecti viri periti rerum civilium? **12** quodsi nec earum rerum quae subiectae sensibus sunt ulla divinatio est nec earum quae artibus continentur nec earum quae in philosophia disseruntur nec earum quae in re publica versantur, quarum rerum sit nihil prorsus intellego. nam aut omnium debet esse, aut aliqua ei materia danda est in qua versari possit. sed nec omnium divinatio est, ut ratio docuit, nec locus nec materia invenitur cui divinationem praeficere possimus. vide igitur ne nulla sit divinatio. est quidam Graecus vulgaris in hanc sententiam versus:

bene qui coniciet, vatem hunc perhibebo optumum.

num igitur aut quae tempestas inpendeat vates melius coniciet quam gubernator aut morbi naturam acutius quam medicus aut belli administrationem prudentius quam inperator coniectura adsequetur?

13 Sed animadverti, Quinte, te caute et ab iis coniecturis quae haberent artem atque prudentiam et ab iis rebus quae sensibus aut artificiis perciperentur abducere divinationem eamque ita definire: divinationem esse earum rerum praedictionem et praesensionem quae essent fortuitae. primum eodem revolveris, nam et medici et gubernatoris et imperatoris praesensio est rerum fortuitarum. num igitur aut haruspex aut augur aut vates quis aut somnians melius coniecerit aut e morbo evasurum aegrotum aut e periculo navem aut ex insidiis exercitum quam medicus, quam gubernator, quam imperator? **14** atqui ne illa quidem divinantis esse dicebas, ventos aut imbres inpendentes quibusdam praesentire signis (in quo nostra quaedam Aratea memoriter a te pronuntiata sunt), etsi haec ipsa fortuita sunt: plerumque enim, non semper eveniunt. quae est igitur aut ubi versatur fortuitarum rerum praesensio, quam divinationem vocas? quae enim praesentiri aut arte aut ratione aut usu aut coniectura possunt, ea non divinis tribuenda putas, sed peritis. ita relinquitur ut ea fortuita divinari possint quae nulla nec arte nec sapientia provideri possunt, ut si quis M. Marcellum illum qui ter consul fuit multis annis ante dixisset naufragio esse periturum, divinasset profecto: nulla enim arte alia id nec sapientia scire potuisset. talium ergo rerum, quae in fortuna positae sunt, praesensio divinatio est.

15 Potestne igitur earum rerum quae nihil habent rationis quare futurae sint esse ulla praesensio? quid est enim aliud fors, quid fortuna, quid casus, quid eventus, nisi cum sic aliquid cecidit, sic evenit ut vel <non cadere atque evenire vel> aliter cadere atque evenire potuerit? quo modo ergo id quod temere fit, caeco casu et volubilitate fortunae, praesentiri et praedici potest? **16** medicus morbum ingravescentem ratione providet, insidias imperator, tempestates gubernator; et tamen ii ipsi saepe falluntur qui nihil sine certa ratione opinantur; ut agricola cum florem oleae videt, bacam quoque se visurum putat—non sine ratione ille quidem, sed non numquam tamen fallitur. quodsi falluntur ii qui nihil sine aliqua probabili coniectura ac ratione dicunt, quid existimandum est de coniectura eorum qui extis aut avibus aut ostentis aut oraclis aut somniis futura praesentiunt? nondum dico quam haec signa nulla sint, fissum iecoris, corvi cantus, volatus aquilae, stellae traiectio, voces furentium, sortes, somnia; de quibus singulis dicam suo loco; nunc de universis. **17** qui potest provideri quicquam futurum esse quod neque causam habet ullam neque notam cur futurum sit? solis defectiones itemque lunae praedicuntur in multos annos ab iis qui siderum motus numeris persequuntur; ea praedicunt enim quae naturae necessitas perfectura est: vident ex constantissimo motu lunae quando illa e regione solis [facta] incurrat in umbram terrae, quae est meta noctis, ut eam obscurari necesse sit, quandoque eadem luna subiecta atque opposita soli nostris oculis eius lumen obscuret, quo in signo quaeque errantium stellarum quoque tempore futura sit, qui exortus quoque die signi alicuius aut qui occasus futurus sit. haec qui ante dicunt quam rationem sequantur vides.

18 Qui thesaurum inventum <iri> aut hereditatem venturam dicunt quid sequuntur, aut in qua rerum natura inest id futurum? quod si haec eaque quae sunt eiusdem generis habent aliquam talem necessitatem, quid est tandem quod casu fieri aut forte fortuna putemus? nihil enim est tam contrarium rationi et constantiae quam fortuna, ut mihi ne in deum quidem cadere videatur ut sciat quid casu et fortuito futurum sit. si enim scit, certe illud eveniet; sin certe eveniet, nulla fortuna est; est autem fortuna; rerum igitur fortuitarum nulla praesensio est. **19** aut si negas esse fortunam, et omnia quae fiunt quaeque futura sunt ex omni aeternitate definita dicis esse fataliter, muta definitionem divinationis, quam dicebas praesensionem esse rerum fortuitarum. si enim nihil fieri potest, nihil accidere, nihil evenire, nisi quod ab omni aeternitate certum fuerit esse futurum rato tempore, quae potest esse fortuna? qua sublata qui locus est divinationi, quae a te fortuitarum rerum est dicta praesensio? quamquam dicebas omnia quae fierent futurave essent fato contineri. anile sane et plenum superstitionis fati nomen ipsum; sed tamen apud Stoicos de isto fato multa dicuntur; de quo alias; nunc quod necesse est.

20 Si omnia fato, quid mihi divinatio prodest? quod enim is qui divinat praedicit, id vero futurum est. ut ne illud quidem sciam quale sit quod Deiotarum, necessarium nostrum, ex itinere aquila revocavit. qui nisi revertisset, in eo conclavi ei cubandum fuisset quod proxuma nocte corruit; ruina igitur oppressus esset. at id neque si fatum fuerat, effugisset nec, si non fuerat, in eum casum incidisset. quid ergo adiuvat divinatio, aut quid est quod me moneant aut sortes aut exta aut ulla praedictio? si enim fatum fuit classes populi Romani bello Punico primo alteram naufragio, alteram a Poenis depressam interire, etiamsi tripudium solistumum pulli fecissent L. Iunio et P. Claudio consulibus, classes tamen interissent. sin cum auspiciis obtemperatum esset, interiturae classes non fuerunt, non interierunt fato. vultis autem omnia fato; nulla igitur est divinatio. **21** quodsi fatum fuit bello Punico secundo exercitum populi Romani ad lacum Trasumennum interire, num id vitari potuit, si Flaminius consul iis signis iisque auspiciis quibus pugnare prohibebatur paruisset? certe <non> potuit. aut igitur non fato interiit exercitus (mutari enim fata non possunt) aut, si fato (quod certe vobis ita dicendum est), etiamsi obtemperasset auspiciis, idem eventurum fuisset. ubi est igitur ista divinatio Stoicorum, quae, si fato omnia fiunt, nihil nos admonere potest ut cautiores simus? quoquo enim modo nos gesserimus, fiet tamen illud quod futurum est; sin autem id potest flecti, nullum est fatum; ita ne divinatio quidem, quoniam ea rerum futurarum est; nihil autem est pro certo futurum quod potest aliqua procuratione accidere ne fiat.

22 Atque ego ne utilem quidem arbitror esse nobis futurarum rerum scientiam. quae enim vita fuisset Priamo, si ab adulescentia scisset quos eventus senectutis esset habiturus? abeamus a fabulis, propiora videamus. clarissimorum hominum nostrae civitatis gravissimos exitus in Consolatione collegimus. quid igitur, ut omittamus superiores, Marcone Crasso putas utile fuisse tum, cum maxumis opibus fortunisque florebat, scire sibi interfecto Publio filio exercituque deleto trans Euphratem cum ignominia et dedecore esse pereundum? an Cn. Pompeium censes tribus suis consulatibus, tribus triumphis, maximarum rerum gloria laetaturum fuisse, si sciret se in solitudine, <scelere> Aegyptiorum trucidatum iri amisso exercitu, post mortem vero ea consecutura quae sine lacrimis non possumus dicere? **23** quid vero Caesarem putamus, si divinasset fore ut in eo senatu quem maiore ex parte ipse cooptasset, in curia Pompeia, ante ipsius Pompei simulacrum, tot centurionibus suis inspectantibus, a nobilissumis civibus, partim etiam a se omnibus rebus ornatis, trucidatus ita iaceret ut ad eius corpus non modo amicorum, sed ne servorum quidem quisquam accederet, quo cruciatu animi vitam acturum fuisse? certe igitur ignoratio futurorum malorum utilior est quam scientia. **24** nam illud quidem dici, praesertim a Stoicis, nullo modo potest: 'non isset ad arma Pompeius, non transisset Crassus Euphratem, non suscepisset bellum civile Caesar; non igitur fatalis exitus habuerunt.' vultis autem evenire omnia fato. nihil ergo illis profuisset divinare, atque etiam omnem fructum vitae superioris perdidissent: quid enim posset iis esse laetum exitus suos cogitantibus? ita quoquo sese verterint Stoici, iaceat necesse est omnis eorum sollertia. si enim id quod eventurum est vel hoc vel illo modo potest evenire, fortuna valet plurimum; quae autem fortuita sunt certa esse non possunt. sin autem certum est quid quaque de re quoque tempore futurum sit, quid est quod me adiuvent haruspices, <qui> cum res tristissumas portendi dixerunt, **25** addunt ad extremum omnia levius casura rebus divinis procuratis? si enim nihil fit extra fatum, nihil levari re divina potest. hoc sentit Homerus, cum querentem Iovem inducit quod Sarpedonem filium a morte contra fatum eripere non posset. hoc idem significat Graecus ille in eam sententiam versus:

quod fore paratum est, id summum exsuperat Iovem.

totum omnino fatum etiam Atellanio versu iure mihi esse inrisum videtur; sed in rebus tam severis non est iocandi locus. concludatur igitur ratio: si enim provideri nihil potest futurum esse eorum quae casu fiunt, quia esse certa non possunt, divinatio nulla est; sin autem idcirco possunt provideri, quia certa sunt et fatalia, rursus divinatio nulla est; eam enim tu fortuitarum rerum esse dicebas.

26a Sed haec fuerit nobis tamquam levis armaturae prima orationis excursio; nunc comminus agamus experiamurque si possimus cornua commovere disputationis tuae.

26b Duo enim genera divinandi esse dicebas, unum artificiosum, alterum naturale: artificiosum constare partim ex coniectura, partim ex observatione diuturna; naturale, quod animus arriperet aut exciperet extrinsecus ex divinitate, unde omnes animos haustos aut acceptos aut libatos haberemus. artificiosa divinationis illa fere genera ponebas: extispicum eorumque qui ex fulgoribus ostentisque praedicerent, tum augurum eorumque qui signis aut ominibus uterentur, omneque genus coniecturale in hoc fere genere ponebas. **27** illud autem naturale aut concitatione mentis edi et quasi fundi videbatur aut animo per somn[i]um sensibus et curis vacuo provideri. duxisti autem divinationem omnem a tribus rebus, a deo, a fato, a natura. sed tamen cum explicare nihil posses, pugnasti commenticiorum exemplorum mirifica copia. de quo primum hoc libet dicere: hoc ego philosophi non esse arbitror, testibus uti qui aut casu veri aut malitia falsi fictique esse possunt; argumentis et rationibus oportet quare quidque ita sit docere, non eventis, iis praesertim quibus mihi liceat non credere.

28 Ut ordiar ab haruspicina, quam ego rei publicae causa communisque religionis colendam censeo—sed soli sumus; licet verum exquirere sine invidia, mihi praesertim de plerisque dubitanti—inspiciamus, si placet, exta primum. persuaderi igitur cuiquam potest ea quae significari dicuntur extis cognita esse ab haruspicibus observatione diuturna? quam diuturna ista fuit? aut quam longinquo tempore observari potuit, aut quo modo est conlata inter ipsos quae pars inimica, quae pars familiaris esset, quod fissum periculum, quod commodum aliquod ostenderet? an haec inter se haruspices Etrusci, Elii, Aegyptii, Poeni contulerunt? at id, praeterquam quod fieri non potuit, ne fingi quidem potest; alios enim alio more videmus exta interpretari nec esse unam omnium disciplinam.

29 Et certe si est in extis aliqua vis quae declaret futura, necesse est eam aut cum rerum natura esse coniunctam aut conformari quodam modo numine deorum vique divina. cum rerum natura tanta tamque praeclara in omnes partes motusque diffusa quid habere potest commune non dicam gallinaceum fel (sunt enim qui vel argutissima haec exta esse dicant), sed tauri opimi iecur aut cor aut pulmo quid habet naturale quod declarare possit quid futurum sit? **30** Democritus tamen non inscite—nugatur ut physicus, quo genere nihil adrogantius:

quod est ante pedes nemo spectat, caeli scrutantur plagas—

verum is tamen habitu extorum et colore declarari censet haec dumtaxat: pabuli genus et earum rerum quas terra procreet vel ubertatem vel tenuitatem; salubritatem etiam aut pestilentiam extis significari putat. o mortalem beatum, cui certo scio ludum numquam defuisse! huncine hominem tantis delectatum esse nugis, ut non videret tum futurum id veri simile, si omnium pecudum exta eodem tempore in eundem habitum se coloremque converterent? sed si eadem hora aliae pecudis iecur nitidum atque plenum est, aliae horridum et exile, quid est quod declarari possit habitu extorum et colore? **31** an hoc eiusdem modi est quale Pherecydeum illud quod est a te dictum, qui, cum aquam ex puteo vidisset haustam, terrae motum dixit futurum? parum, credo, inpudenter, quod, cum factus es[se]t motus, dicere audent quae vis id effecerit; etiamne futurum esse aquae iugis colore praesentiunt? multa istius modi dicuntur in scholis, sed credere omnia vide ne non sit necesse. **32** verum sint sane ista Democritea vera: quando ea nos extis exquirimus, aut quando aliquid eius modi ab haruspice inspectis extis audivimus? ab aqua aut ab igni pericula monent; tum hereditates, tum damna denuntiant; fissum familiare et vitale tractant; caput iecoris ex omni parte diligentissime considerant; si vero id non est inventum, nihil putant accidere potuisse tristius. **33a** haec observari certe non potuerunt, ut supra docui; sunt igitur artis inventa, non vetustatis, si est ars ulla rerum incognitarum.

33b Cum rerum autem natura quam cognationem habent? quae ut uno consensu iuncta sit et continens (quod video placuisse physicis eisque maxume qui omne quod esset unum esse dixerunt), quid habere mundus potest cum thesauri inventione coniunctum? si enim extis pecuniae mihi amplificatio ostenditur idque fit natura, primum exta sunt coniuncta mundo, deinde meum lucrum natura rerum continetur. nonne pudet physicos haec dicere? ut enim iam sit aliqua in natura rerum contagio, quam esse concedo (multa enim Stoici colligunt: nam et musculorum iecuscula bruma dicunt augeri, et puleium aridum florescere brumali ipso die et inflatas rumpi vesiculas et semina malorum, quae in iis mediis inclusa sint, in contrarias partis se vertere; iam nervos in fidibus aliis pulsis resonare alios; ostreisque et conchyliis omnibus contingere ut cum luna pariter crescant pariterque decrescant; arboresque ut hiemali tempore cum luna simul senescente, quia tum exsiccatae sint, tempestive caedi putentur. **34a** quid de fretis aut de marinis aestibus plura dicam, quorum accessus et recessus lunae motu gubernantur? sescenta licet eiusdem modi proferri, ut distantium rerum cognatio naturalis appareat)—demus hoc: nihil enim huic disputationi adversatur. num etiam, si fissum cuiusdam modi fuerit in iecore, lucrum ostenditur? qua ex coniunctione naturae et quasi concentu atque consensu, quam συμπάθειαν Graeci appellant, convenire potest aut fissum iecoris cum lucello meo aut meus quaesticulus cum caelo, terra rerumque natura?

34b Concedam hoc ipsum, si vis, etsi magnam iacturam causae fecero, si ullam esse convenientiam naturae cum extis concessero. **35** sed tamen eo concesso qui evenit ut is qui impetrire velit convenientem hostiam rebus suis immolet? hoc erat quod ego non rebar posse dissolvi. at quam festive dissolvitur! pudet me non tui quidem, cuius etiam memoriam admiror, sed Chrysippi, Antipatri, Posidoni, qui idem istuc quidem dicunt quod est dictum a te, ad hostiam deligendam ducem esse vim quandam sentientem atque divinam quae toto confusa mundo sit. illud vero multo etiam melius, quod et a te usurpatum est et dicitur ab illis: cum immolare quispiam velit, tum fieri extorum mutationem, ut aut absit aliquid aut supersit; **36a** deorum enim numini parere omnia. haec iam, mihi crede, ne aniculae quidem existimant. an censes, eundem vitulum si alius delegerit, sine capite iecur inventurum, si alius, cum capite? haec decessio capitis aut accessio subitone fieri potest, ut se exta ad immolatoris fortunam accommodent? non perspicitis aleam quandam esse in hostiis deligendis, praesertim cum res ipsa doceat? cum enim [tristissuma] exta sine capite fuerunt, quibus nihil videtur esse dirius, proxuma hostia litatur saepe pulcherrime, ubi igitur illae minae superiorum extorum? aut quae tam subito facta est deorum tanta placatio?

36b Sed adfers in tauri opimi extis immolante Caesare cor non fuisse; id quia non potuerit accidere, ut sine corde victuma illa viveret, iudicandum esse tum interisse cor cum immolaretur. **37** qui fit ut alterum intellegas, sine corde non potuisse bovem vivere, alterum non videas, cor subito non potuisse nescio quo avolare? ego enim possum vel nescire quae vis sit cordis ad vivendum, vel suspicari contractum aliquo morbo bovis exile et exiguum et vietum cor et dissimile cordis fuisse; tu vero quid habes quare putes, si paulo ante cor fuerit in tauro opimo, subito id in ipsa immolatione interisse? an quod aspexerit vestitu purpureo excordem Caesarem, ipse corde privatus est? urbem philosophiae, mihi crede, proditis, dum castella defenditis; nam dum haruspicinam veram esse vultis, physiologiam totam pervertitis. caput est in iecore, cor in extis: iam abscedet, simul ac molam et vinum insperseris; deus id eripiet, vis aliqua conficiet aut exedet: non ergo omnium interitus atque ortus natura conficiet, et erit aliquid quod aut ex nihilo oriatur aut in nihilum subito occidat. quis hoc physicus dixit umquam? 'Haruspices dicunt.' his igitur quam physicis credendum potius existumas.

38 Quid, cum pluribus deis immolatur, qui tandem evenit ut litetur aliis, aliis non litetur? quae autem inconstantia deorum est, ut primis minentur extis, bene promittant secundis? aut tanta inter eos dissensio, saepe etiam inter proxumos, ut Apollinis exta bona sint, Dianae non bona? quid est tam perspicuum quam, cum fortuito hostiae adducantur, talia cuique exta esse, qualis cuique obtigerit hostia? 'At enim id ipsum habet aliquid divini, quae cuique hostia obtingat, tamquam in sortibus quae cui ducatur.' mox de sortibus; quamquam tu quidem non hostiarum causam confirmas sortium similitudine, sed infirmas sortis conlatione hostiarum. **39** an cum in Aequimelium misimus qui adferat agnum quem immolemus, is mihi agnus adfertur qui habet exta rebus accommodata, et ad eum agnum non casu sed duce deo servus deducitur? nam si casum in eo quoque esse dicis quasi sortem quandam cum deorum voluntate coniunctam, doleo tantam Stoicos nostros Epicureis inridendi sui facultatem dedisse; non enim ignoras quam ista derideant. **40** et quidem illi facilius facere possunt; deos enim ipsos iocandi causa induxit Epicurus perlucidos et perflabilis et habitantis tamquam inter duos lucos sic inter duos mundos propter metum ruinarum, eosque habere putat eadem membra quae nos, nec usum ullum habere membrorum. ergo hic circumitione quadam deos tollens, recta non dubitat divinationem tollere. sed non, ut hic sibi constat, item Stoici: illius enim deus, nihil habens nec sui nec alieni negoti, non potest hominibus divinationem inpertire; vester autem deus potest non inpertire, ut nihilo minus mundum regat et hominibus consulat. **41** cur igitur vos induitis in eas captiones quas numquam explicetis? ita enim, cum magis properant, concludere solent: 'si di sunt, est divinatio; sunt autem di; est ergo divinatio.' multo est probabilius: '<si est divinatio, sunt di;> non est autem divinatio; non sunt ergo di.' vide quam temere committant ut si nulla sit divinatio, nulli sint di. divinatio enim perspicue tollitur, deos esse retinendum est. **42a** atque hac extispicum divinatione sublata omnis haruspicina sublata est. ostenta enim sequuntur et fulgura.

42b Valet autem in fulguribus observatio diuturna, in ostentis ratio plerumque coniecturaque adhibetur. quid est igitur quod observatum sit in fulgure? caelum in sedecim partis diviserunt Etrusci. facile id quidem fuit, quattuor quas nos habemus duplicare, post idem iterum facere, ut ex eo dicerent fulmen qua ex parte venisset. primum id quid interest, deinde quid significat? nonne perspicuum est ex prima admiratione hominum, quod tonitrua iactusque fulminum extimuissent, credidisse ea efficere rerum omnium praepotentem Iovem? itaque in nostris commentariis scriptum habemus: 'Iove tonante fulgurante comitia populi habere nefas.' **43a** hoc fortasse rei publicae causa constitutum est: comitiorum enim non habendorum causas esse voluerunt. itaque comitiorum solum vitium est fulmen, quod idem omnibus rebus optumum auspicium habemus si sinistrum fuit. sed de auspiciis alio loco, nunc de fulgoribus.

43b Quid igitur minus a physicis dici debet quam quicquam certi significari rebus incertis? non enim te puto esse eum qui Iovi fulmen fabricatos esse Cyclopas in Aetna putes; **44** nam esset mirabile quo modo id Iuppiter totiens iaceret cum unum haberet; nec vero fulminibus homines quid aut faciendum esset aut cavendum moneret. placet enim Stoicis eos anhelitus terrae qui frigidi sint, cum fluere coeperint, ventos esse; cum autem se in nubem induerint eiusque tenuissimam quamque partem coeperint dividere atque disrumpere idque crebrius facere et vehementius, tum et fulgores et tonitrua existere; si autem nubium conflictu ardor expressus se emiserit, id esse fulmen. quod igitur vi naturae, nulla constantia, nullo rato tempore videmus effici, ex eo significationem rerum consequentium quaerimus? scilicet, si ista Iuppiter significaret, tam multa frustra fulmina emitteret! **45a** quid enim proficit cum in medium mare fulmen iecit, quid cum in altissimos montis, quod plerumque fit, quid cum in desertas solitudines, quid cum in earum gentium oras in quibus haec ne observantur quidem?

45b 'At inventum est caput in Tiberi.' quasi ego artem aliquam istorum esse negem! divinationem nego. caeli enim distributio, quam ante dixi, et certarum rerum notatio docet unde fulmen venerit, quo concesserit; quid significet autem nulla ratio docet. sed urges me meis versibus:

nam pater altitonans stellanti nixus Olympo
ipse suos quondam tumulos ac templa petivit
et Capitolinis iniecit sedibus ignis.

tum statua Nattae, tum simulacra deorum Romulusque et Remus cum altrice belua vi fulminis icti conciderunt, deque his rebus haruspicum extiterunt responsa verissuma. **46** mirabile autem illud, quod, eo ipso tempore quo fieret indicium coniurationis in senatu, signum Iovis biennio post quam erat locatum in Capitolio conlocabatur. 'Tu igitur animum induces'—sic enim mecum agebas—'causam istam et contra facta tua et contra scripta defendere?' frater es; eo vereor—verum quid tibi hic tandem nocet? resne quae talis est an ego qui verum explicari volo?—itaque nihil contra dico, a te rationem totius haruspicinae peto. sed te mirificam in latebram coniecisti: quod enim intellegeres fore ut premerere cum ex te causas unius cuiusque divinationis exquirerem, multa verba fecisti te, cum res videres, rationem causamque non quaerere, quid fieret, non cur fieret, ad rem pertinere. quasi ego aut fieri concederem aut esset philosophi causam cur quidque fieret non quaerere! **47** et eo quidem loco et Prognostica nostra pronuntiabas et genera herbarum, scammoniam aristolochiamque [radicem], quarum causam ignorares, vim et effectum videres. dissimile totum: nam et prognosticorum causas persecuti sunt et Boëthus Stoicus, qui est a te nominatus, et noster etiam Posidonius, et si causae non reperiantur istarum rerum, res tamen ipsae observari animadvertique potuerunt. Nattae vero statua aut aera legum de caelo tacta quid habent observatum ac vetustum? 'Pinarii Nattae nobiles; a nobilitate igitur periculum.' hoc tam callide Iuppiter cogitavit! 'Romulus lactens fulmine ictus; urbi igitur periculum ostenditur ei quam ille condidit.' quam scite per notas nos certiores facit Iuppiter! 'At eodem tempore signum Iovis conlocabatur quo coniuratio indicabatur.' et tu scilicet mavis numine deorum id factum quam casu arbitrari, et redemptor qui columnam illam de Cotta et de Torquato conduxerat faciendam, non inertia aut inopia tardior fuit, sed a deis inmortalibus ad istam horam reservatus est!

48 Non equidem plane despero ista esse vera, sed nescio et discere a te volo. nam cum mihi quaedam casu viderentur sic evenire ut praedicta essent a divinantibus, dixisti multa de casu, ut Venerium iaci posse casu quattuor talis iactis, sed quadringentis centum Venerios non posse casu consistere. primum nescio cur non possint, sed non pugno; abundas enim similibus. habes et respersionem pigmentorum et rostrum suis et alia permulta. idem Carneadem fingere dicis de capite Panisci; quasi non potuerit id evenire casu et non in omni marmore necesse sit inesse vel Praxitelia capita! illa enim ipsa efficiuntur detractione, neque quicquam illuc adfertur a Praxitele; sed cum multa sunt detracta et ad liniamenta oris perventum est, tum intellegas illud quod iam expolitum sit intus fuisse. **49a** potest igitur tale aliquid etiam sua sponte in lapicidinis Chiorum extitisse. sed sit hoc fictum; quid, in nubibus numquam animadvertisti leonis formam aut hippocentauri? potest igitur, quod modo negabas, veritatem casus imitari.

49b Sed quoniam de extis et de fulgoribus satis est disputatum, ostenta restant ut tota haruspicina sit pertractata. mulae partus prolatus est a te, res mirabilis propterea quia non saepe fit, sed si fieri non potuisset, facta non esset. atque hoc contra omnia ostenta valeat: numquam quod fieri non potuerit esse factum; sin potuerit, non esse mirandum. causarum enim ignoratio in re nova mirationem facit; eadem ignoratio si in rebus usitatis est, non miramur. nam qui mulam peperisse miratur, is, quo modo equa pariat aut omnino quae natura partum animantis faciat, ignorat. sed quod crebro videt non miratur, etiamsi cur fiat nescit; quod ante non vidit, id si evenit, ostentum esse censet. utrum igitur cum concepit mula an cum peperit, ostentum est? **50a** conceptio contra naturam fortasse, sed partus prope necessarius.

50b Sed quid plura? ortum videamus haruspicinae; sic facillume quid habeat auctoritatis iudicabimus. Tages quidam dicitur in agro Tarquiniensi, cum terra araretur et sulcus altius esset impressus, extitisse repente et eum adfatus esse qui arabat. is autem Tages, ut in libris est Etruscorum, puerili specie dicitur visus sed senili fuisse prudentia. eius adspectu cum obstipuisset bubulcus clamoremque maiorem cum admiratione edidisset, concursum esse factum, totamque brevi tempore in eum locum Etruriam convenisse. tum illum plura locutum multis audientibus, qui omnia verba eius exceperint litterisque mandarint. omnem autem orationem fuisse eam qua haruspicinae disciplina contineretur; eam postea crevisse rebus novis cognoscendis et ad eadem illa principia referendis. haec accepimus ab ipsis, haec scripta conservant, hunc fontem habent disciplinae.

51 Num ergo opus est ad haec refellenda Carneade, num Epicuro? estne quisquam ita desipiens qui credat exaratum esse deum dicam an hominem? si deum, cur se contra naturam in terram abdiderat, ut patefactus aratro lucem aspiceret? quid, idem nonne poterat deus hominibus disciplinam superiore e loco tradere? si autem homo ille Tages fuit, quonam modo potuit terra oppressus vivere? unde porro illa potuit, quae docebat alios, ipse didicisse? sed ego insipientior quam illi ipsi qui ista credunt, qui quidem contra eos tam diu disputem. vetus autem illud Catonis admodum scitum est, qui mirari se aiebat quod non rideret haruspex haruspicem cum vidisset. **52a** quota enim quaeque res evenit praedicta ab istis? aut si evenit quippiam, quid adferri potest cur non casu id evenerit?

52b Rex Prusias, cum Hannibali apud eum exsulanti depugnari placeret, negabat se audere quod exta prohiberent. 'Ain tu?' inquit, 'carunculae vitulinae mavis quam imperatori veteri credere?' quid, ipse Caesar cum a summo haruspice moneretur ne in Africam ante brumam transmitteret, nonne transmisit? quod ni fecisset, uno in loco omnes adversariorum copiae convenissent. quid ego haruspicum responsa commemorem (possum equidem innumerabilia), quae aut nullos habuerint exitus aut contrarios? **53** hoc civili bello, di immortales, quam multa luserunt quae nobis in Graeciam Roma responsa haruspicum missa sunt, quae dicta Pompeio! etenim ille admodum extis et ostentis movebatur. non lubet commemorare, nec vero necesse est, tibi praesertim qui interfuisti; vides tamen omnia fere contra ac dicta sint evenisse. sed haec hactenus; nunc ad ostenta veniamus.

54 Multa me consule a me ipso scripta recitasti, multa ante Marsicum bellum a Sisenna collecta attulisti, multa ante Lacedaemoniorum malam pugnam in Leuctris a Callisthene commemorata dixisti. de quibus dicam equidem singulis quoad videbitur; sed dicendum etiam est de universis. quae est enim ista a deis profecta significatio et quasi denuntiatio calamitatum? quid autem volunt di inmortales primum ea significantes quae sine interpretibus non possimus intellegere, deinde ea quae cavere nequeamus? at hoc ne homines quidem probi faciunt, ut amicis inpendentis calamitates praedicant quas illi effugere nullo modo possint, ut medici quamquam intellegunt saepe, tamen numquam aegris dicunt illo morbo eos esse morituros; omnis enim praedictio mali tum probatur, cum ad praedictionem cautio adiungitur. **55a** quid igitur aut ostenta aut eorum interpretes vel Lacedaemonios olim vel nuper nostros adiuverunt? quae si signa deorum putanda sunt, cur tam obscura fuerunt? si enim ut intellegeremus quid esset eventurum, aperte declarari oportebat aut ne occulte quidem, si ea sciri nolebant.

55b Iam vero coniectura omnis, in qua nititur divinatio, ingeniis hominum in multas aut diversas aut etiam contrarias partis saepe diducitur. ut enim in causis iudicialibus alia coniectura est accusatoris, alia defensoris et tamen utriusque credibilis, sic in omnibus iis rebus quae coniectura investigari videntur anceps reperitur oratio.

55c Quas autem res tum natura, tum casus adfert—non numquam etiam errorem creat similitudo—magna stultitia est earum rerum deos facere effectores, causas rerum non quaerere. **56** tu vates Boeotios credis Lebadiae vidisse ex gallorum gallinaceorum cantu victoriam esse Thebanorum, quia galli victi silere solerent, canere victores. hoc igitur per gallinas Iuppiter tantae civitati signum dabat? an illae aves, nisi cum vicerunt, canere non solent? at tum canebant nec vicerant. 'Id enim est,' inquies, 'ostentum.' magnum vero, quasi pisces, non galli cecinerint! quod autem est tempus quo illi non cantent, vel nocturnum vel diurnum? quodsi victores alacritate et quasi laetitia ad canendum excitantur, potuit accidisse alia quoque laetitia qua ad cantum moverentur. **57** Democritus quidem optumis verbis causam explicat cur ante lucem galli canant: depulso enim de pectore et in omne corpus diviso et mitificato cibo, cantus edere quiete satiatos; qui quidem silentio noctis, ut ait Ennius,

> favent faucibus russis
> cantu, plausuque premunt alas.

cum igitur hoc animal tam sit canorum sua sponte, quid in mentem venit Callistheni dicere deos gallis signum dedisse cantandi, cum id vel natura vel casus efficere potuisset?

58 Sanguine[m] pluisse senatui nuntiatum est, Atratum etiam fluvium fluxisse sanguine[m], deorum sudasse simulacra. num censes his nuntiis Thalen aut Anaxagoran aut quemquam physicum crediturum fuisse? nec enim sanguis nec sudor nisi e corpore. sed et decoloratio quaedam ex aliqua contagione terrena maxume potest sanguini similis esse, et umor adlapsus extrinsecus, ut in tectoriis videmus austro, sudorem videtur imitari. atque haec in bello plura et maiora videntur timentibus, eadem non tam animadvertuntur in pace; accedit illud etiam, quod in metu et periculo cum creduntur facilius tum finguntur inpunius. **59** nos autem ita leves atque inconsiderati sumus ut si mures corroserint aliquid, quorum est opus hoc unum, monstrum putemus. ante vero Marsicum bellum quod clipeos Lanuvii, ut a te dictum est, mures rossent, maxumum id portentum haruspices esse dixerunt; quasi vero quicquam intersit, mures diem noctem aliquid rodentes scuta an cribra corroserint! nam si ista sequimur, quod Platonis Politian nuper apud me mures corroserunt, de re publica debui pertimescere, aut si Epicuri de voluptate liber rosus esset, putarem annonam in macello cariorem fore.

60 An vero illa nos terrent, si quando aliqua portentosa aut ex pecude aut ex homine nata dicuntur? quorum omnium, ne sim longior, una ratio est. quicquid enim oritur, qualecumque est, causam habeat a natura necesse est, ut, etiamsi praeter consuetudinem extiterit, praeter naturam tamen non possit existere. causam igitur investigato in re nova atque admirabili, si poteris; si nullam reperies, illud tamen exploratum habeto, nihil fieri potuisse sine causa, eumque errorem quem tibi rei novitas attulerit naturae ratione depellito. ita te nec terrae fremitus nec caeli discessus nec lapideus aut sanguineus imber nec traiectio stellae nec faces visae terrebunt. **61** quarum <rerum> omnium causas si a Chrysippo quaeram, ipse ille divinationis auctor numquam illa dicet facta fortuito naturalemque rationem omnium reddet; nihil enim fieri sine causa potest, nec quicquam fit quod fieri non potest, nec si id factum est quod potuit fieri, portentum debet videri; nulla igitur portenta sunt. nam si, quod raro fit, id portentum putandum est, sapientem esse portentum est: saepius enim mulam peperisse arbitror quam sapientem fuisse. illa igitur ratio concluditur: nec id quod non potuerit fieri factum umquam esse, nec quod potuerit id portentum esse; ita omnino nullum esse portentum. **62a** quod etiam coniector quidam et interpres portentorum non inscite respondisse dicitur ei qui [cum] ad eum rettulisset quasi ostentum quod anguis domi vectem circumiectus fuisset: 'Tum esset,' inquit, 'ostentum, si anguem vectis circumplicavisset.' hoc ille responso satis aperte declaravit nihil habendum esse quod fieri posset ostentum.

62b C. Gracchus ad M. Pomponium scripsit, duobus anguibus domi conprehensis, haruspices a patre convocatos. qui magis anguibus quam lacertis, quam muribus? quia sunt haec cotidiana, angues non item; quasi vero referat quod fieri potest quam id saepe fiat. ego tamen miror, si emissio feminae anguis mortem adferebat Ti. Graccho, emissio autem maris anguis erat mortifera Corneliae, cur alteram utram emiserit; nihil enim scribit respondisse haruspices, si neuter anguis emissus esset, quid esset futurum. 'At mors insecuta Gracchum est.' causa quidem, credo, aliqua morbi gravioris, non emissione serpentis; neque enim tanta est infelicitas haruspicum ut ne casu quidem umquam fiat quod futurum illi esse dixerint. **63** nam illud mirarer, si crederem, quod apud Homerum Calchantem dixisti ex passerum numero belli Troiani annos auguratum; de quoius coniectura sic apud Homerum, ut nos otiosi convertimus, loquitur Agamemnon:

Ferte, viri, et duros animo tolerate labores,
auguris ut nostri Calchantis fata queamus
scire ratosne habeant an vanos pectoris orsus.
namque omnes memori portentum mente retentant,
qui non funestis liquerunt lumina fatis.
Argolicis primum ut vestita est classibus Aulis,
quae Priamo cladem et Troiae pestemque ferebant,
nos circum latices gelidos fumantibus aris
aurigeris divom placantes numina tauris

sub platano umbrifera, fons unde eman[ab]at aquai,
vidimus inmani specie tortuque draconem
terribilem, Iovis ut pulsu †penetraret ab ara;
qui platani in ramo foliorum tegmine saeptos
corripuit pullos. quos cum consumeret octo,
nona super tremulo genetrix clangore volabat,
cui ferus inmani laniavit viscera morsu.
64 hunc, ubi tam teneros volucris matremque peremit,
qui luci ediderat genitor Saturnius idem
abdidit et †duro formavit† tegmine saxi.
nos autem timidi stantes mirabile monstrum
vidimus in mediis divom versarier aris.
tum Calchas haec est fidenti voce locutus:
'Quidnam torpentes subito obstipuistis, Achivi?
nobis haec portenta deum dedit ipse creator
tarda et sera [a]nimis, sed fama ac laude perenni.
nam quot avis taetro mactatas dente videtis,
tot nos ad Troiam belli exanclabimus annos;
quae decumo cadet et poena satiabit Achivos.'
edidit haec Calchas, quae iam matura videtis.

65 quae tandem ista auguratio est ex passeribus annorum potius quam aut mensuum aut dierum? cur autem de passerculis coniecturam facit, in quibus nullum erat monstrum, de dracone silet, qui, id quod fieri non potuit, lapideus dicitur factus? postremo quid simile habet passer annis? nam de angue illo qui Sullae apparuit immolanti, utrumque memini, et Sullam cum in expeditionem educturus esset immolavisse, et anguem ab ara extitisse, eoque die rem praeclare esse gestam non haruspicis consilio sed imperatoris.

66 Atque haec ostentorum genera mirabile nihil habent quae cum facta sunt, tum ad coniecturam aliqua interpretatione revocantur, ut illa tritici grana in os pueri Midae congesta aut apes quas dixisti in labris Platonis consedisse pueri, non tam mirabilia sint quam coniecta belle; quae tamen vel ipsa falsa esse, vel ea quae praedicta sunt fortuito cecidisse potuerunt. de ipso Roscio potest illud quidem esse falsum, ut circumligatus fuerit angui, sed ut in cunis fuerit anguis non tam est mirum, in Solonio praesertim, ubi ad focum angues nundinari solent. nam quod haruspices responderint nihil illo clarius, nihil nobilius fore, miror deos immortales histrioni futuro claritatem ostendisse, nullam ostendisse Africano. **67** atque etiam a te Flaminiana ostenta collecta sunt: quod ipse et equus eius repente conciderit, non sane mirabile hoc quidem; quod evelli primi hastati signum non potuerit, timide fortasse signifer evellebat quod fidenter infixerat. nam Dionysi equus quid attulit admirationis quod emersit e flumine quodque habuit apes in iuba? sed quia brevi tempore regnare coepit, quod acciderat casu, vim habuit ostenti. 'At Lacedaemoniis in Herculis fano arma sonuerunt, eiusdemque dei Thebis valvae clausae subito se aperuerunt, eaque scuta quae fuerant sublime fixa sunt humi inventa.' horum cum fieri nihil potuerit sine aliquo motu, quid est cur divinitus ea potius quam casu facta esse dicamus?

68 'At in Lysandri statuae capite Delphis extitit corona ex asperis herbis, et quidem subito.' itane, censes ante coronam herbae extitisse quam conceptum esse semen? herbam autem asperam credo avium congestu, non divino satu; iam quicquid in capite est, id coronae simile videri potest. nam quod eodem tempore stellas aureas Castoris et Pollucis Delphis positas decidisse neque eas usquam repertas esse dixisti, furum id magis factum quam deorum videtur. **69** simiae vero Dodonaeae improbitatem historiis Graecis mandatam esse demiror. quid minus mirum quam illam monstruosissumam bestiam urnam evertisse, sortes dissupavisse? et negant historici Lacedaemoniis ullum ostentum hoc tristius accidisse! nam illa praedicta Veientium, si lacus Albanus redundasset isque in mare fluxisset, Romam perituram, si repressus esset, Veios ** ita aqua Albana deducta ad utilitatem agri suburbani, non ad arcem urbemque retinendam. 'At paulo post audita vox est monentis ut providerent ne a Gallis Roma caperetur; ex eo Aio Loquenti aram in Nova Via consecratam.' quid ergo, Aius iste Loquens, quom eum nemo norat, et aiebat et loquebatur et ex eo nomen invenit, posteaquam et sedem et aram et nomen invenit, ommutuit? quod idem dici de Moneta potest, a qua praeterquam de sue plena quid umquam moniti sumus?

70 Satis multa de ostentis; auspicia restant et sortes—eae quae ducuntur, non illae quae vaticinatione funduntur, quae oracla verius dicimus; de quibus tum dicemus, cum ad naturalem divinationem venerimus. restat etiam de Chaldaeis; sed primum auspicia videamus. 'Difficilis auguri locus ad contra dicendum.' Marso fortasse, sed Romano facillumus. non enim sumus ii nos augures qui avium reliquorumve signorum observatione futura dicamus. et tamen credo Romulum, qui urbem auspicato condidit, habuisse opinionem esse in providendis rebus augurandi scientiam (errabat enim multis in rebus antiquitas), quam vel usu iam vel doctrina vel vetustate immutatam videmus; retinetur autem et ad opinionem vulgi et ad magnas utilitates rei publicae mos, religio, disciplina, ius augurium, collegi auctoritas. **71a** nec vero non omni supplicio digni P. Claudius L. Iunius consules, qui contra auspicia navigaverunt? parendum enim religioni fuit nec patrius mos tam contumaciter repudiandus. iure igitur alter populi iudicio damnatus est, alter mortem sibi ipse conscivit. 'Flaminius non paruit auspiciis, itaque periit cum exercitu.' at anno post Paulus paruit; num minus cecidit in Cannensi pugna cum exercitu?

71b Etenim ut sint auspicia—quae nulla sunt—haec certe quibus utimur, sive tripudio sive de caelo, simulacra sunt auspiciorum, auspicia nullo modo. 'Q. Fabi, te mihi in auspicio esse volo.' respondet: 'Audivi.' hic apud maiores adhibebatur peritus, nunc quilubet. peritum autem esse necesse est eum qui silentium quid sit intellegat; id enim silentium dicimus in auspiciis quod omni vitio caret; **72** hoc intellegere perfecti auguris est. illi autem qui in auspicium adhibe[n]tur, cum ita imperavit is qui auspicatur, 'Dicito, <si> silentium esse videbitur,' nec suspicit nec circumspicit; statim respondet silentium esse videri. tum ille: 'Dicito, si pascentur.' 'Pascuntur.' quae aves, aut ubi? attulit [inquit] in cavea pullos is qui ex eo ipso nominatur pullarius. haec sunt igitur aves internuntiae Iovis! quae pascantur necne quid refert? nihil ad auspicia; sed quia, cum pascuntur, necesse est aliquid ex ore cadere et terram pavire (terripavium primo, post terripudium dictum est; hoc quidem iam tripudium dicitur)—cum igitur offa cecidit ex ore pulli, tum auspicanti tripudium solistimum nuntiatur. **73** ergo hoc auspicium divini quicquam habere potest quod tam sit coactum et expressum? quo antiquissumos augures non esse usos argumento est quod decretum collegi vetus habemus, omnem avem tripudium facere posse. tum igitur esset auspicium, si modo esset ei liberum se ostendisse; tum avis illa videri posset interpres et satelles Iovis. nunc vero inclusa in cavea et fame enecta si in offam pultis invadit et si aliquid ex eius ore cecidit, hoc tu auspicium aut hoc modo Romulum auspicari solitum putas? **74a** iam de caelo servare non ipsos censes solitos qui auspicabantur? nunc imperant pullario; ille renuntiat fulmen sinistrum, auspicium optumum quod habemus ad omnis res praeterquam ad comitia. quod quidem institutum rei publicae causa est, ut comitiorum vel in iudiciis populi vel in iure legum vel in creandis magistratibus principes civitatis essent interpretes.

74b 'At Ti. Gracchi litteris Scipio et Figulus consules, cum augures iudicassent eos vitio creatos esse, magistratu se abdicaverunt.' quis negat augurum disciplinam esse? divinationem nego. 'At haruspices divini, quos cum Ti. Gracchus, propter mortem repentinam eius qui in praerogativa referenda subito concidisset, in senatum introduxisset, non iustum rogatorem fuisse dixerunt.' **75** primum vide ne in eum dixerint qui rogator centuriae fuisset; is enim erat mortuus, id autem sine divinatione coniectura poterant dicere. deinde fortasse casu, qui nullo modo est ex hoc genere tollendus. quid enim scire Etrusci haruspices aut de tabernaculo recte capto aut de pomerii iure potuerunt? equidem adsentior C. Marcello potius quam App. Claudio, qui ambo mei collegae fuerunt, existimoque ius augurum, etsi divinationis opinione principio constitutum sit, tamen postea rei publicae causa conservatum ac retentum. **76a** sed de hoc loco plura in aliis, nunc hactenus.

76b Externa enim auguria, quae sunt non tam artificiosa quam superstitiosa, videamus. omnibus fere avibus utuntur, nos admodum paucis; alia illis sinistra sunt, alia nostris. solebat ex me Deiotarus percontari nostri augurii disciplinam, ego ex illo sui. di inmortales, quantum differebat! ut quaedam essent etiam contraria. atque ille iis semper utebatur, nos, nisi dum a populo auspicia accepta habemus, quam multum iis utimur? bellicam rem administrari maiores nostri nisi auspicato noluerunt; quam multi anni sunt cum bella a proconsulibus et a propraetoribus administrantur, qui auspicia non habent? **77** itaque nec amnis transeunt auspicato nec tripudio auspicantur. ubi ergo avium divinatio? quae, quoniam ab iis qui auspicia nulla habent bella administrantur, ad urbanas res retenta videtur, a bellicis esse sublata. nam ex acuminibus quidem, quod totum auspicium militare est, iam M. Marcellus ille quinquiens consul totum omisit, idem imperator idem augur optumus. et quidem ille dicebat, si quando rem agere vellet, ne impediretur auspiciis, lectica operta facere iter se solere. huic simile est quod nos augures praecipimus, ne iuges auspicium obveniat, ut iumenta iubeant diiungere. **78a** quid est aliud nolle moneri a Iove, nisi efficere ut aut ne fieri possit auspicium aut, si fiat, videri?

78b Nam illud admodum ridiculum, quod negas Deiotarum auspiciorum quae sibi ad Pompeium proficiscenti facta sint paenitere, quod fidem secutus amicitiamque populi Romani functus sit officio; antiquiorem enim sibi fuisse laudem et gloriam quam regnum et possessiones suas. credo id quidem, sed hoc nihil ad auspicia; nec enim ei cornix canere potuit recte eum facere quod populi Romani libertatem defendere pararet; ipse hoc sentiebat, sicuti sensit. **79** aves eventus significant aut adversos aut secundos. virtutis auspiciis video esse usum Deiotarum, quae vetat spectare fortunam dum praestetur fides. aves vero <si> prosperos eventus ostenderunt, certe fefellerunt. fugit e proelio cum Pompeio: grave tempus! discessit ab eo: luctuosa res! Caesarem eodem tempore hostem et hospitem vidit: quid hoc tristius? is cum ei Trocmorum tetrarchian eripuisset et adseculae suo Pergameno nescio cui dedisset eidemque detraxisset Armeniam a senatu datam, cumque ab eo magnificentissumo hospitio acceptus esset, spoliatum reliquit et hospitem et regem. sed labor longius; ad propositum revertar. si eventa quaerimus, quae exquiruntur avibus, nullo modo prospera Deiotaro; sin officia, a virtute ipsius, non ab auspiciis petita sunt.

80 Omitte igitur lituum Romuli, quem in maximo incendio negas potuisse comburi; contemne cotem Atti Navi. nihil debet esse in philosophia commenticiis fabellis loci; illud erat philosophi potius, totius augurii primum naturam ipsam videre, deinde inventionem, deinde constantiam. quae est igitur natura quae volucris huc et illuc passim vagantis efficiat ut significent aliquid et tum vetent agere, tum iubeant aut cantu aut volatu? cur autem aliis a laeva, aliis a dextra datum est avibus ut ratum auspicium facere possint? quo modo autem haec aut quando aut a quibus inventa dicemus? Etrusci tamen habent exaratum puerum auctorem disciplinae suae; nos quem? Attumne Navium? at aliquot annis antiquior Romulus et Remus, ambo augures, ut accepimus. an Pisidarum aut Cilicum aut Phrygum ista inventa dicemus? placet igitur humanitatis expertis habere divinitatis auctores?

81 'At omnes reges, populi, nationes utuntur auspiciis.' quasi vero quicquam sit tam valde quam nihil sapere vulgare, aut quasi tibi ipsi in iudicando placeat multitudo! quotus quisque est qui voluptatem neget esse bonum? plerique etiam summum bonum dicunt. num igitur eorum frequentia Stoici de sententia deterrentur? aut num plerisque in rebus sequitur eorum auctoritatem multitudo? quid mirum igitur si in auspiciis et in omni divinatione inbecilli animi superstitiosa ista concipiant, verum dispicere non possint?

82 Quae autem est inter augures conveniens et coniuncta constantia? ad nostri auguri [in] consuetudinem dixit Ennius:

tum tonuit laevum bene tempestate serena.

at Homericus Aiax apud Achillem querens de ferocitate Troianorum nescio quid hoc modo nuntiat:

prospera Iuppiter his dextris fulgoribus edit.

ita nobis sinistra videntur, Graiis et barbaris dextra meliora. quamquam haud ignoro quae bona sint sinistra nos dicere, etiamsi dextra sint; sed certe nostri sinistrum <ita> nominaverunt externique dextrum, quia plerumque id melius videbatur. haec quanta dissensio est! **83a** quid, quod aliis avibus utuntur, aliis signis, aliter observant, alia respondent, non necesse est fateri partim horum errore susceptum esse, partim superstitione, multa fallendo?

83b Atque his superstitionibus non dubitasti etiam omina adiungere: Aemilia Paulo Persam perisse, quod pater omen accepit; Caecilia se sororis filiae sedes suas tradere; iam illa 'favete linguis' et 'praerogativam, omen comitiorum'—hoc est ipsum esse contra se copiosum et disertum. quando enim ista observans quieto et libero animo esse poteris, ut ad rem gerendam non superstitionem habeas, sed rationem ducem? itane, si quis aliquid ex sua re atque ex suo sermone dixerit et eius verbum aliquod apte ceciderit ad id quod ages aut cogitabis, ea res tibi aut timorem adferet aut alacritatem? **84** cum M. Crassus exercitum Brundisii inponeret, quidam in portu caricas Cauno advecta[n]s vendens 'Cauneas' clamitabat. dicamus, si placet, monitum ab eo Crassum, caveret ne iret; non fuisse periturum si omini paruisset. quae si suscipiamus, pedis offensio nobis et abruptio corrigiae et sternumenta erunt observanda.

85 Sortes restant et Chaldaei, ut ad vates veniamus et ad somnia. dicendum igitur putas de sortibus. quid enim sors est? idem prope modum quod micare, quod talos iacere, quod tesseras, quibus in rebus temeritas et casus, non ratio nec consilium valet. tota res est inventa fallaciis aut ad quaestum aut ad superstitionem aut ad errorem. atque ut in haruspicina fecimus, sic videamus clarissumarum sortium quae tradatur inventio. Numerium Suffustium Praenestinorum monumenta declarant, honestum hominem et nobilem, somniis crebris, ad extremum etiam minacibus, cum iuberetur certo in loco silicem caedere, perterritum visis, inridentibus suis civibus, id agere coepisse. itaque perfracto saxo sortis erupisse in robore insculptas priscarum litterarum notis. is est hodie locus saeptus religiose propter Iovis pueri, qui lactens, cum Iunone Fortunae in gremio sedens, mammam adpetens, castissime colitur a matribus. **86** eodemque tempore in eo loco ubi Fortunae nunc sit<a est> aedes, mel ex olea fluxisse dicunt, haruspicesque dixisse summa nobilitate illas sortis futuras, eorumque iussu ex illa olea arcam esse factam eoque conditas sortis, quae hodie Fortunae monitu tolluntur. quid igitur in his potest esse certi quae Fortunae monitu pueri manu miscentur atque ducuntur? quo modo autem istae positae in illo loco? quis robur illud cecidit, dolavit, inscripsit? 'Nihil est,' inquiunt, 'quod deus efficere non possit.' utinam sapientis Stoicos effecisset, ne omnia cum superstitiosa sollicitudine et miseria crederent! sed hoc quidem genus divinationis vita iam communis explosit; fani pulchritudo et vetustas Praenestinarum etiam nunc retinet sortium nomen, atque id in volgus. **87a** quis enim magistratus aut quis vir inlustrior utitur sortibus? ceteris vero in locis sortes plane refrixerunt. quod Carneadem Clitomachus scribit dicere solitum, nusquam se fortunatiorem quam Praeneste vidisse Fortunam.

87b Ergo hoc divinationis genus omittamus, ad Chaldaeorum monstra veniamus. de quibus Eudoxus, Platonis auditor, in astrologia iudicio doctissimorum hominum facile princeps, sic opinatur, id quod scriptum reliquit, Chaldaeis in praedictione et in notatione cuiusque vitae ex natali die minime esse credendum. **88** nominat etiam Panaetius, qui unus e Stoicis astrologorum praedicta reiecit, Anchialum et Cassandrum, summos astrologos illius aetatis qua erat ipse, cum in ceteris astrologiae partibus excellerent, hoc praedictionis genere non usos. Scylax Halicarnassius, familiaris Panaeti, excellens in astrologia idemque in regenda sua civitate princeps, totum hoc Chaldaeicum praedicendi genus repudiavit. **89** sed ut ratione utamur omissis testibus, sic isti disputant qui haec Chaldaeorum natalicia praedicta defendunt: vim quandam esse aiunt signifero in orbe, qui Graece ζωδιακός dicitur, talem ut eius orbis una quaeque pars alia alio modo moveat inmutetque caelum perinde ut quaeque stellae in his finitumisque partibus sint quoque tempore, eamque vim varie moveri ab iis sideribus quae vocentur errantia, cum aut[em] in eam ipsam partem orbis venerint in qua sit ortus eius qui nascatur, aut in eam quae coniunctum aliquid habeat aut consentiens (ea triangula illi et quadrata nominant). etenim cum tempore anni tempestatumque caeli conversiones commutationesque tantae fiant accessu stellarum et recessu, cumque ea vi solis efficiantur quae videmus, non veri simile solum, sed etiam verum esse censent, perinde utcumque temperatus sit aër, ita pueros orientis animari atque formari, ex eoque ingenia, mores, animum, corpus, actionem vitae, casus cuiusque eventusque fingi.

90 O delirationem incredibilem (non enim omnis error stultitia dicenda est)! quibus etiam Diogenes Stoicus concedit aliquid, ut praedicere possint dumtaxat qualis quisque natura et ad quam quisque maxume rem aptus futurus sit; cetera quae profiteantur negat ullo modo posse sciri: etenim geminorum formas esse similis, vitam atque fortunam plerumque disparem. Procles et Eurysthenes, Lacedaemoniorum reges, gemini fratres fuerunt. at ii nec totidem annos vixerunt (anno enim Procli vita brevior fuit), multumque is fratri rerum gestarum gloria praestitit. **91** at ego id ipsum quod vir optumus Diogenes Chaldaeis quasi quadam praevaricatione concedit, nego posse intellegi. etenim cum, ut ipsi dicunt, ortus nascentium luna moderetur, eaque animadvertant et notent sidera natalicia Chaldaei, quaecumque lunae iuncta videantur, oculorum fallacissimo sensu iudicant ea quae ratione atque animo videre debebant. docet enim ratio mathematicorum, quam istis notam esse oportebat, quanta humilitate luna feratur terram paene contingens, quantum absit a proxuma Mercuri stella, multo autem longius a Veneris, deinde alio intervallo distet a sole, cuius lumine conlustrari putatur; reliqua vero tria intervalla infinita et inmensa, a sole ad Martis, inde ad Iovis, ab eo ad Saturni stellam, inde ad caelum ipsum, quod extremum atque ultumum mundi est. **92a** quae potest igitur contagio ex infinito paene intervallo pertinere ad lunam vel potius ad terram?

92b Quid, cum dicunt id quod iis dicere necesse est, omnis omnium ortus quicumque <eodem tempore> gignantur in omni terra quae incolatur eosdem esse eademque omnibus qui eodem statu caeli et stellarum nati sint accidere necesse esse, nonne eius modi <ea> sunt ut ne caeli quidem naturam interpretes istos caeli nosse appareat? cum enim illi orbes qui caelum quasi medium dividunt et aspectum nostrum definiunt (qui a Graecis ὁρίζοντες nominantur, a nobis 'finientes' rectissume nominari possunt) varietatem maxumam habeant aliique in aliis locis sint, necesse est ortus occasusque siderum non fieri eodem tempore apud omnis. **93** quodsi eorum vi caelum modo hoc, modo illo modo temperatur, qui potest eadem vis esse nascentium, cum caeli tanta sit dissimilitudo? in his locis quae nos incolimus post solstitium Canicula exoritur, et quidem aliquot diebus; at apud Trogodytas, ut scribitur, ante solstitium; ut, si iam concedamus aliquid vim caelestem ad eos qui in terra gignuntur pertinere, confitendum sit illis eos qui nascuntur eodem tempore posse in dissimilis incidere naturas propter caeli dissimilitudinem, quod minime illis placet; volunt enim illi omnis eodem tempore ortos qui ubique sint nati eadem condicione nasci.

94 Sed quae tanta dementia est, ut in maxumis motibus mutationibusque caeli nihil intersit qui ventus, qui imber, quae tempestas ubique sit? quarum rerum in proxumis locis tantae dissimilitudines saepe sunt ut alia Tusculi, alia Romae eveniat saepe tempestas, quod qui navigant maxume animadvertunt cum in flectendis promunturiis ventorum mutationes maxumas saepe sentiunt. haec igitur cum sit tum serenitas, tum perturbatio caeli, estne sanorum hominum hoc ad nascentium ortus pertinere non dicere, quod [non] certe pertinet, illud nescio quid tenue, quod sentiri nullo modo, intellegi autem vix potest, quae a luna ceterisque sideribus caeli temperatio fiat, dicere ad puerorum ortus pertinere? quid, quod non intellegunt seminum vim, quae ad gignendum procreandumque plurimum valeat, funditus tolli, mediocris erroris est? quis enim non videt et formas et mores et plerosque status ac motus effingere a parentibus liberos? quod non contingeret, si haec non vis et natura gignentium efficeret, sed temperatio lunae caelique moderatio. **95** quid, quod uno et eodem temporis puncto nati dissimilis et naturas et vitas et casus habent, parumne declara[n]t nihil ad agendam vitam nascendi tempus pertinere? nisi forte putamus neminem eodem tempore ipso et conceptum et natum quo Africanum. num quis igitur talis fuit?

96a Quid, illudne dubium est quin multi, cum ita nati essent ut quaedam contra naturam depravata haberent, restituerentur et corrigerentur ab Natura, cum se ipsa revocasset, aut arte atque medicina, ut quorum linguae sic inhaererent ut loqui non possent, eae scalpello resectae liberarentur? multi etiam naturae vitium meditatione atque exercitatione sustulerunt, ut Demosthenem scribit Phalereus, cum 'rho' dicere nequiret, exercitatione fecisse ut planissume diceret. quodsi haec astro ingenerata et tradita essent, nulla res ea mutare posset.

96b Quid, dissimilitudo locorum nonne dissimilis hominum procreationes habet? quas quidem percurrere oratione facile est, quid inter Indos et Persas, Aethiopas <et> Syros differat corporibus, animis, ut incredibilis varietas dissimilitudoque sit. **97a** ex quo intellegitur plus terrarum situs quam lunae tactus ad nascendum valere. nam quod aiunt quadringenta septuaginta milia annorum in periclitandis experiundisque pueris quicumque essent nati Babylonios posuisse, fallunt: si enim esset factitatum, non esset desitum; neminem autem habemus auctorem qui id aut fieri dicat aut factum sciat. videsne me non ea dicere quae Carneades, sed ea quae princeps Stoicorum Panaetius dixerit?

97b Ego autem etiam haec requiro: omnesne qui Cannensi pugna ceciderint uno astro fuerint (exitus quidem omnium unus et idem fuit)? quid, qui ingenio atque animo singulares, num astro quoque uno? quod enim tempus quo non innumerabiles nascantur? at certe similis nemo Homeri. **98** et, si ad rem pertinet, quo modo caelo adfecto conpositisque sideribus quodque animal oriatur, valeat id necesse est non in hominibus solum verum in bestiis etiam; quo quid potest dici absurdius? Lucius quidem Tarutius Firmanus, familiaris noster, in primis Chaldaeicis rationibus eruditus, urbis etiam nostrae natalem diem repetebat ab iis Parilibus quibus eam a Romulo conditam accepimus, Romamque, in iugo cum esset luna, natam esse dicebat, nec eius fata canere dubitabat. **99** o vim maxumam erroris! etiamne urbis natalis dies ad vim stellarum et lunae pertinebat? fac in puero referre ex qua adfectione caeli primum spiritum duxerit; num hoc in latere aut in caemento, ex quibus urbs effecta est, potuit valere? sed quid plura? cotidie refelluntur. quam multa ego Pompeio, quam multa Crasso, quam multa huic ipsi Caesari a Chaldaeis dicta memini, neminem eorum nisi senectute, nisi domi, nisi cum claritate esse moriturum! ut mihi permirum videatur quemquam exstare qui etiam nunc credat iis quorum praedicta cotidie videat re et eventis refelli.

100a Restant duo divinandi genera quae habere dicimur a natura, non ab arte, vaticinandi et somniandi; de quibus, Quinte, inquam, si placet, disseramus.

100b 'Mihi vero,' inquit, 'placet; his enim quae adhuc disputasti prorsus adsentior, et, vere ut loquar, quamquam tua me oratio confirmavit, tamen etiam mea sponte nimis superstitiosam de divinatione Stoicorum sententiam iudicabam. haec me Peripateticorum ratio magis movebat et veteris Dicaearchi et eius qui nunc floret Cratippi, qui censent esse in mentibus hominum tamquam oraclum aliquod, ex quo futura praesentiant, si aut furore divino incitatus animus aut somno relaxatus solute moveatur ac libere. his de generibus quid sentias et quibus ea rationibus infirmes audire sane velim.'

101 Quae cum ille dixisset, tum ego rursus quasi ab alio principio sum exorsus dicere: Non ignoro, inquam, Quinte, te semper ita sensisse, ut de ceteris divinandi generibus dubitares, ista duo, furoris et somni, quae a libera mente fluere viderentur, probares. dicam igitur de istis ipsis duobus generibus mihi quid videatur, si prius et Stoicorum conclusio rationis et Cratippi nostri quid valeat videro. dixisti enim et Chrysippum et Diogenem et Antipatrum concludere hoc modo: 'si sunt di neque ante declarant hominibus quae futura sint, aut non diligunt homines, aut quid eventurum sit ignorant, aut existumant nihil interesse hominum scire quid sit futurum, aut non censent esse suae maiestatis praesignificare hominibus quae sint futura, aut ea ne ipsi quidem di significare possunt. **102** at neque non diligunt nos (sunt enim benefici generique hominum amici); neque ignorant ea quae ab ipsis constituta et designata sunt; neque nostra nihil interest scire ea quae futura sint (erimus enim cautiores, si sciemus); neque hoc alienum ducunt maiestate sua (nihil est enim beneficentia praestantius); neque non possunt futura praenoscere. non igitur di sunt nec significant nobis futura; sunt autem di; significant ergo. et non, si significant futura, nullas dant vias nobis ad significationum scientiam (frustra enim significarent); nec, si dant vias, non est divinatio; est igitur divinatio.'

103 O acutos homines! quam paucis verbis confectum negotium putant! ea sumunt ad concludendum quorum iis nihil conceditur. conclusio autem rationis ea probanda est, in qua ex rebus non dubiis id quod dubitatur efficitur. videsne Epicurum, quem hebetem et rudem dicere solent Stoici, quem ad modum quod in natura rerum omne esse dicimus id infinitum esse concluserit? 'quod finitum est,' inquit, 'habet extremum': quis hoc non dederit? 'quod autem habet extremum, id cernitur ex alio extrinsecus': hoc quoque est concedendum. 'at quod omne est, id non cernitur ex alio extrinsecus': ne hoc quidem negari potest. 'nihil igitur cum habeat extremum, infinitum sit necesse est.' **104** videsne ut ad rem dubiam <a> concessis rebus pervenerit? hoc vos dialectici non facitis, nec solum ea non sumitis ad concludendum quae ab omnibus concedantur, sed ea sumitis, quibus concessis, nihilo magis efficiatur quod velitis. primum enim hoc sumitis: 'si sunt di, benefici in homines sunt.' quis hoc vobis dabit? Epicurusne, qui negat quicquam deos nec alieni curare nec sui? an noster Ennius, qui magno plausu loquitur adsentiente populo,

ego deum genus esse semper dixi et dicam caelitum,
sed eos non curare opinor quid agat humanum genus?

et quidem cur sic opinetur rationem subicit, sed nihil est necesse dicere quae sequuntur; tantum sat est intellegi id sumere istos pro certo quod dubium controversumque sit. **105** sequitur porro nihil deos ignorare, quod omnia sint ab iis constituta. hic vero quanta pugna est doctissumorum hominum negantium esse haec a dis inmortalibus constituta! 'at nostra interest scire ea quae eventura sint.' magnus Dicaearchi liber est nescire ea melius esse quam scire. negant id esse alienum maiestate deorum, scilicet casas omnium introspicere, ut videant quid cuique conducat! **106** 'neque non possunt futura praenoscere.' negant posse ii quibus non placet esse certum quid futurum sit. videsne igitur quae dubia sint, ea sumi pro certis atque concessis? deinde contorquent et ita concludunt: 'non igitur et sunt di nec significant futura'; id enim iam perfectum arbitrantur. deinde adsumunt: 'sunt autem di,' quod ipsum non ab omnibus conceditur. 'significant ergo.' ne id quidem sequitur; possunt enim non significare et tamen esse di. 'nec si significent, non dant vias aliquas ad scientiam significationis.' at id quoque potest, ut non dent homini, ipsi habeant; cur enim Tuscis potius quam Romanis darent? 'nec, si dant vias, nulla est divinatio.' fac dare deos—quod absurdum est; quid refert, si accipere non possumus? extremum <est>: 'est igitur divinatio.' sit extremum, effectum tamen non est; ex falsis enim, ut ab ipsis didicimus, verum effici non potest. iacet igitur tota conclusio.

107 Veniamus nunc ad optumum virum, familiarem nostrum Cratippum. 'si sine oculis,' inquit, 'non potest exstare officium et munus oculorum, possunt autem aliquando oculi non fungi suo munere, qui vel semel ita est usus oculis ut vera cerneret, is habet sensum oculorum vera cernentium. item igitur si sine divinatione non potest officium et munus divinationis exstare, potest autem, cum quis divinationem habeat, errare aliquando nec vera cernere, satis est ad confirmandam divinationem semel aliquid ita esse divinatum nihil ut fortuito cecidisse videatur. sunt autem eius generis innumerabilia; esse igitur divinationem confitendum est.' festive et breviter! sed cum bis sumpsit quod voluit, etiamsi faciles nos ad concedendum habuerit, id tamen quod adsumit concedi nullo modo potest. **108** 'si,' inquit, 'aliquando oculi peccent, tamen quia recte aliquando viderunt, inest in iis vis videndi; item si quis semel aliquid in divinatione dixerit, is etiam cum peccet, tamen existumandus est habere vim divinandi.' vide, quaeso, Cratippe noster, quam sint ista similia; nam mihi non videntur. oculi enim vera cernentes utuntur natura atque sensu; animi, si quando vel vaticinando vel somniando vera viderunt, usi sunt fortuna atque casu; nisi forte concessuros tibi existumas eos qui somnia pro somniis habent, si quando aliquod somnium verum evaserit, non id fortuito accidisse. sed demus tibi istas duas sumptiones (ea quae λήμματα appellant dialectici, sed nos Latine loqui malumus), <adsumptio> [praesensio] tamen (quam πρόσληψιν iidem vocant) non dabitur. **109** adsumit autem Cratippus hoc modo: 'Sunt autem innumerabiles praesensiones non fortuitae.' at ego dico nullam (vide quanta sit controversia!); iam adsumptione non concessa, nulla conclusio est. at impudentes sumus qui, cum tam perspicuum sit, non concedamus. quid est perspicuum? 'Multa vera,' inquit, 'evadere.' quid quod multo plura falsa? nonne ipsa varietas, quae est propria fortunae, fortunam esse causam, non naturam esse docet? deinde si tua ista conclusio, Cratippe, vera est (tecum enim mihi res est), nonne intellegis eadem uti posse et haruspices et fulguratores et interpretes ostentorum et augures et sortilegos et Chaldaeos, quorum generum nullum est ex quo non aliquid sicut praedictum sit evaserit? ergo aut ea quoque genera divinandi sunt, quae tu rectissume inprobas, aut si ea non sunt, non intellego cur haec duo sint quae relinquis. qua ergo ratione haec inducis, eadem illa possunt esse quae tollis.

110 Quid vero habet auctoritatis furor iste quem divinum vocatis, ut quae sapiens non videat, ea videat insanus, et is qui humanos sensus amiserit, divinos adsecutus sit? Sibyllae versus observamus, quos illa furens fudisse dicitur. quorum interpres nuper falsa quadam hominum fama dicturus in senatu putabatur eum quem re vera regem habebamus appellandum quoque esse regem, si salvi esse vellemus. hoc si est in libris, in quem hominem et in quod tempus est? callide enim qui illa composuit perfecit ut quodcumque accidisset praedictum videretur, hominum et temporum definitione sublata. **111** adhibuit etiam latebram obscuritatis, ut iidem versus alias in aliam rem posse accommodari viderentur. non esse autem illud carmen furentis cum ipsum poëma declarat (est enim magis artis et diligentiae quam incitationis et motus), tum vero ea quae ἀκροστιχίς dicitur, cum deinceps ex primis <cuiusque> versus litteris aliquid conectitur, ut in quibusdam Ennianis 'Q. Ennius fecit.' id certe magis est attenti animi quam furentis. **112a** atque in Sibyllinis <excerptis> ex primo versu cuiusque sententiae primis litteris [illius sententiae] carmen omne praetexitur. hoc scriptoris est, non furentis, adhibentis diligentiam, non insani. quam ob rem Sibyllam quidem sepositam et conditam habeamus, ut—id quod proditum est a maioribus—iniussu senatus ne legantur quidem libri valeantque ad deponendas potius quam ad suscipiendas religiones; cum antistitibus agamus ut quidvis potius ex illis libris quam regem proferant, quem Romae posthac nec di nec homines esse patientur.

112b 'At multi saepe vera vaticinati, ut Cassandra

iamque mari magno

eademque paulo post

eheu videte!'

113 num igitur me cogis etiam fabulis credere? quae delectationis habeant quantum voles, verbis sententiis numeris cantibus adiuventur; auctoritatem quidem nullam debemus nec fidem commenticiis rebus adiungere. eodemque modo nec ego Publicio nescio cui nec Marciis vatibus nec Apollinis opertis credendum existimo; quorum partim ficta aperte, partim effutita temere numquam ne mediocri quidem cuiquam, non modo prudenti probata sunt.
114 'Quid,' inquies, 'remex ille de classe Coponi nonne ea praedixit quae facta sunt?' ille vero, et ea quidem quae omnes eo tempore ne acciderent timebamus. castra enim in Thessalia castris conlata audiebamus, videbaturque nobis exercitus Caesaris et audaciae plus habere, quippe qui patriae bellum intulisset, et roboris propter vetustatem; casum autem proeli nemo nostrum erat quin timeret, sed ita ut constantibus hominibus par erat, non aperte. ille autem Graecus quid mirum si magnitudine timoris, ut plerumque fit, a constantia atque a mente atque a se ipse discessit? qua perturbatione animi, quae sanus cum esset timebat ne evenirent, ea demens eventura esse dicebat. utrum tandem, per deos atque homines, magis veri simile est vesanum remigem an aliquem nostrum qui ibi tum eramus, me, Catonem, Varronem, Coponium ipsum, consilia deorum inmortalium perspicere potuisse?

115 Sed iam ad te venio,

o sancte Apollo, qui umbilicum certum terrarum obtines,
unde superstitiosa primum saeva evasit vox fera.

tuis enim oraclis Chrysippus totum volumen inplevit partim falsis, ut ego opinor, partim casu veris, ut fit in omni oratione saepissime, partim flexiloquis et obscuris ut interpres egeat interprete et sors ipsa ad sortes referenda sit, partim ambiguis et quae ad dialecticum deferenda sint. nam cum illa sors edita est opulentissumo regi Asiae,

Croesus Halyn penetrans magnam pervertet opum vim,

hostium vim se perversurum putavit, pervertit autem suam; **116** utrum igitur eorum accidisset, verum oraclum fuisset. cur autem hoc credam umquam editum Croeso? aut Herodotum cur veraciorem ducam Ennio? num minus ille potuit de Croeso quam de Pyrrho fingere Ennius? quis enim est qui credat Apollinis ex oraclo Pyrrho esse responsum

ai<i>o te, Aeacida, Romanos vincere posse?

primum Latine Apollo numquam locutus est; deinde ista sors inaudita Graecis est; praeterea Pyrrhi temporibus iam Apollo versus facere desierat; postremo, quamquam semper fuit, ut apud Ennium est,

stolidum genus Aeacidarum,
bellipotentes sunt magis quam sapientipotentes,

tamen hanc amphiboliam versus intellegere potuisset, 'vincere te Romanos' nihilo magis in se quam in Romanos valere; nam illa amphibolia quae Croesum decepit vel Chrysippum potuisset fallere, haec vero ne Epicurum quidem.

117 Sed, quod caput est, cur isto modo iam oracla Delphis non eduntur? <cur> non modo nostra aetate, sed iam diu tam otiosa iacent ut nihil possit esse contemptius? hoc loco cum urgentur, evanuisse aiunt vetustate vim loci eius unde anhelitus ille terrae fieret quo Pythia mente incitata oracla ederet. de vino aut salsamento putes loqui, quae evanescunt vetustate! de vi loci agitur, neque solum naturali, sed etiam divina; quae quo tandem modo evanuit? 'Vetustate,' inquies. quae vetustas est quae vim divinam conficere possit? quid tam divinum autem quam adflatus e terra mentem ita movens ut eam providam rerum futurarum efficiat, ut ea non modo cernat multo ante sed etiam numero versuque pronuntiet? quando ista vis autem evanuit? an postquam homines minus creduli esse coeperunt? **118** Demosthenes quidem, qui abhinc annos prope trecentos fuit, iam tum φιλιππίζειν Pythiam dicebat, id est quasi cum Philippo facere. hoc autem eo spectabat, ut eam a Philippo corruptam diceret; quod licet existimare in aliis quoque oraclis Delphicis, aliquid non sinceri fuisse. sed nescio quo modo isti philosophi superstitiosi et paene fanatici quidvis malle videntur quam se non ineptos: evanuisse mavultis et extinctum esse id quod, si umquam fuisset, certe aeternum esset, quam ea quae non sunt credenda non credere.

119 Similis est error in somniis; quorum quidem defensio repetita quam longe est! divinos animos censent esse nostros, eosque esse tractos extrinsecus, animorumque consentientium multitudine conpletum esse mundum; hac igitur mentis et ipsius divinitate et coniunctione cum externis mentibus cerni quae sint futura. contrahi autem animum Zeno et quasi labi putat atque concidere, et <id> ipsum esse dormire. iam Pythagoras et Plato, locupletissimi auctores, quo in somnis certiora videamus, praeparatos quodam cultu atque victu proficisci ad dormiendum iubent; faba quidem Pythagorei utique abstinere, quasi vero eo cibo mens, non venter infletur! sed nescio quo modo nihil tam absurde dici potest quod non dicatur ab aliquo philosophorum. **120** utrum igitur censemus dormientium animos per sene ipsos in somniando moveri an, ut Democritus censet, externa et adventicia visione pulsari? sive enim sic est sive illo modo, videri possunt permulta somniantibus falsa pro veris. nam et navigantibus moveri videntur ea quae stant, et quodam obtutu oculorum duo pro uno lucernae lumina. quid dicam insanis, quid ebriis quam multa falsa videantur? quodsi eius modi visis credendum non est, cur somniis credatur nescio. nam tam licet de his erroribus, si velis, quam de somniis disputare, ut ea quae stant, <si> moveri videantur, terrae motum significare dicas aut repentinam aliquam fugam, gemino autem lucernae lumine declarari dissensionem ac seditionem moveri. **121** iam ex insanorum aut ebriorum visis innumerabilia coniectura trahi possunt quae futura videantur. quis est enim qui totum diem iaculans non aliquando conliniet? totas noctes somniamus—neque ulla est fere qua non dormiamus—et miramur aliquando id quod somniarimus evadere? quid est tam incertum quam talorum iactus? tamen nemo est quin saepe iactans Venerium iaciat aliquando, non numquam etiam iterum ac tertium; num igitur, ut inepti, Veneris id inpulsu fieri malumus quam casu dicere? quodsi ceteris temporibus falsis visis credendum non est, non video quid praecipui somnus habeat in quo valeant falsa pro veris. **122a** quodsi ita natura paratum esset ut ea dormientes agerent quae somniarent, alligandi omnes essent qui cubitum irent; maiores enim quam ulli insani efficerent motus somniantes. quodsi insanorum visis fides non est habenda quia falsa sunt, cur credatur somniantium visis, quae multo etiam perturbatiora sunt, non intellego; an quod insani sua visa coniectori non narrant, narrant qui somniaverunt?

122b Quaero etiam, si velim scribere quid aut legere aut canere vel voce vel fidibus aut geometricum quiddam aut physicum aut dialecticum explicare, somniumne expectandum sit an ars adhibenda, sine qua nihil earum rerum nec fieri nec expediri potest. atqui ne si navigare quidem velim, ita gubernem ut somniaverim; praesens enim poena sit. **123** qui igitur convenit aegros a coniectore somniorum potius quam a medico petere medicinam? an

Aesculapius, an Serapis potest nobis praescribere per somnum curationem valetudinis, Neptunus <gubernationem> gubernantibus non potest? et si sine medico medicinam dabit Minerva, Musae scribendi, legendi, ceterarum artium scientiam somniantibus non dabunt? at si curatio daretur valetudinis, haec quoque quae dixi darentur; quae quoniam non dantur, medicina non datur; qua sublata tollitur omnis auctoritas somniorum.

124 Sed haec [quoque] in promptu fuerint; nunc interiora videamus. aut enim divina vis quaedam consulens nobis somniorum significationes facit, aut coniectores ex quadam convenientia et coniunctione naturae, quam vocant συμπάθειαν, quid cuique rei conveniat ex somniis, et quid quamque rem sequatur intellegunt, aut eorum neutrum est, sed quaedam observatio constans atque diuturna est, cum quid visum secundum quietem sit, quid evenire et quid sequi soleat. primum igitur intellegendum est nullam vim esse divinam effectricem somniorum. atque illud quidem perspicuum est, nulla visa somniorum proficisci a numine deorum; nostra enim causa di id facerent ut providere futura possemus. **125** quotus igitur est quisque qui somniis pareat, qui intellegat, qui meminerit? quam multi vero qui contemnant eamque superstitionem inbecilli animi atque anilis putent? quid est igitur cur his hominibus consulens deus somniis moneat eos qui illa non modo cura, sed ne memoria quidem digna ducant? nec enim ignorare deus potest qua mente quisque sit, nec frustra ac sine causa quid facere dignum deo est, quod abhorret etiam ab hominis constantia. ita si pleraque somnia aut ignorantur aut negleguntur, aut nescit hoc deus aut frustra somniorum significatione utitur; at horum neutrum in deum cadit; nihil igitur a deo somniis significari fatendum est.

126 Illud etiam requiro, cur, si deus ista visa nobis providendi causa dat, non vigilantibus potius det quam dormientibus. sive enim externus et adventicius pulsus animos dormientium commovet, sive per se ipsi animi moventur, sive quae causa alia est cur secundum quietem aliquid videre, audire, agere videamur, eadem causa vigilantibus esse poterat. idque si nostra causa di secundum quietem facerent, vigilantibus idem facerent, praesertim <cum> Chrysippus Academicos refellens permulto clariora et certiora esse dicat quae vigilantibus videantur quam quae somniantibus. fuit igitur divina beneficentia dignius, cum consulerent nobis, clariora visa dare vigilanti quam obscuriora per somn[i]um. quod quoniam non fit, somnia divina putanda non sunt. **127a** iam vero quid opus est circumitione et anfractu, ut sit utendum interpretibus somniorum, potius quam derecto deus, siquidem nobis consulebat, 'hoc facito, hoc ne feceris' diceret idque visum vigilanti potius quam dormienti daret?

127b Iam vero quis dicere audeat vera omnia esse somnia? 'aliquot somnia vera,' inquit Ennius, 'sed omnia non necesse est.' quae est tandem ista distinctio? quae vera, quae falsa habet? et si vera a deo mittuntur, falsa unde nascuntur? nam si ea quoque divina, quid inconstantius deo? quid insidiosius autem est quam mentes mortalium falsis et mendacibus visis concitare? sin vera visa divina sunt, falsa autem et inania humana, quae est ista designandi licentia, ut hoc deus, hoc natura fecerit potius quam aut omnia deus, quod negatis, aut omnia natura? quod quoniam illud negatis, hoc necessario confitendum est. **128** naturam autem eam dico, qua numquam animus insistens agitatione et motu esse vacuus potest. is cum languore corporis nec membris uti nec sensibus potest, incidit in visa varia et incerta ex reliquiis, ut ait Aristoteles, inhaerentibus earum rerum quas vigilans gesserit aut cogitaverit; quarum perturbatione mirabiles interdum existunt species somniorum. quae si alia falsa, alia vera, qua nota internoscantur scire sane velim. si nulla est, quid istos interpretes audiamus? sin quaepiam est, aveo audire quae sit; sed haerebunt. **129a** venit enim iam in contentionem utrum sit probabilius, deosne immortalis, rerum omnium praestantia excellentis, concursare omnium mortalium qui ubique sunt non modo lectos verum etiam grabatos et, cum stertentem aliquem viderint, obicere iis visa quaedam tortuosa et obscura, quae illi exterriti somn[i]o ad coniectorem mane deferant, an natura fieri ut mobiliter animus agitatus, quod vigilans viderit, dormiens videre videatur. utrum philosophia dignius, sagarum superstitione ista interpretari an explicatione naturae?

129b Ut, si iam fieri possit vera coniectura somniorum, tamen isti qui profitentur eam facere non possint: ex levissimo enim et indoctissimo genere constant. Stoici autem tui negant quemquam nisi sapientem divinum esse posse. **130** Chrysippus quidem divinationem definit his verbis: vim cognoscentem et videntem et explicantem signa quae a dis hominibus portendantur; officium autem esse eius praenoscere dei erga homines mente qua sint quidque significent, quemadmodumque ea procurentur atque expientur. idemque somniorum coniectionem definit hoc modo: esse vim cernentem et explanantem quae a dis hominibus significentur in somnis. quid ergo, ad haec mediocri opus est prudentia an et ingenio praestanti et eruditione perfecta? talem autem cognovimus neminem. **131a** vide igitur ne etiamsi divinationem tibi esse concessero—quod numquam faciam—neminem tamen divinum reperire possimus.

131b Qualis autem ista mens est deorum, si neque ea nobis significant in somnis quae ipsi per nos intellegamus, neque ea quorum interpretes habere possimus? similes enim sunt dei, si ea nobis obiciunt quorum nec scientiam neque explanatorem habeamus, tamquam si Poeni aut Hispani in senatu nostro loquerentur sine interprete. **132** iam vero quo pertinent obscuritates et aenigmata somniorum? intellegi enim a nobis di velle debebant ea quae nostra causa nos monerent. 'Quid, poëta nemone, <nemo> physicus obscurus?' **133** ille vero nimis etiam obscurus Euphorion, at non Homerus: uter igitur melior? 'Valde Heraclitus obscurus, minime Democritus.' num igitur conferendi? mea causa me mones quod non intellegam: quid me igitur mones? ut si quis medicus aegroto imperet ut sumat

terrigenam, herbigradam, domiportam, sanguine cassam,

potius quam hominum more 'cocleam' diceret. nam Pacuvianus Amphio

quadrupes tardigrada agrestis humilis aspera
capite brevi cervice anguina aspectu truci,
eviscerata, inanima cum animali sono

cum dixisset obscurius, tum Attici respondent:

non intellegimus, nisi si aperte dixeris.

at ille uno verbo 'testudo'; non potueras hoc igitur a principio, citharista, dicere? **134** defert ad coniectorem quidam somniasse se ovum pendere ex fascea lecti sui cubicularis (est hoc in Chrysippi libro somnium). respondit coniector thesaurum defossum esse sub lecto. fodit, invenit auri aliquantum, idque circumdatum argento; misit coniectori quantulum visum est de argento. tum ille 'Nihilne,' inquit, 'de vitello?' id enim ei ex ovo videbatur aurum declarasse, reliquum argentum. nemone igitur umquam alius ovum somniavit? cur ergo hic nescio qui thesaurum solus invenit? quam multi inopes digni praesidio deorum nullo somnio ad thesaurum reperiendum admonentur! quam autem ob causam tam est obscure admonitus, ut ex ovo nasceretur thesauri similitudo, potius quam aperte thesaurum quaerere iuberetur, sicut aperte Simonides vetitus est navigare? **135a** ergo obscura somnia minime consentanea maiestati deorum.

135b Ad aperta et clara veniamus, quale est de illo interfecto a copone Megaris, quale de Simonide, qui ab eo quem humarat vetitus est navigare, quale etiam de Alexandro, quod a te praeteritum esse miror. qui, cum Ptolomaeus, familiaris eius, in proelio telo venenato ictus esset eoque vulnere summo cum dolore moreretur, Alexander adsidens somno est consopitus. tum secundum quietem visus ei dicitur draco is quem mater Olympias alebat radiculam ore ferre et simul dicere quo illa loci nasceretur (neque is longe aberat ab eo loco), eius autem esse vim tantam ut Ptolomaeum facile sanaret. cum Alexander experrectus narrasset amicis somnium, emissi sunt qui illam radiculam quaererent; qua inventa et Ptolomaeus sanatus dicitur et multi milites qui erant eodem genere teli vulnerati. **136a** multa etiam sunt a te ex historiis prolata somnia, matris Phalaridis, Cyri superioris, matris Dionysi, Poeni Hamilcaris, Hannibalis, P. Deci; pervulgatum iam illud de praesule, C. Gracchi etiam et recens Caeciliae, Baliarici filiae, somnium. sed haec externa ob eamque causam ignota nobis sunt, non nulla etiam ficta fortasse: quis enim auctor istorum?

136b De nostris somniis quid habemus dicere? tu de emerso me et equo ad ripam, ego de Mario cum fascibus laureatis me in suum deduci iubente monumentum. omnium somniorum, Quinte, una ratio est; quae, per deos inmortalis, videamus ne nostra superstitione et depravatione superetur. **137** quem enim tu Marium visum a me putas? speciem, credo, eius et imaginem, ut Democrito videtur. unde profectam imaginem? a corporibus enim solidis et a certis figuris vult fluere imagines. quod igitur Mari corpus erat? 'Ex eo,' inquit, 'quod fuerat.' ista igitur me imago Mari in campum Atinatem persequebatur? 'Plena sunt imaginum omnia; nulla enim species cogitari potest nisi pulsu imaginum.' **138** quid ergo, istae imagines ita nobis dicto audientes sunt ut simul atque velimus accurrant? etiamne earum rerum quae nullae sunt? quae est enim forma tam invisitata, tam nulla, quam non sibi ipse fingere animus possit, ut quae numquam vidimus ea tamen informata habeamus, oppidorum situs, hominum figuras? **139** num igitur cum aut muros Babylonis aut Homeri faciem cogito, imago illorum me aliqua pellit? omnia igitur quae volumus nota nobis esse possunt; nihil est enim de quo cogitare nequeamus. nullae ergo imagines obrepunt in animos dormientium extrinsecus, nec omnino fluunt ullae, nec cognovi quemquam qui maiore auctoritate nihil diceret. animorum est ea vis eaque natura ut vigeant vigilantes nullo adventicio pulsu, sed suo motu incredibili quadam celeritate. hi cum sustinentur membris et corpore et sensibus, omnia certiora cernunt, cogitant, sentiunt. cum autem haec subtracta sunt desertusque animus languore corporis, tum agitatur ipse per sese. itaque in eo et formae versantur et actiones, et multa audiri, multa dici videntur. **140** haec scilicet in inbecillo remissoque animo multa omnibus modis confusa et variata versantur, maxumeque reliquiae rerum earum moventur in animis et agitantur de quibus vigilantes aut cogitavimus aut egimus, ut mihi temporibus illis multum in animo Marius versabatur recordanti quam ille gravem suum casum magno animo, quam constanti tulisset; hanc credo causam de illo somniandi fuisse. tibi autem de me cum sollicitudine cogitanti subito sum visus emersus e flumine. inerant enim in utriusque nostrum animis vigilantium cogitationum vestigia. at quaedam adiuncta sunt, ut mihi de monumento Mari, tibi quod equus in quo ego vehebar mecum una demersus rursus apparuit. **141a** an tu censes ullam anum tam deliram futuram fuisse ut somniis crederet, nisi ista casu non numquam forte temere concurrerent?

141b Alexandro draco loqui visus est. potest omnino hoc esse falsum, potest verum, sed ut verum sit, non est mirabile. non enim audivit ille draconem loquentem, sed est visus audire, et quidem, quo maius sit, cum radicem ore teneret, locutus est; sed nihil est magnum somnianti. quaero autem cur Alexandro tam inlustre somnium, tam certum, nec huic eidem alias, nec multa ceteris. mihi quidem praeter hoc Marianum nihil sane quod meminerim; frustra igitur consumptae tot noctes tam longa in aetate! **142a** nunc quidem propter intermissionem forensis operae et lucubrationes detraxi et meridiationes addidi, quibus uti antea non solebam, nec tam multum dormiens ullo somnio sum admonitus, tantis praesertim de rebus, nec mihi magis unquam videor, quam cum aut in foro magistratus aut in curia senatum video, somniare.

142b Etenim (ex divisione hoc secundum est) quae est continuatio coniunctioque naturae, quam, ut dixi, vocant συμπάθειαν, eius modi ut thesaurus ex ovo intellegi debeat? nam medici ex quibusdam rebus et advenientis et crescentis morbos intellegunt, non nullas etiam valetudinis significationes, ut hoc ipsum, pleni enectine simus, ex quodam genere somniorum intellegi posse dicunt. thesaurus vero et hereditas et honos et victoria et multa generis eiusdem qua cum somniis naturali cognatione iunguntur? **143** dicitur quidam, cum in somnis complexu Venerio iungeretur, calculos eiecisse. video sympathian: visum est enim tale obiectum dormienti, ut id quod evenit naturae vis, non opinio [erroris] effecerit. quae igitur natura obtulit illam speciem Simonidi, a qua vetaretur navigare? aut quid naturae copulatum habuit Alcibiadis quod scribitur somnium? qui paulo ante interitum visus est in somnis amicae esse amictus amiculo. is cum esset proiectus inhumatus ab omnibusque desertus iaceret, amica corpus eius texit suo pallio. ergo hoc inerat in rebus futuris et causas naturalis habebat, an et ut videretur et ut eveniret casus effecit?

144 Quid, ipsorum interpretum coniecturae nonne magis ingenia declarant eorum quam vim consensumque naturae? cursor ad Olympia proficisci cogitans visus est in somnis curru quadrigarum vehi. mane ad coniectorem. at ille 'Vinces,' inquit, 'id enim celeritas significat et vis equorum.' post idem ad Antiphontem. is autem 'Vincare,' inquit, 'necesse est; an non intellegis quattuor ante te cucurrisse?' ecce alius cursor—atque horum somniorum et talium plenus est Chrysippi liber, plenus Antipatri; sed ad cursorem redeo—ad interpretem detulit aquilam se in somnis visum esse factum. at ille: 'Vicisti; ista enim avi volat nulla vehementius.' huic eidem Antipho 'Baro,' inquit, 'victum te esse non vides? ista enim avis insectans alias avis et agitans semper ipsa postrema est.' **145** parere quaedam matrona cupiens, dubitans essetne praegnans, visa est in quiete obsignatam habere naturam; rettulit. negavit eam, quoniam obsignata fuisset, concipere potuisse. at alter praegnantem esse dixit; nam inane obsignari nihil solere. quae est ars coniectoris eludentis ingenio? an ea quae dixi et innumerabilia quae conlecta habent Stoici quicquam significant nisi acumen hominum ex similitudine aliqua coniecturam modo huc, modo illuc ducentium? medici signa quaedam habent ex venis et ex spiritu aegroti, multisque ex aliis futura praesentiunt; gubernatores, cum exsultantis lolligines viderunt aut delphinos se in portum conicientes, tempestatem significari putant. haec ratione explicari et ad naturam revocari facile possunt, ea vero quae paulo ante dixi nullo modo.

146 'At enim observatio diuturna (haec enim pars una restat) notandis rebus fecit artem.' ain tandem? 'Somnia observari possunt.' quonam modo? sunt enim innumerabiles varietates: nihil tam praepostere, tam incondite, tam monstruose cogitari potest quod non possimus somniare. quo modo igitur haec infinita et semper nova aut memoria conplecti aut observando notare possumus? astrologi motus errantium stellarum notaverunt; inventus est enim ordo in iis stellis qui non putabatur. cedo tandem qui sit ordo aut quae concursatio somniorum. quo modo autem distingui possunt vera somnia a falsis, cum eadem et aliis aliter evadant et isdem non semper eodem modo? ut mihi mirum videatur, cum mendaci homini ne verum quidem dicenti credere soleamus, quo modo isti, si somnium verum evasit aliquod, non ex multis potius uni fidem derogent quam ex uno innumerabilia confirment.

147 Si igitur neque deus est effector somniorum neque naturae societas ulla cum somniis neque observatione inveniri potuit scientia, effectum est ut nihil prorsus somniis tribuendum sit, praesertim cum illi ipsi qui ea vident nihil divinent, ii qui interpretantur coniecturam adhibeant, non naturam, casus autem innumerabilibus paene saeculis in omnibus plura mirabilia quam in somniorum visis effecerit, neque coniectura, quae in varias partis duci possit, non numquam etiam in contrarias, quicquam sit incertius. **148a** explodatur <igitur> haec quoque somniorum divinatio pariter cum ceteris.

148b Nam, ut vere loquamur, superstitio fusa per gentis oppressit omnium fere animos atque hominum inbecillitatem occupavit. quod et in iis libris dictum est qui sunt de natura deorum, et hac disputatione id maxume egimus. multum enim et nobismet ipsis et nostris profuturi videbamur si eam funditus sustulissemus. nec vero (id enim diligenter intellegi volo) superstitione tollenda religio tollitur. nam et maiorum instituta tueri sacris caerimoniisque retinendis sapientis est, et esse praestantem aliquam aeternamque naturam et eam suspiciendam admirandamque hominum generi pulchritudo mundi ordoque rerum caelestium cogit confiteri. **149** quam ob rem ut religio propaganda etiam est quae est iuncta cum cognitione naturae, sic superstitionis stirpes omnes eligendae. instat enim et urget et quo te cumque verteris persequitur, sive tu vatem sive tu omen audieris, sive immolaris sive avem aspexeris, si Chaldaeum, si haruspicem videris, si fulserit, si tonuerit, si tactum aliquid erit de caelo, si ostenti simile natum factumve quippiam; quorum necesse est plerumque aliquid eveniat, ut numquam liceat quieta mente consistere. **150a** perfugium videtur omnium laborum et sollicitudinum esse somnus. at ex eo ipso plurumae curae metusque nascuntur; qui quidem ipsi per se minus valerent et magis contemnerentur, nisi somniorum patrocinium philosophi suscepissent, nec ii quidem contemptissimi sed in primis acuti et consequentia et repugnantia videntes, qui prope iam absoluti et perfecti putantur. quorum licentiae nisi Carneades restitisset, haud scio an soli iam philosophi iudicarentur. cum quibus omnis fere nobis disceptatio contentioque est, non quod eos maxume contemnamus, sed quod videntur acutissime sententias suas prudentissimeque defendere.

150b Cum autem proprium sit Academiae iudicium suum nullum interponere, ea probare quae simillima veri videantur, conferre causas et quid in quamque sententiam dici possit expromere, nulla adhibita sua auctoritate iudicium audientium relinquere integrum ac liberum, tenebimus hanc consuetudinem a Socrate traditam eaque inter nos, si tibi, Quinte frater, placebit, quam saepissime utemur. 'Mihi vero,' inquit ille, 'nihil potest esse iucundius.' quae cum essent dicta, surreximus.

COMMENTARY

1–7 Introduction

Cicero had witnessed Caesar's assassination on the Ides of March (*Att.* 4.14[368].4; §23) and participated in the session of the senate on March 17 that yielded the compromise whereby the Liberators were granted amnesty and Caesar's *acta* were recognized as valid (*Att.* 14.14[368].2; *Phil.* 1.1, 2.89, and 3.30). In the aftermath of Caesar's public funeral, where Antony roused the passions of the urban plebs (cf. Mahy 2013, 339–40; van der Blom 2016, 264–67), the trend of opinion turned sharply against the Liberators, who could no longer move freely about the City (*Ad Brut.* 1.15[23].5). Distressed by these developments, Cicero retired to his country estates, as he reports to Atticus on April 7 (*Att.* 14.1[355]). Probably before his departure, Cicero put the finishing touches to *Div.*, adding allusions to Caesar's assassination (see above 30–31) and also this passage (§§1–7).

Though Cicero had a *liber prohoemiorum* from which he drew the prefaces to some of his philosophical books (*Att.* 16.6[414].4), no one could mistake this example for one of those ready-made proems. Cutting into the middle of the dialogue on divination, it exemplifies how Caesar's assassination has disrupted everything, not least Cicero's philosophical project. It also serves to defend Cicero against any charge of pursuing philosophy at the expense of politics, by making it clear that this work was conceived and begun when he was at leisure and that his further philosophical writing will be pursued in time left over from public service. He also raises the claim that his study of philosophy has equipped him with a perspective on events of the recent past and enabled him to endure Caesar's dictatorship with moderation. Cf. Ruch 1958, 176–77; Steel 2005, 138; Schofield 2008, 76–82. Durand 1903, 183, suggested that in a modern book such material might be presented in an "Afterword" ("*Postface*").

1–4a Inventory of Philosophical Books

This list can be seen as a "reading order," with the introductory *Hortensius* placed first (so Altman 2008, 105; further comments on the order: Altman 2016, xx–xxix). Next Cicero gives pride of place to the foundational works of his "philosophical encyclopedia": *Academici libri* (a work of epistemology,

"Academic" in the sense of setting out the position of the Skeptical Academy, to which Cicero adhered), *De finibus* (a work of theoretical ethics), and *Tusculan Disputations* (a work of practical ethics). Next the theological trilogy *De natura deorum*, the current work, and the planned *De fato*. Then, indicating a chronological break, he adds the earlier *De republica* (a work written in emulation of Plato's *Republic* but taking the earlier Roman Republic as the ideal), justified as political philosophy in the style of certain named Greek authors. Only then does he name the *Consolatio* (written to console himself over the death of his daughter Tullia) as of personal significance but perhaps benefiting others. *Cato maior de senectute* is paired with it as another work of consolation. Then, associatively it seems, the eulogy of Cato Uticensis is added as an example of a philosophical life, and finally the three rhetorical works. These last items beginning with the eulogy receive special justifications since they are more loosely connected with philosophy. Several items are omitted: *De inventione*, from which he later distanced himself (*De orat.* 1.5); the *Partitiones oratoriae*, which could be viewed as a kind of epitome of *De orat.* (cf. Arweiler 2003, 78–81); *De legibus*, which remained unpublished; the *Paradoxa Stoicorum*, which he seems to have regarded as a jeu d'esprit (*Parad.* 3: *ludens*); *De optimo genere oratorum*, a preface to a projected translation of speeches by Demosthenes and Aeschines that was apparently never executed; the project was perhaps set aside in favor of *Orator* and published posthumously from his papers; see further Berry 1996, 69; Ronconi 1998.

1 The first sentence compactly narrates three stages that have preceded this writing: the search (*quaerenti*), the plan (*nulla maior . . . meis civibus*), and the execution (*quod . . . me . . . consecutum*). Characteristically, Cicero emphasizes the important points by placing them at the beginning or end of their respective clauses and by separation of related words (hyperbaton), on which see Devine and Stephens 2006, ch. 6; Powell 2010.

Quaerenti mihi multumque et diu cogitanti: A common Ciceronian introductory formula, going all the way back to *Inv.* 1.1 (*saepe et multum hoc mecum cogitavi*) and famously instantiated at *De orat.* 1.1 (*cogitanti mihi saepe numero et memoria vetera repetenti*). The topos serves to emphasize the importance of the subject (cf. Lévy 1995, 158) and assigns the speaker the thoughtful and deliberate persona of a man unlikely to fall into *temeritas*, which, for an Academic, is the greatest disgrace (*N.D.* 1.1; cf. Lévy 2018).

. . . prodesse quam plurimis . . . : As elsewhere, Cicero presents his philosophical writing as a public benefit, not a mere private amusement;

cf. *Luc.* 6: *ut plurimis prosimus enitimur*; *Tusc.* 1.5: *ut, si occupati profuimus aliquid civibus nostris, prosimus etiam . . . otiosi*; §7 below: *ut . . . prodessemus civibus nostris.*

. . . ne quando intermitterem consulere rei publicae . . . : The activity benefits, in particular, the state itself (cf. *N.D.* 1.7: *ipsius rei publicae causa philosophiam nostris hominibus explicandam putavi*), albeit it will give way to direct work for the state (§7).

. . . optimarum artium vias . . . : *via* is "a way of achieving" (+ gen.): *OLD* s.v. 8a. *bonae artes* are "cultural pursuits, liberal studies": *OLD* s.v. *bonus* 6a. Cicero represents this as a general cultural project, since he wants to list not only his philosophical but also (§3 *fin.*) his rhetorical treatises.

nam leads off the enumeration (expected after *conpluribus . . . libris*): *OLD* s.v. 6.

et . . . et set the two works *Hortensius* and *Academici libri* in parallel; they are also framed as a unit by their verbs at beginning and end (*cohortati sumus . . . ostendimus*).

cohortati sumus . . . inscriptus Hortensius: *cohortor* ("encourage, exhort") is used as the equivalent of προτρέπω of encouraging the pursuit of philosophy. The προτρεπτικὸς λόγος ("exhortatory discourse") was a genre of Greek philosophical writing to which Aristotle, Epicurus, Cleanthes, et al. contributed; cf. Düring 1961; p. 109 Usener; *SVF* 1:481 and 568. Cicero entitled his version *Hortensius*; see further above 14.

quod genus philosophandi . . . Academicis libris ostendimus: For Cicero, the leading attribute of his favorite philosophy, Academic Skepticism, is the avoidance of something negative (*minime adrogans*); cf. already *Inv.* 2.10: *quod maximum est, ut ne cui rei temere atque adroganter assenserimus.* The two qualities consistency and elegance are closely linked (*et . . . et*): by consistently denying truth-value to impressions, the Skeptic achieves a neat, compact position; cf. Reid 1885 on *Luc.* 146. Similarly, at *Tusc.* 4.6, the philosophy of the Academy and its derivatives is said to be *elegans*, whereas for Cicero Epicurus *sentit . . . nihil umquam elegans* (*Div.* 1.62). For Cicero's notions of *elegantia* cf. in general Stucchi 2013. In June 45, the four *Academic Books* replaced Cicero's previous treatment of epistemology in the *Catulus* and *Lucullus*, altered in view of criticisms that the subject matter was too learned for the interlocutors; see above 15 and n34 and 26–27.

2 cumque fundamentum . . . intellegi posset: For the foundational significance of determining the ultimate good, cf. *Fin.* 5.15; "of evils" is added because pain and its status is also an important topic of ethics (cf. *Fin.* 1.29 *fin.*; Allen 2014, 250–52). By using *perpurgatus* ("cleaned up, got out of the way": *OLD* s.v. *perpurgo*), Cicero suggests that this was essentially a preliminary task, and indeed the focus will be on the next item in the series. The emphasis here is simply on the debate of each philosophy pro and contra without any mention of the possibility of (something like) truth emerging (cf. *Luc.* 7) or of Cicero's own view being expressed (cf. *Fin.* 1.12: *quid nobis probaretur*).

totidem subsecuti libri Tusculanarum . . . virtutem se ipsa esse contentam: *Tusc.* is the only item in the list provided with a table of contents, Cicero characteristically choosing to make the practical work "the centrepiece of the whole account" (Schofield 2002, 102); see further Gildenhard 2007, 81–82. **qui totam philosophiam maxime inlustrat** "that lends utmost distinction to the whole of philosophy" (*OLD* s.v. *illustro* 3); similarly of the Stoic position at *Off.* 3.20: *splendidius haec ab iis disserentur*; cf. details at *Fin.* 5.84. The topic of the sufficiency of virtue to procure happiness had also been dealt with by M. Brutus (*Tusc.* 5.21; fragments at Garbarino 2003, 93–95; cf. Sedley 1997) as well as in *Fin.* 3–5.

3 quibus rebus editis . . . satis factum toti huic quaestioni: *edo* here has the sense "set out, expound," as at *Brut.* 20, not "publish"; hence Ernesti's deletion of *rebus* is unnecessary. The books of *De natura deorum* were not only *perfecti* ("completed") but also published, as Quintus' remark at 1.8 suggests, but Cicero perhaps expresses the matter this way to avoid potential confusion by repeating a form of *edo* in a different sense. Cicero likes to emphasize comprehensiveness of treatment (cf. *Fin.* 1.12: *omnem quaestionem de finibus bonorum et malorum fere a nobis explicatam esse his litteris arbitramur*), but these three projects seem to be virtually trying to outbid one another: *N.D.* is asserted to comprise *omnis eius loci quaestio*, but the matter will be *plane . . . cumulateque perfecta* by the present work (for the phrasing cf. *Brut.* 126: *praeclare incohata multa, perfecta non plane*); but still not enough, by the projected *De fato*, "abundant attention will have been given to the entire matter" (*OLD* s.v. *satisfacio* 3b). On the decision to write *De fato*, see §19 below.

atque his libris . . . tractatus uberrime: *De republica* was composed in the late 50s and circulated just after Cicero's departure for Cilicia (*Fam.* 8.1[77].4: Caelius to Cicero, May 26, 51, on the work's reception). Cicero's claim that he was holding the rudder of state (*gubernacula rei publicae*) when it was written is evidently overstated; perhaps he means that he was relatively independent in comparison with his life under Caesar's dictatorship, when his influence was further reduced; cf. also on §6b. **magnus locus . . . tractatus uberrime:** An evaluative clause loosely attached to the foregoing; the label "clausal apposition" is sometimes applied to such phenomena; see Pinkster 2015, 1072–74. **magnus locus** "an important topic": *OLD* s.v. *locus* 24a. *familia* (literally, "members of a household") is an informal designation of a philosophical school (already so used by Cicero at *Leg.* 3.14 and *Tusc.* 1.55); *schola* (cf. §31) or *secta* would have been possible. At *Leg.* 3.14, he lists the other Peripatetics he has in mind, viz., Dicaearchus and Demetrius of Phalerum; see further Dyck 2004b ad loc. **-tatus uberrime:** A sonorous double cretic signals the conclusion of the period.

nam quid ego de Consolatione . . . profuturam puto: The *Consolatio*, surviving only in sparse fragments, was written soon after the death of his beloved daughter Tullia, from complications after childbirth in February 45. Cicero later admitted that it was a mistake to write it when his grief was in full spate (*Tusc.* 4.63; cf. 3.76) and that it reduced only the outer manifestation (*maeror*) but not the inner pain (*dolor*): *Att.* 12.28(267).2.—After *quae* Plasberg suggested insertion of *quoniam*, which would smoothe the construction a bit and allow punctuation with comma rather than semicolon after *medetur.*

interiectus est . . . de senectute misimus: This is the first mention of *Cato maior de senectute*, written perhaps at the end of 45 and/or beginning of 44 (cf. Powell 1988, 267–68), a consolation this time not for bereavement, but for the onset of old age. **interiectus est** "was inserted," evidently between *N.D.* and *Div.*, in spite of their closely related subject matter. One suspects, accordingly, an external cause. Here alone in the list the dedicatee is mentioned: Atticus would have turned 65 in November or December of 45 (cf. R. Feger, *RE* Suppl. 8:503.47–504.8); perhaps Cicero wrote the little dialogue to cheer his friend up. On Atticus, see Shackleton Bailey 1965–70, 1:3–59; Perlwitz 1992; Welch 1996; Cappello 2016; Pina Polo 2016, 105; Nelsestuen 2019. In a letter dated May 11, 44, Cicero raises the possibility that the work might cure his own current moroseness (*Att.* 14.21[375].3).

in primisque quoniam philosophia . . . ponendus est: Perhaps the mention of the elder Cato prompted Cicero to recall his panegyric of his descendant Cato Uticensis, undertaken on Brutus' request shortly after word arrived of his suicide at Utica (spring 46; *Orat.* 35). Publishing it was a minor act of defiance under Caesar's dictatorship, and it triggered ripostes (*Anticatones*) by both Aulus Hirtius and Caesar himself. Its inclusion here is perhaps not so surprising when one considers that Stoic philosophy was the informing principle of Cato's life (as Cicero represents it; for a different view, cf. Drogula 2019) and Cicero's tendency to assign *exempla* of Roman statesmen the place-value of philosophical arguments. See further Dyck (forthcoming).

4a cumque Aristoteles . . . quintus Orator: Cicero appeals to the precedent of Aristotle and Theophrastus, each of whom published a *Rhetoric*, Theophrastus additionally *On Style, On Delivery, On Judicial Speeches*, and *Rhetorical Precepts.* **cum subtilitate tum copia** "not only with subtlety [expected in philosophical writing] but also abundance [the stylistic quality Cicero prized]" (the following *cum* is the preposition). With the named Greeks as precedent, Cicero fleshes out his list with his three major rhetorical treatises, *De oratore*, published in 55, *Brutus*, and *Orator*, these latter two appearing in 46. At *Orat.* 148 Cicero conceives such "domestic literature" as a counterpart to his public speeches. By *Off.* 1.3, he is keen to show that his philosophical books now constitute a corpus more or less equivalent to his oratorical one: *te hortor . . . ut non solum orationes meas sed hos etiam de philosophia libros, qui iam illis fere se aequarunt, studiose legas.* **erunt:** Sc. *in eundem librorum numerum referendi.* This move may also help to raise the status of philosophical writing in the eyes of Roman readers; cf. Woolf 2015, 87.

4b–7 The Current Position

Cicero "was heading toward the rest" (*ad reliqua . . . tendebamus:* §4b) when the picture was suddenly and dramatically changed (sc. by Caesar's assassination), and Cicero could play a role in the state once again; and so, while still planning to complete the projected philosophical corpus, he will have to do it in his spare time. Within this basic frame, he inserts another justification of his writing on philosophy under Caesar's dictatorship. This adopts a different tone, however, in comparison with his previous philosophical prefaces: "the sense of urgency and desperation" is gone, since in view of his return to active politics—a more comfortable role—philosophical writing "is no longer his only option," as Baraz 2012, 190, observes.

4b Adhuc haec erant . . . inlustratus pateret: Cicero now explains that the corpus just described was part of a plan to treat the whole of philosophy in Latin. It is not clear exactly when he formed this plan. His resumption of work on philosophy in 46–45 seems to have been initially tentative but then continued when his first efforts were positively received (*Fin.* 1.2). He has by now dealt with epistemology, ethics, and physics, to which the ancients reckoned theology; and an additional theological work (*De fato*) has been promised (§3). One contribution to logic (the *Topica*) would follow in the summer, and another such work (on dialectics) was projected (*Top.* 7), but was never executed. **qui non Latinis litteris inlustratus pateret** "that has not been made accessible in Latin." Cf. the position before Cicero set to work: *philosophia iacuit . . . nec ullum habuit lumen litterarum Latinarum* and his own resolution: *quae inlustranda et excitanda nobis est* (*Tusc.* 1.5).

quod enim munus . . . ac coercenda sit?: One expects an explanation of the interruption to follow immediately upon the preceding description (*ad reliqua alacri tendebamus animo*), but in fact that is postponed until the last sentence of §7 (*nunc quoniam de re publica consuli coepti sumus . . .*). Instead, Cicero takes up from §1 the idea of benefit to the state (*munus* "gift" or "duty") and expands the value judgment (*maius meliusve* vs. *maior*). Schäublin (1991, 343) suspects that this material (§§4b–7) has replaced an earlier version. On the effect of "elid[ing] any clean-cut distinction between philosophy . . . and public service," cf. Woolf 2015, 65; Lévy 2012, 71–72. **quam si docemus . . . ac coercenda sit?:** Only gradually did Cicero come to embrace the role of *praeceptor iuventutis Romanae*. An important turning point is *Orat.* 143–46, where he stages a little dialogue with himself justifying his taking on the role of teacher; a further step down this path is represented by *Tusc.*; cf. Lévy 2012, 72–73. The Romans generally thought that youth was a vulnerable time of life (cf. Eyben 1993, 19–24). Cicero could be sympathetic to the young (cf. *Cael.*; Humpert 2001, esp. 271–76) but could also voice sharp criticism, as in our passage; cf. his complaint about the *perdita iuventus* in the run-up to the civil war (*Att.* 7.7[130].6). **his praesertim moribus atque temporibus:** This implies Cicero's oft-repeated assessment, famously encapsulated in the expostulation *o tempora! o mores!* (*Catil.* 1.2). For his evaluation of the moral climate of his times and strategies for counteracting it, cf. Braun 2003; Mueller-Goldingen 2003; and Gärtner 2003. This view was not exclusive to Cicero, however, but was shared notably by Sallust; cf. Earl 1961, 41–59; Mutschler 2003; and other papers in Haltenhoff, Heil, and Mutschler 2003.

5 nec vero id effici . . . late patere poterit industria: Cicero evidently aims to train the next generation of Rome's leaders; cf., e.g., *Sest.* 96 and 136, where he explicitly offers lessons for the young. Realizing, as he says at *Hort.* fr. 89 G. (similarly 88), *abhorrere a multitudine philosophiam*, Cicero will content himself with a few (*pauci* as opposed to *omnes*), on the assumption that they are of good quality; cf. the anecdote at *Brut.* 191: the poet Antimachus is content to have a single person listen to him reading his poem, since that one is Plato. **late patere poterit industria:** Cicero's confidence that the young who are so equipped will be able to display their hard work over a wide field contrasts with the picture he painted as a young man of a nobility hostile to hard-working *novi homines* (*Ver.* 5.181).

equidem ex iis etiam . . . plures quam rebar esse cognovi: *equidem* ("I for one"), characteristic of the conversational style of Cicero's *philosophica* (von Albrecht 2003, 87), shifts the topic, as Cicero goes on to describe the feedback loop whereby his readers' enthusiasm (*studium*) for reading spurs on Cicero's for writing. **fructum capio laboris mei** "I derive satisfaction from my work"; cf. *OLD* s.v. *fructus* 6. *acquiesco* can mean to "find (mental) peace, comfort or relief in": *OLD* s.v. 4, citing *Att.* 7.11(134).5 (as the civil war was brewing): *acquiesco . . . et scribens ad te et legens tua.* C. Matius was one of the elderly persons who encouraged Cicero's philosophical writing (*Fam.* 11.27[348].5). Cicero surely also had Atticus in mind, who later reported having found comfort in *Tusc.* 1 (cf. *Att.* 15.2[379].4, May 18, 44) and *Sen.* (*Att.* 16.11[420].3). **rebar:** The word had fallen out of general use but is employed by Cicero (also at §35) to lend a certain archaic patina and grandeur; cf. *De orat.* 3.153; for details on usage of *reor*, cf. Lebek 1970, 31.

5–6a magnificum illud . . . perfecero: *magnificum . . . gloriosum* "a splendid thing and glorious for Romans" is an emphatic nominal sentence with the verb "to be" elided and *illud* serving as a placeholder for the following *ut*-clause; cf. 1.1: *magnifica quaedam res et salutaris*; §19; §§35–36; Dyck 1996, 50; and 2004b on *Leg.* 1.42. *homo* is regularly used in ethnic designations but is not to be rendered in English; cf. *OLD* s.v. 4b. **ut Graecis de philosophia litteris non egeant:** At the same time that he worked to shape his philosophical corpus, Cicero was also at pains to shape the public perception of it (cf. *Att.* 2.1.[21].3 for his similar work on the corpus of consular speeches). Cicero's philosophical project has some of the trappings of a cultural war, seeking to replace major works of Greek literature with Latin equivalents; cf. *Fin.* 1.4–5; *Tusc.* 2.6: *quodsi haec studia traducta erunt ad nostros, ne bibliothecis quidem Graecis egebimus* with Citroni 2003: 150–57; Görler 2017, 221–22; similarly apropos of oratory in *Brutus*; cf. Dyck (forthcoming). He thus finds a patriotic justification for writing on philosophy; cf. Luciani 2010, 95. **Graecis de philosophia litteris** "Greek literature on philosophy," the noun and epithet encircling the prepositional phrase to create a self-contained sense-unit.

6b Ac mihi quidem explicandae philosophiae . . . agerem reperiebam: *casus gravis civitatis* ("grave state crisis") is, as he immediately clarifies, a reference to the civil war, in the aftermath of which Cicero resorted to philosophical writing when he could neither defend the state (*tueri . . . rem publicam*) nor sit idle; *meo more* may imply "according to my ideas" or "policies." Cicero's letters on the threshhold and at the early stages of the civil war show that he harbored no illusions that what was at issue was the preservation of the Republic; cf. *Att.* 7.7(130).7; 9.10(177).2–3; 9.11(178).3; 10.7(198).1. He paints the position in dark colors at *Fam.* 5.15(252).3 (to Lucceius); ibid. 9.8(254).2 (to Varro; a more optimistic version at *Ac.* 1.11); *Att.* 13.10(318).1; *Off.* 3.3–4. Nevertheless, he was prepared to advocate a peaceful settlement at virtually any price; see further Gelzer 1969, 243–46. This explanation of his turn to philosophy is a bit odd, however, in that he now ignores *De oratore* and *De republica*, both published in the 50s. Cf. Baraz 2012, 191, pointing out that although Cicero had been intensively engaged with it previously, he now makes "philosophy appear [merely] as one of many potential activities, and his decision [to pursue it] more the result of a process [of discovery] than a natural step" (my insertions). The reason may perhaps be that he wishes to portray a sharp break between his activities before and after the civil war and hence represents *De republica* as closely tied to political work (cf. §3: *cum gubernacula rei publicae tenebamus*).

dabunt igitur mihi veniam . . . ut me meae paeniteret: At issue is the judgment of Cicero's position under Caesar's dictatorship. Not without pride, he claims to have avoided the extremes of anger on the one side and fawning on the other. This perhaps gives a sense of what Cicero meant when he commented on his entertainment of the dictator (and 2,000 followers) at one of his villas (perhaps the one at Puteoli): *homines visi sumus*, i.e., he kept his self-respect, unequal though the relation may have been (*Att.* 13.52[353].2). **unius . . . homini . . . alterius:** In this passage Cicero refers obliquely to Caesar, whose legacy is contested, with an uneasy truce holding between the Liberators and Caesar's former followers. By the fall, however, Cicero will throw caution to the winds and repeatedly denounce Caesar by name in *De officiis*.

id enim ipsum a Platone . . . aliquando a singulis: Connected with *enim* is the reason for Cicero's equanimity in trying times: he saw that a constitutional change had occurred, as predicted by the theory of Plato, for whom the three forms, oligarchy, democracy, and monarchy, are prone to shift from one to another in no fixed cycle. Cicero prefers to cite Plato, who first formulated the theory (cf. *Rep.* 1.65–68, citing Plato, *Rp.* 8.562c–563d; cf. also *Plt.* 291d–92a and 302c–e). It later formed the basis of Polybius' system of six constitutions recurring in a fixed cycle, with the addition of defective versions of the three basic ones (viz., tyranny, oligarchy, and ochlocracy): Polyb. 6.3.5–4.10. After the outbreak of the civil war, on May 2, 49, Cicero predicted Caesar's decline based upon Plato's comments on tyrants (*Att.* 10.8[199].6); cf. Gildenhard 2006, 206.

7 quod cum accidisset . . . qua re cumque possemus: *quod* refers to the shift from oligarchy to monarchy, even though Caesar declined the most overt symbol of monarchy—the diadem offered him by Antony at the Lupercalia of 44 (cf. *Phil.* 2.84–87). Describing himself as *orbati* ("orphaned"), Cicero aims to stir sympathy for his position and also to emphasize the familial connection he felt to the *res publica*; cf. Baraz 2012, 192. He uses *renovare* ("renew") advisedly: at *N.D.* 1.6 he was at pains to show critics that he had long cultivated an interest in philosophy. **ut et animus . . . et prodessemus civibus nostris:** Cicero now admits that his occupation with philosophy was not merely to provide an altruistic public benefit, as appeared to be the case in §1, but it also had the function of relieving his mind of *molestiae* ("distress"), most directly addressed in *Consol.* and *Tusc.* 3. **hac potissimum re:** Sc. *philosophia*. With *ut . . . prodessemus civibus nostris* he returns, by ring composition, to the theme of the opening. **qua re cumque** "by whatever means," *quicumque* being often in tmesis, especially in verse: *OLD* s.v. *init.*

in libris enim . . . substitutam putabamus: At *Brut.* 330 Cicero speaks of Eloquence as a grown-up maiden (*adultam virginem*) who must be guarded at home; on the personification see further Stroup 2010: 261–64. So here the private activity of philosophizing substitutes for such public acts as pronouncing his opinion (*sententiam dicere*) at a meeting of the senate or holding forth in a public assembly (*contionari*); Cicero envisions a similar substitution in a letter to Varro (9.2[177].5, April 22, 46) and speaks of M. Marcellus as having made such a substitution at *Brut.* 249–51. **pro rei publicae procuratione** "for the administration of the state": *OLD* s.v. *procuratio* 2b; for a different sense, cf. on §21 *fin.* As Baraz 2012, 194, notes, "it is only here, in *De Divinatione*, that he can afford, in retrospect, to be honest with himself about the exact nature and the implied limitations of this substitution."

nunc quoniam de re publica . . . revertamur: It is now open to Cicero to play a role in public deliberations once again, as he had at the senate's meeting of March 17 (see on §§1–7). That being so, he now reverts to his previous policy of devoting only "leftover time" to philosophical writing (*subsiciva tempora*: *Leg.* 1.8–9). **tantum huic studio . . . quantum vacabit a publico officio:** Cf. Cic. *Cons.* F 10.78 Courtney: *quod patria vacat, id studiis nobisque* [sc. *Musis*] *sacrasti*, where the plain abl. (*patria*) reflects poetic syntax. **haec alias pluribus:** A formula for postponement not necessarily implying that Cicero has a specific plan to pursue the topic in another work (some have thought of *Off.* in this connection).

8–26a "Preliminary Sortie"

In this "preliminary sortie" (*levis armaturae prima orationis excursio*: §26a), Cicero puts forward some general objections to divination; then after summarizing and critiquing Quintus' presentation in Book 1 (§§26–27), he attacks in detail the two species of divination, artificial and natural (§§28–99 and 110–48 respectively, with an intermezzo at §§100–109 containing Quintus' reaction and a refutation of the syllogisms of Chrysippus and Cratippus). In our passage, Cicero offers three basic objections: (a) divination lacks a subject matter of its own (§§9–14); (b) there can be no art of predicting random events (§§15–18); (c) if events are fated, rather than random, advance knowledge of the outcomes would not benefit the human race (§§19–25).

8 Nam cum de divinatione . . . in bibliotheca quae in Lycio est adsedimus: The first book narrated the conversation the brothers held while walking in the "Lycium" or upper gymnasium (essentially a building in a courtyard used for educational purposes) of Cicero's villa at Tusculum (1.8); it was named after the famous gymnasium outside of Athens that served as the headquarters for Aristotle's school. They now repair to its library for the continuation (the outfitting of this library was a major project, discussed in detail with Atticus in the early 60s: *Att.* 1.5[1].7, 8[4].2, 9[5].2, 1.10[6].3, 1.3[8].2, 1.4[9].3, 1.1[10].5; see Houston 2014, 28–29). For the Tusculan villa "conceived as a place separated in both space and thought from the business of Rome," cf. Bishop 2019, 21. Similar transitions from walking to sitting mark the change from Book 2 to 3 of *De orat.* (2.20, 3.18) and from Book 1 to 2 of *Leg.* (1.15, 2.1); cf. also *'Considamus igitur,'* spoken by Cicero's character to mark the onset of his lecture (*Fat.* 4). **de divinatione:** *divinatio* was used by Cicero as early as his first criminal defense (*S.Rosc.* 96) in the sense of "guesswork." Cicero uses the word in our work as an equivalent of Greek μαντική (*mantikē*) and claims that the Latin word is superior in making a connection with *divinus*, rather than μανία (*mania* "madness"), claimed by Plato (*Phaedr.*

244a–c) as the etymology of the Greek word (cf. 1.1). He thus aimed to connect this work with a particular Greek tradition of theoretical writing, but the equivalence is problematic; see Santangelo 2012, 41–47; above 20.

Adcurate tu quidem . . . et Stoice Stoicorum sententiam defendisti: *adcurate* ("meticulously") repays the compliment Quintus had bestowed on the verses quoted from the *De consulatu suo* (1.22: *accuratissime*); for such praise cf. *Arch.* 18: *accurate cogitateque*; *Brut.* 86: *accurate . . . eleganterque.* **Quinte:** The address with praenomen, which is regularly used in Cicero's dialogues, is found throughout *Div.*, except in the conclusion (§150b), where the more formal *Quinte frater* lends focus (cf. *De orat.* 1.1, 2.1, 3.1 and 13; *Mil.* 102; *Leg.* 3.26). On Cicero's practices in naming his brother in various genres, cf. Dickey 2002, 257–61. Marcus is—notoriously—never named by his brother or any other interlocutor in a dialogue with his praenomen; cf. Dickey 1997; Bishop 2019, 297. **Stoice:** To say that the subject has been treated "in the Stoic manner" is barbed, since the Stoics were known for a thin, thorny style that Cicero disapproved; cf. *Fin.* 3.3: *Stoicorum . . . non ignoro quam sit subtile vel spinosum potius disserendi genus*; similarly 4.79 of their *disserendi spinae*; *De orat.* 1.83, 2.159, 3.66. Hence Cicero experimented by presenting Stoic arguments in a rhetorical style, most explicitly in *Parad.*

quodque me maxime delectat . . . claris et inlustribus: Quintus' speech catered for Cicero's intended readers in two respects: the Roman examples (*nostris exemplis*) and the fact that they are chosen from a higher social stratum (*claris et inlustribus*) will tend to involve upper-class Romans in the argument. Quintus had, in fact, criticized Chrysippus for using humble examples (1.39); from a strictly philosophical point of view, the distinction is, of course, irrelevant. **et iis quidem claris et inlustribus:** Cicero uses *et is quidem* to add emphatic attributes; cf. Solodow 1978, 110–19.

dicendum est mihi . . . et mihi ipse diffidens: Speaking as a Skeptic (see on §§1–4a), Cicero assumes a characteristically cautious persona, in contrast to the confidence with which a dogmatist puts forward his positions (cf., e.g., *N.D.* 1.18 of the Epicurean Velleius: *fidenter sane, ut solent isti, nihil tam verens quam ne dubitare aliqua de re videretur, tamquam modo ex deorum concilio . . . descendisset*). Cicero explains at *Luc.* 7: *omnis cognitio multis est obstructa difficultatibus . . . ut non sine causa antiquissimi et doctissimi invenire se posse quod cuperent diffisi sunt.* **nihil ut adfirmem:** The Skeptic abstains from advancing positive doctrine; cf. the description of Socrates' procedure at *Ac.* 1.16: *hic . . . ita disputat ut nihil affirmet, ipse refellat alios*;

similarly Arcesilas as described ibid. 45; *Luc.* 8. Cotta, the Skeptical speaker in *N.D.*, constructs a similar persona for himself (1.60; 3.1 and 4, etc.); cf. Wynne 2014; so, too, here at 1.7 (Cicero as author).

si enim aliquid certi . . . divinationem nego!: A "somewhat forced" pun on the technical sense of *divino* ("practice divination") and the common one ("make a guess"); cf. Woolf 2015, 79 (source of the quoted words); *OLD* s.v. 1a and b: "I would be practicing the diviner's art while denying its existence." **aliquid certi** "something certain"; for the genitive cf. Pinkster 2015, 1019–22.

9 etenim me movet illud . . . divinatio esset: Carneades (214/13–129/28) was one of antiquity's leading Skeptics, much admired by Cicero; cf. *Fin.* 5.4, set at the Academy in Athens (the character Cicero is the speaker): *ego illa moveor exhedra, modo enim fuit Carneadis*). On him, cf. Bett 1989 and 1990; Schofield 1999, 334–50; Thorsrud 2010, 70–80. Our passage = F 9 Mette, comprising all allusions to him in *Div.* Since, like Socrates, Carneades left no writings, Cicero knows his views via his pupil Clitomachus (cf. §87; *Luc.* 98, 102, 108; *Tusc.* 3.54). **quarumnam rerum divinatio esset** "To what matters does divination belong?," i.e., "What is its subject matter?," with possessive gen. as predicate, a construction often repeated in the sequel; cf. Pinkster 2015: 208(t); *NLS* 72.1(1)(iii). Modeling his approach on Socrates' challenge to claims to arts of poetic interpretation, rhetoric, and generalship in Plato's dialogues (*Ion*, *Gorgias*, and *Laches* respectively; cf. Timpanaro 1988, 332; Woolf 2015, 79), Carneades argued that divination has no proper subject matter and therefore no status as an art (τέχνη, *ars*); cf. above 25; 1.23: *quid, quaeris, Carneades . . . qua arte perspici possint?* Cicero grants divination status as an *ars* for the sake of argument at *Fat.* 11b. Cf. *Luc.* 91 for Carneades' similar criticism of dialectic.

earumne quae sensibus perciperentur . . . divinatio adhibetur: Marcus' argument is carried largely by questions, many with a bias toward a negative response ("railroading" *num*; cf. *OLD* s.v. 3), with a few assertions. The first potential field for the operation of divination is the realm of sense perception. But this is already claimed by the five senses, which are enumerated for clarity and emphasis. **provisione aut permotione mentis . . . natura ipsa:** *provisio* is used of precognition in general (cf. *OLD* s.v. a), whereas *permotio* points to natural divination, which Marcus takes as his example; cf. 1.89: *quid Asiae rex Priamus nonne et Helenum filium et Cassandram filiam divinantes habebat, alterum auguriis, alteram mentis incitatione et permotione divina?* The alterative explanation is *natura*, i.e., the five senses; cf.

§108 (*oculi vera cernentes utuntur natura atque sensu*), where the dichotomy between divination and the senses helps to refute Cratippus' justification of divination. **nescio qui ille divinus** "such and such diviner" (*OLD* s.v. *ille* A5). **oculis captus:** Slow to develop a technical vocabulary in medicine, Latin describes various afflictions with a form of *captus* + the ablative of the affected part; cf. *OLD* s.v. *capio* 22. **ut Tiresias fuit:** Marcus follows his brother's lead in citing an illustrious example, albeit he later distances himself from the mythological (§113). The point is that the subject's ability to discriminate colors or tones will be impaired by the loss of sight or hearing, and divination can offer no substitute. **ad nullam igitur . . . divinatio adhibetur:** The emphatic conclusion is drawn, shutting divination out of the realm perceived by the senses.

atqui ne in iis quidem rebus quae arte tractantur . . . sed a musicis: From the senses in general, Cicero moves on to the various *artes* ("skilled disciplines") that benefit human beings, beginning with medicine and music. Information from a seer cannot replace the specialist knowledge of the physician or musician. In Republican Latin a *vates* is a "prophet, seer"; cf. *OLD* s.v. 1; Bendlin, *BNP* s.v. The argument is a bit tendentious, however, since there was a form of divination used in the treatment of disease, viz., divination from dreams (cf. §123 with notes). **fidibus aut tibiis:** The principal string and wind instruments frequently appear in combination; cf. *Rep.* 2.69; *Leg.* 2.22 and 38; *Off.* 1.145; Quint. *Inst.* 1.10.14 and 11.3.59.

10 Eadem in litteris . . . quarum est disciplina: Cicero extends the argument to other departments of knowledge, beginning with astronomy.

num censes . . . non hariolorum: Marcus resumes the interrogation with "railroading" *num* (see on §9 [*earumne quae sensibus perciperentur*]), which recurs three times in this chapter and the next, as Marcus presses his brother to accept successive limitations on the diviner's scope. The size and distance (and hence speed of motion) of the sun and moon were among the major problems discussed by Greek astronomers (cf. *Inv.* 1.8 on the *solis magnitudo* as a standard philosophical issue). Both Aristarchus of Samos (third century) and Hipparchus (second century) contributed books *On the Size and Distances of the Sun and Moon*; see further Evans 1998, 67–73. **tantus quantus videatur:** Epicurus' view, dismissed as naive at *Luc.* 82 (cf. *Fin.* 1.20 *fin.*), where Cicero cites a figure offered by the *mathematici* for the size of the sun (relative to earth); similarly, *N.D.* 2.92. See in general Bakker 2016, 236–39 and 262–63 (on Epicurus' acceptance of any theory that agrees with appearances and rejection of mathematical proofs offered by astronomers when competing theories explain appearances equally well). That the moon's light is reflected from the sun was already posited by Anaxagoras (mid-fifth century) as the explanation for lunar eclipses (59 B 18 D.–K.). Cf. *Rep.* 6.17 = 21 P.: *luna radiis solis accensa* (similarly 6.16 = 20 P.: *luce lucebat aliena*); *N.D.* 2.103; §91: *luna . . . distet a sole, cuius lumine conlustrari putatur.* **sol, luna quem motum habeat:** A reference, perhaps, not only to their orbits, but also to the regularity of their motion, from which other inferences could be drawn; cf. §17: *ex constantissimo motu lunae*; *N.D.* 2.43–44. As usual in Latin, the verb agrees with the nearer inanimate subject; cf. Pinkster 2015, 1254. **quinque stellae quae errare dicuntur:** The canonical "five planets" of the ancients were Mercury, Venus, Mars, Jupiter, and Saturn, the others having been discovered in modern times. Cicero identifies them by the traditional name (= "wanderers"), though he denies its accuracy (*Cons.* F 10.8 Courtney), cited at 1.17: *quae* [sc. *stellae*] *verbo et falsis Graecorum vocibus errant*; similar criticism at *Tusc.* 1.62 and *N.D.* 2.51; hence here *quae errare dicuntur*; similarly §89, *Rep.* 1.22, *N.D.* 2.119. There follow geometry and theoretical ethics, each punctuated with a proprietary claim. **qui divini habentur** varies *qui divinare dicuntur*. **divini** is a substantive ("diviners"); cf. *vates*, *harioli*, and *haruspex* elsewhere in this context; cf. also *Fat.* 15: *Chrysippus . . . falli sperat Chaldaeos ceterosque divinos*; *OLD* s.v. *divinus* 6. **sunt enim ea mathematicorum, non hariolorum:** *mathematicus* = mathematician; cf. *OLD* s.v. 1, citing inter alia *Luc.* 82; similarly §91. *hariolus*, on the other hand, is an old word for a diviner: the first element, also seen in *haruspex*, may correspond to Greek χορδή ("entrails") and similar words in Indo-European (a connection with the Sumerian ideogram for liver [HAR] is untenable, however); the suffix *-lo-* is found, e.g., in *figulus*; see E.–M. s.v. *haru-*, *har-*; Turfa 2012, 256.

de illis vero rebus . . . propria philosophorum: For *vero* calling attention to a new point, cf. Kroon 1995, 319–25. It is odd that ethics is treated initially as if it were the whole of philosophy and ethicists as the only philosophers. As his example of a philosophical question on which a diviner would not be expected to pronounce Marcus chooses the problem of the classification of goods, evils, and indifferents, explored in detail in *De finibus*. Only after citing examples of practical ethics does Marcus add the other departments of philosophy. One suspects that he may originally have planned for ethical problems to stand as his sole example of philosophy (ethics being the department of philosophy of greatest interest to the Romans; see further Dyck 2004b on *Leg.* 1.58–62) but then decided to add examples from physics and logic. Marcus offers an illustration of the futility of looking for ethical guidance from omens at §§78–79.

11 quid, de officio . . . non ad divinos referri solent: These are all points Cicero will explore in *De officiis* (relations with others in Book 1 [esp. §§50–58], use of external goods in Book 2), the former also in *De amicitia*. With *sapientes* he evidently means respected Romans (*viri boni*), not Stoic sages, on the rarity of whom see §61 with n.; cf. *Fin.* 3.64, where *vir bonus* and *sapiens* appear side by side as equivalents; *Amic.* 18–19; *Off.* 3.17–18.

quid, quae a dialecticis . . . dialectici dicent, non divini: The two remaining divisions of philosophy, physics and logic/dialectic, now follow. Under physics, Cicero identifies two problems (which we would call "cosmological"): (a) the number of worlds, the Epicureans having posited a multiplicity of them (fr. 301 Usener; cf. *Hort.* fr. 79 G.); (b) the origin of the world, for which the Epicureans offered a mechanical explanation in the collision of atoms, in contrast to Plato's creator, the demiurge (cf. *N.D.* 1.18–20 and 54; Sedley 2007, chs. 4–5). Under logic, he similarly focuses on two paradoxes, both said to have been invented by Eubulides of Megara, a contemporary of Aristotle and student of Euclid; cf. *Hort.* (fr. 26 G.); L–S 37 E, H: (a) the "liar paradox," i.e., the fact that someone who claims to be a liar may be telling the truth (cf. *Luc.* 95–97; Gel. 18.2.10; other testimonies cited by Pease ad loc.); (b) the *sorites* ("the accumulator," more commonly called "the heap"), i.e., the fact that a heap can arise by addition of tiny increments without a single identifiable act as the cause (cf. *Luc.* 49; Burnyeat 1982). The translation of Greek terminology was a major problem Cicero wrestled with in composing his *philosophica*; see above 32. Here he offers an equivalent for *sorites* (*acervalis* [sc. *ratio*]) but decides it is unnecessary after all.

quid, cum quaeritur . . . periti rerum civilium?: On questions of political philosophy the haruspices' advice is likewise redundant (even though they could be consulted about particular phenomena that might have a bearing on issues of state, such as the strange rumblings heard in Italy in early 56 and discussed by Cicero in *Har.*). **qui sit optimus rei publicae status** "What is the best constitution?" Cf. *Q.fr.* 3.5.(25).1, describing *De republica* as *de optimo statu civitatis et de optimo cive.* The *principes* here will be the "leading men" of the state, further specified as *delecti viri periti rerum civilium.*

12 quodsi nec earum rerum . . . nihil prorsus intellego: Cicero summarizes the findings of §§9–11: divination pertains neither to objects of perception (*quae subiectae sensibus sunt*) nor the subject matter of established disciplines, including philosophy and practical politics. This leads back to Carneades' problem (*quarumnam rerum divinatio esset*: §9), with no answer in prospect. **nihil prorsus intellego:** *nihil* is a stronger (and colloquial) equivalent of *non* (Hofmann 2003, 208), further strengthened by *prorsus*: "I completely fail to understand."

nam aut omnium . . . ne nulla sit divinatio: Divination is neither an all-encompassing art nor one that has its own identifiable subject matter (*materia*). **ut ratio docuit** "as our argument has shown" (sc. §§9–11). **nec locus . . . praeficere possimus:** *locus* here is a "subject" (*OLD* s.v. 24a). *divinatio* is personified, as if it were a magistrate that one might "put in charge of" (*praeficere*) a portfolio; similar metaphor at *Fin.* 1.20: *erit hoc quasi atomis provincias dare.* For the subjunctive of tendency in the relative clause, cf. on §19 (*nisi quod . . . rato tempore*). **vide igitur ne nulla sit divinatio** "perhaps, then, there is no divination": *OLD* s.v. *video* 17a. In the sequel, Marcus will repeatedly hammer home this point, the nonexistence of divination.

est quidam Graecus . . . optumum: A well-known tag; to Atticus Cicero needs to cite only the first three words (in Greek) to conjure it up (*Att.* 7.13[136].4). **in hanc sententiam** "to this effect" (since he is translating, rather than quoting the *ipsissima verba*); cf. §25: *in eam sententiam.* **bene qui coniciet, vatem hunc perhibebo optumum** "I shall call a good guesser the best seer," an iambic senarius = Cic. fr. 45 Bl., rendering Euripides F 973 Kn. (play unknown), sometimes attributed to Menander (fr. inc. 941 Körte): μάντις δ᾽ ἄριστος ὅστις εἰκάζει καλῶς.

num igitur . . . coniectura adsequetur?: Another leading question introduced by *num* (cf. on §§9 and 10). On the basis of the quoted verse, Cicero throws the diviner into the general category of those who offer predictions of the future and compares the results: the diviner will not be as good at predicting the weather as the ship's pilot or treating a disease as the physician or managing a war as the general. Though *vatis* is the transmitted nominative here, this is likely to be a scribal error: *vates* is the transmitted nominative at §13. These are, however, the only two instances of the nom. sg. in *Div.*, and the form in *-is* can be defended with reference to Pl. *Mil.* 911. **prudentius** "with greater skill"; see on §13 *init.* **coniectura:** A juxtaposition of two things and hence an inference from one to the other (*OLD* s.v.); it is the basis of the interpretation of dreams and of portents generally (cf. *OLD* s.v. 3; *TLL* 4:316.27–59); cf. 1.73: *facta coniectura etiam in Dionysio est . . . quod ostentum habuit hanc vim, ut Dionysius paucis post diebus regnare coeperit.* Its Greek equivalent is στοχασμός; see further Hankinson 1988, 146n92; Wardle 2006, 165.

13 Sed animadverti, Quinte . . . quae essent fortuitae: Turning now to Quintus' definition of divination, Marcus claims that his brother formulated it cautiously (*caute*) so as to separate divination from other areas in which conjectures are made, an apparent reference to 1.111–12, where Quintus differentiates between divination and predictions of natural or political occurrences. The relevance here of a science or skill (*ars*), proficiency in a subject (*prudentia* [cf. §11: *physicorum est ista prudentia*; *OLD* s.v. 2]), or the skilled professions (*artificia*, such as those of the physician or the ship's pilot) is obvious. The remaining item is a problem, however. There is no passage in which Quintus argues for a dichotomy between perceptibles and *res fortuitae*; indeed, both should be in the same category; cf. Schäublin 1989, 49–50. Marcus has, however, argued for the separation of divination from the objects of sense perception (§9). That may explain the presence of perceptibles here. **divinationem esse earum rerum praedictionem et praesensionem quae essent fortuitae:** Similarly §19: *quam* [sc. *divinationem*] *dicebas praesensionem esse rerum fortuitarum* (for the juxtaposition of *praedictio* and *praesensio*, cf. *N.D.* 2.7). Actually, Quintus defined divination as *earum rerum quae fortuitae putantur praedictio atque praesensio* (1.9). This divergence has been traced to error (Denyer 1985, 6; Schofield 1986, 62) or deceit (Schultz 2014, 69); cf. also Timpanaro 1988, XCIII; Begemann 2015, 276. In fact, however, under the Stoic definition of chance, the two definitions are the same: "the Stoics [say] that chance is a cause unclear to human reason" (οἱ Στωικοὶ [τὴν τύχην] ἄδηλον αἰτίαν ἀνθρωπίνωι λογισμῶι: *SVF* 2:966; similarly 965, 967, 970, 971). Quintus' version merely calls attention to the way in which the Stoic definition differs from the ordinary; cf. Hankinson 1988, 155; Struck 2016, 199–200. Quoting the definition in this form, though not incorrect per se, does, however, enable Marcus to win some easy victories in the following "preliminary sortie," where, ignoring the special Stoic sense of chance, he traps Quintus between the two concepts of randomness and fate, the latter disallowed as an explanation of divination because of this definition, the former disallowed as providing no scope for prediction. This move is in line with the kinds of rhetoric Cicero regularly deploys in his speeches, and he draws no sharp distinction between rhetorical and philosophical discourse; cf. Krostenko 2000, 371–73; Begemann 2012, 78n377; Beard 2012, 37n68. Marcus' refutation in the "preliminary sortie" also includes, however, the stronger point that fate, understood as a fixed chain of causation, is at odds with the traditional Roman practice of divination, which assumes that outcomes can be altered if the human actors change their behavior. **praesensionem:** Augustine (*Civ.* 5.9) later replaced *praesensio* ("perception in advance") with *praescientia* ("foreknowledge").

primum eodem revolveris . . . quam imperator?: No benefit has been realized by Quintus' cautious definition: "you wind up in the same place" (*eodem revolveris*; cf. *Luc.* 18: *ita imprudens* [Philo] *eo quo minime volt revolvitur*). Hence the refutation is repeated from §12, since the same difficulty is entailed. The seer, whether relying on art (*haruspex aut augur* [respectively seers who prophesy from signs in entrails or provided by birds]) or nature (*aut vates quis aut somnians* [an inspired prophet or a person who has a dream thought to be prophetic]), is nonetheless locked in an unequal competition with the physician or ship's pilot. For *conicio* + acc. and inf. ("form a conclusion about"), cf. *OLD* s.v. 13 *fin.* Compared to Greek, Latin does not have a rich vocabulary, but in Cicero's hands it is a flexible instrument, as here *evado* serves for "escape" in three very different areas. **aut e periculo . . . quam gubernator:** Quintus had, however, opined that in Homer Calchas had been placed in charge of the fleet *auspiciorum . . . scientia, non locorum* (1.87).

14 atqui ne illa quidem divinantis . . . non semper eveniunt: At 1.13–15 Quintus had cited passages from Cicero's *Prognostica* (translated from Aratus' *Phaenomena*) describing various natural signs associated with meteorological phenomena; he had not claimed them as divination but similar to it (cf. Kany-Turpin 2003, 367–71). **memoriter** "with good memory, accurately" (*OLD* s.v.); cf. §35, where Marcus praises Quintus' memory of doctrines (since he cannot praise the doctrines themselves); cf. his previous praise of Quintus' presentation as done *adcurate* (§8). **haec ipsa** "even these points," i.e., the correspondence of certain signs to certain atmospheric phenomena: *OLD* s.v. *ipse* 8–9.

quae est igitur . . . sed peritis: Not diviners, but experts, *periti*, sc. in the various types of subject matter (used differently by Quintus of expert diviners at 1.77 and 78, as by Marcus at §71), are seen to exercise skill in prediction based on the named methods *ars, ratio, usus, coniectura*, whereby *ars* is a combination of *ratio* ("deduction": cf. Frank 1992, 312) and *usus* ("experience"), whereas *coniectura* might be called "intelligent guessing" (cf. on §12).

ita relinquitur ut . . . praesensio divinatio est: Marcus has relentlessly pushed divination outside the mainstream *artes*. It receives what is left over (*ita relinquitur . . .*) after their subject matters have been subtracted, viz., the fortuitous, of which he offers an example. Denyer 1985, 3, however, challenges Marcus' Other Sciences argument on the ground that "there are many other areas in which foreknowledge would be desirable but in which scientific knowledge of effects from causes is simply unavailable." **si quis M. Marcellum illum . . . divinasset profecto:** M. Claudius Marcellus (*RE* s.v. Claudius 225), cos. 166, 155, 152, died in a shipwreck in 148 on an embassy to the Numidian king Massinissa. At *Pis.* 44 Marcellus' shipwreck is ascribed to *fortuna*, as it is implicitly here (since Cicero would allow this, if correctly predicted well in advance, as an instance of divination under Quintus' definition). This example recurs at *Fat.* 33 to illustrate the New Academy's "weak" conception of truth that involves no chain of causes anchored in the order of nature: even Apollo could not know of such a past event that left no traces, much less a future event; cf. Schallenberg 2008, 208–09. **M. Marcellum illum** "the M. Marcellus," with defining relative clause: *OLD* s.v. *ille* 3a. **multis annis ante** is specified to exclude the kinds of short-term prediction from weather and other patterns that Marcus accepts (cf. §145).

15 Potestne igitur earum rerum . . . esse ulla praesensio?: Having created this subject matter for divination, things for the occurrence of which there is no explanation (*ratio*; cf. Frank 1992, 151, and for the genitive on §8 *fin.*), Cicero now inquires whether there can be such a science at all, the two quantifiers *nihil* and *ulla* exerting pressure toward a negative answer. In the sequel what Cicero here paraphrases as "events that lack a rationale for their occurrence" are called *res incertae* or *incognitae*; cf. §§33a, 43b.

quid est enim aliud fors . . . cadere atque evenire potuerit?: In this company, *eventus* will be "an event relating to a particular person or thing, fate" (*OLD* s.v. 3a). This is a variation of the point raised apropos of weather signs at §14: *plerumque . . . non semper eveniunt*. Here after *vel* the words *non cadere atque evenire vel*, which appear as a correction in V, are adopted; they can easily have dropped out by saltation (i.e., by a scribe's eye skipping from *vel* to *vel*), and it seems doubtful that a scribe of the high Middle Ages would have been able to hit upon the required sense; cf. Timpanaro 1988, 336.

quo modo ergo . . . praedici potest?: The very terms in which the question is posed (*temere, caeco casu, volubilitate fortunae*) suggest that the problem is insoluble. Fortune was appropriately depicted in art poised on a globe or with a spinning wheel; see further Pease ad loc. *praesentiri* and *praedici* are taken up from the definition of divination at §13 (*praedictio, praesensio*).

16 medicus morbum ingravescentem . . . non numquam tamen fallitur: The physician, the general, and the ship's pilot return as examples of experts guided by *ratio* (cf. §§12, 13), i.e., they can cite a justification (*ratio*) for their action (cf. Frank 1992, 297), to whom the farmer, in his evaluation of ripening crops, is now added. Quintus had already pointed to the fallibility of such predictions (in extenuation of diviners) at 1.24; cf. also *N.D.* 3.14. **providet** "takes steps in advance to deal with": *OLD* s.v. *provideo* 3a. **non sine ratione ille quidem:** Contrasting *quidem* typically requires the support of a pronoun, hence it will prompt the appearance of *ille*; cf. Solodow 1978, 38–39.

quodsi falluntur ii . . . somniis futura praesentiunt?: The expected conclusion of the *a fortiori* argument: if these experts sometimes err on the basis of *probabilis coniectura ac ratio*, how much more likely that seers would do so, who have a much less solid basis for their predictions! A *probabilis coniectura* is a "plausible guess" (*OLD* s.v. *probabilis* 2). **oraclis:** In older Latin generally the instrumental deverbative suffixes *-culum* and *-clum* are found side by side (cf. Leumann 1977, 102); hence *oraclum* and *oraculum* are both used by Cicero.

nondum dico quam haec signa nulla sint . . . nunc de universis: *nondum dico quam haec signa nulla sint* "I am not at this stage arguing that these signs are worthless." This is the first hint of a plan whereby the current argument is a preliminary to detailed discussion of the individual types of divination. Here, to heighten the absurdity, Cicero lists not the names of the different species of divination (haruspicy, augury, astrology, etc.) but the particular signs on which they are based, beginning with the cleft of the liver (*fissum iecoris*), which was, in fact, used by the haruspices as a major criterion; cf. on §32; Wardle 2006, 141–42. The five items with limiting genitive are arranged in chiastic order (abba, etc.), with the two unmodified terms (*sortes somnia*) appended. **corvi cantus, volatus aquilae:** Cf. 1.12: *Iuppiterne . . . corvum ab dextera canere iussisset.* These two examples, with a chiastic arrangement of birds and behavior, correspond to the two types of bird-signs, *oscines* and *alites*; cf. on §80. **stellae traiectio:** A shooting star; cf. 1.2: *traiectiones . . . stellarum*; §60.

17 qui potest provideri . . . cur futurum sit?: *qui* is the old abl. or instrumental functioning as an adverb: "how"; cf. *OLD* s.v. *qui*[2]. Quintus might at this point object that it has not been shown that the phenomena have no cause (*causa*), merely that there is no *ratio* accessible to ordinary humans for their occurrence (Augustine will take a similar line at *Civ.* 5.9; see above 36). *nota* is any distinguishing mark, in this case, one pointing to an event that may be expected to take place in the future; cf. *OLD* s.v. 8a. The denial of a (valid) *nota* anticipates the argument at §18; cf. also §128.

solis defectiones itemque lunae . . . quam rationem sequantur vides: Astronomy provides an illustration of how a successful prediction can be made by use of reason. **in multos annos** "into many years," i.e., many years in advance, a use of *in* + acc. to indicate "a terminal point of something conceived as going through several stages": *OLD* s.v. *in* 2c. *numeri* here are "numerical calculations," the basis of the astronomical predictions of the Babylonians and their successors; cf. *OLD* s.v. *numerus* 2c; *Div.* 1.36 with Pease's note. Quintus had identified the first successful prediction of a solar eclipse as taking place in the reign of Astyages of Persia, a misremembrance for Cyaxares (Hdt. 1.74): 1.112 with Pease's note. **quae naturae necessitas perfectura est** "what the laws of nature are going to bring to completion"; cf. *Fat.* 48, where it is hypothesized that the atoms fall because of gravity *necessitate naturae.* **vident ex constantissimo motu lunae:** *video* has the metaphorical sense "ascertain by inquiry": *OLD* s.v. 17. Cf. on §10 (*sol, luna quem motum habeat*). **e regione solis** "directly opposite the sun": *OLD* s.v. *regio* 2b; cf. *N.D.* 2.103: *cum est e regione solis*. The following *facta* is difficult; no satisfactory emendation has so far been proposed; possibly it is a variant for *perfectura* in the previous line that crept into the text; hence it is deleted here, as suggested by Timpanaro 1988 ad loc. **umbram terrae, quae est meta noctis** "the earth's shadow, which is the cone of night"; similarly *Rep.* 1.22; *N.D.* 2.49: *umbra terrae soli officiens noctem efficit*. Pliny (*Nat.* 2.51) explains that a shadow may have several possible shapes and that if the material is less than the light, the resulting shadow is a cone (*meta*). See illustration at Bakker 2016, 244. **subiecta atque opposita soli** "placed beneath [i.e., in conjunction with] and in front of the sun," i.e., between the earth and the sun; cf. Pease on *N.D.* 2.104. **nostris oculis:** Dative of disadvantage; cf. Pinkster 2015, 892–96. **signo** "sign" (of the zodiac): *OLD* s.v. *signum* 13b. **quaeque errantium stellarum** "each of the planets"; cf. on §10 (*quinque stellae quae errare dicuntur*). **qui exortus . . . qui occasus futurus sit:** Knowing the risings and settings of the signs of the zodiac as well as the "aspect" (as indicated above) is, of course, important for both weather prediction and astrology. **quam rationem sequantur vides:** It is obvious what (reasoning or observations) astronomers are acting in accordance with (*sequantur*: *OLD* s.v. *sequor* 10a).

18 Qui thesaurum inventum . . . aut forte fortuna putemus?: Marcus now turns to discovery of a treasure or coming into a legacy, typical subjects of diviners' predictions (cf. §§32, 134, 142). Verbal echoes of the previous argument underline that the two methods of prediction are diametrically opposed. If the basis for the astronomers' prediction is clear, the question regarding the diviners is *quid sequuntur?* This question will be pursued in detail at §§33–35. Marcus' assumption here and throughout his refutation is that the sign used by the seer is the cause of the predicted phenomenon. Though this was not in general the Stoic theory, in which the signs were merely arbitrary communications devices (cf. Denyer 1985, esp. 9–10), the dialogue stages a debate between Quintus and Marcus, and the former also usually fails to distinguish clearly between cause and sign; see above 23–24. **inventum <iri>:** Lambin's restoration for *inventurum* (which would require an expressed subject) has been generally accepted; though the form is relatively rare in Cicero, cf. §22 *trucidatum iri.* Marcus spoke of a *naturae necessitas* guiding the prediction of the eclipse (§17), but inquires *in qua rerum natura* the discovery of the treasure or the arrival of the legacy inheres. If there is some such necessity (*aliquam talem necessitatem*) in these predictions, what room is left for chance? In fact, the Stoics had an understanding of chance as "a cause obscure to human understanding" that would not exclude causal determinism, but Cicero either did not know about this or chose not to address it in *Div.*; see on §13. **forte fortuna** "by chance," *fortuna* merely strengthenining *forte*, as often; cf. *OLD* s.v. *fors* 1b.

nihil enim est tam contrarium rationi . . . quid casu et fortuito futurum sit: Here *ratio* is reinforced by its characteristic *constantia*; cf. *N.D.* 2.34: *recta ratio constansque*; 3.92 *neque id dicitis superstitiose atque aniliter sed physica constantique ratione.* **ne in deum quidem cadere** "not even fall within the scope of the deity" (*OLD* s.v. *cado* 23c). To use "god" in the singular, as here, without implying a commitment to monotheism was dubbed "henotheism" by F. Max Müller; see Versnel 1990–93, 1:35–37. Chrysippus and Carneades both placed similar restrictions on divine foreknowledge; cf. *SVF* 2:1183; *Fat.* 32 = Carneades F 10 Mette: *itaque dicebat Carneades ne Apollinem quidem futura posse dicere nisi ea quorum causas natura ita contineret ut ea fieri necesse esset.* As might have been expected, Augustine took strong exception to the denial of divine foreknowledge: *ita et Dei praescientiam negat et omnem prophetiam luce clariorem conatur evertere vanis argumentationibus* etc. (*Civ.* 5.9); see above 36.

si enim scit . . . fortuitarum nulla praesensio est: Foreknowledge would imply determinism and exclude chance. But Marcus takes the existence of chance as the agreed premise (in view of the definition at §13; see ad loc.), which therefore excludes the possibility of foreknowledge. He thus supplies the answer to the question posed at §15. **rerum . . . fortuitarum nulla praesensio est:** Cf. Sharples 1991, 182: "The Stoics would agree that undetermined events cannot be foreknown, but deny that any such undetermined events exist."

19 aut si negas . . . praesensionem esse rerum fortuitarum: If Quintus now wishes to deny that chance plays a role and adopt the determinist perspective, he must, according to Marcus, alter the definition of divination at §13. **definita . . . fataliter** "determined by fate" (*OLD* s.v. *definio* 4).

si enim nihil fieri potest . . . est dicta praesensio?: Cicero's rhetorical questions with emphatic anaphora of *nihil* drive home the incompatibility of fortune and determinism and the fact that the definition of divination they have been using presupposes fortune. **nisi quod . . . rato tempore** "except what was set from all eternity to occur at a fixed time"; for the relative clause of tendency, cf. G–L §631.2; for *ratus*, *OLD* s.v. 3a.

quamquam dicebas omnia . . . nunc quod necesse est: *dicebas omnia . . . fato contineri*: Sc. 1.125–26, where Quintus quoted an argument likely to have been derived from Chrysippus; cf. Bobzien 1998, 72. **anile sane et plenum superstitionis:** Another emphatic nominal sentence; cf. on §§5–6a. A marginalized group, old women were thought to be especially prone to superstition; cf. 1.7 (*anili superstitione*) with Schultz 2014 ad loc.; §36a (*aniculae*), varied by *sagae* §129; cf. *N.D.* 1.18, 55, and 94, 3.12; *anilis* at §125; cf. also *Hort.* fr. 48 G.: *avia mea dicebat hoc quod Stoici . . . mater autem, mulier sapiens, non existimavit. superstitio* and *religio* tend to become binary opposites, the former disapproved and characterized as "other": excessive, foreign, or private and, if private, potentially leading to *coniuratio* against the state (cf. Nagy 2002); Christianity, though branded as *superstitio* in the first century CE, eventually achieved a reversal of labels (while keeping the dichotomy); see further Grodzynski 1974; Sachot 1991; Margel 2006; Gordon 2008; Santangelo 2013, 38–47; Rüpke 2016, ch. 4. **fati nomen ipsum** "the very word 'fate'" (*OLD* s.vv. *nomen* 5; *ipse* 7); for the defining genitive, cf. Pinkster 2015, §11.61; cf. *Fat.* 6: *si fati omnino nullum nomen . . . esset.* **de quo alias:** By the time he wrote 1.127 (perhaps even *N.D.* 3.19), Cicero had decided that a separate treatise would be required to deal adequately with fate (*cum fato omnia fiant, id quod alio loco ostendetur*); cf. also §3. **quod necesse est** proves to be that fate is incompatible with the traditional view of divination, according to which the signs are warnings given by the gods to enable the human actors to adjust their behavior.

20 Si omnia fato, quid mihi divinatio . . . id vero futurum est: Cf. the similar point at *N.D.* 3.14: *quid igitur iuvat aut quid adfert ad cavendum scire aliquid futurum, cum id certe futurum sit?* There follow examples of signs that were either obeyed (Deiotarus) or ignored (L. Iunius, P. Claudius, C. Flaminius). But if fate controls everything, it makes no difference: the same outcomes would have ensued no matter what the individuals had done, and divination fails to provide any benefit. **vero** "in fact": *OLD* s.v. 2.

ut ne illud quidem sciam . . . in eum casum incidisset: Deiotarus was a tetrarch (one of four monarchs ruling a divided realm) of Galatia with whom the Tullii had long had ties of friendship (*necessarium nostrum*); on his career and relations with Rome, see Sullivan 1990, 51 and 164–69 with attached notes. In an extant speech Cicero had recently defended Deiotarus on a charge of murder before Caesar. At 1.26–27 Quintus narrated this anecdote as having been heard from the king himself (*ut ex ipso audiebam*), perhaps at the time of Quintus' legateship under his brother in Cilicia (51–50). Quintus invoked the incident as an example of salutary obedience to auspices: because he turned back after seeing an adverse omen, Deiotarus evaded death when the building where he had planned to lodge collapsed. **ut ne illud quidem sciam quale sit:** *ut . . . sciam* is a result clause with the object *illud* as a placeholder for the following *quod*-clause: "Therefore I do not even know how to characterize . . . ," i.e., he finds it puzzling, because, on the given premise, it was futile, since if fate is controlling, it is irrelevant whether the king had turned back or not: his death was in any case predetermined. This is a version of the "Idle Argument" that Cicero cites together with refutations by Chrysippus and Carneades at *Fat.* 28–33. For details, cf. Bobzien 1998: 182–98, refined by Weidemann 2019: 257–67; on §21 *fin.*

quid ergo adiuvat divinatio . . . aut ulla praedictio?: Marcus states the conclusion in the form of a rhetorical question and extends it from augury to other methods of divination. **ulla** lends emphasis and with *praedictio* effects the double cretic; cf. §15 *init.*

si enim fatum fuit classes . . . non interierunt fato: Further examples that Quintus had cited as confirming the power of auspices (1.29), whereas Marcus, on the premise that fate is controlling, denies that disobedience to omens had anything to do with the outcomes. Both consuls of the year 249 lost fleets near Sicily in the First Punic War: P. Claudius Pulcher, who notoriously threw the chickens that refused to eat (and thus failed to provide a favorable omen [a *tripudium solistumum*; see further §71b *sive tripudio sive de caelo*]) into the sea, was defeated in a naval battle near Drepanum, whereas L. Iunius' fleet was dashed against rocks during a storm; for sources cf. *MRR* 1:214; cf. Beck 2005, 90–91; Ladewig 2014, 107–8; detailed account by Bleckmann 2002, 186–201; see further on §71. **L. Iunio et P. Claudio consulibus:** Dative of advantage, not ablative.

vultis autem . . . est divinatio: *vultis* (plural) implicates the Stoics generally in Quintus' position. **nulla . . . est divinatio** is the conclusion Marcus is keen to draw; cf. §12 *vide . . . ne nulla sit divinatio*; §18 *rerum . . . fortuitarum nulla praesensio est*. But here *divinatio* has the slightly different sense of the bundle of practices and expectations of benefit that surround the use of divination, not the predictive power per se.

21 quodsi fatum fuit . . . idem eventurum fuisset: Another example cited by Quintus (1.77–78), after the Sullan annalist Coelius Antipater (*FRH* 15 F *14b), was that of the luckless consul C. Flaminius, who lost an army and his own life to Hannibal in the disastrous battle at Lake Trasimennus (217); cf. *MRR* 1:242 and further on his allegedly ill-omened *via dolorosa*, Rosenstein 1990, 77–78; Konrad 2004, 169–81. **si Flaminius . . . auspiciis quibus pugnare prohibebatur paruisset:** A notable collection of voiced and unvoiced labials; for alliteration in Latin generally, cf. Wilkinson 1963, 25–28. *pareo* is "pay attention to, act in accordance with"; cf. §125; *OLD* s.v. 2c. The following words *certe potuit* provide an unwanted answer to the question, since the same point is made about the unaltered outcome as in the previous examples. Some editors have accordingly deleted the words as a marginal response by a (Christian?) reader that crept into the text. Though Ax attempted to defend the transmitted text on the assumption that *certe potuit* is an objection raised by Quintus, in that case one would expect a riposte from Marcus before he continues *aut igitur non fato interiit . . .* (Ax's attempts to explain the sequel are unconvincing). More plausible is Pearce's insertion of *non* before *potuit*, which was revived by Magnaldi 1995, 64–65, and is adopted here.

ubi est igitur ista divinatio Stoicorum . . . accidere ne fiat: That Stoic divination of yours (*ista divinatio Stoicorum*, where *iste*, with its second-person deixis [cf. *OLD* s.v. 2], keeps Quintus in the picture) is either irrelevant to human life, because, if fate is controlling, the outcome cannot be altered even if known in advance, or, if it can be altered, it is not fated; and there will be no divination either (Marcus hammers home the point yet again), since there is no certain future event if the outcome is alterable. **quoquo enim modo . . . quod futurum est:** The so-called "Idle Argument" invoked by Skeptics against fate, stated in greater detail at *Fat.* 28–29; cf. Bobzien 1998, 182–98. Chrysippus had a reply, however, claiming that the prediction and the taking of precautions are "co-fated" (*confatalia*): *Fat.* 30 = *SVF* 2:956; see further Gourinat 2005, 233–35. **procuratione** "by expiatory sacrifice": *OLD* s.v. *procuratio* 4; cf. §25: *rebus divinis procuratis*; for a different sense, cf. on §7.

22 Atque ego ne utilem quidem . . . futurarum rerum scientiam: A change in point of view, the preceding having been from the point of view of the system of cause and effect, now from that of the human actor, whom the foreknowledge of future events would not help. Aristotle's pupil Dicaearchus had expatiated on this topic (§105 = F 17 We = 32 Mirhady). This argument was already put forward by Cotta at *N.D.* 3.14: *saepe autem ne utile quidem est scire quid futurum sit.*

quae enim vita fuisset Priamo . . . quos eventus senectutis esset habiturus?: Since Aristotle (*EN* 1100a6–8), Priam, king of Troy, has been the paradigm of the person whose life was spoiled by the misfortunes that assailed him at its end; Cicero dilates on them at *Tusc.* 1.85 (and adds Pompey as a Roman counterpart at 86).

abeamus a fabulis, propiora videamus: For the rejection of *fabulae*, cf. on §113 *init.*; for the transitional formula *propiora videamus*, cf. 1.43 and *N.D.* 3.80.

clarissimorum hominum . . . in Consolatione collegimus = F 15 Vitelli (it is unclear, however, whether in the sequel the words *an Cn. Pompeium . . . amisso exercitu* constitute a verbatim quotation, as Vitelli supposes). On the *Consolatio*, see above 14–15 and on §3.

quid igitur . . . esse pereundum?: M. Crassus was one of Rome's wealthiest men and also a prominent politician (until his death one of the so-called triumviri who dominated politics in the 50s); on him, cf. Ward 1977. Cicero put on record his moral disapproval of the man in several works of the 40s beginning with the criticism *tacito nomine* at *Parad.* 6 (*quod solus sapiens dives*) and concluding with *De off.* 1.109; 3.73 and 75. For the disastrous Roman defeat by the Parthians at Carrhae in June 53, when Crassus' arrogance and carelessness led to the loss of his army and his own life and that of his son Publius, see sources at *MRR* 2:230; narrative by Bivar 1983, 48–56. For the Romans' distancing from Crassus in the aftermath, cf. on §84 *init.*; Morrell 2017, 177–81. The terms in which Crassus is described (*maxumis opibus fortunisque florebat . . . interfecto . . . filio exercituque deleto . . . cum ignominia et dedecore esse pereundum*) make him seem like a Roman Priam.

an Cn. Pompeium censes . . . non possumus dicere?: Pompey's three triumphs (alluded to at *Pis.* 58) and three consulships became a topos; cf. Sen. *Ben.* 5.16.4: *Cn. Pompeius . . . pro tribus consulatibus, pro triumphis* *tribus . . .* **si sciret:** One might expect *si scisset* ("if he had known"), the past unreal construction (conjectured here by Lambin), but the distinction is not always observed, even by Cicero; cf. H–S 332. **in solitudine, <scelere> Aegyptiorum** "in solitude, by the crime of the Egyptians"; *scelere* can easily have dropped out by saltation after *solitudine.* For *in solitudine* without specification Timpanaro (1988, 339) compares *Amic.* 87 (*si . . . posset contingere ut aliquis nos deus . . . in solitudine uspiam collocaret*). For a narrative of Pompey's actions after Pharsalus that led to this dénouement, see Seager 2002, 167-68. Pompey was thus deprived of the comfort of dying among friends and loved ones, the remoteness increasing the pathos of the deaths of both him and Crassus (*trans Euphratem*). Contrast the prophesies given to both men that they would die in honor at home: §99. Cicero refers euphemistically to the fact that Pompey was beheaded, the head being presented to Caesar to confirm his death; cf. Plut. *Pomp.* 79–80. At *Tusc.* 1.12, Crassus and Pompey are paired as examples of wretched deaths.

23 quid vero Caesarem putamus . . . vitam acturum fuisse?: Caesar is the third of the three so-called triumviri who controlled politics at Rome from 59 to the death of Crassus and with whom Cicero later settled scores on moral grounds at *Off.* 3.73–83. Cicero's portrait here is dubious in several respects: Caesar put no stock in haruspices, having ignored a soothsayer's warning not to set sail for Africa before the winter solstice (cf. §52 below); nor did he fear death, having declared that he had lived long enough "for nature or for glory" (*vel naturae . . . vel gloriae*: *Marc.* 25). Cicero seems to assimilate Caesar to the fearful tyrant Dionysius described at *Tusc.* 5.57–63. See also above 30. Cicero paints the scene of Caesar's assassination in such detail that it is assumed that he must have been an eyewitness. **senatu quem maiore ex parte cooptasset:** Sc. to replenish the ranks depleted by the civil war; see further Syme 1939, ch. 6; Pinkernell-Kreidt 1997, 333–34. This is the first of a series of aggravating circumstances that would, Cicero supposes, have made the assassination still more galling. **curia Pompeia:** An annex of the Porticus Pompei, later walled up by Augustus; cf. Richardson 1992 and Coarelli, *LTUR* s.v. **ante ipsius Pompei simulacrum:** Ironically, Caesar had restored Pompey's statues that had been pulled down by the mob, earning Cicero's praise; cf. Plut. *Cic.* 40.4–5; *Caes.* 57.4. **tot centurionibus suis inspectantibus:** Cicero complained of intimidation of the senate by Antony (*Phil.* 1.27) but claimed that the presence of arms had been more discreet under Caesar (ibid. 2.108). **a nobilissumis civibus, partim etiam a se omnibus rebus ornatis:** The fact that after the civil war such later conspirators as Brutus and Cassius had been granted pardon and preferment by Caesar was bitterly recalled by Caesar's partisans after the assassination; cf. *Fam.*

11.28(349).3 (Matius to Cicero). **ne servorum quidem quisquam accederet:** Not initially at least; finally three slaves transported the body back to Caesar's house; cf. Suet. *Jul.* 82.3; App. *BC* 2.118/498. **cruciatu animi** "mental agony." Cicero's previous use of this expression was in reporting Caesar's proposed punishment of the captured Catilinarian conspirators by confiscation of their property: *ut omnis animi cruciatus et corporis egestatem ac mendicitas consequatur* (*Catil.* 4.10). In spite of their political differences, Cicero thus shows a certain amount of empathy for Caesar.

certe igitur ignoratio . . . utilior est quam scientia: When the topic was introduced, it was the "knowledge of things in the future" (*futurarum rerum scientiam*: §22 *init.*), but now it is specified as "knowledge of future evils," since knowledge of future goods might be cheering rather than a source of fear (cf. *Tusc.* 3.23).

24 nam illud quidem dici . . . exitus suos cogitantibus?: *nullo modo* ("by no means") is an emphatic colloquial negation; cf. Hofmann 2003, 209. The supposition that foreknowledge could beneficially inhibit behavior (*non isset . . . non transisset . . . non suscepisset*) is not available to the Stoics with their belief in fate: *vultis autem evenire omnia fato* (similarly §20 *fin.*). **omnem fructum vitae superioris perdidissent** "they would have completely forfeited the enjoyment of their previous life" (i.e., before the final catastrophe), *fructus* having its original sense (as the noun corresponding to *fruor*; cf. *OLD* s.v. 1). The point was explicit in the case of Pompey and Caesar (*censes . . . laetaturum fuisse . . . quid . . . putamus . . . quo cruciatu animi vitam acturum fuisse*: §§22–23), implicit in that of Crassus. **exitus suos cogitantibus:** The present participle with object, occupying final position, bears the principal weight in this sentence; it is typical of the late Cicero to exploit this property of the participle to the full; cf. on §58 (*timentibus*); Laughton 1964, 45.

ita quoquo sese verterint Stoici, iaceat necesse est omnis eorum sollertia "Thus wherever the Stoics turn, all their cleverness must be defeated," i.e., because they attempt to maintain the mutually exclusive tenets of fate and divination as traditionally understood and practiced; cf. *OLD* s.vv. *verto* 12 and *iaceo* 5a.

si enim id quod eventurum est . . . certa esse non possunt: Since the binary terms *hic* and *ille* provide contrast (*OLD* s.v. *hic* 7), *vel hoc vel illo modo potest evenire* is a colloquial way of describing the fortuitous. **fortuna valet plurimum** "fortune rules." **quae autem fortuita sunt certa esse non**

possunt: Once again, the boundary between the fixed and the fortuitous is absolute (cf. §18).

24–25 sin autem certum est . . . re divina potest: *sin* ("but if") introduces the alternative possibility. The haruspices are singled out exempli gratia, but the same would apply to other types of diviners (except astrologers). **qui** was rightly supplied by Baiter and Kayser to restore a connection between the two clauses; it can easily have dropped out before *quom* (the archaic spelling of *cum*). **omnia levius casura** "all will be mitigated" (literally, "will fall out more mildly"). **rebus divinis procuratis** "if divine affairs have been attended to." The Romans held the conception of the *pax deorum*, "a 'pact' granted by a god or gods (conferring freedom from divine anger, approval of current activities, etc.)": *OLD* s.v. *pax* 2. This could be disturbed by some human failing, e.g., a ritual deficiency; if so, it had to be restored by carrying out an atonement (*piaculum*), usually an animal sacrifice, that might be prescribed by a priest; cf. Wissowa 1912, 392–94; Rosenberger 1998, 141–54; Santangelo 2011; Satterfield 2015; Champion 2017, XI. Viewed anthropologically, such expiations served to define the group and reaffirm its identity and cohesiveness: Rosenberger 1998, 243. **si enim nihil . . . re divina potest:** Cicero explains why he doubts the efficacy of the haruspices' help: if determinism is total, an appeasement of the gods will have no effect. **re divina** "by cult activity," more specifically, "sacrifice"; cf. Livy 31.5.3: *senatus . . . decrevit uti consules maioribus hostiis rem divinam facerent*; *OLD* s.v. *divinus* 2.

25 hoc sentit Homerus . . . summum exsuperat Iovem: A strong tradition, represented by the verse Cicero cites in his own rendering (fr. 55 Bl., an iambic senarius; the Greek original is not extant), placed fate above the deities; see Pease ad loc., citing such views from a number of authors, but also Stat. *Theb.* 1.213, who makes the fates subject to Jupiter. However, *Iliad* 16.431–38 does not really fit Marcus' argument. There Zeus pities Sarpedon, his son by a mortal woman, fated to be slain by Patroclus, but it is said that he *could* overrule fate (436–37, 441–43); he is merely deterred from doing so by Hera's argument that other deities would then have licence to do the same (446–49). The Olympian deities were overlaid onto an older set of folk beliefs involving fate (*moira*), and the two were never fully reconciled; cf. Greene 1944, 13–15; Burkert 1985, 129–30. For other examples of Cicero's distortion of poetic citations to fit his argument, cf. Jocelyn 1973. For Latin *fatum*, cf. Otto, *RE* s.v. **eripere non posset:** Past sequence of tenses in spite of preceding *querentem . . . inducit*, since this is historical present; cf. H–S 551. **in eam sententiam:** See on §12 (*in hanc sententiam*).

totum omnino fatum . . . non est iocandi locus: It is unusual for Cicero to cite Atellan farce (named for the Oscan town Atella, located near Capua); cf. Zillinger 1911, 42. This reference = Atell. inc. fr. XI Frassinetti, but nothing more is known about the verse in question. Cicero offers some general guidelines for appropriate jokes at *Off.* 1.104.

concludatur igitur ratio . . . fortuitarum rerum esse dicebas: *concludatur . . . ratio* "Let the argument be brought to a conclusion": *OLD* s.v. *concludo* 6. Either divination is impossible because events occur randomly and are not fixed (*certa*), or events are fated and thus fixed, but that contradicts the definition of *divinatio* at §13. The point about the benefit of predictions, argued since §22, is dropped.

26a Sed haec fuerit . . . cornua commovere disputationis tuae: Cicero uses military metaphors to describe the course of the argument: a preliminary sortie (*prima . . . excursio*) of light-armed troops (*velites*) preceded the hand-to-hand (*comminus*) fighting, in which the goal is to roll up the two wings (*cornua*: *OLD* s.v. *cornu* 8) of the enemy battle line. There is a similar depreciation of his initial argument against prophetic dreams at §124 *init.*

26b–27 Review of Quintus' Presentation in Book 1, praeparatio *of Marcus' Reply*

Marcus begins with Quintus' basic division of the subject into the two *genera* technical and natural divination (1.12, 34, etc.). He abstracts from the different species of technical divination a *genus coniecturale* ("an inferential type"), not so formulated by Quintus. He also touches on the theory of the soul that Quintus offered to explain natural divination (1.110) as well as Quintus' general theory of divination (1.125). Finally, Marcus offers a *praeparatio* (Lausberg 1990, §854) or preview of the approach he will take, denying the veracity of Quintus' examples and demanding an explanation for the phenomena.

26b Duo enim genera divinandi . . . aut libatos haberemus: The bipartite division, first found in Plato (*Phaedr.* 244a–e), was put forward by Quintus at 1.12 and 34, the latter drawing the distinction within technical divination between *coniectura* and *observatio diuturna* (Marcus will have more to say about the latter; cf. §§28, 42b, 124, 146). Quintus' account of natural divination begins merely by citing dreams and prophecies (1.12), the latter specified as *per furorem* at 1.34. Only later (1.70 [citing Cratippus] and 110) does he explain the underlying theory. Marcus, on the other hand, engages with the theory from the beginning, in particular with Cratippus' doctrine giving a single account for both species of natural divination. Now Cicero considered Cratippus *Peripateticorum . . . princeps* (*Tim.* 1), albeit he was not head of the school (on him, see further Moraux 1973, 223–56; Gottschalk 1987, 1095–97; Dorandi 1994). Unsurprisingly, therefore, Cratippus' theory is in recognizable contact with Aristotle (*Gen. an.* 736b27–28) in that it posits that the soul has entered the body "from outside" (*extrinsecus*, θύραθεν) from the divine nature (*ex divinitate*; similarly Aristotle speaks of the soul as divine [θεῖον]). The doctrine is, however, also attested for other philosophers: Plato (*Phlb.* 30a), Pythagoras (Cic. *Sen.* 78), and the Stoics (Epict. 1.14.5–6). In his version, Marcus leaves open whether the soul's exercise of divinatory power is active or passive (*arriperet aut exciperet*). He is also ambivalent about how to express the process by which the souls derive from the deity, "drawn off or received or skimmed" (*haustos aut acceptos aut libatos*), corresponding to Quintus' *tractos et haustos* (1.70). This discrepancy led Roth to delete *aut acceptos* and M. Seyffert to substitute (from *Tusc.* 5.38) *decerptos* for *acceptos*; but the preceding *exciperet* argues for the retention of *acceptos*.

artificiosa divinationis . . . in hoc fere genere ponebas: Marcus paraphrases Quintus' introduction of the category at 1.12 and generalizes to *omne . . . genus coniecturale* ("every inferential type"). **qui ex fulgoribus . . . praedicerent:** He first uses this paraphrase; only later does he introduce the technical term *fulgurator* (§109). In the oblique cases, our mss. offer *fulgur-* and *fulgor-* promiscuously. **ostentis:** Of the words for "prodigy," the most general, *ostentum* (transparently derived from *ostendo* "show"), is the overwhelming favorite here, occurring twenty-two times in this Book, followed by *portentum* (ten times), and *monstrum* (four times); *prodigium*, however, fails to appear; *signum*, *miraculum*, and *dirum* would also be possible designations; cf. Engels 2007, 57.

27 illud autem naturale . . . curis vacuo provideri: Quintus' two types of natural divination involve a departure from the usual state in the direction of either a surplus or deficit of mental activity, as described here on the basis of 1.34: *concitatione quadam animi aut soluto liberoque motu futura praesentiunt.* **quasi fundi:** The basic idea is of "pouring" a liquid, hence to "pour out (sounds), produce a stream of (poetry, etc.)": *OLD* s.v. *fundo* 1, 5c; at §110 Cicero uses the word in this way without *quasi.* **videbatur:** Sc. *tibi*, still reviewing Quintus' presentation.

duxisti autem divinationem omnem . . . commenticiorum exemplorum mirifica copia: Quintus offered an account of three causes of divination based on Posidonius (frr. 103 and 107 E.–K.; cf. Kidd 1988 ad locos): *a deo*, based on the gods' providential care for humankind (1.82–83); *a natura*, as a function of the human soul (1.60–64, 118, and 129–31); and *a fato* (1.125–27). See Schultz 2014, on 1.125. **explicare nihil posses:** At 1.16 Quintus had candidly admitted *quae causa sit nescio* (similarly 1.85–86) and had resisted looking for causes rather than outcomes (1.12, 35), but toward the end of his presentation, he settled on fate as the cause (1.126), a fact that Marcus ignores here. Marcus does not pull punches, claiming at once "an amazing supply of bogus examples" (*commenticiorum exemplorum mirifica copia*); similarly *Fat.* 5: *quaedam etiam Posidonius (pace magistri dixerim) comminisci videtur; sunt quidem absurda.* In the sequel, Marcus will repeatedly doubt the veracity of Quintus' examples, e.g., §§46 and 66.

de quo primum hoc . . . mihi liceat non credere: A lecture on what befits a philosopher (contrast the harsh criticism of philosophers at §119 *fin.*); cf. *N.D.* 3.6 (Cotta to Balbus): *a te . . . philosopho rationem accipere debeo religionis*; Marcus returns to the topic at §46 *fin.* The reliability of witness testimony was, of course, a constant topic of debate in the lawcourts, and the rhetorical schools therefore developed a repertory of arguments pro and contra; cf. Quint. *Inst.* 5.7. What Marcus offers here is a variation of the general denial of the credibility of witnesses such as Cicero particularly deployed if a number of witnesses were expected to testify against his client; cf., e.g., *Scaur.* 14–17. **non eventis:** An emphatic contradiction of Quintus' approach; cf. 1.12: *quarum quidem rerum* [sc. the predictions of diviners] *eventa magis arbitror quam causas quaeri oportere*; at 1.84 Quintus claims that *ratio* as well as *eventa* are on his side. A similar line was taken by Stoics who argued that divination is an art "on account of certain results" (διά τινας ἐκβάσεις): *SVF* 1:174 (Zeno), 2.191 (Chrysippus), F 7 and 27 E.–K. (Posidonius). At §99 Marcus asserts that each day diviners' predictions are refuted *re et eventis.* **iis praesertim:** *praesertim* is used, like *quidem* (see on §8 [*et iis quidem*]), to attach an emphatic qualifier to a pronoun: "especially those . . ."; cf. §28: *mihi praesertim*; §53: *tibi praesertim*; *OLD* s.v. *praesertim* 1.

28–99 Refutation of Technical Divination

The refutation of Quintus' case for technical divination proceeds via the following stages (cf. MacKendrick 1989, 190–93):

I. *Disciplina Etrusca*
   A. Extispicy (28–42a)
   B. Interpretation of thunder and lightning strikes (42b–49a)
   C. Interpretation of portents (49b–69)
II. Auspices (70–84)
III. Divination by lots (85–87a)
IV. Astrology (87b–99)

28–42a Extispicy

The first type of technical divination Marcus addresses is the bundle of practices that went under the name of the *disciplina Etrusca*. As its name indicates, this was a foreign art, but it was nonetheless incorporated into the official procedures of the Roman state. Its practitioners were called haruspices. These seers were the scions of aristocratic Etruscan families but were by the late Republic supported by the Roman state and consulted to interpret the entrails of animals sacrificed on state occasions and to interpret thunder, lightning, and other occurrences thought to be portents. Under the Republic, they seem not to have attained the status of a public priesthood of the Roman people but had to be summoned from Etruria by the senate for consultation (cf. §11 *fin.*; on §52b [*a summo haruspice*]). There were also private haruspices available for hire (cf. 1.132). See further Rosenberger 1998, 52–54; Corbeill 2012, 244–52; on their gradual acceptance as a tool of the Roman state, Briquel 2014. The threefold division of types of haruspicy may go back to the Etruscans' sacred books; cf. Guillaumont 1996, 50. Marcus begins with extispicy, the haruspices' most publicly prominent role. This section can be analyzed as follows:

1. Groundrules for the discussion (28)
2. Origin of extispicy in "long-continued observation"?
3. Extispicy and the laws of nature I (29)
   a. Democritus' theory (30)
   b. Digression: Pherecydes' prediction of an earthquake (31)
   c. Democritus' information is not what soothsayers are meant to predict (32).
4. Extispicy and the laws of nature II: Stoic theory of *sympatheia* with examples (33–34)
5. How is the sacrificer matched to the appropriate victim?
   a. Divine guidance I (35)
      (1) Change at the moment of sacrifice

(2) Digression: Caesar's sacrifice of a bull without a heart (36–37)
(3) Problem of different results with successive sacrifices (*litatio*: 38)
b. Divine guidance II (39)
6. Comparison of Stoic and Epicurean theology (40–42a)

After setting the basic conditions for the discussion, Marcus seeks to discredit the claimed empirical basis of extispicy with the argument that what to the Roman soothsayer may seem a god-given method proves, on closer inspection, to be culture-specific (a similar argument was adduced by Greek sophists against social conventions in general). Marcus refutes Democritus' theory of extispicy, even though it was of historical interest only and would not justify extispicy as generally practiced, since Quintus had cited it in support of his case (1.131). Marcus next reports the Stoic theory of *sympatheia* and cites examples underpinning it, some of which he undermines by ridicule. The brunt of his criticism is directed, however, at the nexus between the sacrificer and the sacrificial victim: how could the latter be chosen in such a way that its entrails would predict the sacrificer's future position? The section concludes with reflections on the general relation of divination to belief in the gods, Marcus claiming that divination would more easily undermine than form a basis for such belief.

28 Ut ordiar ab haruspicina . . . extra primum: Marcus' strategy here closely tracks that of Cotta in *N.D.*, who is prepared to accept the gods and state religious practices because they are hallowed by tradition (3.5–7) but asserts the right to question them in private conversation (1.61). *haruspicina*, first attested at *Fam.* 6.18(218).1 (ca. January 45), alternates with *disciplina Etrusca* as the designation of the haruspices' art; Marcus will contrast it with *physiologia* at §37. **rei publicae causa:** Quintus made the case for accepting divination on this ground at 1.25b–33 and 95–103a. Cf. §74a (more briefly §43a): *quod* [the fact that lightning on the left is a favorable sign except for public assemblies] . . . *institutum rei publicae causa est, ut comitiorum vel in iudiciis populi vel in iure legum vel in creandis magistratibus principes civitatis essent interpretes*, i.e., the point is to keep such meetings under tight control of the leading citizens (similarly *Leg.* 2.20–21). Such control had, however, suffered a blow when Caesar as consul of 59 ignored the *obnuntiationes* (announcements of unfavorable omens) made by his colleague M. Bibulus and then the following year P. Clodius as tribune of the plebs carried legislation restricting the right of *obnuntiatio*; for a summary of events, cf. Guillaumont 1984, 58–77; Wiseman, *CAH* 9:368–78; Weinstock, *RE* s.v. *Obnuntiatio*. **licet verum exquirere . . . de plerisque dubitanti:** Cicero was well aware that public and private speech offered different possibilities.

Marcus thus notes that he is exempt from the kind of social pressure exerted by Lucullus at *Luc.* 62 (cf. ibid. 144: *quid me . . . in invidiam et tamquam in contionem vocas . . . ?*), "Cicero" at *Fin.* 2.74, or Balbus at *N.D.* 2.2 and 168; cf. also Lact. *Inst.* 2.3.2 (a fragment generally assigned to the lacuna at *N.D.* 3.65): *intellegebat Cicero falsa esse quae homines adorarent. nam cum multa dixisset quae ad eversionem religionum valerent, ait tamen 'non esse illa vulgo disputanda, ne susceptas publice religiones disputatio talis exstinguat.'* On the need to conduct a candid conversation on religion in private, see further Scheid 2007, 60–63. **mihi praesertim de plerisque dubitanti:** For *mihi praesertim* see on §27 *fin.* (*iis praesertim*). This takes up §8: *dubitans plerumque* as well as the doubt expressed by Panaetius and the comments of Cicero as author (1.6–7 = T 137 Alesse; cf. *Luc.* 107 = T 136 Alesse). Such doubt is what separates the Skeptic from the dogmatist; cf. *Luc.* 8: *nec inter nos et eos qui se scire arbitrantur quicquam interest nisi quod illi non dubitant quin ea vera sint.* Contrast the attitude of Quintus: *non dubitans dixerim . . . esse certe divinationem* (1.125); similarly the astrologers *non veri simile solum, sed etiam verum esse censent* (§89). **inspiciamus, si placet, exta primum:** *si placet* is a polite insertion making contact with his interlocutor: "if you please." Another pun, on *inspicio* in the ordinary sense ("look into") vs. the technical soothsayer's sense of "examining for significant marks," for which cf. 1.112; *TLL* 7:1953.59–65. Marcus begins with extispicy as the haruspices' most prominent public role; he will later claim that their entire doctrine collapses in light of the refutation of this practice (§42a).

persuaderi igitur cuiquam potest . . . unam omnium disciplinam: *persuaderi . . . cuiquam potest*: The intransitive *persuadeo* can be used in the passive, but only impersonally; in English, however: "Can anyone be persuaded . . . ?" The argument from *observatio diuturna* is clearly applicable to astronomy/astrology, a point that appears in the author's preface (1.2) and that Marcus is inclined to concede (§146). Quintus did, however, claim it for other forms of divination as well (1.12, etc.) and thus opened himself up to this attack. **conlata inter ipsos:** The feminine agrees with *quae pars* (Lambin's *conlatum* is sometimes adopted, unnecessarily); *inter ipsos* = "among themselves" (*OLD* s.v. *ipse* 10). **quae pars inimica, quae pars familiaris esset** "what part [sc. of the liver] pertains to the enemy, what part to the sacrificer," a military context being assumed; cf. *OLD* s.v. *familiaris* 2b; Oakley 1997–2005, 2:487. Marcus offers these as examples of the kinds of questions haruspices would have to settle. **an haec inter se . . . contulerunt?:** Marcus ridicules the idea that the widely scattered soothsayers would have compared notes; hence, for him, the idea of observation over a long period of time does not stand up. There are, on the one hand, parallels between Etruscan and Near Eastern extispicy (cf. Thulin 1905–9, 2:33–35; Nougayrol 1955; Turfa 2012, 255–58) as well as between Greek and Etruscan (cf. van der Meer 1987, 157–64). But on the other hand, recent tests of specimens of mitochondrial DNA suggest that, though "there might have been a genealogical link between modern Tuscans and the inhabitants of what Herodotus [1.94; cf. Briquel 1991] considered the Etruscans' homeland, Western Anatolia, . . . even under the unrealistic assumption of complete reciprocal isolation for millennia, the likely separation of the Tuscan and Anatolian gene pools must be placed long before the onset of Etruscan culture": Ghirotto et al. 2013: 5–6. Similarities should, rather, be explained by "some sort of knowledge exchange" between Mesopotamian and Etruscan diviners during the first millennium BCE: Turfa 2012, 257. Such influences thus seem less far-fetched than Marcus suggests. **Elii, Aegyptii, Poeni:** As part of his argument for the validity of divination based upon its wide diffusion (1.87b–94), Quintus had pointed in particular to the cultivation of extispicy at Telmesus in Caria and Elis in the Peloponnese (1.91). This passage is our sole evidence for cultivation of haruspicy by the Egyptians and Carthaginians (the former possibly based on a misreading of Hdt. 2.40). **alios enim alio more . . . nec esse unam omnium disciplinam:** It is possible that there were regional variations; Marcus mentions some differences in the interpretation of bird-signs and thunder at §§76 and 82 but offers no specifics about differences in extispicy.

29 Et certe si est in extis aliqua vis . . . vique divina: Here Marcus moves from the diviners' own account of the origin of their doctrine (long-continued observation) to theories of a possible cause for the phenomena: that the entrails contain a sort of power (*vis*) that is somehow (*quodam modo*) connected with either nature (*rerum natura*) or the power of the gods (*numine deorum*), Posidonius' three possibilities (cf. on §27) thus being reduced to two by conflation of fate and the gods; for the two alternatives, cf. Guillaumont 1996, 64. Marcus takes up nature at §§29–34, divine power at §§35–39; see above on §§28–42a. **vi . . . divina:** The phrase is commonly used in expositions of Stoic cosmology with reference to the "divine force," identified with reason (*logos*), that interpenetrates the universe; cf. *N.D.* 1.36, 2.14 and 54; *Div.* 1.118 and §§35, 117, and 124.

cum rerum natura . . . quid futurum sit?: *rerum natura . . . diffusa*: A Stoic definition of nature; cf. *SVF* 2:549 (= *N.D.* 2.115) and 937 (= Plut. *Stoic. rep.* 1050c). Marcus accepts the general Stoic theory of a natural "sympathy" of phenomena of the universe (cf. §§33b–34). What he challenges is that the signs used by the diviners and the things that they predict are sympathetically connected. **gallinaceum fel . . . tauri opimi iecur:** Marcus contrasts the largest and smallest of the sacrificial animals used by the Romans in a hierarchy corresponding to their market value, the *taurus opimus* ("prime bull") being used for important state sacrifices (cf. Wissowa 1912, 410–16); hence the *a fortiori* argument here. That chickens' entrails were studied for purposes of divination is confirmed by Pliny (*Nat.* 10.49; cf. Thulin 1905–9, 2:19). **quid habet naturale . . . quid futurum sit?:** *naturale* ("natural feature"), followed by the subjunctive of tendency; cf. on §19 (*nisi quod . . . rato tempore*).

30 Democritus tamen non inscite . . . extis significari putat: Democritus of Abdera (b. 460/57) was a major cosmologist and developer of the atomic theory; see further Schultz 2014, 63; his views will also be discussed at §§57, 120, and 137, his style at §133. At 1.131 Quintus cited 68 A 138 D.–K. **non inscite** appears five times in Cicero's *philosophica*, the litotes making this an urbane compliment ("cleverly"); cf. §62a. **nugatur ut physicus . . . adrogantius:** Apart from *Att.* 5.21(114).14, this is Cicero's sole use of *nugor*, a comic word ("talk nonsense"; cf. *OLD* s.v.); it is taken up in the sequel (*tantis delectatum est nugis*). The assertion that natural philosophers (*physici*; cf. *N.D.* 1.83) are arrogant may surprise, but this is in line with Cicero's general attitude toward dogmatists (see on §1); cf. *Rep.* 1.15 (in contrast to Socrates); *Luc.* 55 (Lucullus to Cicero): *confugis ad physicos eos qui maxime in Academia inridentur*; ibid. 117 (Cicero): *sed sit ingenio divino: quem unum e physicis potissimum probabit?*; ibid. 122–28a; *Tim.* 1: *multa sunt a nobis in Academicis conscripta contra physicos.* **quod est ante . . . caeli scrutantur plagas:** A trochaic septenarius from Ennius, *Iphigenia* fr. 187 J. = *TRF* and *FRL* 82.3. At *Rep.* 1.30 Laelius had cited this and the two preceding verses to discredit C. Sulpicius Gallus and his astronomical interests and others who would pursue such at the expense of public affairs:

astrologorum signa in caelo quid sit observationis,
cum Capra aut Nepa aut exoritur nomen aliquod beluarum,
quod est ante pedes nemo spectat, caeli scrutantur plagas.

("As regards the star-readers' signs in the sky, what observation there is, / when Capella or Scorpio or some other constellation named after beasts appears: / what is before one's feet nobody watches, they scrutinize the expanses of the sky": tr. Goldberg and Manuwald.) Jocelyn 1967 ad loc. regards Ennius' verses as possibly part of an adaptation of Eur. *IA* 919–74 (Achilles' denunciation of Greek leaders in turn, including Calchas at 956–58). Marcus cites Ennius' satirical description to set the tone. He could, however, have treated Democritus as an ally (as he did at *Luc.* 73), since he evidently framed his sober, physiological account of the entrails as indicative of available fodder and the general state of agriculture and health, in contrast to the extravagant claims of soothsayers.

o mortalem beatum . . . habitu extorum et colore?: *o mortalem beatum*: For the evaluative exclamatory accusative with the interjection *o*, cf. Pinkster 2015, 363–64. Marcus dispenses ironic congratulations to Democritus, who, perhaps because of his promotion of *euthumia* ("good spirits"), had the reputation of being the "laughing philosopher" (cf. *De orat.* 2.235 and other references at 68 A 21 D.–K.). **cui certo scio ludum numquam defuisse** "He never failed to have his joke" (tr. Falconer). **huncine hominem . . . delectatum esse nugis:** An exclamatory accusative and infinitive sentence, marked, as usual, by *-ne* attached to the first or most important word, usually, as here, a pronoun; cf. Pinkster 2015, 365–67. Marcus pretends that in his preoccupation with trifles (*nugae*), the philosopher overlooked the consequence of his theory—that the entrails of all animals sacrificed at the same time and place would have the same characteristics. **aliae . . . aliae:** A colloquialism for *alius . . . alius*; cf. Lucr. 3.918: *aliae . . . rei*; *OLD* s.v. *alius init.* The variety of characteristics of the entrails of victims slaughtered simultaneously refutes the theory. *nitidus* and *horridus* are respectively "smooth and bright" and "rough" (*OLD* s.vv. 4a and 1a) and are opposed elsewhere, both literally (Var. *R.* 3.16.20) and metaphorically (*De orat.* 3.51, *Orat.* 36).

31 an hoc eiusdem modi . . . vide ne non sit necesse: *Pherecydeum illud* "that anecdote of Pherecydes": such allusion by an adjectival form is depreciatory; cf. §32; *ista Democritea.* It is, however, taken up by *qui*, as if the name itself had preceded. This example, which Quintus had cited at 1.112 (explicitly *not* as an example of divination), is one of several miraculous stories told about Pherecydes of Syrus (*fl.* 554); others included predicting a shipwreck and the capture of a city. This was a "floating anecdote" also attributed, with the place-name changed from Syrus to Metapontum, to Pythagoras: 7 A 6 D.–K.; see further Riedweg 2005, 9. **credo**, as often, signals irony (cf. *OLD* s.v. 8c): "It was, I suppose, not brazen enough, upon the occurrence of an earthquake, for them [sc. the *physici*; cf. §30] to dare to pronounce on the force that produced it . . ." **futurum esse:** Sc. *motum (terrae).* **in scholis** "in lectures," sc. on physics, one of the three major branches of philosophy. **credere omnia . . . non sit necesse:** A continuation of the skepticism of §27 *fin.* (*quibus mihi liceat non credere*). **vide ne:** See above on §12 (*vide igitur ne nulla sit divinatio*).

32 verum sint sane ista Democritea vera . . . tum damna denuntiant: The concessive or "positing" subjunctive (cf. Pinkster 2015, 509–10), here in emphatic position: "But let us suppose that they *are* true." **ista Democritea** "those observations of Democritus that you cite [sc. 1.131]": the second-person deixis of the pronominal adj. brings Quintus back into the picture but may also be pejorative (*OLD* s.v. *iste* 1, 3). Even on this assumption, Democritus does not help the case for divination, since the correlating phenomena (the abundance or scarcity of fodder, etc.) are obvious and require no predictive skill. Extispicy, as traditionally practiced, pronounces on very different matters, of which Marcus cites examples. **ab aqua aut ab igni pericula:** The asyndeton marks a sharp contrast. The haruspices assigned different parts of the liver to different deities and inferred divine anger from the markings they found there; cf. Pliny *Nat.* 11.195; Pease ad loc.; van der Meer 1987, 141–46 (attested names of liver gods). **monent:** Sc. haruspices, to be supplied from the preceding *ab haruspice.* **tum hereditates tum damna:** This subject matter points to private haruspices; cf. 1.132: *eos qui quaestus causa hariolentur.*

fissum familiare et vitale tractant: Marcus moves now from the subject matter of the haruspices' predictions to the phenomena that they used as the basis. A *fissum* ("cleft") in the liver was a major concern of both the Etruscan and Near Eastern soothsayers. There was, above all, the major *fissum* that divided the two lobes of the liver. It would be natural to take this as the *fissum vitale,* i.e., the one "concerning life and death" (*OLD* s.v. *vitalis* 1a). If Thulin 1905–9, 2:40–41 is right that the *pars inimica* and the *pars familiaris* (cf. §28) were not the separate lobes (as Blecher 1905, 197, supposed) but that that division cut across the two lobes, then the *fissum familiare et vitale* will be the portion of the "vital fissure" that is in the *pars familiaris,* i.e., pertains to the person offering sacrifice; cf. van der Meer 1987, 147–52, working out the details for the bronze liver of Piacenza; for a different view, cf. Pease ad loc. (Hottinger's proposed change of *vitale* to *hostile* and Kayser's deletion of *vitale* are both implausible.) Other clefts in the liver were also of interest to the soothsayers, however; cf. Thulin 1905–9, 2:41.

caput iecoris . . . accidere potuisse tristius: What the ancients called the "head" of the liver was a protrusion shaped like a three-sided pyramid, the *processus caudatus* (caudate lobe; see illustration of the bronze liver of Piacenza at Beard, North, and Price 1998, 2:7.4b) as well as van der Meer 1987, 8, fig. 7, an actual sheep's liver); this was, as Cicero says, much studied by the haruspices, and if it was completely missing, as in the sacrifice that preceded the battle at the Veseris river in 340 BCE (Livy 8.9.1: *Decio caput* *iocineris a familiari parte caesum haruspex dicitur ostendisse*) or Caesar's sacrifice (1.119; cf. on §§36b–37), it was the direst of omens; cf. Thulin, 1905–9, 2:30–34, citing parallels, including Near Eastern ones.

33a haec observari . . . ars ulla rerum incognitarum: *observari* is evidently a shorthand for *longinquo tempore observari*, Marcus referring back (*ut supra docui*) to his strictures on the idea of long-continued observations by the haruspices resulting in a pool of knowledge on which they could draw (§28). For Marcus, the haruspices' teachings are the "inventions of an art," though he at once raises doubts that there can be any such art, since extispicy is based upon no secure knowledge (*si est ars ulla rerum incognitarum*; cf. §43b *rebus incertis*); this goes back to Marcus' understanding of Quintus' definition of divination as *earum rerum praedictionem et praesensionem quae essent fortuitae* (§13). For the general point cf. *Luc.* 146: *artem sine scientia esse non posse; Fin.* 2.26: *omnium artium recte dici potest commune esse ut in aliqua scientia versentur.* He thus suggests that the Stoics' claim for haruspicy is at odds with their definition of a *technē*; cf. Lévy 1997, 340. Similar doubts were raised by Carneades (*qua arte perspici possint:* 1.23). At §45b, he will clarify what he means by the haruspices' "art."

33b Cum rerum autem natura quam cognationem habent?: *rerum . . . natura* "the natural order": *OLD* s.v. *natura* 14b. With this question Marcus begins his refutation of Quintus' suggestion that there is a sympathetic connection between all elements of nature such that the phenomena of the sacrificial entrails could mirror and predict other events (1.118). This implies a close kinship (*cognatio*) that Marcus will now explore.

quae ut uno consensu . . . unum esse dixerunt: *rerum . . . natura* (see above) is the antecedent of *quae*. The *ut*-clause is concessive (*OLD* s.v. *ut* 35). **uno consensu . . . continens** "has been joined and linked by a single sympathetic bond": *OLD* s.vv. *consensus* 3b, *continens* 2c. **placuisse physicis** "was a view held by natural philosophers" (*OLD* s.v. *placeo* 3). As often, *is* connected with *et* or *-que* adds an amplification or qualification (ibid. s.v. *is* 7). **qui omne quod esset unum esse dixerunt:** Possibly Cicero is thinking of Xenophanes (cf. *Luc.* 118: *Xenophanes . . . unum esse omnia*), whom he seems to have regarded as the father of the Eleatic school (ibid. 129), which is usually rather thought to have comprised Parmenides, Zeno of Elea, and Melissus (cf. *OCD* s.v. Eleatic school). The perfect tenses (*placuisse . . . dixerunt*) show that the point is of historical interest only, not a theory currently held. In Cicero's source, presumably Posidonius, this was a nod to the predecessors of Stoic pantheism; see also Pease 1920–23 ad loc.

quid habere mundus potest . . . natura rerum continetur: As his example Marcus takes a type of occurrence the haruspices might predict (already used as an example at §§18 and 32), the discovery of a treasure, and personalizes it as "my profit" (*meum lucrum*). Marcus raises doubts based implicitly on the problem of the "high" and the "low," the entrails being somehow conjoined with the world (*exta sunt coniuncta mundo*) and Marcus' treasure embedded in the natural order (*meum lucrum natura rerum continetur*). Similarly at *Fat.* 28 Cicero speaks of "fortuitous causes not embedded in nature and the world" (*fortuitae . . . causae . . . non inclusae in rerum natura atque mundo*). Cicero may have been the first to raise the problem of how natural phenomena could be related not to other natural phenomena but aspects of human culture such as a person's wealth; cf. Kany-Turpin 2003, 372. Similarly Carneades and Panaetius queried whether the gods intervened personally to create the right divinatory signs (1.12; Panaetius T 138 Alesse), except that here the order of nature substitutes for the gods. It has been thought that Posidonius may have introduced a second degree of sympathy connecting individual persons and particular phenomena, such as a liver; cf. Kany-Turpin 2003, 374n41.

nonne pudet physicos haec dicere?: Here and elsewhere (e.g., *Fin.* 1.48; *N.D.* 1.83) Cicero uses the language of shaming to constrain philosophical discourse. In the sequel, he will aim this specifically at three named Stoic philosophers (§35). But this rhetorical move preempts the demonstration of why this is unacceptable. From the Stoic point of view, there is a chain of physical causes; that event *x* caused event *y*, which, from Marcus' individual point of view, involved his financial gain, would not necessarily invalidate the causal chain.

ut enim iam sit . . . quam esse concedo: Cicero struggles to render the Greek συμπάθεια. Just above he had tried *cognatio* ("kinship"; cf. §34a); here (as well as §§58 and 92; and *Fat.* 5 and 7) we find *contagio* (*OLD* s.v. 3 "a sympathetic influence"; *contagio* in this sense has been thought to be a corruption of *cognatio* [cf. Luck 1978, approved by Sedley 1993, 314n6], but *contagio* seems to be too firmly rooted in the tradition to be eliminated); we also find *coniunctio naturae* ("a natural bond"), *concentus* ("harmony"), *consensus* ("agreement"), and *convenientia naturae* ("natural agreement": §34a); he finally resorts to the Greek word (§143). It is essentially the view that the universe is a single large organism the parts of which are mutually dependent and interactive; for background and details see Hahm 1977, ch. 5; Struck 2016, 177–85, showing how "a cluster of ideas that had been used to speak of emotional connection between individuals, and then connections within living bodies, can be transported to describing connections between parts of the cosmos" (185); cf. also Pfeffer 1976, 70–71; Pohlenz 1978–80, 1:101–2 and 2:58; Talanga 1986, 87–90; Sharples 1996, 50. In spite of his polemic against the *physici* (§30), Marcus shows some respect for the Stoic theory, since it is bolstered by empirical evidence, but he is only prepared to go a certain distance with the Stoics, as is clear by §35. Similarly, at *N.D.* 3.28 Cotta allows the existence of the cosmic sympathy but not a connection with the Stoics' divine Logos; at *Fat.* 5 the sympathy is again acknowledged, but not a controlling fate (*naturae contagio valet, quam ego non tollo, vis est nulla fatalis*).

multa enim Stoici colligunt: The Stoics were great collectors; cf. 1.37: *collegit innumerabilia oracula Chrysippus*; ibid. 39: *Chrysippus multis et minutis somniis colligendis*; Lévy 1997, 338 and n. 68. Cicero does not say exactly where he found these but cites three specific philosophers at §35: Chrysippus (*SVF* 2:1211), Antipater (*SVF* 3 Antip. 39), and Posidonius (F 106 E.–K.). The final example of the moon and the tides (§34a) can, however, only derive from Posidonius, an acknowledged expert in this area (F 210.10–13 and 215 E.–K.); hence it is assumed that all the examples derive from him. The dividing line between science and folk belief is, however, in some cases rather thin, and Marcus declines to take a stand on details; cf. Kidd 1988, 425.

nam et musculorum iecuscula bruma dicunt augeri: The first of the examples of *distantium rerum cognatio naturalis* (§34a); Cicero offers other examples at *Fat.* 5. Marcus distances himself at once, with the double diminutive ("the liverkins of mousies," tr. Kidd 1988, 424) scornfully underlining the smallness; Cicero complains of Posidonius' ridiculous examples at *Fat.* 5 (quoted on §27). Other references to this phenomenon (Plin. *Nat.* 11.196 and 29.59 and Plut. *Qu. conv.* 4.5 [670b]) connect it with the moon, rather than the winter; hence Kidd conjectured *luna* for *bruma* here, but withdrew the suggestion on the ground that "Cicero appears to be grouping winter phenomena first" (1988, 425). *dicunt* (A[corr.]) is adopted here for smoothness instead of *dicuntur*, which counts as the transmitted text; it seems natural to assume that the Stoics continue as subject, and the following accusative and infinitive would otherwise force one to supply *dicunt*; cf. Timpanaro 1988, 345.

et puleium aridum . . . in contrarias partis se vertere: The pennyroyal (*puleium*; Linnaeus' *Mentha pulegium*) was used by the ancients primarily for medicinal and culinary purposes (cf. Pease ad loc.). This bit of lore is also attested at Plin. *Nat.* 2.108 and 18.227 and [Arist.] *Probl.* 925a19. The pennyroyal does not, however, have sacs (*vesiculae*, literally "little bladders"), so either there is a misunderstanding on the part of Cicero or his source or the name was applied in antiquity to a different plant.

iam nervos in fidibus aliis pulsis resonare alios: *iam* ("further") marks the transition to a new point: *OLD* s.v. 8a. An apparent allusion to the phenomenon of overtones; cf. [Arist.] *Probl.* 919b15. The reference at Suet. p. 278.20–23 Roth = Gel. 9.7 appears to be based on a misunderstanding of our passage or its source, wrongly supposing that the winter solstice was the cause (cf. Pease ad loc.).

ostreisque et conchyliis . . . pariterque decrescant: Cf. Arist. *HA* 544a18–21; *PA* 680a31–34; Plin. *Nat.* 2.109 and 221. The Romans took a particular interest, since they had developed a taste for shellfish; cf. Lucil. 1222–23 W. = 1224–25 K. *apud* Gel. 20.8.4.

arboresque ut hiemali tempore . . . caedi putentur: The belief was that when the moon had set, the wood was harder; cf. Theophr. *HP* 5.1.3; Cato, *Agr.* 31.2. **cum luna simul senescente:** The metaphorical deployment of *senesco* avoids repetition of *decresco*; cf. *N.D.* 2.95: *lunae . . . tum crescentis, tum senescentis.*

34a quid de fretis . . . lunae motu gubernantur?: Cf. on §33b (*multa enim Stoici colligunt*); S.E. *M.* 9.79.

sescenta licet eiusdem modi proferri: *sescenti*, literally "six hundred" (**sexcenti*), with reduction of the consonant cluster *ksk* to *sk*, as in the name *Sestius*; cf. Adams 2013, 171. It is used for a very large number; cf. *OLD* s.v. 2.

demus hoc . . . terra rerumque natura?: After the lengthy parenthesis detailing the Stoics' evidence, Marcus repeats his concession from §33b (*quam esse concedo*) but by his skeptical questions implicitly disputes that this commits him to believe that a marking on the liver could be connected, on the one hand, with the natural order or, on the other hand, with his own personal profit, the insignificance of which is reinforced by the diminutives *lucellum* and *quaesticulus*, the latter already used by the satirist Lucilius (341 W = 315 K). Cf. the similar argument regarding predictive dreams at §142b. **qua ex coniunctione . . . Graeci appellant:** After trying out various Latin equivalents, Cicero appears to capitulate and accept Greek συμπάθεια as a technical term (cf. §143).

34b Concedam hoc ipsum . . . cum extis concessero: Emphasizing his generosity, Marcus says "I will grant even this," *ipse* emphasizing an extreme element (cf. *OLD* s.v. 9a). **etsi magnam iacturam causae fecero** "although I shall do so at great cost to my case," a legal metaphor; this contrasts with the previous concession (*nihil . . . huic disputationi adversatur*). A verbal noun from *iacio*, *iactura* is the "act of throwing overboard" and by easy extension any sacrifice or loss; cf. Zellmer 1976, 210–11. The effect of the future perfect *concessero* is to represent the result as something definite or guaranteed; cf. Pinkster 2015, 467n132.

35 sed tamen eo concesso . . . rebus suis immolet?: The sacrificial entrails (b) are, as it were, the point of entry for the divine (or the cosmos) (a) into human affairs (c). Having conceded a connection between (a) and (b), Marcus moves to harden the border between (b) and (c). **qui evenit** "how does it happen"; cf. on §17 *init.* **is qui impetrire velit:** *impetrio* is to "seek a favorable omen" for some contemplated action; cf. *OLD* s.v. as well as 1.3 with Schultz 2014 ad loc. At §36a the agent noun *immolator* replaces the relative clause.

hoc erat . . . dissolvitur!: *dissolvo* is to "clear up (a problem or sim.), solve, unravel" (*OLD* s.v. 4). **non rebar:** See above on §5 *fin.* **festive** "neatly," colloquial and ironic; cf. Krostenko 2001, 72–75.

pudet me . . . confusa mundo sit: The language of shaming is invoked again (cf. §33b), and again substitutes for an argument. Marcus maintains politeness by sparing Quintus harsh criticism and instead praising his memory (cf. §14 *memoriter*); however, he thus implicitly makes his brother the mere mouthpiece of the named Stoics. Cf. §§69, 109, and 117, where Marcus criticizes Quintus' sources rather than his brother himself. **Chrysippi Antipatri Posidoni** See on §33b (*multa enim Stoici colligunt*). **idem istuc . . . quod est dictum a te:** Sc. 1.118. Some nuance is lost in Marcus' paraphrase: Quintus' cautious *potest dux esse vis quaedam* disappears, and the attribute *divina* is added to *vis*, but Quintus elsewhere speaks of *vim . . . divinam* (1.80). **vim quandam sentientem atque divinam:** Cf. 1.12: *vis et natura quaedam*; 1.118: *vis quaedam sentiens. vis* perhaps renders *dynamis* in Stoic texts and refers to "the general power that precipitates all forms of action in the world"; cf. Struck 2016, 192–95 (the quoted words from 194) and 206–7.

35–36a illud vero multo etiam melius . . . numini parere omnia: For the emphatic nominal sentence, cf. on §5 (*magnificum illud . . . gloriosum*). This praise of the alternative explanation, a sudden change in the character of the entrails at the moment of sacrifice, is, of course, sarcastic and is immediately deflated with the derisive comment *haec iam, mihi crede, ne aniculae quidem* *existimant.* **deorum . . . numini parere omnia** "all things obey the power of the gods"; similarly §86 *(nhil est . . . quod deus efficere non possit)*; *N.D.* 3.92.

36a haec iam, mihi crede, ne aniculae quidem existimant: Here and in §37 the colloquial formula *mihi crede* serves to strengthen the asseveration; cf. Hofmann 2003, 279–80; Adams 2016, 204, noting that the pronoun is emphatic. The *aniculae* may believe in fate (cf. on §19 [*anile sane et plenum superstitionis*]), but even they have abandoned the notion that the gods can do anything.

an censes . . . ad immolatoris fortunam accommodent?: There still remains the difficulty pointed out at the beginning of §35 of explaining how the victim's entrails will match the fortunes of the sacrificer, with the agent noun *immolator* substituting here for *is qui impetrire velit* of the earlier passage (the only occurrence of *immolator* in classical Latin). Marcus points out the absurdity of assuming any such instant substitution of attributes of the entrails. For supposed divine actions occurring *subito*, cf. §§37, 67, and 68.

non perspicitis . . . res ipsa doceat?: The use of the second person plural, including Quintus in the group of Stoics, mitigates somewhat the sting of the criticism. *alea* was a Roman game that involved throwing dice and moving pieces on a board; hence it comes to denote a "risk" in general, as here; cf. *OLD* s.v. 1 and 2; Purcell 1995. Any intrusion of chance would, of course, be fatal to Stoic determinism; thus Quintus was keen to dismiss chance as an explanation as early as 1.23.

cum enim [tristissuma] exta . . . deorum tanta placatio?: *tristissuma* is hardly wanted when the explanation *quibus nihil videtur esse dirius* follows; hence Hottinger's deletion on the assumption that it was inserted by a reader who recalled *nihil putant accidere potuisse tristius* (§32). Or did Cicero himself write the word but forget to delete it when he added the relative clause? Marcus' examples illustrate that the entrails of successive sacrificial animals can show altogether different features (cf. §30, rejecting Democritus' theory on this ground). Now this is a problem only if the *immolator* and the deity are the same, as Marcus clearly assumes, the typical situation being that the sacrifice is repeated if the desired omen is not obtained the first time (*proxuma hostia litatur pulcherrime*, where *proxuma hostia* is abl. of means and *lito* "sacrifice, offer in propitiation" is impersonal passive; cf. *TLL* 7:1511.32–34). On Roman *litatio*, see further Schilling 1962. But if the sign changes, there is the problem Marcus points out of a sudden, inexplicable shift in the divine attitude, baleful signs disclosing the threats (*minae*) of angry gods and favorable ones that the gods have been appeased. For *deorum . . . placatio* as the basis of the Roman state, cf. *N.D.* 3.5.

36b–37 Sed adfers . . . nescio quo avolare?: This and its counterpart at 1.119 is one of several passages Cicero added to the work after the Ides of March (see above 30–31). Quintus' account is more circumstantial, including details of Caesar's sacrifices on successive days: on the first, the bull whose heart could not be recovered; on the second, a "headless liver" (cf. on §32); the two are turned into alternative accounts of the same sacrifice at App. *BC* 2.116/488. Quintus gives the chronological indication "on the first day on which he sat in the golden chair," which identified the occasion for Cicero's first readers; this is generally assumed to have occurred early in 44 (see further Wardle 2006, 393–94). Both V. Max. 1.6.13 and Pliny *Nat.* 11.186 depend on our text. **id quia non potuerit . . . interisse cor cum immolaretur:** In *oratio obliqua*, quoting Quintus' interpretation from 1.119 *fin.* **alterum . . . alterum** set the two halves of Quintus' argument in opposition: he understands that physiology demands the presence of a heart in such an animal, but he nonetheless believes in its sudden disappearance. **nescio quo** "somewhere or other" (literally, "I know not where") is depreciatory and emphasizes the awkward consequence of the theory.

37 ego enim possum . . . in ipsa immolatione interisse?: Marcus can escape the dilemma by either of two routes: as a Skeptic, he can say that he does not know the function (*vis*: *OLD* s.v. 14) of the heart in a living organism (similar distancing at §30: *nugatur ut physicus*), or he can adopt the naturalistic explanation that there was a heart, but one too shrunken and shrivelled to be recognized as such (cf. Democritus' naturalistic explanation of the qualities of entrails at §30). **tu vero quid habes . . . in ipsa immolatione interisse?:** Quintus must evidently rely on divine causation, rather than either of the plausible approaches Marcus has just outlined. For *subito* with the implication of divine intervention, cf. Marcus' summary of Quintus' position just below and §§67–68. **in ipsa immolatione** "at the very moment of sacrifice" (*OLD* s.v. *ipse* 8).

an quod aspexerit . . . corde privatus est?: Marcus' *reductio ad absurdum* of Quintus' position (a parody of the kind of analogy posited by diviners between events of the sacrifice and the state of the world at large): "since he saw that Caesar was out of his mind (*excordem*) with his purple garb, the bull itself was deprived of its heart (*corde*)," a play on the literal and metaphorical meanings of *cor* (on the latter of which *excors* is based); for a similar imputation of mindlessness, cf. *N.D.* 2.56 (*qui vacare mente putat* [sc.

mundum] *is ipse mentis expers habendus est*). For the use of purple as a status symbol in the Roman Republic and Caesar's attempt to restrict it, cf. Reinhold 1970, 45–56. According to the account of Cicero's friend the historian T. Ampius Balbus (*FRH* 34 F 1 = Suet. *Jul.* 77), Caesar himself had launched such a pun when the state of the entrails was reported to him: *nec pro ostento ducendum si pecudi cor defuisset* ("it should not be held to be an omen if a beast lacked a brain/heart"). For similar instances of defiance of omens on Caesar's part, cf. on §52.

urbem philosophiae . . . physiologiam totam pervertitis: Again, the second person plural mitigates the sting of the criticism somewhat, directed at Stoics in general (cf. §36a: *non perspicitis . . . res ipsa doceat?*). Marcus returns to a military metaphor (cf. §26a). As early as 1.10, he has depicted his brother as taking up a defensive position (*arcem tu quidem Stoicorum . . . Quinte, defendis*), but he criticizes the current strategy as a perversion of priorities, since *physiologia*, defined at *N.D.* 1.20 (and by Quintus at 1.90) as *naturae ratio*, could claim status as one of the three major subdivisions of philosophy, whereas divination was subordinate to it. Similar idea at *N.D.* 1.70: *graviorem . . . plagam accipiebat ut leviorem repelleret.* There may be implicit criticism of the fact that Stoic writings generally laid heavy emphasis on divination; cf. Struck 2016, 173–74. **mihi crede**: Cf. on §36a. **dum haruspicinam veram esse vultis** "while claiming that the art of the haruspices is valid" (*OLD* s.v. *volo* 18b).

caput est in iecore . . . in nihilum subito occidat: Marcus summarizes Quintus' position point by point and then shows what the consequences must be (*ergo*). **simul ac molam et vinum insperseris:** The *mola* or *mola salsa* was the mixture of ground barley and salt sprinkled on the victim before sacrifice; hence the verb for sacrifice itself, *immolare*; wine was later added as a reinforcement of the offering. On Roman sacrificial ritual in general, cf. Latte 1960, 386–92; Scheid 2003, ch. 6; on its social function of organizing a hierarchy of beings, cf. Scheid 2012b. **deus id eripiet . . . aut exedet:** Quintus had preferred to leave the modality vague (*extorum fieri mutatio potest*: 1.118; *in ipso immolationis tempore eas partes quae absint interisse*: 1.119), but Marcus emphasizes that *deus* or *vis aliqua* must be invoked as the cause, not the ordinary processes of nature. **conficiet aut exedet** "will consume or eat up" (cf. *OLD* s.v. *conficio* 13a). **non ergo omnium interitus atque ortus natura conficiet:** *ortus* is Davies' conjecture for transmitted *obitus*; it is expected in light of the following *aut ex nihilo oriatur* and is generally accepted (either here or as a substitute for *interitus*) in spite of Pease's attempt to defend the transmitted text. **aut ex nihilo oriatur aut in nihilum subito occidat:** A principle of physics from early times (cf., e.g., Parmen. 28 B 8.7–11 D.–K.), established definitively by Aristotle's theory of matter at *Gen. et corr.* 318a9–319a17; cf. Düring 1966, 376–77 and, on the historical background, Solmsen 1960, 74–91. The principle was most famously enunciated by Lucr. 1.149–50: *principium cuius hinc nobis exordium sumet, / nullam rem e nilo gigni divinitus umquam*; cf. also Cic. *Fat.* 18 and 25 and other passages cited by Pease ad loc.

quis hoc physicus . . . credendum potius existumas: *quis hoc physicus:* The word order falls into a standard pattern, with the interrogative adj. as host of the unstressed pronoun and the related noun postponed; cf. Adams 1994b, 115–16 and 148–49. **'Haruspices dicunt'** is best taken as Quintus' riposte, to which Marcus then replies; cf. §§45b *init.*, 137, 146. Though Marcus can be skeptical of the *physici* (cf. §30: *nugatur ut physicus*), he nonetheless sees them as better qualified than the haruspices to explain events of the natural world (cf. §11: *physicorum est ista prudentia*); similarly §58.

38 Quid, cum pluribus . . . aliis non litetur?: A separate victim had to be offered to each individual deity; cf. Thulin 1905–9, 2:8. **litetur aliis, aliis non litetur** "some are successfully propitiated but not others" (for *lito* with dative of the deity in impersonal passive construction, cf. *TLL* 7.2:1511.39), an attractive chiastic disposition of verbs and their adjuncts.

quae autem inconstantia . . . bene promittant secundis?: This problem with repeated sacrifice was already highlighted at §36a *fin.*

aut tanta inter eos dissensio . . . Dianae non bona?: Marcus gives the problem concrete form with the example of the twins Apollo and Diana, who might have been expected to be in agreement.

quid est tam perspicuum . . . qualis cuique obtigerit hostia?: This picks up and rephrases the point *non perspicitis aleam quandam esse in hostiis deligendis . . . ?*(§36a). On *perspicuus*, a favorite word of Cicero's, its background and register, cf. Kinsey 1969. Once again, Marcus wants to introduce chance (*fortuito*), which the Stoics must, of course, resist. **talia cuique exta esse, qualis cuique obtigerit hostia** "each one has such entrails as the victim that has fallen to each."

'At enim id ipsum . . . quae cuique ducatur': Quintus counters "But even this has a divine element . . ."; for this point and Marcus' reply, cf. §35 and below. **tamquam . . . ducatur** "as in the case of lots, the one that is drawn for each person."

mox de sortibus . . . conlatione hostiarum: Marcus will take up lot-divination, which was slighted by Quintus in Book 1 (cf. 1.12 and 34), at §§85–87a. Far from admitting that lot-divination strengthens the case for divine guidance in the choice of a sacrificial victim, Marcus insists that the analogy actually works the other way around, to the detriment of lot-divination, i.e., because the selection of victims is so obviously haphazard.

39 an cum in Aequimelium . . . duce deo servus deducitur?: Marcus illustrates the point with a concrete example. The Aequim(a)elium was an open space on the slope of the Capitoline between the Forum Romanum and the Forum Boarium, a natural place to accommodate trade in animals. There, according to legend, the grain dealer Spurius Maelius had a home that was leveled after he was killed in 438 for plotting to seize power. For the sources see Richardson 1992 and Santorio, *LTUR* s.v. Aequim(a)elium. From Marcus' point of view, this scenario involves two improbable suppositions: (1) that the entrails of the victim will match the situation of the sacrificer (*exta rebus accommodata*; cf. §35: *qui evenit ut is qui impetrire velit convenientem hostiam rebus suis immolet?*); and (2) that the slave will be guided to the animal *duce deo* (a possibility likewise raised at §35: *ad hostiam deligendam ducem esse vim quandam sentientem atque divinam quae toto confusa mundo sit*). **duce deo servus deducitur:** The word order, juxtaposing *deo* and *servus*, heightens the incongruity; similarly §56: *per gallinas Iuppiter*. The chiastic pattern *duc- de- . . . deduc-* is also notable.

nam si casum . . . quam ista derideant: *casus* ("chance") is, of course, Marcus' explanation (cf. §38: *fortuito*). Quintus, on the other hand, has claimed the intervention of *vis quaedam* (1.118), specified as *divina* by Marcus (§35), and has urged the analogy of the lots used in divination (§38). The upshot is the monstrosity *casum . . . quasi sortem quandam cum deorum voluntate coniunctam*, which he now attributes to the Stoics (who, however, would hardly admit the influence of *casus*). The Epicureans were indeed given to mocking what they regarded as the weak points in Stoicism, as Velleius does at *N.D.* 1.18–23 and 52–55; cf. ibid. 2.74 (Balbus is speaking): *salem istum, quo caret vestra natio in inridendis nobis*. For divination as a particular target, cf. *N.D.* 2.162. **Stoicos nostros:** It may surprise that Marcus is prepared to identify with the Stoics to this extent, but Cicero has, in general, greater sympathy for Stoicism than Epicureanism (cf. also *Tusc.* 1.78: *num quid . . . est causae, quin amicos nostros Stoicos dimittamus?*). Thus he has made concessions to the Stoic theory of *contagio* (§§33b–34) and at *N.D.* 3.95 was prepared to allow that Balbus' (Stoic) argument on the gods "seemed more inclined to a likeness to the truth." Indeed, Cicero regarded his Skepticism as giving him license to "follow" what he regarded as probable opinions (*Luc.* 99; *Off.* 2.7–8), and at §148, he embraces belief in the deity based on something like the Stoic argument from the design of the universe.

40 Taking the Epicurean ridicule of and/or polemic against the Stoics as his starting point, Cicero inserts here a brief account of the Epicurean view of the deity in relation to divination and the Stoic deity.

et quidem illi . . . propter metum ruinarum: The idea that Epicurus introduced the gods as a joke (*iocandi causa*) differs a bit from Cotta's view that Epicurus merely accepted the gods in order to avoid being branded an atheist (*invidiae detestandae gratia*: *N.D.* 1.123; similarly ibid. 3.3: *ne quid invidiae subeat*; cf. Sedley 2013c, 145–47), but both regard Epicurus' theism as unserious (cf. *N.D.* 3.3: *ludere videtur*). Marcus confirms this claim by selecting features that make the Epicurean gods look ridiculous. *perlucidus* "translucent" is a description offered at *N.D.* 1.75 and 123. On the other hand, *perflabilis* ("permeable") appears here for the first time in extant Latin, perhaps a "burlesque enhancement" ("enchérissement burlesque"), as Kany-Turpin 2004 suggests ad loc. **tamquam inter duos lucos sic inter duos mundos:** Romulus established an asylum on the Capitoline in the saddle between the two crests; anyone who wanted could come there to gain citizenship in the newly founded city; cf. Livy 1.8.5, D.H. 2.15.4; Str. 5.3.2; Richardson 1992 and Wiseman, *LTUR* s.v. Asylum; Dench 2005, 12–25 and 96–107. The comparison to such outcasts is hardly flattering to the Epicurean deities. The gods' sheltering in the μετακόσμια ("spaces between the worlds") is alluded to in passing at *N.D.* 1.18 (*tamquam modo . . . ex Epicuri intermundiis descendisset*), but oddly not in Velleius' exposition of Epicurean theology; and Cotta ignores the point in his refutation (*N.D.* 1.114); see further Essler 2011, 235–40. **propter metum ruinarum:** I.e., the basic downward movement of the atoms; cf. L–S 11 with notes.

eosque habere putat . . . usum ullum habere membrorum: Similar argument at *N.D.* 1.92, 99, 111–13, even though Philodemus had supplied some details of the gods' activities (*De dis* 3, cols. 14–15); cf. also Demetrius Laco coll. XVII–XVIII, responding to critics, with Santoro 2000, 153–57.

ergo hic circumitione . . . et hominibus consulat: *hic . . . hic*: References to Epicurus as the previous subject. **circumitione** "by a round-about route": *OLD* s.v. *circumitio* 7b; similarly at §127a (*quid opus est circumitione . . . ?*); at *N.D.* 1.122–23 Cotta makes it clear that Epicurus has made the gods redundant by abolishing their role in the world and hence the basis for worship. In contrast to that, Epicurus has eliminated divination directly (*recta* [sc. *via*], restored here for transmitted *recte*, an easy error); cf. *OLD* s.v. *recta*; Epicur. pp. 261–62 Usener; for the contrast, cf. §127a: *circumitione et anfractu . . . derecto.* **sed non . . . item Stoici:** Unlike the Epicureans, the Stoics cannot derive rejection of divination directly from their theology (it is, in fact, compatible with their theology, as Marcus goes on to argue). **nihil habens nec sui nec alieni negoti:** This follows from the *beatitudo*, which, together with eternal existence, was the primary attribute of the Epicurean gods (Epicurus, *Key Doctrines* 1; *Ep. Hdt.* 77; *Ep. Pyth.* 97; *Ep. Men.* 123; Dem. Lac. col. XXV; *N.D.* 1.45), a reaction against belief in divine intervention; cf. Merlan 1967. At *N.D.* 1.52 Velleius criticizes Stoic providence as destructive of this divine blessedness. **non potest . . . inpertire . . . potest non inpertire:** The word order is decisive in differentiating the relation of the Epicurean and Stoic gods to divination: the former "cannot impart" (*non potest . . . inpertire*) divination to humans (because he is by definition inactive and uninvolved in human affairs); on the other hand, "it is possible [for the latter] not to impart" (*potest non inpertire*) divination and nonetheless fulfill the functions of providential government claimed by the Stoics (cf. *N.D.* 2.133–67). This argument was begun at §§22–24 by asserting that knowledge of the future is not beneficial to humans, a point taken up at §105 and culminating at §106: *possunt enim non significare et tamen esse di.*

41 cur igitur vos . . . quas numquam explicetis? "Why, then, do you (Stoics) involve yourselves in such sophistries as you would never untangle?" Cf. *OLD* s.v. *captio* 2.

ita enim . . . deos esse retinendum est: Syllogisms were not merely a shorthand to which the Stoics resorted when they were in a hurry (*cum magis properant*), as Marcus suggests; a similar assumption of a quick result from a syllogism is implied at §§103 (*quam paucis verbis confectum negotium putant!*) and 106 (*id enim iam perfectum arbitrantur*). Rather, syllogisms had the function of stimulating thought or summarizing a complex argument before or after its presentation; cf. Schofield 1983, 52–54. At *Fin.* 4.7, Cicero criticizes Stoic discourse on the deeper ground that it is too thin to carry conviction (similarly, *N.D.* 2.20). The syllogism making the existence of divination follow from the existence of the gods was put forward by Balbus (*N.D.* 2.12; similarly *Leg.* 2.32) and argued for by Quintus at 1.82–83 (= Chrysippus, *SVF* 2:1192). Marcus does not refute those arguments here (the refutation is postponed to §§101–6) but merely turns the syllogism on its head, claiming that the reverse is more probable (*probabilius*): *<si est divinatio, sunt di;> non est autem divinatio; non sunt ergo di* (the bracketed words have been added to complete the syllogism; our ms. tradition sometimes mishandles such material; cf. on §15). But did the Stoics rashly (*temere*) commit to that proposition, as Marcus asserts? In fact, the Stoics had other arguments for the existence of the gods, detailed at *N.D.* 2.4–44, and hence would hardly have endorsed a syllogism making the existence of the gods depend solely upon the existence of divination; cf. also Schultz 2014, 69–70. **divinatio . . . perspicue tollitur** "divination is unquestionably eliminated" (cf. *OLD* s.v. *perspicue* 3; on §38 [*quid est tam perspicuum . . . ?*]), as it was by Epicurus (§40). **deos esse retinendum est:** Though at 1.8 Marcus claimed that Cotta's discourse in *N.D.* 3 aimed to refute the Stoic arguments, but not to destroy religion, only at §148 does he explain why he wants to retain the gods. Cf. Ciafardone 2017, who explores how the theism of this passage squares with Cicero's professed Skepticism.

42a atque hac extispicum . . . et fulgura: *extispicum divinatio* is "divination by means of entrails," the genitive expressing the medium; cf. §77 *avium divinatio*; §148a *somniorum divinatio*; *OLD* s.v. *divinatio* 1. Marcus overstates his result (*omnis haruspicina sublata est*), but immediately turns to the other, less prominent branches of the haruspices' art.

42b–47 Thunder and Lightning Strikes

This section can be outlined as follows:

1. Claim of long-continued observation of lightning (42)
2. Etruscan division of the heaven into sixteen regions
3. Alternatives to divine intervention
    a. The fear of early peoples led them to attribute lightning to Jupiter.
    b. The prohibition of assemblies was probably for political reasons (43).
    c. Natural philosophers explain with reference to the behavior of the clouds and winds (44).
    d. The attribution to Jupiter makes no sense (45).
4. Quintus' examples:
    a. Head of Summanus located with the diviners' help: supernatural explanation not required
    b. Marcus' verses and actions as consul (46)
        (1) Ridicule of diviners' predictions
        (2) Chance is a possible explanation for the timing of the installation of Jupiter's statue (47).

Marcus argues that the belief that thunder and lightning are of divine origin is carried over from early humans' fear of these phenomena. He offers an alternative explanation in line with the current scientific understanding of conducive atmospheric conditions. He ridicules the traditional belief, referring to the manufacture of the thunderbolt by the Cyclopes as something no one would believe and claiming that the traditional story attributes a single thunderbolt to Jupiter, which he would hardly waste, as is so often seen to be the case. The haruspices' ability to locate the head of the statue of the god Summanus, knocked down by lightning, shows merely that because they divided the sky into sixteen regions they could determine the source of the lightning and the angle of impact and so estimate where the head might be found, i.e., an inference based on reasoning, not the supernatural. Finally he discusses his poem *De consulatu suo*, from which Quintus had cited the description of the haruspices' prophecy and installation of the statue of Jupiter. Marcus ridicules the haruspices' predictions quoted there and asserts that the arrival of Jupiter's new statue coincided with the revelation of the conspiracy purely by chance.

42b Valet autem in fulguribus . . . coniecturaque adhibetur: The two remaining branches of *haruspicina*, though both falling within technical divination (1.12), follow different methods. *fulgura* are "flashes of lightning" (< *fulgeo* "flash"); Quintus had remarked that their interpretation was based upon long observation (ibid.). **ratio . . . coniecturaque** = "inferential reasoning"; cf. Frank 1992, 312. For *coniectura* cf. on §12 *fin.*

quid est igitur . . . qua ex parte venisset: Pliny *Nat.* 2.143 confirms the Etruscans' division of the heavens into sixteen parts for observing lightning (and probably also the flight of birds; cf. Livy 1.34.9; Thulin 1905–9, 1:15); cf. Weinstock 1951, 145–47. The Romans, on the other hand, as Marcus indicates, divided the heavens into four parts (cf. Var. *L.* 7.7). Though the Etruscan division may have been a complication of an original four-part system (up-down, right-left; cf. Weinstock 1951, 145), it is, *pace* Marcus, unlikely that the Etruscans borrowed from Roman augury. The influence, if such there was, is likely to have been, in line with the general cultural pattern, the other way around; cf. Briquel 1986, 69. Van der Meer 1987, 29, concludes that "the *distributio caeli* into sixteen regions is a local development or invention. Foreign influence in its genesis can hardly be proved." **ut ex eo . . . venisset:** *ex eo* "on that basis." *fulmen* contains the root of *fulgeo* plus deverbative suffix *-men* denoting the product of the action (i.e., **fulg-men*, with expected simplification of the consonant cluster), hence "lightning that strikes, a thunderbolt": *OLD* s.v. 1; Leumann 1977, 218 and 370. At §45b Marcus shows how this system can be applied.

primum id quid interest . . . praepotentem Iovem?: *nonne perspicuum est . . .* : The question introduced with *nonne* guides the reader/interlocutor toward a positive response; cf. §36a: *non perspicitis . . . ?*; § 38: *quid est tam perspicuum . . . ?* Cicero adopts an explanatory model that was developed by Democritus (68 A 75 D.–K.) and given currency by Epicurus (Lucr. 1.151–54, 5.1161 ff., 6.83 ff.) and the Stoics (Cleanthes, *SVF* 1:528 = *N.D.* 2.14 and 3.16), albeit the other authors invoked it to explain the origin of religion in general. **rerum omnium praepotentem Iovem:** *praepotens*, a word of the high style, was a favorite of Cicero's, found twelve times in his speeches and treatises (PHI). It is unusual for it to be construed, like *potens*, with a gen. (cf. *OLD* s.vv. *praepotens* a, *potens* 2): "overlord of the universe" or the like. The word helps to effect a rare triple cretic. Romans thought of Jupiter as the primary hurler of lightning; the Etruscans evidently assigned that role to their corresponding god, Tinia, as argued by Capdeville 1989, who shows that the differentiation of nine Etruscan deities hurling lightning by Pliny (*Nat.* 2.138) probably rests on a misunderstanding.

42b–43a itaque in nostris commentariis . . . nunc de fulgoribus: A small digression prompted by Cicero's recollection of a phrase in the augural books (*in nostris commentariis*), on which see Linderski 1986, 2242–44. Cicero knew this material well, having been elected to the board of augurs in 53 or early 52 (cf. Linderski 1972, 190–99 = 1995, 240–49; Rüpke 2008, §3290). **'Iove tonante fulgurante comitia populi habere nefas':** Cf. *N.D.* 2.65: *Iove fulgente tonante*, the more archaic and perhaps more precise phrasing; cf. Regell 1893, 12 and n. 5; Timpanaro 1988, 352. The two participles in asyndeton point to simultaneous action; cf. Guittard 2003, 459.

43a hoc fortasse rei publicae causa . . . nunc de fulgoribus: Cicero adds this explanation of lightning as a bad omen in the case of elections alone, whereas it was otherwise auspicious if it occurred on the left. He suspects a political motive, as a result of which this sign becomes, from one point of view (though not Cicero's), "too convenient and contrivable" (Driediger-Murphy 2019, 119). Certainly in the late Republic reports of adverse omens (*obnuntiationes*) by magistrates were frequently used (by the *principes civitatis*, as Marcus notes at §74) to forestall or invalidate popular assemblies and the legislation they carried; cf. Burckhardt 1988, ch. 4; de Libero 1992, 56–64; Lintott 1999, 103–4; above on §28. That this was the original purpose is doubtful, however. In early times the Romans may have been guided by practical motives, since if a storm threatened, it might be difficult to assemble a large body of citizens. Cf. also Wissowa 1912, 533, who thinks that thunder was originally a universally negative omen but retained this quality only for elections. **vitium** is an "augural impediment": *OLD* s.v. 6; this was perhaps the original sense of the word, as argued by Paschall 1936. **si sinistrum fuit:** Cf. on §82. **de auspiciis alio loco:** Sc. §§70–83, as well as the treatise *De auguriis* (pp. 94–95 Garbarino).

43b Quid igitur minus . . . rebus incertis?: Marcus thus draws the consequences from the fact that the soothsayer is using *res incertae* or *res incognitae* as the basis for prediction (§33a with note). For the *physici* being held to a higher standard, cf. §33b: *nonne pudet physicos haec dicere?* **quicquam certi** "anything definite"; for the genitive cf. on §8 *fin.*

non enim te puto . . . in Aetna putes: For the type of argument, suggesting that the interlocutor is too sophisticated to believe in myths, cf. *Tusc.* 1.10: *dic quaeso: num te illa terrent, triceps apud inferos Cerberus, Cocyti fremitus, travectio Acherontis . . . ?* For the subjunctive of tendency, cf. on §19 (*nisi quod . . . rato tempore*). Hesiod depicted the thunderbolt as the product of the Cyclopes' forge (*Th.* 139–41); Aeschylus situated the forge on Aetna (*PV* 365–69); for the localization, cf. also Cic. *Ver.* 5.146. See in general Teuchefeu-Meynier, *LIMC* s.v. Kyklops, Kyklopes. With their theory of *sympatheia*, by which the whole universe is divine or interpenetrated by a divine power, the Stoics could hold that thunderbolts were of divine origin but without the mythological narrative, a possibility Marcus does not entertain; cf. Timpanaro 1988, 352.

44 nam esset mirabile . . . aut cavendum moneret: Two unreal apodoses illustrate the folly of the belief Quintus was too clever to hold. Marcus regards the manufacture of the thunderbolt as a one-off: Hes. *Th.* 141 uses aorists to describe the Cyclopes' actions, so Marcus' interpretation is defensible, albeit artworks depict the Cyclopes engaged in a serial manufacturing process (see previous note). Marcus claims that the thunderbolt could therefore not be used frequently or for the purpose of warning human beings. Lucretius (6.411–16) offers the different criticism that Jupiter could not release several different thunderbolts simultaneously. **nec vero fulminibus . . . aut cavendum moneret:** *fulminibus* is emphatic, hammering home the point that if Jupiter meant to issue warnings, he would hardly use so crude a communications device. **aut faciendum . . . aut cavendum:** Marcus attributes to thunderbolts the force of law, since they could be taken as favorable or unfavorable omens; see further on §80 (*quae est igitur natura*).

placet enim Stoicis . . . id esse fulmen: In contrast to the mythological explanation is the scientific one, which the Stoics themselves endorse (= *SVF* 2:699; similarly *SVF* 1:117 = D.L. 7.153–54). **placet . . . Stoicis** "the

Stoics hold"; cf. on §33b (*placuisse physicis*). **anhelitus terrae . . . ventos esse:** That the winds are flowing air is a doctrine well attested since Arist. *Mete.* 349a16–17. **anhelitus terrae**, literally "the breath of the earth," with underlying personification. The phrase recurs at §117 with reference to the mephitic gases supposed to have caused the Pythia's trances; similarly *anhelitus . . . terrarum* at 1.115. Pliny, too, allows that winds can be produced by the "exhalation of the earth" (*anhelitu terrae*: *Nat.* 2.114). Though Marcus points out that the earth's exhalations are cold (*qui frigidi sint*, subj. because part of the report of the Stoic doctrine), he fails to explain what sets them in motion (the heat of the sun according to Anaximander 12 A 24 D.–K.); see Pease ad loc. for further references. **cum autem se . . . tonitrua existere:** Pliny, *Nat.* 2.112, offers a similar description of different levels of disruption and the phenomena thereby produced: *si in nube luctetur flatus aut vapor, tonitrua edi, si erumpat ardens, fulmina, si longiore tractu nitatur, fulgetras.* In our passage, *fulgores et tonitrua* are "flashes of lightning and thunder" (*OLD* s.vv. *fulgor* 3 and *tonitrus* a), whereas *fulmen* is the thunderbolt (cf. on §42b). The same triad reappears at Sen. *N.Q.* 2.11.3: *de tonitruo fulminibusque ac fulgurationibus.* **nubium conflictu:** Cf. Sen. *N.Q.* 1.1.6: *quemadmodum nubes conlisae mediocriter fulgurationes efficiunt, maiore impetu impulsae fulmina*; see Pease ad loc. for further references.

quod igitur vi naturae . . . significationem rerum consequentium quaerimus?: Marcus draws the conclusion that the kinds of consequences claimed by soothsayers would hardly follow from this natural process. This will, in fact, be his general procedure: to offer, if possible, an explanation based on natural occurrences that excludes the need for a supernatural explanation, just as at §§9–10 he shunted the soothsayers aside whenever one of the other arts was available. **nulla constantia, nullo rato tempore** "with no consistency, at no fixed time" (for *rato tempore* see on §19). The implication is that these are chance occurrences, in implicit contrast with astronomical phenomena, which recur at fixed intervals and are thus predictable; cf. §§17 and 89. **significationem rerum consequentium** "indication of coming events," such as the soothsayers were keen to find.

44–45a scilicet, si ista Iuppiter . . . haec ne observantur quidem?: As often, *scilicet* ("doubtless") is ironic, calling attention to the absurdity of the proposition; cf. *OLD* s.v. 4. The premise is that such vain activity is at odds with our concept of divine intelligence; similarly at §102: *frustra . . . significarent.* These arguments against the haruspices' lore about thunderbolts are paralleled in Lucretius (6.396, 421–22; cf. also 2.1100–1104): *cur etiam loca sola petunt frustraque laborant* [sc. the gods who hurl thunderbolts] . . .

altaque cur plerumque petit loca [sc. Jupiter] *plurimaque eius / montibus in summis vestigia cernimus ignis?* Sen. *N.Q.* 2.51 similarly concluded that either thunderbolts signify nothing or we have no idea what they signify. **in desertas solitudines** "into deserted lands," a pleonastic description; *solitudo*, like other Latin abstracts, is concretized in the plural; cf. *OLD* s.v. 4a.

45b 'At inventum est caput in Tiberi': This refers to the incident cited by Quintus at 1.16 when in the year 278 a clay statue of the god Summanus, displayed in the pediment of the temple of Capitoline Jupiter, was struck by lightning, and the head was found in the Tiber thanks to the haruspices' advice (similarly Livy per. 14). Perhaps as a result of this incident, Summanus received his own temple by the Circus Maximus; cf. MacBain 1982, 47; Orlin 1997, 20–21. On Summanus, cf. Capdeville 1989, 1176, who argues convincingly against a foreign origin (*aliter* Weinstock, *RE* s.v. Summanus); García Hernández 1992 argues that the deity should be identified with Lucifer, the morning star.

quasi ego artem . . . nulla ratio docet: Cf. §33a, conceding an art, but with the stipulation *si est ars ulla rerum incognitarum.* **caeli distributio** "the division of the sky into parts": *OLD* s.v. *distributio* 3a. **certarum rerum notatio** "the observation of certain things" may seem vague; hence Schäublin (1987, 182) conjectured *certarum reg<ion>um notatio* (a nearer specification of *caeli distributio*). This is worth considering, but it is possible that Marcus means implicitly to contrast "reliable" and "unreliable"; cf. §43b *init.* **unde fulmen venerit, quo concesserit** "where the lightning bolt came from and where it went" (*OLD* s.v. *concedo* 1b). In other words, their elaborate subdivision of the heavens (§42b) enabled the haruspices to judge the trajectory of the lightning but not to assign a meaning (*quid significet*).

sed urges me . . . extiterunt responsa verissuma: Quintus had cited the poem *De consulatu suo* (F 10 Courtney) at length at 1.17–22. Here Marcus selects vv. 36–38 for verbatim quotation and adds a prose summary of vv. 39–48. **altitonans** "thundering on high," a word already used by Ennius (*An.* 554 Sk.) to render Homer's epithet for Zeus ὑψιβρεμέτης (*Il.* 1.354 etc.); cf. *altisonus* at F 17.1 Courtney, borrowed from Enn. *An.* 586. *stellans*, too, is a poetic word ("adorned with stars, starry"), first attested in *De consulatu suo* but taken up by later poets; see *OLD* s.v. **suos quondam tumulos ac templa petivit:** The lightning strike occurred in the year 65 (as is shown by the consuls named in v. 33; cf. on §47 *fin.*). The *tumuli* will be the two crests of the Capitoline. Lucretius may have had this incident in mind when he pointed out that Jupiter destroys his own statues and temples (6.416–

20). **statua Nattae:** It is uncertain which Pinarius Natta was represented; cf. on §47. **Romulusque et Remus cum altrice belua:** A shorthand for *statuaeque Romuli et Remi* etc. The statue of the twins with the she-wolf that suckled them was a type dating back to a monument erected by the Ogulnii in 297 (Livy 10.23.12); cf. Wiseman 1995, 72–76. But laboratory analysis of the casting technique argues that the extant Capitoline she-wolf dates from the twelfth century; cf. Carruba and De Masi 2006.

46 mirabile autem illud . . . in Capitolio conlocabatur: *mirabile autem illud*: For the type of sentence, see on §§5–6a (*magnificum illud*). It was only toward the end of Cicero's consulship (63) that the new cult statue of Jupiter, ordered two years previously, was ready for installation; this coincided with the "proof of the conspiracy" (*indicium coniurationis*) on December 3; cf. *Catil.* 3.20; *Cons.* vv. 60–65. This sentence illustrates the transformative power of a prefix: *loco* = "award a contract," *colloco* = "put in place" (*OLD* s.vv. 5 and 1 respectively).

'Tu igitur animum induces . . . contra scripta defendere?': A paraphrase of Quintus' appeal at 1.22. On Quintus' tactic of enlisting his brother's actions and poetry on his side, cf. Woolf 2015, 68–69; Bishop 2019, 286–98. *animum inducere* is to "bring oneself" (to do something, sc. against one's better judgment or the like); cf. *OLD* s.v. *induco* 12a. Similarly, Balbus attempted to constrain Cotta's reply to his presentation of Stoic theology by reference to the fact that Cotta was a civic leader and a priest (*principem civem et pontificem*: *N.D.* 2.168).

frater es . . . rationem totius haruspicinae peto: *frater . . . vereor*: Santangelo 2013, 26, understands: "I am your brother and I have to respect you—but how could you possibily take that argument seriously in the first place?" On the inhibition (*verecundia*), which is on display here (*vereor*), cf. Kaster 2005, ch. 1, esp. 26–27. The passage is reminiscent of Marcus' reply to Atticus, when he inquired too closely into the relation of "poetry and truth" (*Dichtung und Wahrheit*) in the poem *Marius* at *Leg.* 1.3–4. The implication is that public oratory may entail some use of religious arguments to persuade the audience but that the current discussion is on a different level (cf. §28: *soli sumus* etc.); cf. also *Fin.* 4.74, differentiating the current (philosophical) discussion from the kinds of arguments (about the Stoic paradoxes) he had once used in a forensic speech (*Pro Murena*). **verum quid tibi hic tandem nocet?:** Cf. §34a (Marcus' assessment of the state of his case in light of a concession): *demus hoc: nihil enim huic disputationi adversatur.* **qui verum explicari volo:** In his dialogues, Cicero tends to depict himself as a seeker of truth; cf.

Fin. 1.13: *verum enim invenire volumus, non tamquam adversarium aliquem convincere.* **rationem . . . peto:** Similarly Cotta at *N.D.* 3.13: *rumoribus . . . mecum pugnas, Balbe, ego autem a te rationes requiro.*

sed te mirificam in latebram . . . ad rem pertinere: Cicero can use *latebra* literally ("hiding place" < *lateo*), as at *Cael.* 62 (of Clodia's agents delegated to seize poison at the baths): *non invenio quae latebra togatis hominibus esse posset*, but more frequently in a metaphorical sense ("subterfuge"), as here and at §111: *latebram obscuritatis*; similarly *Fin.* 2.107: *latebram haberes. mirificam* is ironic, as at §27 (*commenticiorum exemplorum mirifica copia*). **quod . . . intellegeres fore ut premerere** "since you realized that you would be hard-pressed": *intellegeres* is subj., since it is the reason supplied by Marcus for his brother's behavior; *fore ut* + subj. substitutes for the future passive infinitive; cf. Pinkster 2015, 533. **multa verba fecisti . . . ad rem pertinere:** *verba facere* is a colloquial substitute for a verb of speaking (cf. H–S 754–56) but also allows for the addition of the (emphatic) quantitative adj. Quintus argued along such lines at 1.12, 15–16, 23, 35, 85–86, urging acceptance of divination based upon results (*eventa*) even in default of an account of the causes (*causae*); when at 1.109 Quintus offered to produce a cause, he merely repeated the claim of "long observation"; cf. Timpanaro 1988, 313–14 n. 253. See also Allen 2001, 162-67, who compares the Stoics' focus on results with their apparent model, Empirical medicine.

quasi ego aut fieri concederem . . . non quaerere!: Marcus objects on grounds of both content and procedure: he refuses to accept the veracity of Quintus' examples (*quasi ego . . . fieri concederem*; cf. again the *commenticia exempla* of §27; *credere omnia vide ne non sit necesse* [§31], etc.); and he refuses to allow the parameters of debate to be narrowed so as to exclude the investigation of causes (cf. §27 *fin.*). As Marcus had previously insisted upon an account that would satisfy a natural philosopher (*physicus*: §§33b, 37, 43b), so here a philosopher in general. For the idea, cf. Arist. *Met.* 1003b3–5 and other passages cited by Bonitz 1870 s.v. φιλόσοφος. On Marcus' exclusionist move, see further Hankinson 1988, 152–53.

47 et eo quidem loco . . . vim et effectum videres: *et eo quidem loco* shows "extending *quidem*" attracted to a pronominal adj. (cf. Solodow 1978, 110 and 112): "At that point, moreover, . . ." At 1.13–15 Quintus quoted weather signs from several passages of the *Prognostica*, the second part of the rendering of the *Phaenomena* of Aratus of Soli (315–240) that Cicero produced in his youth; for details, see Schultz 2014 ad locos. He went on to mention the purgative effects of scammony (*scammonia*) and aristolochia as an antidote for snakebite (1.16) and claimed that knowledge of their power (*quid . . . possit*) is enough; one need not inquire into the cause. **scammoniam aristolochiamque [radicem]:** In the text as transmitted, *radicem* must be taken as an appositive with *aristolochiam* (so evidently *TLL* 2:584.35). Contrast 1.16: *quid scammoniae radix . . . quid aristolochia.* Hence Lambin wanted to change our passage to *scammoniae aristolochiaeque radicem*, whereas Timpanaro (1988, 355) would retain *scammoniam* but alter *aristolochiam* to *aristolochiae.* I suspect, rather, that *radicem* should be deleted as a gloss inserted on the basis of 1.16.

dissimile totum . . . observari animadvertique potuerunt: With another emphatic nominal sentence (*dissimile totum*) Marcus rejects Quintus' analogy between weather signs preceding certain meteorological phenomena (the province of the *gubernator* according to §12) and the signs used by diviners to predict future events, because, as explained below, divinatory signs provide no opportunity for long-continued observation. In addition, the causes of meteorological events can be investigated, as Quintus himself acknowledged with reference to the work of the second-century Stoic Boethus of Sidon (1.13; *SVF* 3 Boeth. 4), to which Marcus now adds that of his teacher Posidonius (*N.D.* 1.6; F 109 E.–K.; cf. Kidd 1988 ad loc.).

Nattae vero statua . . . callide Iuppiter cogitavit!: For *vero* calling attention to a new point, cf. on §10 *fin.* Marcus alludes to vv. 39–40 of *De consulatu suo*: *tum species ex aere vetus venerataque Nattae / concidit, elapsaeque vetusto numine leges* ("then the ancient, venerated bronze likeness of Natta collapsed, and the laws with their ancient divine aura melted") and the haruspices' pronouncement as recorded at vv. 49–50: *civilem generosa stirpe profectam / volvier in gentem cladem* ("a slaughter of citizens originating in a noble family is being plotted against the people"). Both Catiline and his lieutenant P. Cornelius Lentulus Sura were of noble lineage. Marcus offers ironic praise for Jupiter's cleverness in signifying a danger emanating from the nobility by the destruction of the statue of a member of the *gens Pinaria*, one of Rome's oldest aristocratic families. **cogitavit** "thought out" (*OLD* s.v. *cogito* 3c) is the transmitted text and should be retained (with Christ and Timpanaro). It is surprising how many editors have adopted Markland's *<ex>cogitavit* in spite of the fact that it substitutes an heroic clausula (which Cicero tends to avoid; cf. Laurand 1911) for his fifth-favorite rhythm (cretic plus double trochee).

'Romulus lactens . . . certiores facit Iuppiter!: *Romulus lactens*: cf. on §45b (*Romulusque et Remus*). *Cons.* 42–46 detailed the fate of Romulus and Remus (*parvos Mavortis semine natos*), likewise blasted by a thunderbolt (*flammato* *fulminis ictu*), and hence the danger to the city and its monuments (52–53). **urbi . . . ei quam ille condidit** "for the city that he founded," with hyperbaton of the determinative pronominal adj.; cf. Devine and Stephens 2006, §6.2. The comment, *quam scite* varies *tam callide* (cf. §§30, 62a: *non inscite*). **per notas** "by tokens" or "signs" (*OLD* s.v. *nota* 8); cf. §17 *init. certiorem facere* is to "inform": *OLD* s.v. *certus* 12b. Cicero varies the order with *Iuppiter* in final position (and thus secures the double cretic).

'At eodem tempore . . . ad istam horam reservatus est!: *Cons.* 54–65 narrates the haruspices' prophecy that the installation of a new statue of Jupiter facing east would secure the city against the impending (internal) threat and that this finally came to pass during Cicero's consulate; similarly, in prose style, *Catil.* 3.20. **conlocabatur . . . indicabatur:** the imperfect tense is used for parallel events unfolding in the past; cf. Pinkster 2015, 416–19. The evidence was provided (*indicabatur*) by the Allobroges (*Cons.* 65: *vocibus Allobrogum . . . patebat*), as narrated in detail in *Catil.* 3. **et tu scilicet mavis . . . :** For *et* "introducing an indignant exclamation, usually in the form of an ironical question," cf. *OLD* s.v. 15; for *scilicet* signaling irony, cf. on §§44–45a. Actually, Cicero himself had claimed this as the obvious interpretation of the events (*Catil.* 3.21). **numine deorum . . . casu:** These are the two competing interpretative models that will be explored in the sequel. **columnam illam:** A shorthand for the column plus the statue of Jupiter placed on top of it: *Cons.* 63: *Iuppiter excelsa clarabat sceptra columna*. **de Cotta et de Torquato:** I.e., the two consuls of 65, L. Aurelius Cotta and L. Manlius Torquatus (*MRR* 2:157), who issued the contract.

48 Non equidem plane despero . . . discere a te volo: Marcus' Skepticism has two faces: (a) the aggressive rejection/refutation of dogmatic assertions; (b) Socratic-style confession of ignorance. Here he makes a rather sharp turn from (a) to (b).

nam cum mihi quaedam casu . . . abundas enim similibus: After his lengthy quotation from *De consulatu suo*, Quintus countered the interpretation of the simultaneous installation of the statue and revelation of the Catilinarian conspiracy as a chance occurrence by citing a series of examples. The first of these, the hundred successive occurrences of the "Venus throw" (1.23), i.e., four dice each showing a different number, is hypothetical and therefore ineffective, and Marcus' reply *nescio cur non possint* would be hard for Quintus to counter. The boundary between the improbable and the impossible was murky in antiquity, probability theory having been invented only in the mid-seventeenth century; cf. Wardle 2006, 161–62. Sambursky 1956 explains the thinking that kept the ancients from the experimentation and quantification that could have led to the theory.

habes et respersionem . . . et alia permulta: Quintus' next examples aimed to show that "chance cannot imitate truth" (§49a). First he observed that colors splashed randomly onto a tablet could resemble a face, but hardly the beauty of (Apelles') Coan Venus. Next he claimed that a pig might produce the letter *A* with its snout, but could not write out Ennius' *Andromacha* (1.23; cf. *N.D.* 2.93 for the [rejected] possiblity that letters scattered at random could produce Ennius' *Annals*). The point seems to be that there is a sharp line dividing nature and culture. Again, these are hypothetical examples, and Marcus does not find them worthy of a reply. **permulta** may contain a hint of fatigue. For the "urbane" intensifier *per-*, which Cicero often uses in his less formal writing in preference to the fussier comparative and superlative forms, cf. André 1951.

48–49a idem Carneadem fingere . . . sed sit hoc fictum: Quintus cited as his final example an anecdote mentioned by Carneades (1.23, F 9 Mette): when a rock was split in the quarries of Chios, a small head of the god Pan emerged. This may have occurred, Quintus opined, but the head will not have been of such artistry as to be worthy of Scopas (1.23). Marcus replies, using instead Praxiteles as the standard for excellence in sculpture, and alluding to a theory of artistic production that was currently held: the work of art was a core that was already present in the block; the artist merely peeled away the covering; see examples cited by Pease ad loc. On Cicero's attitude toward art in general, cf. Berry 2012. **Praxitelia capita** "heads in the style of Praxiteles." **neque quicquam illuc adfertur a Praxitele:** Schäublin 1987, 183, proposed deleting *a Praxitele* on the ground that this is a generic description of the process, but surely the transmitted text can stand as an elaboration based upon the hypothetical example. **sua sponte** varies the preceding *casu*. **sit hoc fictum:** Cf. §32 (*sint sane ista Democritea vera*) with note.

49a quid, in nubibus . . . veritatem casus imitari: Marcus counters Quintus' examples, all either hypothetical or of dubious veracity, with an example from common experience, viz., the clouds imitating shapes of various creatures, as an example of chance imitating reality. **formam . . . hippocentauri:** The centaur (*hippocentaurus*, though *centaurus* is also found) seems an odd example of *veritas*; it was, however, a traditional example of a shape clouds could assume; cf. Aristoph. *Nub.* 946; Arist. *Insomn.* 461b19–21.

49b–69 Portents

This section mostly argues that the particular examples cited by Quintus can be explained by natural causes and therefore need not be regarded as portents. Marcus inserts an exhortation to seek a natural cause and not to shortcircuit that process by immediately positing a divine cause (60). The details:

1. A mule's foaling: not impossible, hence not a portent (49b)
2. Digression: origin of haruspicy (50)
   a. Story of Tages
   b. Criticism, culminating in Cato's comment on haruspices (51)
3. Obedience to/trust in or defiance of omens by military commanders (52)
   a. Hannibal and Prusias
   b. Caesar
   c. Pompey (53)
4. General questions about portents (54)
   a. Why do the gods give warnings requiring an interpreter?
   b. Why warn of things that cannot be avoided?
   c. Fastening on the gods preempts the search for causes (55).
5. Quintus' other examples
   a. Crowing of cocks as a portent of Boeotian victory at Leuctra (56)
      (1) Jupiter would not have used them as his messengers.
      (2) Crowing is not unnatural behavior for them.
   b. Shower of blood, sweating statues (58)
      (1) Natural explanations are available.
      (2) In stressful times, people are more credulous.
   c. Mice gnawing shields as a portent of the Social War (59)
      (1) Not unnatural behavior
      (2) *Reductio ad absurdum*
   d. Digression: exhortation to seek a physical cause; Chrysippus cited (60–61)
   e. Snake-portents (62)
      (1) Tiberius Gracchus' portent: nothing unnatural occurred (62).
      (2) Calchas' prophecy of the duration of the Trojan War (63)
      (3) A snake appears to Sulla before battle (65).
   f. Portents given to infants (66)
      (1) Midas
      (2) Plato
      (3) Roscius

g. Leaders receive portents of future disaster or success.
    (1) Flaminius
    (2) Dionysius
h. Portents prior to Leuctra at Thebes, Sparta, Delphi, and Dodona (67)
i. Warnings to Romans (69)
    (1) The oracle of Veii
    (2) Aius Locutius
    (3) Juno Moneta

49b Sed quoniam de extis . . . tota haruspicina sit pertractata: With these words, Marcus turns to the third division of soothsaying, the interpretation of prodigies; cf. on §§28–99. **ostenta:** See on §26b *fin.*

mulae partus prolatus est . . . non esse mirandum: Quintus had reported at 1.36 on *partus hic mulae*, where *hic* suggests a fairly recent occurrence. In fact, the most recent attested example occurred in the year 50 and was interpreted (by the haruspices, according to Quintus) as a possible portent of disaster; cf. Obseq. 65: *L. Paulo C. Marcello consulibus mula pariens discordiam civium, bonorum interitum, mutationem legum, turpes matronarum partus significavit*; cf. MacBain 1982, 103 (prodigy list for the relevant period); for the reported occurrences cf. Wülker 1903, 15–16. This was considered an impossibility (*adynaton*) and hence to portend a severe disturbance of the world-order; cf. Rosenberger 1998, 104–5 and 107–9; Rosenberger in Rüpke and Belayche 2004–6, 86; Rosenberger 2007, 295. Attentiveness to portents tended to be heightened at times of anxiety (cf. §58). This is the first of the portents discussed by Marcus that clustered around the recent civil war; a desire to come to terms with these may have been one motive for Cicero's composition of *Div.*; see above 19–20. **propterea quia non saepe fit:** *propterea quia* is found elsewhere in Cicero only at *Fin.* 1.53. In general, such double causal expressions were eschewed by Cicero after his early speeches but reappear in his late *philosophica*; cf. von Albrecht 2003, 100. Marcus' argument here is based upon a distinction between the rare and the impossible (see above on §48 [the "Venus throw"]) and reflects Chrysippus' position (§61). Though a mule, the offspring of a donkey stallion and horse mare, is almost always sterile, there are cases of such births; they may cause wonderment because of their rarity (*res mirabilis propterea quia non saepe fit*) but are not impossible. Hence Marcus formulates a principle that would apply "against all prodigies" (*contra omnia ostenta*), since the assumption is that these are unnatural occurrences (cf. §50a: *contra naturam*).

causarum enim ignoratio . . . ostentum esse censet: Here Marcus adds another factor, ignorance, into the mix. Quintus had professed ignorance of the causes of the phenomena he discussed and claimed that such knowledge was unnecessary (cf. on §46 [*multa verba fecisti . . . ad rem pertinere*]). Here Marcus shows how such ignorance contributes to superstitious thinking. One may be ignorant of the precise process of a mare's foaling, but since this is a commonplace occurrence, it causes no wonderment. But since the mule's foaling is a rarity, that fact plus the ignorance of the process leads to wonderment and hence the classification as an *ostentum*.

49b–50a utrum igitur . . . partus prope necessarius: Had he revised more carefully before publishing, Cicero might have wished to delete this argument, claiming that the *ostentum* is at the moment of conception, not parturition, since it goes against his previous, stronger claim that something that can occur is not an *ostentum* at all.

50b Sed quid plura? . . . quid habeat auctoritatis iudicabimus: *quid plura?* is a formula found eleven times in Cicero's corpus for cutting an argument short (cf., e.g., §99). Quintus had mentioned the *Etruscorum . . . et haruspicini et fulgurales et tonitruales libri* (1.72; cf. Guillaumont 1986, 128 and n. 97), but not their origin. This was reserved for Marcus' speech, since the story of Tages lends itself to ridicule. The insertion of this digression into the middle of the discussion of prodigies has been criticized (by Sander 1908, 15–17). Though the eschewing of rigid structures may be part of the charm of this "easy-going dialogue," as Pease (1920–23, 435) argued, it is surprising that at §§53 *fin.*–54 he proceeds as if *ostenta* were a fresh topic; see ad §53 *fin.* **quid . . . auctoritatis:** see above §8 *fin.*

Tages quidam dicitur . . . qui arabat: *Tages* is the new focus, while *quidam* shows that Roman readers are not expected to know the name. The story of the miraculous appearance of the man-child Tages and his revelation of the Etruscan prophetic lore is at first narrated in simple style, then subjected to criticism. The testimonies for Tages were collected by Thulin 1906, 3–6, and subjected to critical scrutiny by Wood 1980, who argues that Cicero distorts for polemical purposes; cf. Leighton 2004, 75–78. In the meantime Wood's identification, followed by Leighton, of Tages and Tarchon on a mirror from Tuscania has been exploded by Cristofani 1985. **dicitur** carefully distances Marcus from the anecdote. **cum . . . sulcus altius esset impressus:** This adds a realistic cause not found in other versions of the story. **cum terra araretur . . . eum . . . qui arabat:** The imperfect is the appropriate tense for an action that was in progress but interrupted by a specific occurrence (expressed by the perfect infinitives *extitisse* and *adfatus esse*); cf. Pinkster 2015, 420. **qui arabat:** The descriptive relative clause is replaced by *bubulcus* in the next sentence; cf. §§35–36a, where *is qui impetrire velit* is taken up by *immolator*. This figure is identified by John Lydus (sixth cent.: *Ost.* 3) with Tarchon, a companion, son, or brother of Tyrrhenus, the founder of Tarquinii.

is autem Tages . . . haruspicinae disciplina contineretur: Though Cicero names his source as "the books of the Etruscans," he evidently knew no Etruscan. He may, however, have gained some knowledge of their contents from three of his friends: (1) A. Caecina, son of the homonymous client whom Cicero defended (probably) in 69; he participated on Pompey's side in the civil war and wrote a pamphlet attacking Caesar; exiled in the sequel, he corresponded with Cicero, who tried to procure his recall (cf. *Fam.* 6.6[234], 6.8[235], and 6.7[237]); for his writings on divination, cf. Hohti 1975, 427–29; on his family in general, cf. Ramelli 2003, 196–98; (2) P. Nigidius Figulus, a polymath who counseled Cicero during his consulate (Plut. *Cic.* 30.3) and later also opposed Caesar in the civil war; in the aftermath, in spite of Cicero's efforts to procure his recall (*Fam.* 4.13[225]), he died in exile; the translation Cicero produced from the *Timaeus* was part of a project meant to honor Nigidius' memory (*Tim.* 1); Lydus (*Ost.* p. 110.6–10 Wachsm.) cites Nigidius for some lore about earthquakes from Tages; cf. Rawson 1985, 309–12, who doubts this information but allows that some of the Nigidian material "may possibly already have been in an Etruscan source" (312); for Nigidius' extant fragments, cf. Liuzzi 1983; (3) Varro, from whom Censorinus (4.13) may have his information on Tages. See further Guillaumont 1986, 122–25, who also considers Tarquitius Priscus, used as a source by Pliny but not known to have been available to Cicero. For writings on Etruscan divination known to Romans, see in general Harris 1971, 5–6. **clamoremque maiorem** "a loud shout," the comparative being used in Latin to express an intense quality without necessarily having an explicit *comparandum*; cf. Pinkster 2015, 47. **concursum esse factum:** English requires a personal construction: "people made a beeline." **totam . . . Etruriam:** The concept is underlined by the long-range hyperbaton (cf. Powell 2010, 174–76). Wood 1980, 342, doubts this picture "of 'all Etruria' rushing to the summons of a peasant bellow." **tum illum plura locutum multis audientibus:** Wood 1980, 342, notes that this description "contradicts everything we know of the aristocratic control exercised over divination in early Italy." **exceperint litterisque mandarint** "they took down and published": *OLD* s.v. *excipio* 6. Weinstock 1950, 45–46, suspects that with the Tages legend "an old story" was "used to lend authenticity to recent apocryphal writings."

eam postea crevisse . . . illa principia referendis "it afterward expanded by accrual of new knowledge compared against the same first principles." Interesting that, in spite of the existence of a revelation contained in authoritative sacred books, the *disciplina* was not thought of as a closed system but one open to further development.

haec accepimus . . . fontem habent disciplinae: The previous reference (*ut in libris est Etruscorum*) is reinforced by this tricolon with anaphora of a form of *hic.* **ab ipsis**, i.e., the Etruscans themselves, not merely secondhand reports; cf. *OLD* s.v. *ipse* 5.

51 Num ergo opus est . . . num Epicuro?: Upon the recital of the origin of the haruspical lore follows the devastating critique. For "railroading" *num*, cf. on §9. As early as 1.7 Carneades appeared as the primary adversary of divination; Epicurus is paired with him at 1.62, 109, etc.; see above on §40 *fin.*

estne quisquam . . . deum dicam an hominem?: Cf. *N.D.* 1.123 (of Epicurus, supposed to have retained the gods only to avert ill will): *neque enim tam desipiens fuisset ut homunculi similem deum fingeret . . .* ; for the "subjunctive of tendency" cf. §19 (*nisi quod . . . rato tempore*). To have been "dug up by a plough" (*exaratum*) is a problem whether one assumes that Tages was divine or human, as Marcus goes on to argue, such use of dilemmas being characteristic of Cicero's speeches (especially in his weaker cases); cf. Craig 1993.

si deum, cur . . . superiore e loco tradere?: The Romans distinguished sharply between the gods of cult, thought of as residing in heaven (hence often referred to as *caelites*; cf. *OLD* s.v. *caeles* 2), and the chthonic deities of the underworld. Thus Tages, dug up from the earth, confounds the usual categories. One would expect Tages, "as a god" (*deus*, a complement) to expound his teaching from a higher position (vis-à-vis humans), corresponding to the hierarchical relationship, just as a magistrate would take his seat on a platform (the *tribunal*) when he performed public duties; cf. *Ver.* 2.1.14: *hanc ego causam cum agam . . . de loco superiore*; cf. Krostenko 2000, 359.

si autem homo . . . ipse didicisse?: Tages the human raises no less daunting problems, viz., his survival underground and the source of his teachings. *homo* (predicate) is the new focus. **ille Tages** is anaphoric: "the aforementioned Tages." **ipse** effects a contrast to the "others," who received his teachings: *OLD* s.v. *ipse* 1.

sed ego insipientior . . . contra eos tam diu disputem: With barely concealed disgust, Marcus upbraids his own folly in indulging in so lengthy a refutation, *insipientior* taking up the preceding *desipiens*.

vetus autem illud Catonis . . . haruspicem cum vidisset: Cato's remark had become a "winged word" (Cicero cited it without attribution at *N.D.* 1.71). Its original context unknown, it has been assigned to his *apophthegmata* (p. 109 no. 65 Iordan); cf. Pavis d'Escurac 1981, 31; Blänsdorf 1991, 53; for its implications for the Roman mentality in the late Republic, cf. Engels 2007, 779–80. It went on to be a favorite of the English deists; see above 37 and Gawlick 1963, 664n16. Cato also issued the warning: *haruspicem augurum hariolum Chaldaeum ne quem consuluisse velit* (sc. *vilicus*: *Agr.* 5.4), whereby he seems to be thinking of the mercenary haruspices criticized by Quintus at 1.132 (see Schultz 2014 ad loc.). Reports of deceit practiced by the haruspices on their Roman clients suggest tensions between the two groups; see further MacBain 1982, 53–56; Briquel 1986, 76–78; Briquel 2014, 118–20.

52a quota enim quaeque . . . casu id evenerit?: Marcus draws his conclusion about the *auctoritas* of the teachings (cf. §50b *init.*): its predictions seldom come true, and when they do, do so by chance, a strong position; cf. Hankinson 1988, 146–48. *quotus quisque* "in what proportion to the total is each person who (i.e., there are few people who)": *OLD* s.v. *quotus* 2a.   **quid adferri potest** "what reason can be adduced." As Cicero well knew, it is virtually impossible to exclude chance by proving such a negative.

52b–53 As a test for the proposition just stated, Marcus offers examples in which commanders defied or acted in accord with the advice of diviners, with results opposite to the predictions.

52b Rex Prusias . . . imperatori veteri credere?': After his defeat, Rome's great adversary Hannibal was successively in exile at the court of Antiochus the Great (195–190) and Prusias I of Bithynia (until 183/82). This anecdote was also referred to Antiochus (Plut. *De exilio* 16 = *mor.* 606c); V. Max. 3.7 ext. 6 depends on our passage. If Prusias was the monarch in question, the reference will be to the war he waged (and lost) against Eumenes II of Pergamum (187–183); see further C. Habicht, *CAH* 8:325 and 328. The anecdote could thus have been cited in support of divination, but Marcus chooses to focus on Hannibal's contemptuous dismissal of divinatory signs: "Really? . . . Would you rather place your trust in a bit of calf's flesh than a seasoned commander?" For the contemptuous diminutive (*caruncula*, previously attested at Var. *Men.* 31: *sed quidvis potius homo quam caruncula* *nostra* [sc. *perficiet* or the like]), cf. §33b (*musculorum iecuscula*). Belief in divination was firmly rooted in Asia Minor (cf. 1.25; *Leg.* 2.33); hence the hesitancy of a monarch such as Prusias or Deiotarus (1.26–27, §§20, 78–79) to act contrary to omens.

quid, ipse Caesar . . . adversariorum copiae convenissent: Cf. Suet. *Jul.* 59, including ritual detail: *cum immolanti aufugisset hostia, profectionem adversus Scipionem et Iubam non distulit.* **a summo haruspice:** A unique combination. The epithet is clearly meant to mark this man as authoritative and not a mere *vicanus haruspex* (1.132), but is he the formal head of the *ordo haruspicum*? That is unclear, and indeed it is uncertain whether the haruspices were already organized as a formal body in Rome at this time (§11, which speaks of their being summoned from Etruria for consultation, suggests not; our first indication that they were so organized is Tac. *An.* 11.15: Claudius reporting to the senate *super collegio haruspicum*; cf. also *CIL* VI 2161 [second or third cent. CE], our other dated reference; other [undated] inscriptions are cited by Pease ad loc.). It has been suspected that this might have been Spurinna, the haruspex whose interaction with Caesar at another sacrifice was recounted at 1.119: see Rawson 1991, 307–10; Haack 2003, 56, but also the contrary view of Thulin 1905–9, 3:135. **ante brumam** could be taken as "before winter" or "before the winter solstice." According to *BAfr.* 1.4, Caesar embarked on December 25, the traditional Roman date of the solstice. The matter is complicated, however, by the fact that Caesar's reform of the calendar had not yet been implemented, so that December 25 would have corresponded to July 9 Julian; hence in that sense his departure was indeed *ante brumam*; cf. Pelling 2011, 400–401. For Caesar's defiance of omens on other occasions, cf. on §37 and Suet. *Jul.* 81.4. **quod ni fecisset . . . adversariorum copiae convenisset:** The juncture was effected later; cf. *BAfr.* 20.2: *audiebat enim Scipionem . . . adpropinquare, copias suas cum Labieno et Petreio coniungere.*

quid ego haruspicum responsa . . . aut contrarios?: This confirms the point of §52a about the fewness of the haruspices' successful predictions; similarly §53 and (about the astrologers) §99.

53 hoc civili bello . . . ad ostenta veniamus: *hoc* = "this last, the recent": *OLD* s.v. *hic* 3a; similarly 1.36 *partus hic mulae* with n. on §49b (*mulae partus*). The many false predictions surrounding the civil war may have been one of the motives for the composition of this work; see above 19–20. **di immortales:** Such colloquial oaths lend force to an assertion; cf. Hofmann 2003, 139; similarly §§114 (*per deos atque homines*) and 136b (*per deos inmortalis*). **quam multa luserunt** "how many of them proved deceptive":

OLD s.v. *ludo* 9b. **etenim ille . . . ostentis movebatur:** Unlike the omens given to Caesar, such reports may have contributed to the overconfidence of Pompey's officers, which Cicero did not share (*Att.* 11.4a[214]; *Fam.* 7.3[183].2), and may have led him to commit to battle rashly at Pharsalus; cf. Seager 2002, 166–67; Haack 2003, 61 and n. 85.

non lubet commemorare . . . ad ostenta veniamus: *tibi praesertim, qui interfuisti:* Cf. on §27 *fin.* (*iis praesertim*). Though alone of the family members Quintus did not urge adhesion to Pompey in the civil war, he followed his brother's lead (*Att.* 9.6[172].4; 11.12[223].2) and, like his brother, abandoned the Pompeian cause after Pharsalus, taking up residence in Greece (ibid. 11.11[222].2). **vides tamen omnia . . . dicta sint evenisse:** An even more negative emphasis than above (*quae aut nullos habuerint exitus aut contrarios*: §52b *fin.*). **sed haec hactenus:** A common formula for concluding a topic in less formal writing (twenty-three times in Cicero's treatises and letters). **nunc ad ostenta veniamus:** As if he had not already broached the topic at §49b! Timpanaro (1988, 358) suggested inserting <*rursum*> before *ad ostenta*, but this does not go to the root of the problem, since the next sentences include the acts of Cicero's consulship as one of the topics that he will discuss individually, when, in fact, he already did so at §§45b–47. It seems clear that here, as elsewhere, the text still betrays hasty composition and publication.

54 Multa me consule . . . a Callisthene commemorata dixisti: *multa me consule* is a shorthand for *multa quae me consule evenerunt* (Timpanaro 1988, 358). In this tricolon with anaphora of *multa*, Marcus summarizes the major prodigies and the authorities for them cited by Quintus: (1) the prodigies surrounding his own consulship, cited from the *Cons.* (1.17–22); (2) the prodigies narrated by the historian Sisenna in the run-up to the Social War (1.99 = *FRH* 26 F 6); (3) the prodigies recorded by the Greek historian Callisthenes before the battle of Leuctra (371), at which the Thebans broke the Spartan hegemony (1.74 = *FGrH* 124 F 22). **Marsicum bellum** is the way the Romans regularly referred to the Social War (so already at 1.99 and later at §59), since the Marsi were the prime movers of the war once it had flared up at the Picene town of Asculum; cf. Rosenberger 1992, 35–37.

de quibus dicam . . . de universis: Marcus agrees to discuss Quintus' examples individually but will first reflect on them collectively. This ignores, however, the remarks on what constitutes an *ostentum* at §49b as well as the implications of the foundation of the *disciplina Etrusca* by Tages at §§50b–51; and the events of Cicero's consulship were already discussed; cf. on §53 *fin.*

quae est enim ista . . . quae cavere nequeamus?: *ista . . . significatio et quasi denuntiatio*: *ista* keeps Quintus involved as the sponsor of the view (cf. on §21), and the hyperbaton lends emphasis. *significatio* ("indication") is neutral, but *denuntiatio* ("warning": *OLD* s.v. 1b) adds force (hence *quasi*), since Marcus focuses only on signs portending disasters (*calamitates*), not successes. He thus takes up the argument from §§22–25 (and the assumption that the outcome is unalterable). Marcus raises two objections, of which he discusses the second, the inevitability of the outcome, first. For perspicuity, the transposition of Lambin (1581) is adopted, so that the first *ea* is moved from after *volunt* so as to follow *primum*. **di inmortales** is a common combination, since *di* alone was felt to carry insufficient weight. **sine interpretibus:** At §131 Marcus takes this literally, illustrating the point with a striking analogy.

at hoc ne homines quidem . . . cautio adiungitur: *homines . . . probi* "decent people," whose behavior could serve as a model; for similar focus on *viri boni*, cf. *Off.* 3.17–18. **nullo modo** "by no means"; cf. on §24 *init.* If it is approved for human beings, such as physicians, to withhold prediction of an outcome that is dire but inevitable, this should apply *a fortiori* to the gods. Such advice is only acceptable if accompanied by a warning (*cautio*), i.e., if the outcome can be averted. But Quintus might, of course, have replied that the gods stand in a different relation to human beings and have no need to exercise tact. Cf. also Krostenko 2000, 358.

55a quid igitur aut ostenta . . . nuper nostros adiuverunt?: *Lacedaemonios olim . . . nuper nostros*: The Greek and Roman examples are held in chiastic balance of temporal adverbs and substantives. The Spartans at Leuctra are again cited as parallel to the Roman experience at *Off.* 2.26–28. The warnings to the Spartans prior to Leuctra did them no good; Quintus might, however, have countered that they could have done, had they been heeded. As to the prodigies during the recent civil war, as so far narrated, they encouraged the Pompeians, and so may have helped lead that army to disaster.

quae si signa deorum . . . si ea sciri nolebant: Marcus takes up the other objection from §54, that the gods' messages, if such they are, are obscure: he poses the alternatives that they should either be crystal clear if the gods want them to be understood or not transmitted at all if they are not meant to be understood. Marcus complains similarly about the ambiguity of dreams at §§132–33. **si enim:** Sc. *volebant*, the positive counterpart of the following *nolebant*; it is possible, however, that *volebant* dropped out prior to *ut* **aut ne occulte quidem:** Sc. *declarari oportebat.*

55b Iam vero coniectura . . . anceps reperitur oratio: *Iam vero* marks the transition to a new point: "Moreover." Appended to the complaint about the obscurity of the divine messages is this aside, in which Cicero calls upon his experience as a litigator to clarify the nature of reasoning based upon *coniectura*. According to the doctrine of στάσις or *status* of Hermagoras of Temnos (ca. 150 BCE), a *causa coniecturalis* ("case based upon inference") was one in which the fact of the crime was denied. Two *coniecturae* were therefore in contention, that of the prosecutor and that of the defense, as to what occurred; cf. *Rhet. Her.* 1.10.18; in general, Lausberg 1990, §§150–65. Since divination rests upon inference (*coniectura . . . in qua nititur divinatio*), like a legal issue, it lends itself to being argued several different ways (*anceps reperitur oratio*); cf. Allen 2001, 167. At §§144–45 Marcus offers some striking examples (drawn from dream-interpretation).

55c Quas autem res . . . causas rerum non quaerere "It is a great piece of folly to make the gods responsible for the things that sometimes nature, sometimes chance brings about—the similarity sometimes gives rise to error—and fail to search for their causes." The matter in dashes relieves Marcus of the need to choose between these two factors. *effector*, first attested at *De orat.* 1.150, may have been Cicero's coinage (he has eight of the fourteen attestations in Classical Latin; of later classical authors, only Quintilian and Servius used the word); here it enables him to avoid use of *causa* twice in the sentence. An anonymous reader deleted *rerum* before *non quaerere* in the margin of Lambin's 1581 edition, perhaps rightly. For Marcus, then, divination, with its insistence on divine causation, shortcircuits the search for causes; in the sequel nature and chance will compete with divine intervention as the appropriate explanation of the phenomena adduced by Quintus. Cf. *Fat.* 6: *quid ergo adtinet inculcare fatum, cum sine fato ratio omnium rerum ad naturam fortunamve referatur?*

56 tu vates Boeotios . . . canere victores: An instance of what Marcus has in mind, introduced, as often, in asyndeton (see, e.g., Dyck 1996 on *Off.* 1.36). Marcus cross-refers to Quintus' report at 1.74 that cocks crowing during a rite at the sanctuary of Trophonius at Lebadia led the Boeotian seers to prophesy a Theban victory at Leuctra on the ground that the birds crow when victorious. (On Trophonius and the ritual in his honor, cf. Schultz 2014 ad loc.) Cicero produces a chiastic contrast of attributes and behaviors (*victi silere . . . canere victores*).

hoc igitur per gallinas . . . signum dabat?: An interesting sentence, exhibiting what Powell (2010, 177–78) calls double-focus hyperbaton, i.e., *hoc . . . signum* is focused, but so, too, is *per gallinas*, conveying a tone of incredulity and contempt (indicated, perhaps, by the substitution of *gallinas* "hens" for *galli* above; cf. Timpanaro 1988, 360), especially since *per gallinas* is juxtaposed with *Iuppiter*, Cicero exploiting the incongruous juxtaposition of high and low (reinforced by *tantae civitati*) to assist the work of persuasion.

an illae aves . . . nocturnum vel diurnum?: Marcus queries whether the general pattern claimed (i.e., that the birds crow when victorious) is relevant here. Quintus retorts, "But this is a prodigy," i.e., a supernatural sign. Marcus will have none of it, however, retorting sarcastically (*quasi pisces, non galli cecinerint*) and claiming per contra that cocks are liable to crow at any time of day or night, the frequentative *canto* perhaps containing a hint of annoyance.

quodsi victores alacritate . . . qua ad cantum moverentur: Marcus hesitates to apply *laetitia*, usually thought of as a human emotion (cf. *Tusc.* 4.11–12 etc.), to fowl, first deploying *alacritas* ("liveliness, enthusiasm") and then attaching the apologetic *quasi*. The point is that victory is only one of the conceivable stimuli that could produce such vocal activity. **laetitia . . . alia . . . laetitia:** A subtle semantic shift from "joy" to "source of joy": *OLD* s.v. 1a vs. b.

57 Democritus quidem . . . quiete satiatos = 68 A 158 D.-K. As at §30 above, Democritus offers a down-to-earth explanation and this time wins Marcus' approval (*optumis verbis*). As our passage shows, *pectus* as a receptacle for food can refer to a bird's crop (*OLD* s.v. 2a). **mitificato** "softened" appears only here in Cicero. **cantus edere quiete satiatos** "they have had sleep enough and begin to crow" (tr. Falconer).

qui quidem . . . plausuque premunt alas': *silentio noctis* ("in the silence of night") is sometimes taken to be part of the Ennian quotation. **favent faucibus . . . plausuque premunt alas** "they indulge their russet throats / in song and ply their wings with flapping" (tr. Goldberg and Manuwald, *FRL* Ennius *inc.* F 161, modified = 344–45 J.), two anapaestic dimeters from an unknown tragedy, the first incomplete at the beginning.

cum igitur hoc animal . . . vel casus efficere potuisset?: *canorus* ("songful, vocal") is first applied to birds in our passage (*OLD* s.v. 2a; *TLL* 3:277.59–60). **sua sponte** "on its own, unprompted"; cf. §49a. **quid in mentem venit Callistheni?** "how did Callisthenes get the idea?," his source again substituting for Quintus as the target. See on §54 *init.* **signum . . . cantandi** "the signal to sing"; cf. Caes. *Gal.* 2.21.3: *proeli committendi signum* *dedit.* **cum id vel natura vel casus efficere potuisset:** The alternative explanatory models (cf. §55c) are preferred as more economical; this will be Marcus' general approach to Quintus' examples.

58 Sanguine[m] pluisse . . . deorum sudasse simulacra: Summary of Quintus' claims at 1.98: *quid, cum Cumis Apollo sudavit, Capuae Victoria . . . quid, quod fluvius Atratus sanguine fluxit, quid, cum . . . sanguinis nonnumquam . . . imber defluxit.* Blood prodigies were regularly taken to portend war; cf. Rosenberger 1998, 101. For the attestations of a rain of blood, cf. Wülker 1903, 11; Rosenberger 1998, 118 and n. 161; see ibid. 35 on the rain of blood as one of a limited number of preset cultural patterns to which people tended to adjust their perceptions. For blood in water, Wülker 1903, 13 (the Atratus river—if this is correctly interpreted as a proper name and not the word for "black"—is not attested elsewhere); for sweating statues, cf. Schultz 2014 on 1.74.

num censes his nuntiis . . . crediturum fuisse?: For "railroading" *num*, cf. on §9 (*earumne quae sensibus perciperentur*). **Thalen aut Anaxagoran:** In his treatises, Cicero tends to prefer the Greek accusative endings for Greek names. Once again, the criterion is what a natural philosopher (*physicus*) would find credible, these two being singled out as the most famous; cf. §§33b, 37, 43b.

nec enim sanguis nec sudor . . . sudorem videtur imitari: As at §37 (*sine corde non potuisse bovem vivere*), Marcus begins with a point of physiology. On this basis, he denies that the phenomena are prodigies and offers alternative explanations. *decoloratio* ("a change of color") is first attested here, possibly coined *ad hoc*. Here *contagio* has the literal sense "contact involving some influence on the object touched" (cf. *OLD* s.v. 1), whereas at §33b Cicero had tried it out as an equivalent for *sympatheia.* **in tectoriis** "in the case of stucco buildings" (*OLD* s.v. *tectorium*); for the full form, *opus tectorium*, cf. *Leg.* 2.65. **austro** "when the south wind is blowing," the plain abl. being used very freely of time; cf. examples at Pinkster 2015, 835–37; Cat. *Agr.* 31.2: *vento austro caveto ne quam materiam . . . tractes.* This wind was known for its moisture; cf. Gel. 2.22.14.

atque haec in bello . . . tum finguntur inpunius: As in the case of the mule's foaling (§49b), there is also a psychological angle: there it was ignorance plus the rarity of the event that sparked wonder, here it is the presence of war and its attendant anxiety that amplifies, creating more and larger prodigies and making them more credible (and thus also giving greater scope to invention);

cf. Livy 21.62.1: *Romae aut circa urbem multa ea hieme prodigia facta aut, quod evenire solet motis semel in religionem animis, multa nuntiata et temere credita sunt.* See further Rosenberger 1998, 32–35. **timentibus:** Dative after *videntur*. The substantivized participle bears weight by virtue of its final position in its clause and its rhythm (with *-tur* it forms a cretic + iamb); similarly §24 (*exitus suos cogitantibus*), where see note.

59 nos autem ita leves . . . monstrum putemus: This sentence is sometimes taken to be a question, but the question mark should ordinarily be reserved for sentences containing an explicit marker (*non, nonne, num*, or an interrogrative word); if this is taken as a statement, *nos* will be "we humans" generally. **leves atque inconsiderati** "shallow and unreflective." Romans would not wish to have these predicates attached to them, since they prized *gravitas* and careful deliberation (cf., e.g., *Off.* 1.81). **quorum est opus hoc unum:** Said with mock solemnity. The argument is similar to that apropos of chickens above (§56): an occurrence so common and natural can hardly be viewed as a portent (*monstrum*).

ante vero Marsicum bellum . . . scuta an cribra corroserint!: The climactic item in Quintus' list from Sisenna of prodigies preceding the Social War (for the designation *Marsicum bellum*, cf. on §54 *init.*): *et Lanuvii clipeos—quod haruspicibus tristissumum visum esset—a muribus esse derosos* (1.99). The dilapidated condition of the shields—the neglect possibly related to the building at Rome of the temple of Juno Sospita vowed by C. Cornelius Cethegus (cos. 197; Livy 32.30.10)—could be seen as symbolic of the fraying alliance between Rome and its allies; cf. Garofalo 2019, 47–48. **rossent:** See Timpanaro 1988, 361–62, who shows that this (not *rosissent*) must count as the transmitted text (corrupted to *possent* in the oldest witnesses) and is in line with Cicero's contraction of the pluperfect subjunctive elsewhere. **mures . . . rodentes:** The participial phrase with enclosed adverbial modifier and direct object carries considerable weight in this sentence, the increased exploitation of the active participle being characteristic of Cicero's late style; cf. Laughton 1964, 45. **diem noctem** "night and day"; cf. §56: *tempus . . . nocturnum vel diurnum* of the roosters' habitual activity.

nam si ista sequimur . . . cariorem fore: *ista* "those notions" (with a note of contempt; cf. *OLD* s.v. *iste* 3). **Platonis Politian** "Plato's *Republic*," the fate of the book being taken as an allegory for that of the (Roman) Republic, about which Cicero so often expressed anxiety; cf. testimonies cited by Meier 1966, 1–2. **Epicuri de voluptate liber:** Epicurus probably never wrote a work

On Pleasure (it is not attested elsewhere). Speaking with tongue in cheek, Cicero adopts his opponents' caricature of Epicurus as the "philosopher of the belly" (cf. testimonies collected at Epicur. fr. 409 Usener; Görler 1974, 69–71), the assumption being that "Epicurean pleasure" stands for the pleasures of the table and hence their disappearance symbolizes a scarcity of food and rise in the price of grain.

60 An vero illa . . . ex homine nata dicuntur?: Marcus has already addressed one example, the mule's foaling, at §49b; here he broadens to unusual births in general, human as well as animal, since both kinds were held to be prodigies; see in general Allély 2003; on the treatment of hermaphrodites in particular (cf. 1.98), Brisson 2002. *portentosus* "unnatural, abnormal" is first used here in its literal sense, Cicero having abused Clodius as a *portentosa pestis* at *Dom.* 72: *OLD* s.v. a; *TLL* 10.2: 277.59–60. Though *pecus* is ordinarily used of a farm animal, the word also serves to designate an animal in general, as opposed to a human; cf. *OLD* s.v. *pecus*[2] 2. At §149, in the list of terrors that beset human life (and that this discourse is meant to eliminate), the climactic item is *si ostenti simile natum factumve quippiam.*

quorum omnium . . . non possit existere: *ne sim longior* is a type of formula Cicero uses to cut discussion short; cf., e.g., *N.D.* 1.56: *vereor ne longior fuerim.* The point about a natural cause is repeated from §37. As in the argument about the mule's foaling (§49b), Marcus opposes what is *praeter consuetudinem* to what is *praeter naturam*, the two being often confused in the popular imagination.

causam igitur . . . naturae ratione dispellito: *causam* is taken up from the previous sentence and focalized. Marcus lays out a plan of procedure that follows from the above (*igitur*) in three stages, each marked by a *-to* imperative characteristic of legal language (see further Dyck 2004b on *Leg.* 1.16 with literature): *investigato . . . exploratum habeto . . . depellito.* **exploratum habeto** "consider (it) certain" or "established": *OLD* s.v. *exploratum* 1. **nihil fieri potuisse sine causa:** Cf. on §37 (*aut ex nihilo oriatur aut in nihilum subito occidat*). **eumque errorem quem tibi rei novitas attulerit:** I.e., the error of thinking it a divine prodigy. *terrorem* (Lambin) is sometimes adopted, e.g., by Pease, but Ax rightly defends the transmitted text with reference to §49b: *causarum . . . ignoratio in re nova*; cf. also §85 *ad errorem;* §119: *similis est error in somniis.* **naturae ratione:** this is Cicero's rendering of Gk. φυσιολογία (cf. 1.90; *N.D.* 1.20), i.e., "inquiry into natural causes and phenomena" (LSJ s.v.). *depello* ("drive away") is par excellence a military term, but Cicero saw and exploited its potential application to abstract ideas and attitudes; cf. *Tusc.* 3.25: *nunc aegritudinem, si possumus, depellamus*; *OLD* s.v. 7a. *(rati)one depellito* secures the double cretic.

ita te nec terrae . . . nec faces visae terrebunt: A summary of common prodigies, all previously mentioned: earthquake (1.18 and 35); a division of the sky (1.97); a rain of stones or blood (1.98, §58); a shooting star (*traiectio stellae*: 1.2; cf. §16); a comet or meteor (1.18, 97; cf. Timpanaro 1988, CI). There is a similar but more extensive list, after Cleanthes (*SVF* 1:528), at *N.D.* 2.14.

61 quarum <rerum> omnium causas . . . quam sapientem fuisse: A cunning argument, citing Chrysippus ("that very sponsor of divination"; cf. 1.6 = *SVF* 2:1187) as his key witness. Here Marcus' strategy becomes visible: to divide "technical" from "natural" divination, attacking the former first and finding an ally in Chrysippus, whom Quintus had cited for examples of natural divination (1.37, 39) as well as general arguments supporting divination (1.82–83 = *SVF* 2:1192). The Stoics were committed to the view that physical events such as the ones regarded as portents had antecedent physical causes. Hence Chrysippus, too, would search for physical causes for such events, just as the *physici* do; cf. the similar argument apropos of thunder and lightning at §44. What Marcus does not say here is that Chrysippus also held a theory of fate such that the causes of future events become accessible to inspired prophets or in dreams (1.125–26, explored further in *De fato*). **nihil enim fieri sine causa . . . quod fieri non potest:** Cf. §37, restated at §60. **sapientem esse portentum est:** The Stoics formulated the sage (*sapiens*) as an ethical ideal but emphasized that he appeared very rarely: *SVF* 3:167.34: there have been only one or two; comparing the phoenix, Sen. *Ep.* 42.1 says one may be born every five hundredth year.

illa igitur ratio concluditur . . . nullum esse portentum: *concludere rationem* = "formulate a syllogism" (for a different sense, cf. §25); cf. examples at Merguet 1887–94, 1:474a (the expression is misunderstood here by Schäublin 1987, 185n13). The mention of the famous Stoic may have prompted Marcus to couch his argument in syllogistic form, which he uses sparingly in his philosophical writing; cf., e.g., *Leg.* 1.23, 33, 2.12; *Fin.* 3.27; *Off.* 2.10; see further MacKendrick 1989, index s.v. syllogism.

62a quod etiam coniector quidam . . . quod fieri posset ostentum: Since Plautus (*Poen.* 444), *coniector*, agent noun to *conicio* and related to the noun of process *coniectura* (see Zellmer 1976, 180–82), designates the professional dream-interpreter (though the area could still be specified, as at §123: *a* *coniectore somniorum*; cf. on §§13 and 15 above). Marcus draws confirmation for his conclusion (*nec quod potuerit id portentum esse: §61*) from this "floating anecdote" elsewhere attributed to the Spartan king Leotychidas, son of Ariston (Plut. *Apophth. Lacon. Leotych.* 2 = *mor.* 224e), or, perhaps secondarily, Diogenes the Cynic (Clem. Al. *Strom.* 7.25.1). The least plausible attribution is Cicero's, to a *coniector*, a figure alluded to several times by Quintus (1.45, 72, 132). For a *coniector*, having a professional interest in fostering a belief in divination, would hardly be expected to take so skeptical a line. In Plutarch's version, the seers (μάντεις) are the ones who declare the phenomenon a portent, only to be contradicted by Leotychidas; has Cicero perhaps confused or misremembered this? For *non inscite*, cf. on §30 *init.* **ei qui [cum] ad eum rettulisset:** *cum* was omitted by Davies; one suspects that *ei qui* and *cum* were variants that both wound up in the text. **quod anguis . . . circumiectus fuisset** "that a snake had wrapped itself around a bar in his house." **hoc ille responso:** The demonstrative serves as the focused host of the weak *ille* with resulting division of the phrase *hoc responso*; cf. Adams 1994b, 122–24 and 132–36. **nihil habendum . . . ostentum:** Emphasis falls on the strong negative *nihil* and *ostentum*; the cretic plus trochee rounds off the argument.

62b C. Gracchus ad M. Pomponium . . . quid esset futurum: Not mentioning that this example was cited by Quintus (1.36), Marcus provides the source (C. Gracchus, *epist.* CXXII F 1a Cugusi = *FRH* 11 F 1) and subjects the facts to critical scrutiny. Gracchus will have consulted private haruspices (cf. on §51 *fin.*). The anecdote may be related to the Roman belief in the *genius*, the divine power associated with the head of the household, believed to come into existence at his birth and, originally, to perish at his death; the female counterpart was called the *iuno*; Wissowa 1912, 175–79, esp. 176–77, thought they took the form of snakes, but see the reservations of Flower 2017, 65 and n. 6. On the *genius*, see further Scheid 2003, 165–66; W.-A. Maharam, *BNP* s.v. Genius; Flower 2017 index s.v. *genius*; for the snake as a house-spirit, see Thompson 1955, B593.1. As in the case of the mule foaling, the roosters crowing, or the mice gnawing shields (§§49b, 54–57, 59), Marcus is prepared to allow only an unnatural occurrence to be considered a prodigy, not merely an unusual one. Marcus expresses surprise that Tiberius released either of the snakes if that inevitably entailed the death of either himself or his wife Cornelia. Given, however, that they must both eventually die anyway, Tiberius seized the opportunity to determine the order of death in the way he considered best for the family. **emissio** is first attested at *Tusc.* 2.57; cf. *TLL* s.v.

'At mors insecuta . . . quod futurum illi esse dixerint: Quintus is given a rejoinder, pointing to the fulfillment of the prediction (cf. §45b: '*At inventum est caput in Tiberi*'), but Marcus is unimpressed, insisting again on a rational explanation: *causa quidem, credo, aliqua morbi gravioris non emissione serpentis* "on account of a grave illness, I believe, not the release of the snake," with nonironic *credo*.

63 nam illud mirarer . . . loquitur Agamemnon: Marcus would marvel at (*mirarer*) the story told in the *Iliad* about Calchas' prediction of the number of years of the Trojan War based upon the number of sparrows devoured by a snake as witnessed by the Greek host assembled at Aulis, if he believed it, i.e., he would marvel at the supernatural element in the story, not the prediction; see below. Again, an example cited by Quintus (1.72) is traced more precisely to its source by Marcus, who, indeed, offers a rendering of the whole passage (*Iliad* 2.299–330 = Cic. fr. 23 Bl.). **loquitur Agamemnon:** For the "reproducing" use of the present, cf. Pinkster 2015, 398. Marcus errs in assigning the speech to Agamemnon, rather than Ulysses (perhaps he assumed that the supreme commander was presiding at the meeting, as a Roman consul would). Stroup 2010, 60, argues that the attribution to Agamemnon is a deliberate move by Cicero "to underline the tonal redirection that is involved in any appropriative act of 'translation,'" but it is hard to see how that point could be conveyed by the attribution alone. Nor is this an isolated example of an error in the hastily written *philosophica* of 45–44; cf. *De gloria* fr. 2 Garbarino (words of Hector, not Ajax), *Tusc.* 1.84 (confusion of Cleombrotus with Theombrotus) or 5.115 (mistaken paraphrase of Polyphemus' words to the ram); on §82 below. Cicero also, notoriously, misattributes a speaking part in one of his own dialogues at *Fam.* 7.32(113).2. See further Spahlinger 2005, 189–96. The commentary here will try to bring out the different sensibility underlying Cicero's version but will be relatively brief, since no knowledge of Greek is assumed; for more detailed notes, cf. Pease ad loc. and Chinnici 2000, 25–47.

1 viri: The Roman commander addresses the troops formally, whereas Odysseus calls them "friends" (φίλοι). What in Homer is a request to take out time to consider Calchas' prophecy becomes, in Cicero's hands, an exhortation to the troops to endure sufferings.

2 auguris: His name alone would apparently not identify Calchas for Roman readers; hence this *interpretatio Romana* of his function (cf. 1.87, *auguratum* just above, and §65: *auguratio*), since he based his prophecy on the observation of birds. But this narrows his scope compared to the Homeric figure, who was called upon to utter inspired prophecies in general (cf. *Il.* 1.85–87), i.e., he was a natural, not a systematic, diviner.

2–3 fata queamus / scire: Homer, as always, "eminently plain and direct" (Matthew Arnold [1905, 41]), simply says "so that we may know whether Calchas prophesies truly or not." Cicero, however, in his more elaborate poetic manner, adds a line here compared to his original. *fata* (the "predictions of fate" [Pease]), the subject of the dependent indirect question, is anticipated as the object of *queamus scire*, as often (cf. G–L §468, the so-called "consider the lilies how they grow" construction). **habeant** = "comprise" (*OLD* s.v. *habeo* 13). **ratos** "true" (ibid. s.v. *ratus* 2b), an augural term (1.85, §80). **pectoris orsus** "outpourings of his heart," the first attestation of *orsus*, a rare noun from *ordior* ("begin"); for the idea cf. *Cons.* F 10.28–29 Courtney (= 1.18): *vates oracla furenti / pectore fundebant.*

4 portentum mente retentant: Notable assonance of *-(t)ent/ant*; on the sound here and in the following verse, cf. Wilkinson 1963, 29. Instead of *retentant*, one might have expected first person plural, as in Homer, recalling a shared experience, but that would be harder to fit into a Latin hexameter.

5 qui non funestis liquerunt lumina fatis: A nice chiastic arrangement of liquids and fricatives. Here Homer has a reference to the *keres*, "the spirits that cut short the thread of man's life" (Greene 1944, 16). Unlike Homer, Cicero does not personify them carrying the dead away but renders them with the phrase *funesta fata*, a combination found nowhere else in Classical Latin (PHI). On the other hand, *liquerunt lumina* takes up a similar expression of Ennius (*An.* 137 Sk.): *lumina sic oculis . . . relinquit*; it was also imitated by Lucretius (3.542, 5.989).

6 vestita est . . . Aulis: One of a wide variety of metaphorical applications of *vestio* ("clothe": *OLD* s.v. 2), whereas Homer simply says that the ships "were gathered at Aulis" (ἐς Αὐλίδα . . . ἠγερέθοντο).

7 quae Priamo . . . pestemque ferebant: In Homer, what the ships bore were "evils for Priam and the Trojans" (κακὰ Πριάμωι καὶ Τρωσί: 304), which becomes "disaster and ruin for Priam and Troy," whereby Cicero reaches back for a phrase from the *Cons.*: *volvier in gentem cladem pestemque monebant* (F 10.50 Courtney) and converts the sufferings of the people into a corporate experience for Troy itself; cf. Goldberg 1995, 144–45.

8 latices gelidos fumantibus aris: Cicero supplies the epithets (Homer simply has "round about the fountain by the holy altars"), creating a nice chiastic contrast of cold and warm.

9 aurigeris "covered with gold," first attested here. As early as *Odyssey* 3.384 and 437, there is mention of the gilding of the horns of sacrificial animals, a practice also followed at Rome; cf. Wissowa 1912, 416. Here Homer speaks merely of "perfect hecatombs" (306).

10 umbrifera "shady." Here Cicero found another chance to deploy the compound epithet he had used at *Cons.* F 10.73 Courtney (its first attestation); Homer has "beautiful" (καλῆι).

aquai: Archaism for *aquae*, also used by Cicero at 1.15 (= *Progn.* 4.1 = p. 194 Soubiran) and later by Virgil (*Aen.* 7.464).

11 Homer introduces the portent with the remark, "Then a great sign appeared," which Cicero does not render, preferring to emphasize the shared viewing of the spectacle: *vidimus . . . draconem.* The description of the snake as "tawny" (δαφοινός) is also omitted in the Latin version in favor of the ominous size (*inmani*).

tortu "coil," a word Cicero had used in the description of a serpent translated from Sophocles (fr. 34.42 Bl. = *Tusc.* 2.22); the Homeric equivalent comes later (ἐλελιξάμενος "moving on its coils") when it attacks the mother (316).

12 terribilem: A nice touch, occupying the same enjambed metrical position as the Homeric equivalent (σμερδαλέος: 309), as if a single line could not contain the monster.

Iovis . . . pulsu "set on by Jupiter" (*OLD* s.v. *pulsus* 3a). Again, Homer is, in Arnold's phrase, "eminently . . . direct," making "the Olympian himself" the subject of the verb "hurled" (ἧκε).

†**penetraret** was rightly marked as corrupt by Timpanaro (1988, 364); it should mean "entered," whereas Homer pictures the serpent "darting from under" the altar and "rushing" (ὑπαΐξας, ὄρουσεν: 310); Soubiran has suggested *reptaret* or *properaret.*

13 tegmine: A *tegmen* can be any sort of covering (< *tego*); here the material is specified by the defining gen. *foliorum*; similarly v. 19 *tegmine saxi.* This form is convenient for a fifth foot with a following trochee or spondee; hence it occurs six times in the *Aratea*, always in this position.

15 tremulo . . . clangore "with a trembling cry," whereby *tremulus* indicates fear (*OLD* s.v. 1b). By contrast, Homer humanizes the mother, having her mourn the fate of the chicks (ὀδυρομένη φίλα τέκνα: 315). *clangor* was first used by Cicero in the rendering from Aeschylus at *Tusc.* 2.24 = fr. 33.14 Bl.: *clangorem fundit vastum.*

genetrix: Only here in Cicero; a somewhat surprising use of the word that Ennius had used in a solemn address to Venus: *te sole nata precor, Venus, te genetrix patris nostri* (*An.* 58 Sk.; cf. also, famously, Lucr. 1.1: *Aeneadum genetrix*).

16 cui ferus . . . laniavit viscera morsu: If Homer describes the chicks as "pitiably chirping" (ἐλεεινὰ . . . τετριγῶτας) as they are eaten (314), Cicero, too, adds pathetic touches, qualifying the serpent as *ferus*, deploying the verb *laniare* ("wound savagely, mutilate"), and in the next line applying the epithet *teneros* to the chicks. As in v. 11, the sheer size of the snake is emphasized (*inmani . . . morsu*).

64 17 tam teneros: Timpanaro (1988, 364) suspects, perhaps rightly, that this should be *iam teneros.*

18 qui luci ediderat genitor Saturnius "the Saturnian father who had brought it to the light." Beginning with Ennius (fr. 444 Sk.: *o genitor noster, Saturnie, maxime divom*), *genitor* becomes a common poetic description of Jupiter (cf. *OLD* s.v. 2a). Cicero transfers to this point the idea of "bringing to light" that Homer deployed when he first mentioned the creature (309).

19 †duro formavit† tegmine saxi: It is, as Timpanaro (1988, 364) remarks, unclear what is meant by *formavit*, and he compares Ov. *Met.* 12.23: *fit lapis et servat serpentis imagine saxum.* If that is along the right lines, one might perhaps contemplate *formam duravit tegmine saxi* "he hardened the shape [of the snake] with a covering of stone."

20 timidi stantes: Homer has, rather, "we stood and marvelled" (ἑσταότες θαυμάζομεν: 320); Cicero comes closer to capturing this idea at v. 23 (*torpentes . . . obstipuistis*).

21 versarier "stalking, running rampant," or the like (cf. *OLD* s.v. *verso* 10); the origin of the archaic third conjugation passive infinitive in *-ier* is unclear; for some hypotheses, cf. Leumann 1977, 581–82; Weiss 2009, 446 and n. 81.

22 fidenti voce: Cicero portrays Calchas, like the dogmatist Velleius at *N.D.* 1.18 (quoted on §8), speaking with supreme confidence. Homer, on the other hand, has him speaking "with divine inspiration" (θεοπροπέων: 322).

24 deum . . . creator substitutes for the Homeric formula "counselor Zeus" (μητίετα Ζεύς: 324) and implies a conception of the supreme god very different from that of Homer; cf. Sen. *Phaedr.* 88: *creator caelitum.*

26 nam quot avis . . . videtis: Cicero compresses here, not distinguishing the mother's fate (contrast Homer 327).

27 exanclabimus: A Greek loanword literally meaning to "draw off" a liquid, but already used in Ennian tragedy to mean "endure" (fr. 103 J. = *FRL* 28; 144 J. = *FRL* 52); Cicero also deploys it in the rendering from Sophocles (*Tusc.* 2.20 = fr. 34.2 Bl.) as well as at *Luc.* 108 and *Tusc.* 1.118.

28 poena satiabit Achivos: Cicero introduces the quasi-judicial idea of punishment, not found in Homer.

29 matura videtis "you see that they are due to take place" (*OLD* s.v. *maturus* 7b). Cicero inserts a quasi-visual element, whereas Homer simply says "all these things are now being fulfilled" (τὰ δὴ νῦν πάντα τελεῖται: 330).

65 quae tandem ista auguratio . . . mensuum aut dierum?: The sober critique contrasts with the violence and pathos of the poetic scene. *passer* is difficult to fit into hexameters and therefore was replaced by the generic *avis/aves* in Cicero's translation. Marcus queries the basis for calculation: why should the number of sparrows be associated with the number of years, rather than some other unit of time? This is essentially the same problem that was raised at §29 of the inherent connection of the divinatory sign with the event it predicts. The point is repeated below (*postremo quid simile habet passer annis?*).

cur autem de passerculis . . . lapideus dicitur factus?: This argument follows Aristotle (fr. 145 Rose), who had pointed out that the snake's devouring of the sparrows was a natural occurrence and could hardly be considered a portent (cf. above on the mule's foaling, roosters, mice: §§49b, 54–57, 59) but that the prophecy ignored the metamorphosis of the snake into stone, which would so qualify. For the folktale motif of the transformation of a snake into an object, cf. Thompson 1955, D425.1. **passerculis** "little sparrows," the diminutive providing variety and hinting at the speaker's pity and/or contempt (cf. §33: *musculorum iecuscula*; §52b: *carunculae*).

nam de angue illo . . . haruspicis consilio sed imperatoris: With *nam* providing transition ("again, moveover": *OLD* s.v. 4), Marcus moves on to a fairly recent incident also involving a snake appearing from beneath an altar. This occurred in the year 89 when, during the Social War, Sulla's army was encamped before the Campanian town of Nola. Quintus, too, had juxtaposed the two incidents (1.72) and had appealed both to Sulla's memoirs (*FRH* 22 F 17; cf. Noble 2014, 124–30) and to his brother's own recollection, since Marcus had participated in the campaign in 89 as a raw recruit (*tiro*); on the date cf. Mitchell 1979, 9; Noble 2014, 124n3; Flower 2017, 69–70 n. 16 with literature. The sacrifice, carried out in front of the general's tent (*ante praetorium*: 1.72), aimed at impetrative auspices, i.e., to determine whether the gods were favorably disposed to his planned attack; cf. Keaveney 1983, 51; Rüpke 1990, 148 and n. 32. The field altar used will have been improvised from mounds of earth topped with grass; cf. Reisch, *RE* 1.2:54 ff. While confirming that he recalls the facts of the incident (*memini*), Marcus contradicts his brother's interpretation. Quintus had claimed that, upon seeing the omen, C. Postumius, perhaps his personal *haruspex* (cf. Rawson 1991, 304–5), begged Sulla to offer battle (*oraret illum ut in expeditionem exercitum educeret*: 1.72), an example of an immediate *coniectura* without consultation of sacred books (cf. §50b; Guillaumont 1986, 128). Postumius may have taken this as "a natural sign that Sulla was being acknowledged by a local divinity and that his mission was, therefore, destined to succeed" (Flower 2017, 70). Marcus, however, states that Sulla made sacrifice when he was already on the point of offering battle (*cum in expeditionem educturus esset*) and that the victory was owed to the commander's strategy (*consilium*), not that of the haruspex; cf. Pl. *Lach.* 198e, where Socrates remarks that in war strategy has greater value than divination. Had he been given a reply, Quintus might have pointed out that in his autobiography Sulla often cited portents, oracles, and dreams and used Fortune/the divine as an explanatory tool (cf. *FRH* 22 T 2c, 3, F 4, 6, 9, 11, 12, 14, 15, 22, 24; see further Noble 2014, esp. 224–26). If he was a believer (see Champeaux 1982–87, 2:222–24), he might well have obtained from the omen and the soothsayer's interpretation the boost he needed to carry out his strategy with vigor, even if it had been previously formulated; and even if he was not himself a believer, he might have seen the value of exploiting the sign for the benefit of his troops' morale (for such a move on Caesar's part, see on §84). So the portent might have contributed to the victory after all. **rem praeclare esse gestam** "a splendid victory was won." For *rem gerere* used par excellence in the military sphere, cf. *OLD* s.v. *gero* 9a. Indeed, Sulla was presented that day with a grass crown by his troops, a signal honor (*FRH* 22 F 16 = Plin. *Nat.* 22.12). On the battle, see further Letzner 2000, 123–24; Keaveney 2005, 43.

66 Atque haec ostentorum genera . . . fortuito cecidisse potuerunt: From snake portents connected with death or military events (§§62b–65) Marcus now turns to three omens cited by Quintus that involve infants who receive special treatment from animals, which is taken as a harbinger of future success of one kind or another (1.78–79). **haec ostentorum genera** "the kinds of portents," the demonstrative taken up by the relative clause, as often (cf. *OLD* s.v. *hic*[1] 5b). **ad coniecturam aliqua interpretatione revocantur** "are brought under the heading of prophecy by means of some interpretation" (*OLD* s.v. *revoco* 18a). **ut illa tritici grana in os pueri Midae congesta:** An eighth-century king of Phrygia, Midas was a byword for wealth in Greece by the middle of the following century; on him and his legend, see further Roller 1983. The ants placing grains of wheat on the lips of the sleeping infant is a variant of the folktale in which bees or ants bring honey to an infant's lips and thus mark him out for future greatness; cf. Thompson 1955, B147.3.1.2. The tale is also recounted by Ael. *VH* 12.45 and reproduced (with the similar one of Plato that follows) from Cicero by V. Max. 1.6 ext. 3. **aut apes . . . consedisse pueri:** The full anecdote appears at Ael. *VH* 10.21; there are also allusions to it at Plin. *Nat.* 11.55 and Ael. *VH* 12.45; cf. Riginos 1976, 17–21, who also cites later attestations. **coniecta belle** "neatly guessed"; for the colloquial *belle*, cf. Krostenko 2001, 111–14. **quae tamen vel ipsa . . . fortuito cecidisse potuerunt:** By now Marcus' strategies for denying the supernatural are familiar: either the stories are fiction (cf. §27: *commenticiorum exemplorum mirifica copia*) or the phenomena are chance coincidences.

de ipso Roscio . . . nullam ostendisse Africano: *ipse* lends focus to the actor Roscius as the climactic example of the series; cf. §52: *ipse Caesar*; §99: *huic ipsi Caesari*; *TLL* 7.2:316.67. On Roscius' life and career, cf. Lebek 1996, 36–39; on Cicero's relations with him, Fantham 2002, 364–67; on Cicero's defense of the actor, Dyck (forthcoming). **potest illud quidem esse falsum:** *quidem*, adhering, as often, to a form of *ille*, prepares for the following adversative; cf. Solodow 1978, 36–42. Again, Marcus refuses to commit to the veracity of the story; this time, however, he offers a naturalistic explanation in the event that it is true. **ut circumligatus fuerit angui:** Cf. the folktale motif of the child born with a snake around its neck: Thompson 1955, T552.2. **in Solonio praesertim . . . nundinari solent:** The *Solonius ager* lay a bit south of the twelfth milestone on the road leading from Rome to Ostia; this reference plus *Att.* 2.3(23).3 suggests it was at this time a very rural area; see further Fluss, *RE* s.v. *Solonius ager.* It may be relevant that in 64 a moneyer named L. Roscius Fabatus (relation to the actor unknown) from nearby Lanuvium issued a coin depicting Juno Sospita and a snake (*RRC* no. 412, with comment at pp. 439–40); for a snake-ritual at Lanuvium, cf. Prop. 4.8 with Rein 1919. **nundinari** "throng together, assemble," i.e., as at a market (*nundinae*; cf. *OLD* s.v. *nundinor* 3), applied facetiously to snakes. **miror deos immortales . . . nullam ostendisse Africano:** In spite of the explanation just mooted, Marcus concludes the topic with a reason to be skeptical of the diviners' interpretation, whereby he assumes the Roman valuation of professions, with military commanders at the top and actors at the bottom; cf., e.g., *Mur.* 21–30; Lebek 1996, 39–40. Pease takes this allusion, and the similar one at §95, to "Africanus" as the great Roman par excellence without further specification as referring to the elder Africanus. But Cicero surely means the younger man, whose achievements came more readily to the mind of people of his generation; cf., e.g., *De orat.* 2.250, *Brut.* 77, *Off.* 1.121, *Corn. I* F 27 Cr., *Arch.* 16, and *Phil.* 5.48 and 14.9, where the elder Africanus is qualified as *superior* (similarly *Off.* 3.1). Except for *Parad.* 12, where *maior* and *minor* are contrasted (similarly *Fin.* 5.70: *superior—posterior*), or unless otherwise clarified in context, the younger Africanus is Africanus *tout court* (similarly, for Cicero the *bellum Carthaginiense* is the Third Punic War; cf. *Agr.* 2.90 with Manuwald 2018, 383). In addition, a snake-prodigy was, in fact, associated with the elder Africanus (cf., e.g., Livy 26.19.7).

67 atque etiam a te Flaminiana ostenta . . . quod fidenter infixerat: *atque etiam* is a loose connection often found in Cicero's less formal writing; cf., e.g., Dyck 1996 on *Off.* 1.8. Marcus cross-refers to Quintus' report at 1.77; cf. on §21. Again, he offers an alternative naturalistic explanation for the phenomena. For *Flaminiana ostenta* as depreciatory, see on §31 (*Pherecydeum illud*). **non sane mirabile hoc quidem:** *quidem* lends focus to *hoc*, which is specified in the following *quod*-clause. **evellebat:** Conative imperfect; cf. Pinkster 2015, 420–21. On the incident, see Konrad 2004, 170–71.

nam Dionysi equus . . . vim habuit ostenti: For transitional *nam*, cf. on §65 (*nam de angue illo*). This was the second of two prophecies Quintus narrated predicting special distinction for Dionysius I of Syracuse (1.73; cf. 1.39 for his mother's dream before giving birth). According to Quintus' account, quoted from Philistus (*FGrH* 556 F 58), Dionysius lost a horse when crossing a river, but then the animal reappeared with a swarm of bees in its mane. Since Dionysius began his reign within a few days (*paucis post diebus*: 1.73), the incident was held to be prophetic of his future rule (the swarming bees being taken to represent Dionysius' [future] subjects). Marcus will, of course, have none of this, assigning the cause to chance (*casus*). **quid . . . admirationis** "what cause for wonderment"; a common type of partitive genitive (cf. Pinkster 2015, 1005). **vim habuit ostenti** "it was tantamount to" or "taken to be a portent": *OLD* s.v. *vis* 19.

'At Lacedaemoniis . . . quam casu facta esse dicamus?: Quintus poses an objection (*At*) based upon portents that seemed to presage the battle of Leuctra (371): the alleged spontaneous opening of the doors of the temple of Hercules at Thebes and the fact that the armor on display there all fell to the ground were already cited at 1.73. Again, Marcus suggests that there is no reason to privilege divine intervention over chance as an explanation. **Lacedaemoniis:** Dative of disadvantage; cf. on §17 (*nostris oculis*). **valvae** "a double or folding door" characteristic of temples or palaces: *OLD* s.v. The sounding or movement of arms or other disturbance in the temple of a tutelary deity such as Hercules would, of course, suggest by analogy that war is imminent; cf. Rosenberger 1998, 97–98; Rosenberger in Rüpke and Belayche 2004–6, 86; Rosenberger 2007, 295. **subito** in this sentence and the emphatic *et quidem subito* in the next one are meant to suggest that divine action is the cause (similarly at §§36a and 37). **scuta** are shields, whereas Quintus had spoken more generally of *arma* (1.74). **sine aliquo motu:** Marcus insists that a physical cause must be assumed to explain the phenomena and therefore a coincidence is involved (not divine intervention). One need not restore <*terrae*> *motu* or assume that *motu* alone can mean "earthquake"; Cicero deliberately leaves the point vague (*aliquo motu*).

68 'At in Lysandri statuae capite . . . et quidem subito': The Spartan commander Lysander, who brought Athens to its knees in the final phase of the Peloponnesian War and established oligarchic regimes in many cities under his control, was honored at Delphi with a stone statue in the treasury of the Acanthians (Plut. *Lys.* 1). The crown of weeds (*asperis herbis*: *OLD* s.v. *asper* 4b) that suddenly appeared on this statue—covering the face, according to Plut. *De Pyth. orac.* 8 = *mor.* 397f—was taken as a portent of the eclipse of the Spartan empire, associated par excellence with Lysander. **et quidem subito':** For "extending *quidem*," cf. Solodow 1978, 110–12. The adverb was rightly restored in Lambin's 1573 edition for the transmitted *subita,* so as to match Quintus' claim at 1.75; for the implication, see on §67 *fin.*

itane, censes . . . coronae simile videri potest: Marcus' incredulous response: *itane* "Really?" As usual, he finds a natural rather than supernatural explanation. If the "crown" appeared before its seed was germinated (*OLD* s.v. *concipio* 3c; cf. *N.D.* 2.26), that would be supernatural, but Quintus surely does not believe that (cf. on §43b). **credo avium congestu:** Sc. *extitisse* (with nonironic *credo*). Marcus' alternative explanation is that the weeds were gathered together by birds (*avium congestu*: *OLD* s.v. 1; *congero* is used of the "gathering" of materials for a bird's nest at Pl. *Rud.* 889; cf. *TLL* 4:278.81

and 281.18); this haphazard pile was then taken for a crown (*iam quicquid in capite est, id coronae simile videri potest*). **non divino satu** "not by divine sowing." Here *divino* is the conjecture of Schäublin (1989, 46–47) for transmitted *humano*. In this argument, human or animal action is one explanation (see the following example), whereas the alternative is divine intervention (see above on the miraculous origin of the seed). One must assume either that Cicero himself muddled the argument (so Pease ad loc.) or a reader misunderstood and substituted *humano* for *divino*.

nam quod eodem tempore . . . quam deorum videtur: The golden stars in the temple of Castor and Pollux, mentioned by Quintus at 1.75, were dedicated by Lysander after he defeated the Athenian fleet at Aegospotami (406): Plut. *De Pyth. orac.* 8 = *mor.* 397e–f. Given the precious medium, Marcus' suggestion of theft is the obvious explanation.

69 simiae vero Dodonaeae . . . hoc tristius accidisse!: This was reported at 1.76 by Quintus, who, while not naming a source, declared that this incident was the *maximum . . . portentum* the Spartans received (before Leuctra). Lot-divination at the sanctuary of Zeus at Dodona is confirmed by ca. fourteen hundred lead tablets discovered at the site; they contain queries on one side and the name of the worshipper on the other. Johnston (2008, 70) reconstructs the procedure as follows: the lead sheets were rolled or folded and placed into one jar, while a second jar contained small balls of baked clay that were marked or colored to signify yes or no. The priestess would draw a query from one urn, then a ball from the other, and announce the god's response to the worshipper. In contrast to his brother, Marcus sees in this incident nothing except an ape's usual mischievousness (*improbitas*)—a case of expected animal behavior, like the roosters crowing (§§56–57) or mice gnawing (§59). **illam monstruosissumam bestiam:** The monkey's bad reputation in Latin literature begins as early as *FRL* Enn. *Sat.* F 17: *simia quam similis, turpissima bestia, nobis*; cf. *CGL* 4.144.5 and 5.321.8, glossing *pitecus* as *monstrum*. **et negant historici:** For *et* cf. on §47 (*et tu scilicet mavis*). Again, Marcus chooses to criticize not his brother, but his brother's source (cf. on §§35 and 109), presumably Callisthenes (cf. on §54 *init.*).

nam illa praedicta Veientium . . . urbemque retinendam: At 1.100 Quintus had reported from annals the prophecy that a defector told the Romans besieging Veii (406–396) that the city could not be taken when Lake Albanus, which was relatively nearby, was in flood; if the waters were allowed to drain to the sea, the Romans would suffer disaster; but if they were cut off before reaching the sea, the Romans' safety was assured. **Veios **:** A lacuna was detected at this point by Lambin. The text lacks an expression of disbelief in or scorn for the prophecy. Timpanaro (1988, 367) suggested a supplement along these lines: . . . *Veios, <quisnam vera esse credet? ego quidem maiores nostros frugum ubertate consuluisse magis quam transfugae nescio cui fidem tribuisse puto>; ita aqua Albana* etc. In fact, Lake Albanus was cut off from the sea, but Marcus thinks the project was undertaken for agricultural reasons, not for advantage in Rome's war with Veii. The archaeological remains of the drainageway are dated by Judson and Kahane (1963, 87–88), followed by Coarelli (1991, 39), to the Etruscan period. If this is correct, there could be no causal connection between the prophecy and the construction.

'At paulo post audita vox . . . ommutuit?: In reply to Marcus' denial that the drainage of Lake Albanus had to do with "keeping the citadel and city," Quintus cites an incident that did involve such stakes. There was an altar of Aius Locutius (< *aio*, with the epithet Locutius added later for clarification) on the Nova Via between the temple and grove of Vesta. Quintus had narrated the founding legend at 1.101, according to which a plebeian, one M. Caedicius, heard a voice by night warning that, unless the gate and walls were repaired, the City would be captured by the Gauls. Because of Caedicius' low status, however, his report was ignored by the senate, but after the Gauls sacked the City (390), the prophecy was recalled and led to the foundation of the cult; cf. Livy 5.32.6, 50.5, 52.11; Plut. *Cam.* 30.3; Ogilvie 1965 on Livy 5.32.6–7; Richardson 1992 and Aronow, *LTUR* s.v. Aius Locutius; on Aius and his counterpart Angerona, the goddess of silence, cf. Dubourdieu 2003, 262–71. Marcus mocks the idea that this unknown voice suddenly spoke but then, when honored with an altar and a cult, fell silent (*ommutuit*). Such ad hoc arrangements (nonce-cults) are characteristic of Roman religion, however, the Romans being unwilling to ignore an apparent divine intervention but yet also not wanting to risk identification of the power with a member of the recognized pantheon, for fear of calling down divine wrath if they are wrong in guessing the identity; cf. Wissowa 1904; Otto 1909; Briquel 1993, esp. (on Aius Locutius) 82. The Greeks' vague references to the intervention of a δαίμων (*daimon*) are similarly motivated; cf. Burkert 1985, 180–81.

quod idem dici de Moneta . . . quid umquam moniti sumus?: A separate temple to Juno Moneta was vowed by Camillus in 345 and dedicated in 344 (Livy 7.28.4–6 with Orlin 1997, 153); it became the site of the mint. Quintus had narrated (1.101) the incident in which at the time of an earthquake a voice was heard from Juno's temple advising the sacrifice of a pregnant sow (to Tellus, goddess of the earth) as an appeasement. This occurrence is an outlier in that such "oracular voices" were otherwise heard in nonurban or at any rate unbuilt spaces; cf. Briquel 1993. Hence Poulle 2010, 151, argues that the expiation by means of a pregnant sow was recommended in the prophetic books (the *libri lintei*) that were stored in the temple and by later misunderstanding and on the analogy of Aius Locutius attributed to a voice heard from within the temple. Cicero evidently derives Moneta from *moneo* (*a qua . . . quid umquam moniti sumus?*). The formation is unusual and likely to be archaic (so Latte 1960, 169; cf., e.g., *Educa*, *Potina*, *Cuba*); it is unlikely to be Etruscan (as suggested with a query by *OLD* s.v.). *moneta* of coinage is a later semantic development and not the source of the epithet (so also Poulle 2010, 153). Cicero seems to be right, however, in placing the temple between the *arx* and the Capitolium (*Dom.* 101), rather than on the *arx*; cf. Oakley 1997–2005 on Livy 6.20.13; Giannelli, *LTUR* s.v. Iuno Moneta, aedes; Tucci 2005 and 2014; for a different view cf. Richardson 1992 s.v. Iuno Moneta, Aedes; Arata 2010, 122–29. Marcus applies the same objection that, once institutionalized, the goddess has ceased to warn. **quid . . . moniti sumus?:** *moneo* can be used with plain acc. (*OLD* s.v. 3b), but the retained acc. with the passive (cf. Pinkster 2015, 264–67) is unusual with this verb and is highlighted by the preceding *de sue plena*.

70–84 Augury

This section makes two major points: (a) Marcus wishes to maintain augury in the state interest, i.e., because it enables the upper class to control the holding of public assemblies for legislative, electoral, and judicial purposes (§73); (b) as to Quintus' argument for the validity of augury in view of its wide diffusion, while acknowledging that the practice is widespread, Marcus denies that this is any sort of validation; rather, he unhesitatingly brands foreign augury as superstitious (§76). In general, Marcus takes a somewhat ambivalent attitude toward augury: like Quintus, Marcus regrets that it has fallen into neglect (cf. *Leg.* 2.20: *publici augures . . . disciplinam tenento*), but at the same time he regards prophetic augury as practiced by such legendary figures as Romulus and Attus Navius as a thing of the past, criticizes the errors of antiquity (§70), and embraces the modernizing views of his late augural colleague C. Marcellus (§75; contrast the approach at *Leg.* 2.33). Augury had in fact fallen on hard times in the late Republic, partly perhaps because of competition with other divinatory systems, such as haruspicy or astrology (cf. Montero 2006, 22–29, attributing the decline of augury to the rise of haruspicy as a prestigious public rite), partly because augury had been "tamed": its scope had been narrowed from prediction of the future to confirmation of a planned action, and there was now a board of augurs composed of senior politicians and their scions; gone were the days when a marginal figure such as Attus Navius could shake the Roman state with his pronouncements. The contents may be outlined as follows:

1. Marcus' status as augur is irrelevant (70).
   a. Augury should be retained in the state interest.
   b. Disregard of auspices should be severely punished (71).
2. Current *tripudium* follows the traditional form without the substance (72).
   a. The older practice was far different (73).
   b. The abdication of the consuls of 162 because of a flaw in ritual is not a proof of divination (74).
3. Foreign practice is superstitious (76).
   a. Roman commanders no longer practice auspication in the field (77).
   b. Deiotarus did not follow Pompey because of auspices (78).
   c. Who is the founder of augury (80)?
   d. The claimed universality masks a divergence in practice (81).
4. Omens contained in chance remarks come true by accident (83).

70 Satis multa de ostentis . . . primum auspicia videamus: The transition to a new topic is clearly marked with a standard formula (*satis multa de*); cf. *Mil.* 92; *Orat.* 204; *Luc.* 76; *Top.* 90; *Phil.* 7.16; *Ad Brut.* 1.15(23).10. Marcus gives a clear roadmap: technical divination will be rounded out with auspices (§§70–84), divination by lots (*sortes*: §§85–87a), and astrology (§§87b–99), then will follow natural divination, including oracles (§§110–18), which could also be called *sortes* (*OLD* s.v. *sors* 1b vs. 3); hence the distinction drawn here and the pun at §115 (*ut . . . sors ipsa ad sortes referenda sit*).

'Difficilis auguri locus . . . futura dicamus: Quintus stated his position emphatically at 1.105: *tuae partes sunt, tuum, inquam, auspiciorum patrocinium debet esse*, just as Balbus had sought to blunt the force of Cotta's attack on Stoic theology by reference to his status as a priest (*N.D.* 2.168). Snake-handling and various occult activities were attributed to the Marsi (cf. Piccaluga 1976, 207–10); hence Quintus' criticism of the *Marsus augur* at 1.132. In general, the older religious practices, including a wide scope for augury (including predictions of the future), maintained themselves in fringe areas (cf. 1.105: *eumque* [sc. *Appium*] *tum Pisidam tum Soranum augurum esse dicebant*), whereas, as Marcus indicates, at Rome the official practice had been narrowed to impetrative auspices, seeking approval of a specific contemplated action; cf. 1.105 (Quintus of Appius): *solus . . . multorum annorum memoria* *non decantandi* ["reciting in sing-song fashion," i.e., performing perfunctorily] *augurii sed divinandi tenuit disciplinam.*

et tamen credo Romulum . . . collegi auctoritas: *qui urbem auspicato* [adv. = "after taking the auspices": *OLD* s.v. 1] *condidit*: The point is repeated from 1.3 (cf. also *Rep.* 2.5, 16, 51; *Leg.* 2.33); Quintus quoted Ennius' description of Romulus' augury (1.107–8 = *An.* 72–91 Sk.) and reported the miraculous survival of Romulus' augur's staff (*lituus*) after a fire had ravaged the meeting-place of the Salii, where it had been kept (1.30). Marcus does not dispute that Romulus took an expansive view of augury. Marcus is not, however, prepared to endorse predictive augury on that account, noting that ancient beliefs and practices have been improved upon and superseded in many respects (contrast Quintus' defense of divinatory practices on the ground of antiquity: 1.34–35, 87; cf. Krostenko 2000, 374). Moreover, Marcus takes up a version of the criticism anticipated by Quintus. The latter argued against the possibility that Romulus, like the clever man envisioned by Critias, had invented augury in order to manipulate the masses (1.105 and 107; Critias, *Sisyphus TGrF* 43 F 19.12–15, for the interpretation of which see Sutton 1981). Marcus, on the other hand, thinks the auspices are retained both for their benefit to the state (cf. §43a) and in view of popular opinion (*ad opinionem vulgi*). But Marcus goes on to criticize current practice and cite Romulus as a standard: §§71–73. **ius augurium** "augural law": the adj. *augurius* occurs only in this phrase (*OLD* s.v.; PHI).

71a nec vero non omni supplicio . . . tam contumaciter repudiandus: A rather abrupt shift of tone that Timpanaro (1988, 369) suspects may cover a certain amount of embarrassment. For the luckless consuls of the year 249, see on §20 above. Here Marcus implicitly endorses the capital punishment Cicero had provided for disobeying an augur (*Leg.* 2.21). **parendum . . . religioni fuit** "they ought to have obeyed religious custom": for indicative in an expression of obligation (whereas English emphasizes the nonfulfillment), cf. G–L §254R1; for the sense of *religio*, cf. *OLD* s.v. 8b. **nec . . . tam contumaciter repudiandus** refers to Claudius' throwing of the sacred chickens into the sea when they refused to eat, with the comment that in that case they could drink, previously recorded at *N.D.* 2.7.

iure igitur alter . . . sibi ipse conscivit: Claudius was prosecuted for *perduellio* (treason), a capital offense, but a storm arose and halted the proceedings. Since he could not be tried twice by the same process, he was retried under another form of litigation and condemned to pay a fine of 120,000 sesterces (1,000 for each of the ships he had lost). The main source is sch. Bob. 90.1–8

Stangl; cf. Mommsen 1887–88, 2:321n1; Linderski 1986, 2176–77; for detailed analysis of Claudius' trials and their political background, cf. Bleckmann 2002, 193–201. The other consul of 249, L. Iunius Pullus, also lost a fleet (in a storm on the south coast of Sicily). One suspects, however, that his impiety (for which no details are supplied) may have been assimilated to that of his colleague. In spite of the loss of the fleet, Iunius was able to keep his crew safe and mounted a land expedition in which he seized both the town of Eryx and the temple of Venus Erycina (Polyb. 1.54–55; cf. Konrad 2016, clearing away misunderstandings about Polybius' dating). He was thus able to salvage some of his reputation and is unlikely to have committed the sort of "honor-suicide" that Cicero seems to envision (attested elsewhere only at *N.D.* 2.7, on which V. Max. 1.4[Paris].4 depends). According to one tradition, he was taken captive when Carthalo occupied Aegithalus (Zon. 8.15.14); no further activities are attested after his consulship. See Münzer, *RE* s.v. Iunius 133.

'Flaminius non paruit auspiciis . . . in Cannensi pugna cum exercitu?: For C. Flaminius (cos. 217), who lost his army and his life at the disastrous battle of Lake Trasimennus, see on §21. Quintus' *Flaminius non paruit* is met by Marcus' *Paulus paruit*, i.e., while not disputing Flaminius' impiety and disaster, he shows that his piety did not save L. Aemilius Paulus (cos. 216), who fell along with most of the Roman army at Cannae, the most notorious defeat in Roman history; see on §97 *fin*. The antithesis is a bit strained, however, since Paulus was drawn into disaster by the calamitous decision of his consular colleague C. Terentius Varro, who held command on alternate days, to join battle (Livy 22.45.5) and a religious offense was, in fact, alleged against Varro (V. Max. 1.1.16). For "railroading" *num*, see on §9.

71b Etenim ut sint auspicia . . . auspicia nullo modo: *ut sint auspicia* "on the understanding that there are auspices" (cf. *OLD* s.v. *ut* 31). The emphatic *quae nulla sunt* makes it clear that this is merely granted for the sake of argument; cf. §16: *nondum dico quam haec signa nulla sint.* **haec certe quibus utimur** "at any rate the current ones we use." Marcus is prepared to join in this respect with Quintus' critique of current augural practices (cf. 1.105). **sive tripudio sive de caelo:** *tripudium* is usually a sign taken from "the noisy falling to the ground of corn fed on by the sacred chickens" (*OLD* s.v. 2), though any animal might provide such a sign; see further Regell 1893, 8–9; Foti 2011, 90–92. For a description of such a rite performed in a military context, cf. schol. Verg. Veron. *Aen.* 10.241, cited by Rüpke 1990, 148–49 n. 37; cf. also Mommsen 1887–88, 1:84n5. Cicero offers an etymology of the word at §72; see ad loc. *de caelo* (sc. *servare*) is to watch the sky for omens, an action by a magistrate that brought public business to a halt (until

Caesar as consul of 59 chose to ignore it when his colleague Bibulus took this action); see further Linderski 1995, 490–95; Driediger-Murphy 2019, 133–60. **simulacra . . . auspiciorum** "sham auspices," i.e., the form without the substance, as the following example illustrates; Quintus had made this same point at 1.27–28; cf. also *N.D.* 2.9: *sed neglegentia nobilitatis augurii disciplina omissa veritas auspiciorum spreta est, species tantum retenta.* In view of Marcus' regret over the decline of augury, Pavis d'Escurac (1981, 32) finds "a residue of belief" ("un arrière fond de croyance") beneath his skepticism. Wissowa (1912, 532) notes the general tendency, under pressure of the exigencies of state administration, for the sign to change categories over time from oblative to impetrative, i.e., from the random observation of the behavior of birds to a controlled rite. Scheid remarks (1987–89, 130) that the important point is the auspicant's decision to accept the sign and adds (2012a, 116) that the performance of such a rite is, from the Roman point of view, the perfect model of divination (sc. because chance is excluded). But Driediger-Murphy 2019, esp. ch. 1, argues powerfully that in the late Republic the results were less tightly controlled than scholars have supposed. **auspicia nullo modo** "on no account (genuine) auspices"; for *nullo modo*, see on §24.

'Q. Fabi, te mihi . . . nunc quilubet: Cicero sketches a scenario of current practice, in contrast to old-time augury. The speaker is the person, ordinarily a magistrate (cf. Mommsen 1887–88, 1:89–93, but see also Kunkel and Wittmann 1995, 28–37; Lintott 1999, 103; Berthelet 2015, 103–41), who has initiated the action (in §72 he is called *is qui auspicatur* or *auspicans*). His words constitute a formal stipulation for assistance at auspication; cf. Linderski 1986, 2191. **Q. Fabi:** Fabius is a name that Cicero uses to designate a specific individual, as we would use "John Doe" (cf. *Fat.* 12; *Top.* 14). Such fictive names were used in official texts (thus the *accensus* in the consular commentaries cited by Var. *L.* 6.88 is called C. Calpurnius) and by the jurists (cf. Frier 1985, 166 and n. 113). The praenomen is added here to mark this as a formal address; cf. Dickey 2002, 51–53. **te mihi in auspicio esse volo** "I would like you to assist me in taking the auspices." Cf. *Rep.* 2.16: *qui sibi essent in auspiciis ex singulis tribubus singulos cooptavit augures* [sc. Romulus]; *Leg.* 3.43: *est autem boni auguris meminisse . . . Iovi . . . optimo maximo se consiliarium atque administrum datum, ut sibi quos in auspicio esse iusserit*; Messalla *apud* Gel. 13.15.4 (= fr. 1 Huschke): *nos . . . veterum auctoritatem sumus secuti neque his comitiis in auspicio fuimus.* **'Audivi'** "I comply," a performative utterance. **hic . . . peritus** "this man, an expert"; *adhibebatur* ("used to be brought in"), the imperfect used of a standing practice in the old days. Linderski (1986, 2191) notes that, though *peritus* need not necessarily designate an *augur publicus*, it is likely, in view of the following *hoc intellegere perfecti auguris est*, that Cicero assumed that a public augur would have performed this function in earlier times. **nunc quilubet:** Was augury really so debased in Cicero's time? Dionysius of Halicarnassus (2.6.1–2), though also speaking of a decline in the art of augury since the days of Romulus, speaks of "one of the augurs paid by the state" taking part in the inauguration of magistrates, albeit his report of a favorable bolt of lightning was conventional, not based on an actual occurrence (cf. §72 *init.* with note).

peritum autem esse . . . omni vitio caret: *silentium* has the special sense in augury defined here; similarly Festus p. 474 L. s.v. <*silentio surgere*>: . . . *hoc enim est* <*proprie sil*>*entium omnis vitii in auspiciis vacuitas.* Ceremonial silence was induced by the command *favete linguis* (1.102; Hor. *Carm.* 3.1.2, etc.); by easy extension, this literal silence is broadened to freedom from any phenomenon that might vitiate the ritual. On *vitium*, cf. on §43a.

72 hoc intellegere . . . silentium esse videri: The augural books contained an elaborate register of the "signs from heaven, bird-signs, signs from quadrupeds," etc. that the augur must look out for; cf. Regell 1882. Understanding all of these is, as Marcus says, the task of a perfect augur. **'Dicito, <si> silentium esse videbitur'** "Indicate when 'silence' seems to be present," a use of *si* to introduce "a sustantival cl(ause) expr(essing) a situation, etc., as yet undetermined, s(ome)t(ime)s virtually an indir(ect) qu(estion)," sometimes with indicative: *OLD* s.v. *si* 13. When the magistrate gives this command, the (current, inexpert) attendant replies immediately that it is, without making a proper inspection (*nec suspicit nec circumspicit*), the ceremony being merely carried out for form's sake; cf. §71b: *simulacra . . . auspiciorum.*

tum ille: 'Dicito . . . tripudium solistimum nuntiatur: The feeding of the birds is the next step in the ritual, but again current practice makes this routine, since these are not wild birds but caged chickens, as Marcus explains. *inquit* following *attulit* has been an embarrassment for translators ("someone replies" Falconer; similarly Timpanaro and Schäublin) and was rightly suspected by Christ. In fact, no plausible interlocutor can be supplied to answer Marcus' question, the only interlocutor in the dialogue being Quintus, who is indicated with the second person, and the etymology of *pullarius* (like that of *tripudium* below) surely belongs to Marcus; *inquit* was evidently added by a reader who mistakenly believed the dialogue was continuing. *pullarius* is, as is noted here, formed from *pullus* ("chicken") + –*arius*, used to denote "a dealer in" the particular merchandise; cf. *OLD* s.vv.;

Foti 2011, 93–94. **haec sunt . . . internuntiae Iovis!** "*These* birds, then, are Jupiter's messengers!" The humble and familiar domestic fowl is thus substituted for the eagle in this august role (on birds as divine messengers, see in general Linderski 1986, 2227n316); cf. also on §73. *hic* seems to have depreciatory force here, as it sometimes does (cf. *OLD* 8b on *hoc* + gen.). The cretic plus iamb is Cicero's sixth-favorite clausula. **nihil ad auspicia:** Sc. *pertinet*. That some bits inevitably fall to the ground when the chickens eat was already pointed out by Quintus (*necesse est . . . offa obiecta cadere frustum ex pulli ore cum pascitur*) when he criticized the current system of "forced auspices" (1.27). At this point Marcus offers an etymology of *tripudium* from *terripavium*, which is also reproduced by Festus (pp. 284 and 498 L.). An alternative explanation offered by Festus (p. 498 L.) connects the word with the triple-time dance in honor of Mars (also called *tripudium*); on this theory, the hopping about of the birds would convey the sign; cf. E.–M. s.v. *tripodo*; *OLD* s.v. *tripudium*. **solistimum:** Another technical term from augury, usually taken to be a superlative of *sollus* "complete": *OLD* s.v. *solistimus*; E.–M. s.v. *sollus*; but cf. Dieu 2009, arguing for a connection with Old English *sēlest-* and "favorable" as the original sense.

73 **ergo hoc auspicium . . . coactum et expressum?:** Marcus thus echoes Quintus' criticism of current augural practice (*hoc auspicium*); cf. 1.27–28; Liebeschuetz 1979, 25. **divini quicquam** "any connection with the divine": *OLD* s.v. *divinus* 1; for the construction, cf. on §67 (*quid . . . admirationis*).

quo antiquissumos augures . . . tripudium facere posse: The *decreta* "formed the most recent and constantly growing part of the augural archives" (Linderski 1986, 2244–45); see Regell 1878, 22–24, for discussion of the testimonies. As an augur himself (cf. on §§42b–43a), Marcus had access to and could cite and draw an inference from a decree (he seems not to notice that this decree implicitly contradicts his etymology of *tripudium* based upon current practice; cf. §72 *fin.*). He thus arrives by a different route at the same conclusion as Quintus, who had argued that earlier augural practice was still preserved among outlying peoples (he names the Cilicians, Pamphylians, Pisidians, and Lycians), though it had fallen into desuetude at Rome; Quintus went on to cite Deiotarus' obedience to a sign presented by an eagle to confirm this older practice (1.26–27).

tum igitur esset auspicium . . . Romulum auspicari solitum putas?: *tum*, emphatically repeated, = "in those days." **si modo esset ei liberum se ostendisse** "on the condition that it was open to it [the bird] to show itself."

The conditional *si modo esset ei liberum* is placed in parentheses by most recent editors in order to avoid having *se ostendisse* depend on *esset ei liberum*, which has been thought impossible in Cicero, but that is hardly a natural way of taking the Latin. Timpanaro (1988, 371–72) plausibly argues that Cicero uses this archaism exceptionally here since he is discussing the archaic institution of the augurate. On this premise, the appearance of a bird (*se ostendisse*) would be a sign, and the bird could be taken, as it traditionally was, as the "interpreter and attendant of Jupiter." The birds share the former status with the augurs themselves; cf. *Leg.* 2.20; Linderski 1986, 2226. **satelles Iovis:** Cf. *Marius* F 17.1 Courtney = 20.1 Bl., cited at 1.106, and the rendering from *Prometheus Unbound* at *Tusc.* 2.24 = fr. 33.12 Bl. Seneca, however, challenged this ranking as arbitrary; cf. *N.Q.* 2.32.5: *cur ergo aquilae hic honor datus est, ut magnarum rerum faceret auspicia, aut corvo et paucissimis avibus, ceterarum sine praesagio vox est?* In contrast with the tradition stands the current practice (*nunc vero*), whereby a chicken is kept in a cage, starved, then allowed to feed, whereupon it attacks its food (*in . . . invadit*, also used of a bird eagerly feeding at *N.D.* 2.124). **hoc . . . hoc modo:** A derisive question marked by the emphatic repetition of the pronoun/pronominal adj. used of the current and just described practice with a hint of contempt (cf. on §72 [*haec sunt . . . internuntiae Iovis!*]), in contrast with the august augury of Romulus.

74a iam de caelo servare . . . nunc imperant pullario: For *de caelo servare* cf. on §71b. The older practice is contrasted with the current one, which was illustrated by Marcus' example in §72 ('*Dicito, <si> silentium esse videbitur*'). *ipsos* = "in person," as opposed to using an agent; cf. *OLD* s.v. *ipse* 4. The "command" (*imperant*) is to make a report but does not prejudice the content of the report, as Driediger-Murphy 2019, 118, correctly notes.

ille renuntiat fulmen sinistrum . . . principes civitatis essent interpretes: For *ille* used to change the subject to the other of two parties, cf. *TLL* 7.1:351.67; Joffre 2010, 568–69, connects this usage with the contrasting function of *ille*. After *auspicium optumum* Clark (1918, 361) wanted to delete *quod* as anticipated from the next line, unnecessarily. Marcus again explains the exception whereby lightning on the left is a bad omen for the holding of assemblies as politically motivated; cf. on §43a. **ut . . . principes civitatis essent interpretes:** *interpres* has augural connotations here (cf. *Leg.* 2.20: *interpretes . . . Iovis optumi maxumi, publici augures*), as is emphasized by Linderski 1995, 487.

74b 'At Ti. Gracchi litteris . . . divinationem nego: At *N.D.* 2.10–11 Balbus narrates this incident in detail as his crowning example of the importance of augury and haruspicy. The account given here is a bit truncated, but the version in *N.D.* makes the relation of events clear: when he was already serving as proconsul in Sardinia, Ti. Sempronius Gracchus (cos. 177, 163) realized his error in failing to repeat the auspices when he returned to the scene of the elections after crossing the *pomerium* and entering the city to preside over a meeting of the senate; he therefore explained these circumstances in a letter to the college of augurs (CXII F 1 Cugusi), who in turn reported the matter to the senate, which then obtained the abdication of the consuls of 162, P. Cornelius Scipio Nasica and C. Marcius Figulus; for full testimonies, cf. *MRR* 1:441–42. For procedure in determining and responding to a *vitium*, cf. Mommsen 1887–88, 1:114–16; Linderski 1986, 2158–77. For an argument that the religious component of the incident should be given full weight, cf. Driediger-Murphy 2019, 172–79. **quis negat augurum disciplinam esse?:** Marcus, himself an augur, certainly cannot. Indeed, at *Leg.* 2.20 Cicero said of the public augurs: *disciplinam tenento*. On the *disciplina auguralis*, see further Linderski 1986, 2226–41. **divinationem nego:** But one wonders whether augury, even in the attenuated form in which it was currently practiced, was not still a kind of divination (indicating a prospective breach of the *pax deorum*). This question is never squarely faced, however, since Quintus immediately raises a new objection based on the action of the haruspices, whose status as diviners (*divini*) is clear. For a similar pattern involving Quintus' claim of a counterexample followed by Marcus' concession of an *ars/disciplina* but denial of divination, cf. §45b.

'At haruspices divini . . . non iustum rogatorem fuisse dixerunt': Quintus is not about to allow Marcus to dispatch this example so easily and so calls attention to the earlier phase involving the haruspices. Before a vote was taken in an electoral assembly, one of the thirty-five centuries of voting citizens was selected by lot as the *praerogativa centuria* that would be the first both to vote and to have its vote (which was taken as an omen: 1.103) announced; see further Staveley 1972, 154–55; Jehne 2000; Feig Vishnia 2012, 123; detailed study by C. Meier, *RE* Suppl. 8 s.v. *Praerogativa centuria*. **propter mortem repentinam eius qui in praerogativa referenda subito concidisset:** This person is called the *primus rogator* at *N.D.* 2.10, i.e., he tallies and reports (*refert*) the vote to the presiding magistrate; cf. Staveley 1972, 158; Feig Vishnia 2012, 93. In spite of this, Tiberius carried on with the election undeterred. But then, sensing that, in the people's eyes, the matter had assumed the character of a religious violation (*cum . . . rem . . . illam in religionem populo venisse sentiret*: *N.D.* 2.10; cf. *OLD* s.v. *religio* 3a), he summoned the haruspices to give their opinion to the senate. The haruspices' pronouncement that there was no proper *rogator* could be taken either to refer to the deceased official or to Tiberius himself as presiding officer. For another instance of a consular election invalidated by the lack of a *iustus comitiorum rogator*, sc. the election of M. Claudius Marcellus as suffect consul in 215, cf. Linderski 1986, 2168–71; Driediger-Murphy 2019, 95–96.

75 primum vide ne . . . coniectura poterant dicere: Marcus' first riposte is the nonsupernatural explanation that by *rogator* the haruspices merely meant the deceased man, not Tiberius, a fact that they could have ascertained *sine divinatione*. **vide ne:** Cf. on §12.

deinde fortasse casu . . . de pomerii iure potuerunt?: If, however, by *iniustus rogator* they meant Tiberius, they might have been correct merely by accident (*casu*), a possibility repeatedly raised by Marcus to explain apparently successful divination (cf. §§39, 47, 52a, 55a, 57, 67). He goes on to claim that the Etruscan haruspices will hardly have known the details of Roman augural procedure, such as the two points relevant to the present case. **tabernaculo recte capto** "the tent correctly set up," sc. for augural observations; cf. *OLD* s.v. *tabernaculum* b. The night before the event for which augury was required, the responsible magistrate pitched a tent and defined a field for augural observation (*templum* designated both the chosen spot and the field of observation); cf. Paul. ex Fest. 57.4 L.; Rüpke 1990, 31. **de pomerii iure:** The *pomerium* was the sacred boundary of the city, beyond which urban auspices did not apply; cf. Galsterer, *BNP* s.v. *pomerium*. Though the *pomerium* was actually of Etruscan origin (cf. Thulin 1905–9, 3:113), by Cicero's day the Romans had evidently forgotten that.

75–76a equidem adsentior C. Marcello . . . nunc hactenus: For *equidem*, cf. on §5. C. Claudius Marcellus (pr. 80) and Appius Claudius Pulcher (cos. 54) had both been distinguished members of the college of augurs and authors of books on the *disciplina* but were by now deceased (*mei collegae fuerunt*); see further Dyck 2004b, 344–46. At *Leg.* 2.33, Cicero's character tried to steer a middle course between the two: *neque illi adsentior qui hanc scientiam negat umquam in nostro collegio fuisse* [sc. Marcellus], *neque illi qui esse etiamnunc putat* [sc. Appius]. Quintus had expressed strong approval for Appius' approach (1.105); here, however, Marcus endorses the augury *rei publicae causa* of Marcellus, which does not, in Marcus' view, involve divination; see above. Similarly Quintus says that Appius is the only one who for many years has maintained the discipline *non decantandi augurii sed divinandi* (ibid.); see on §70 ('*Difficilis auguri locus . . . futura dicimus*). Thus the brothers, while agreeing on the arc of the historical trajectory, disagree on whether this is good or bad (though Marcus wavers in his view at §§71–73; see above). **ius augurum:** Orelli conjectured *ius augur<i>um*, but *Dom.*

39 and *Leg.* 2.31 can be invoked to defend the transmitted text. **plura in aliis:** Sc. *libris*. It is natural to think of *De auguriis*; cf. on §43a. One wonders whether it was already completed or merely projected at this time. **nunc hactenus:** A variant of the standard concluding formula *sed haec hactenus*; cf. on §53 *fin.*

76b Externa enim auguria . . . videamus: Quintus had praised foreign augurs for retaining the robust ancient-style predictive augury and criticized current Roman augurs for narrowing the scope of the discipline (1.25–28), a point Marcus will now pursue, starting with the assertion that foreign auguries do not qualify as an art but are mere superstition (on which cf. on §19 *fin.*). Hobbes (2012, 2:86) famously held: "Feare of power invisible, feigned by the mind, or imagined from tales publiquely allowed, RELIGION; not allowed, SUPERSTITION." The idea of religion as state-sanctioned superstition could have been derived from Marcus' treatment of augury, which merely asserts (§74b) that the Roman version is a *disciplina* and in our passage that foreign augury is superstitious, without any attempt to show a fundamental difference.

omnibus fere avibus utuntur . . . alia nostris: Foreign augurs thus adhere more closely to the decree of the augural college (cf. §73) than their current Roman counterparts. **sinistra** is used here in the evaluative sense ("favorable"), not the literal one; cf. *OLD* s.v. *sinister* 3; cf. §82 *fin.*

solebat ex me Deiotarus . . . essent etiam contraria: The explanation of how Cicero knows about foreign augury now follows in asyndeton. On Deiotarus, see on §20. These conversations presumably took place during Cicero's governorship of Cilicia (51–50; *MRR* 2:243, 251–52). For the exclamation *di inmortales*, see on §53. **quantum differebat!:** In Latin a fact that is still true at the present but is embedded in a past narrative can be assimilated, as here, to the past; cf. Pinkster 2015, 413. For an example of "opposite" (*contraria*) significance of signs, cf. §82.

atque ille iis semper utebatur . . . quam multum iis utimur?: Deiotarus' practice in this regard was made clear by Quintus (1.26–27). **nisi dum a populo auspicia accepta habemus:** Conducting state auspices was the exclusive right of elected magistrates; cf. on §71b ('*Q. Fabi, te mihi . . . nunc quilubet*).

bellicam rem administrari . . . qui auspicia non habent?: For *auspicato*, cf. on §70. Marcus infers the "wish" of the ancestors simply from the earlier practice. Balbus makes a complaint along these lines at *N.D.* 2.9

(*bella quibus rei publicae salus continetur nullis auspiciis administrantur* etc.). The change (dating roughly from the beginning of the first century) whereby the promagistrates assumed primary command of Rome's wars was surely deliberate; the next section shows how cumbersome the traditional auspication requirements could be.

77 **itaque nec amnis . . . nec tripudio auspicantur:** The crossing of a boundary such as a river raises the possibility that the auspices previously obtained may be invalidated; hence there was a rite, the *auspicia peremnia* (also referred to at *N.D.* 2.9), involving prayers accompanied by libations, that the previous auspices be extended (Festus pp. 284 and 296 L.); cf. Mommsen 1887–88, 1:97n1; Rüpke 1990, 147. For *tripudium*, see on §71.

ubi ergo avium divinatio? . . . a bellicis esse sublata: Madvig's transposition is adopted here (as it is also by Pease, Timpanaro, and Schäublin), so that this material follows immediately after *nec tripudio auspicantur* (rather than *idem augur optumus*). The transposition has several advantages: (1) it creates a more perspicuous train of thought by closing off the topic of *avium divinatio* and its elimination from military affairs before going on to other matters; (2) it establishes the distinction between *urbanae* and *bellicae res* before the point *quod totum auspicium militare est*; (3) with this order, *nam* can function in an *occupatio*, i.e., anticipating a possible objection about the use of another type of auspication in a military context (*OLD* s.v. *nam* 5); (4) it improves the perspicuity of the following connection *et quidem ille*, which now refers back to the man mentioned in the immediately preceding clause. See also Timpanaro 1988, 374–75. **avium divinatio** = augury, similar construction to *extispicum divinatio* at §42a or *somniorum divinatio* at §148a. **ab iis . . . bella administrantur:** The idea is repeated from §76b *fin.* **ad urbanas res:** Müller's conjecture is adopted for transmitted *ab urbanis*. The transmitted text may have arisen when *res* dropped out before *retenta* and the remaining *ad urbanas* was rewritten to match the following *a bellicis*.

nam ex acuminibus . . . idem augur optumus: For the connection with *nam*, see above. The augury *ex acuminibus*, also mentioned at *N.D.* 2.9, is an obscure sign, perhaps a kind of electric flashing off the tips of an army's spears answered by a flashing in the sun; it may be a type of St. Elmo's fire; see further Mommsen 1887–88, 1:87n6; Pease ad loc.; Rüpke 1990, 149–50. **M. Marcellus . . . idem augur optumus:** M. Claudius Marcellus was, apart from the Scipios, perhaps the most distinguished military commander of the Middle Republic, best known for the capture of Syracuse in the Second Punic War (212); his consulships: 222, 215 (included since he was elected, albeit he did not serve; see on §74b *fin.*), 214, 210, 208. It is assumed that he was coopted to the augural college around the time of his aedileship ("226 or shortly before"): Rüpke 2008, §1206.

et quidem ille dicebat . . . facere iter se solere: *ille* continues the focus on Marcellus. Cicero no doubt has this information from an historian. The closed litter would, of course, prevent him from seeing an oblative sign, such as the *augurium ex acuminibus*; cf. Driediger-Murphy 2019, 88–89. Similarly Livy (34.55.4) reports that the senate limited reports of earthquakes early in the year 193; cf. Rasmussen 2000, 19. For this strategy, see Liebeschuetz 1979, 24–25. **ne impediretur auspiciis:** Similarly, Caesar was not about to be impeded by the warning of the *summus haruspex* (cf. on §52). **facere iter** is "to advance" (usually in military contexts): *OLD* s.v. *iter* 4a.

huic simile est . . . iumenta iubeant diiungere: The *iuges auspicium* was a type of *auspicium ex quadrupedibus*; cf. Paul. ex Fest. p. 92 L.: *iuges auspicium est cum iunctum iumentum stercus fecit.* Cf. Regell 1882, 14, and 1893, 18 and n. 47 (on Serv. *Aen.* 3.537). Dumézil 1966, 94–98 = 1970, 84–88, interprets the phrase *iouxmenta kapiad* on the sixth-century Lapis niger (= *CIL* 1.2^2 1) as *iumenta capiat*, with the previous]*od* interpreted as abl. of the word for "yoke": "let him (sc. the priest's servant [*kalator*]) take the yoked animals from the yoke" so as to avoid their simultaneous dunging and hence a bad omen. Other interpretations are available, however; see Driediger-Murphy 2019, 86n91 with literature.

78a quid est aliud . . . si fiat, videri?: Marcus concludes his review of current practices in Roman auspication with this pointed question, implying again that they are not sincere attempts to determine the divine will but a sham; cf. §71b: *simulacra . . . auspiciorum*. Though Driediger-Murphy 2019, 90 (cf. 112–13), suggests that Marcus "is probably exaggerating to strengthen his case," the status of current auspices is not in dispute between Marcus and Quintus (cf. 1.27–28), so there is no apparent motive for tendentiousness. Elsewhere she admits that "there seems to have been a real breakdown in elite adherence to divinatory customs, conventions, and norms in this period" (2019, 99).

78b Nam illud admodum ridiculum . . . regnum et possessiones suas: Marcus critically reviews Quintus' account of Deiotarus' attitude toward participation in the civil war: *posteaquam a Caesare tetrarchia et regno pecuniaque multatus est, negat se tamen eorum auspiciorum quae sibi ad Pompeium proficiscenti secunda evenerint paenitere . . . sibique eas* *aves quibus auctoribus officium et fidem secutus esset bene consuluisse* (1.27). **auspiciorum quae sibi . . . facta sint paenitere:** Deiotarus' comment is similar to that of Socrates, who said that his divine sign had not warned him prior to going to court or making his speech on the day he was condemned (Pl. *Ap.* 40a–b and 41d, cited at 1.124); but if Plato was the model here, doubts arise that Deiotarus actually said this; cf. Timpanaro 1988, 376. **ad Pompeium proficiscenti:** Deiotarus had good reason to throw in his lot with Pompey, under whose reorganization of the East in 63–62 he had received land in Pontus and the Kingdom of Lesser Armenia as well as the title of "king"; cf. Cimma 1976, 213 and n. 71; Sullivan 1990, 51 and 164; Seager 2002, 61 and 211n94. **amicitiam . . . populi Romani:** "Friend of the Roman people" was an official status granted by a magistrate or promagistrate in consultation with the senate; cf. Mommsen 1887–88, 3:1026; on Pompey's award of it to Deiotarus, cf. Cimma 1976, 232 and n. 112. Cicero improves upon the conventional designation at *Phil.* 2.93: *de rege Deiotaro, populi Romani amicissimo.* **antiquiorem enim sibi . . . possessiones suas:** *antiquior* = "preferable" (*OLD* s.v. *antiquus* 10a). Cicero also attributes such highmindedness to Deiotarus in his defense speech (§36), where he compares the comment of Antiochus III, when forced to cede his territory east of the Taurus, that the Romans had relieved him of an administrative burden. In fact, Deiotarus was not indifferent to territorial interests, as is shown by the fact that upon learning of Caesar's death he immediately reannexed his lost territories and paid a bribe of ten million sesterces to Antony's wife Fulvia in order to be permitted to retain them (*Phil.* 2.94–95). The corrupt bargain was already known to Cicero by April 22 (*Att.* 14.12[366].1). One wonders whether Cicero would have mentioned this had he known about Deiotarus' reappropriation before publication; cf. Durand 1903, 178. Boes 1981, 172, supposes that Cicero passed over the matter in silence out of contempt for Antony and Fulvia.

78b–79 credo id quidem . . . dum praestetur fides: For *quidem* preparing for the following adversative, cf. on §66 (*potest illud quidem esse falsum*); Madvig's substitution of *equidem* is unwanted (it adds an extra short syllable, destroying a cretic). **sed hoc nihil ad auspicia:** Sc. *pertinet*: "but this has nothing to do with auspices." Marcus goes on to clarify that the auspices are amoral: they can only predict the success or failure of a contemplated action; they cannot offer counsel about the right course of action. **recte . . . facere** is to take the morally correct action; cf. *Leg.* 1.19, 2.9–10; *Fin.* 3.24, etc. **ipse hoc sentiebat** "he knew this on his own" (*OLD* s.v. *ipse* 7). **sicuti sensit:** The foregoing imperfect provides the background, whereas *sensit* refers to the specific act of resolving to join Pompey's forces. **virtutis auspiciis**

video esse usum Deiotarum: Cicero speaks metaphorically of the "auspices of virtue," i.e., which of the contemplated actions would be the virtuous one (as opposed to the usual "auspices of success"). Epictetus (*Diss.* 2.7.3) makes a similar point: "Have I not within me the diviner that has told me the true nature of good and of evil, that has set forth the signs characteristic of both of them?" (tr. Oldfather). **quae vetat . . . dum praestetur fides** "which forbids looking to fortune until one has given proof of one's loyalty." For *fidem praestare*, cf. *OLD* s.v. *praesto* 11b. He thus places morally correct action above the external goods, the Peripatetic valuation of goods favored in *Fin.* 5 (but cf. the reservations of Long 2015) and, in a kind of coalition with Stoicism, at *Tusc.* 5.

79 aves vero <si> . . . certe fefellerunt: Quintus stated that Deiotarus had reported favorable omens at his departure to join Pompey (*sibi ad Pompeium proficiscenti secunda evenerint*: 1.27) and mentioned that the sign of an eagle guided the king's action on another occasion (1.26). Marcus comments that if the auspices promised success, they deceived him (*fefellerunt*). He goes on to sketch the dénouement.

fugit e proelio . . . et hospitem et regem: Though Cicero is usually associated with long, periodic sentences, he could use short sentences effectively, as here, where the short narratives, each followed by a brief comment, seem to mirror the rapidity of the unfolding events. Drastic actions tend to be emphasized by a leading verb (cf. Marouzeau 1938, 69), and so it is here with Deiotarus' initial actions, both of which involve the relationship with Pompey: *fugit . . . cum Pompeio . . . discessit ab eo* (Cicero gives the reasons for his abandonment of Pompey at *Deiot.* 13). The following comments (*grave tempus . . . luctuosa res*) give a subjective reaction. Then the order is reversed, with Caesar and his attributes dominating the next phase (*Caesarem . . . hostem et hospitem* [a play on words]) and Deiotarus as a mere observer (*vidit*); the following comment takes, for variety, the form of a rhetorical question: *quid hoc tristius?* After Pharsalus, Deiotarus allied himself with Caesar's legate Domitius Calvinus in the hope of recovering his Pontic possessions, including Lesser Armenia, which Deiotarus had received from Pompey (see on §78b [*ad Pompeium proficiscenti*]) but had been seized by Pharnaces II, son of Mithridates VI. In the summer of 47, coming to Asia Minor from Alexandria, Caesar met Deiotarus, confirmed his status as king, and accepted his hospitality and gifts (this will be the occasion referred to here, which was also the focus of Cicero's defense of the king). After Caesar defeated Pharnaces at Zela, however, he stripped Deiotarus of the tetrarchy of the Trocmi (which Deiotarus had seized a few years previously) as punishment for having taken Pompey's side. Caesar awarded this together with Lesser Armenia to the young prince Mithridates of Pergamum for services in the Alexandrine War; cf. *BAlex.* 78.2–3; Cimma 1976, 269 and n. 26. Marcus alludes to him disparagingly: *adseculae suo Pergameno nescio quo*, *assecula* being, since the *Verrines*, a term for a hanger-on; cf. *OLD* s.v.; for depreciatory *nescio quis* "someone or other" cf. *OLD* s.v. *nescio* 5b. Cf. detailed account by Niese, *RE* s.v. Deiotarus 2. **Armeniam a senatu datam:** The participial adjunct is, of course, from Cicero's point of view, damning. **magnificentissumo hospitio** is likely to be exaggerated; at *Fam.* 9.12(263).2 Cicero tells Dolabella that his speech for the king was light and coarse-spun like the king's own gifts (*levidense crasso filo, cuius modi ipsius solent esse munera*). This is for the sake of the following point: *spoliatum reliquit et hospitem et regem*. In his speech before Caesar, of course, Cicero had put the best face on this: *hospitem agnovisti, regem reliquisti*, i.e., he accepted his hospitality and did not deprive him (altogether) of his realm (*Deiot.* 10; cf. 8).

sed labor longius . . . non ab auspiciis petita sunt: *labor* is used of "slipping" away from the topic (*OLD* s.v. *labor*[1] 9b); cf. *Leg.* 1.52: *labebar longius, nisi me retinuissem*. Marcus then reiterates the distinction drawn in §78 between *eventa* and *officium*, the former sought from bird-signs, but the latter derived from the individual's character. For the emphatic colloquial negation *nullo modo*, cf. on §24.

80 Omitte igitur lituum . . . cotem Atti Navi: Quintus had told of both of these incidents at 1.30–33. The *lituus* was a curved staff free of knots (Livy 1.18.7) of Etruscan origin, as paintings and other monuments show (cf. Thulin 1905–9, 3:113–15), that was carried by augurs as a mark of their office. Romulus' *lituus* was said to have survived the conflagration that followed the Gallic capture of Rome in 390; cf. D.H. 14.2; V. Max. 1.8.11; Plut. *Rom.* 22; Plut. *Cam.* 32. Marcus alludes economically to the tale of Attus Navius, a simple swineherd who accepted and successfully executed the challenge of the king Tarquinius Priscus to cut a whetstone with a razor and thus became the royal augur; a *puteal* or enclosed curbstone in the Forum commemorated the site of the deed. See further Schultz 2014 on 1.31.

nihil debet esse . . . deinde constantiam: Starting at §27 with a complaint about his brother's *commenticiorum exemplorum mirifica copia*, Marcus has repeatedly challenged the credibility of Quintus' evidence; cf. §§46 and 66. At §27 he went on to say that the philosopher's task is to teach with arguments and reasoning. Here he outlines three steps to be applied: to determine (1) the nature of augury, (2) how it was discovered, (3) its consistency.

quae est igitur natura . . . aut cantu aut volatu?: *natura quae volucris . . . efficiat*: subj. of tendency; cf. on §19 (*nisi quod . . . rato tempore*). *vetare* and *iubere* give the bird-signs the typical force of law; cf. *Leg.* 1.18: *lex est ratio . . . quae iubet ea quae facienda sunt, prohibetque contraria.* The two modalities (*cantu . . . volatu*) correspond in augural terminology to two types of signifying birds, *oscines* and *alites*; cf. 1.120; Fest. 214 L.; Paul. ex Fest. 3 L.

cur autem aliis a laeva . . . ratum auspicium facere possint?: The arbitrariness implied here is argued further by comparing foreign practice (§82). For *ratus*, cf. on §63.2–3.

quo modo autem . . . habere divinitatis auctores?: Marcus now moves to point (2), the question of how augury was discovered (see above). *tamen* is elliptical; the implication seems to be: the Etruscans have an absurd story, *but nevertheless* they have one; cf. §50. Attus Navius, though an identifiable early augur, can hardly be the founder of the discipline, since Romulus and Remus, both attested as augurs, were much earlier. The Pisidians, Cilicians, and Phrygians have been named as peoples especially devoted to augury (1.92; cf. also 1.2 and 25, where the Phrygians are omitted; for Quintus' geographical explanation, cf. 1.94). They might thus be thought to be the likely originators of augury. But Marcus retorts with the incredulous question: Do we wish to have people devoid of humanity (or civilization) as sponsors of divine power? Cf. Gordon 2008, 93, on "the Roman habit of identifying their own Empire with the scope of *humanitas*." When juxtaposed with *humanitas*, *divinitas* will be "the divine" or "divine power"; cf. 2.26 (*ex divinitate*) with *OLD* s.v. 2, not a substitute for *divinationis*, as Pease ad loc. supposed. In terms of Quintus' general thesis, viz., that the proof of the gods' existence can be buttressed by the validity of divination (1.9), the Pisidians, etc., would, as the supposed originators of augury, be the prime sponsors of divine power. For the underlying categories, cf. 1.2: *gentem . . . nullam video neque tam humanam atque doctam neque tam inmanem tamque barbaram . . .* Cicero's favorite clausula rounds off the argument.

81 'At omnes reges . . . placeat multitudo!: Cicero had invoked the wide diffusion of divination to argue the importance of the subject in the author's preface (1.2). Quintus took up the point at 1.84 to bolster his case for the authenticity of divination. Marcus launches a two-pronged attack: (1) the consensus is worthless, since the judges are unqualified (§81); (2) the consensus is illusory, since different augural practices are followed in different places (§§82–83a). **quasi vero . . . vulgare** "as if there were anything so immensely widespread as foolishness," quoted with approval by Diderot

(1875, 148). Two colloquialisms add force to this assertion: the intensifier *valde* (cf. Hofmann 2003, 202–3) and *nihil* (ibid. 208). **aut quasi . . . placeat multitudo:** Quintus' disapproval of the judgment of the crowd is shown by his support for optimate policies, in particular his brother's consulship and recall from exile (the latter stand almost cost Quintus his life in a riot on January 23, 57: *Sest.* 75–76). Indeed, Quintus is represented as taking a more extreme optimate view than Marcus on the tribunate of the plebs and on voting laws (*Leg.* 3.17, 19–26, 34–37).

quotus quisque est . . . sequitur eorum auctoritatem multitudo?: For *quotus quisque*, cf. on §52a. In the course of exculpating his client, Cicero had dilated on the prevailing positive valuation of pleasure at *Cael.* 40–42. In ethics, *summum bonum* is the technical term for the ultimate value; Cicero argued against the Epicurean claim that pleasure should be considered as such at *Fin.* 2. The Stoics are singled out for taking the opposite position, rigorously excluding pleasure from the *summum bonum*, as argued by "Cato" in *Fin.* 3 (esp. 16–17), and for their division of humankind into "sages" and "fools" and despising of the latter (cf. *N.D.* 3.11, Cotta addressing the Stoics generally: *placet igitur tantas res opinione stultorum iudicari, vobis praesertim qui illos insanos esse dicatis?*). Because the multitude does not accept Stoic values, speeches before the people should, according to rhetorical doctrine, appeal to interests (*Part.* 91; cf. *Luc.* 144). On Epicureanism at mid-century as "a pervasive cultural phenomenon at Rome and in Italy," cf. Castner 1988, xiv–xv.

quid mirum igitur . . . verum dispicere non possint?: Cf. §148: *superstitio fusa per gentis oppressit omnium fere animos atque hominum inbecillitatem occupavit.* **inbecilli animi:** For the combination, cf. *Ac.* 1.44; for derisive reference to believers in divination cf. §36a (*aniculae*). **superstitiosa ista concipiant** "entertain those superstitious beliefs." For *iste* cf. on §32 *init.* Cf. also *OLD* s.v. *concipio* 9a. **dispicere** "perceive (mentally)," cf. *OLD* s.v. *dispicio* 3b.

82 Quae autem est . . . et coniuncta constantia?: Consistency was the third of the three criteria for belief in augury distinguished at §80; this will be disputed by appealing to comparative evidence.

ad nostri auguri . . . dextra meliora: Ennius' verse (*An.* 541 Sk.; similarly Cic. *Mar.* F 17.12 Courtney = 1.106) is unplaced. *tonuit* is probably impersonal ("it thundered"), though a personal construction with *Iuppiter* would be conceivable. *laevum* is internal accusative, in imitation of the Greek construction in such verses as those quoted below (so Skutsch ad loc.). *bene* = "propitiously": *OLD* s.v. 10, citing this passage. Thunder from a clear sky (*tempestate serena*) was taken by the ancients as a strong sign of divine activity; cf. Cic. *Cons.* F 10.23–24 Courtney; Hor. *C.* 1.34. **Homericus Aiax:** As at §63 Cicero substitutes Agamemnon for Ulysses, so he substitutes Ajax for Ulysses here. If skimming the text, Cicero might have been misled by the fact that the name of Ajax occurs in the nominative case in the same line and before the name Odysseus (*Il.* 9.223). In any case, he correctly identifies the context, the embassy to Achilles, and the tenor of the speech (*querens de ferocitate Troianorum*). **prospera Iuppiter . . . edit** = fr. 26 Bl. Cicero is ostensibly translating *Il.* 9.236–37 ("Zeus, son of Cronus, flashed lightning for them, displaying signs on the right"); the verse does not explicitly identify this as favorable, as Cicero does (*prospera*). It has therefore been suggested that Cicero has conflated this verse with *Il.* 2.353 ("flashing lightning on the right, displaying favorable signs"). This is possible, though Cicero may simply have chosen, for the sake of clarity, to make explicit what was implicit in the Greek. On Cicero's rendering, see further Chinnici 2000, 48–50. **Graiis et barbaris:** Though "chiefly poetic" (*OLD* s.v. 1), *Graius* is sometimes used by Cicero (instead of *Graecus*) when paired or contrasted with another ethnic term; for the origin of *Graius* and *Graecus*, cf. Hadas-Lebel 2012, esp. 69–73.

quamquam haud ignoro . . . haec quanta dissensio est!: Marcus is aware, he says, of the usage by which *sinistra* designates favorable things in general, regardless of position (cf. on §76b *sinistra*), but supposes that the Romans used "left" in this way (Timpanaro's <*ita*> is adopted here for smoothness) and foreigners "right" in accord with the general culture-specific location of good and evil omens; for a different interpretation, cf. Linderski 1995, 494–95.

83a quid, quod aliis avibus . . . multa fallendo?: *aliis avibus utuntur*: This was explained at §76 (*omnibus fere avibus utuntur, nos admodum paucis*). **aliis signis:** I.e., "left" and "right" signify different things, as Marcus just explained. **aliter observant** may refer to orientation in taking auspices: it is known that the Roman augur faced south for the *augurium stativum* (cf. 1.31), but not which way he faced for observation of the sky; cf. Linderski 1986, 2280–81, esp. n. 536. **partim . . . partim . . . multa:** *partim* is treated as a quasi substantive, functioning as subject of *susceptum esse* and being limited by a partitive genitive (*horum*) and taken up by *multa*; see Pinkster 2015, 1300–1301; *OLD* s.v. *partim* 1. For *superstitio*, cf. on §19 *fin.* Having himself denounced dishonest seers (1.132), Quintus is not well placed to mount a defense against Marcus' charge of deceit (*fallendo*).

83b Atque his superstitionibus . . . copiosum et disertum: Besides the broader sense in which it is equivalent to our word "omen," Latin *omen* also had the technical sense of an omen contained in a chance remark (= Greek κληδών); cf. *OLD* s.v. 1 and 2; Engels 2007, 280–82. Quintus had cited the two cases mentioned here: (1) Aemilia Tertia's report of the death of the puppy Persa to her father Aemilius Paulus (cos. II 168), which he formally accepted as a favorable omen for his imminent campaign against the Macedonian king Perseus, whom he famously defeated at the battle of Pydna (cf. *MRR* 1:427); (2) the words with which Metellus' wife Caecilia yielded her *sedes* ("seat" or "home") to her niece, which seemed to presage her death and the niece's subsequent marriage to her uncle (1.103–4; for further detail see Schultz 2014 ad loc.). In our passage, a verb of saying is understood in the clauses *Aemilia . . . perisse* and *Caecilia . . . tradere.* **Aemilia Paulo Persam perisse:** Another notable instance of alliteration; cf. on §21 (*si . . . auspicium quibus pugnare prohibebatur paruisset*). **iam illa:** Sc. *non dubitasti . . . adiungere*, supplied from above. *illa* = "the words" (used in citing; cf. *OLD* s.v. *ille* 13b). **'favete linguis':** The formula calling for silence prior to ritual acts; cf. on §71 above. **'praerogativam, omen comitiorum':** Marcus cites Quintus' words at 1.103 (*praerogativam etiam maiores omen iustorum comitiorum esse voluerunt*); hence the accusative. **hoc est . . . copiosum et disertum:** *hoc* summarizes the preceding direct quotations and should be preceded by a dash to show the relation. *ipse* reinforces the following reflexive: *OLD* s.v. 2.

quando enim ista observans . . . sed rationem ducem?: Quintus had claimed that Marcus himself had observed such superstititious customs both as consul and as a commander, i.e., during his term as governor of Cilicia (1.103), when his troops had proclaimed him *imperator*; cf. *Att.* 5.20(113).3 and 5; *Fam.* 2.10(86).3 and 15.4(110).10; Combès 1966, 74. Marcus, however, objects that following such practices is at odds with the calm, balanced frame of mind one needs for taking action (*ad rem gerendam*: *OLD* s.v. *gero* 9a). Cf. §149 *fin.*: *quorum* [sc. omens of one kind or another] *necesse est plerumque aliquid eveniat, ut numquam liceat quieta mente consistere.*

itane, si quis aliquid . . . aut alacritatem?: With this pointed question Marcus implies that it is folly to allow such chance utterances to influence one's thinking. For *itane* cf. on §68.

84 cum M. Crassus . . . si omini paruisset: In the aftermath of Crassus' disaster at Carrhae (see on §22), the Romans cast about for possible warnings that could have averted the debacle (or indeed scapegoats on whom to foist the blame; cf. 1.29–30 with Driediger-Murphy 2018). One such was this proclamation of a merchant hawking figs imported from Caunus in Caria that chanced to coincide with the embarkation of Crassus' army at Brundisium: *cauneas* (sc. *ficus vendo* or *emite*; such figs were so renowned that the mere mention of the provenance sufficed to identify them; cf. Pease ad loc.). This, according to Marcus, could have been understood as *cave ne eas*. Krostenko 2000, 359n21, explains: there would be iambic shortening of the *-e* in *cave*, then *e* > *i* in a medial syllable and disappearing (e.g., *balineum* > *balneum*; with *v*, of course, as a glide, not a fricative) and elision of *ne eas*. **dicamus** is hortatory subj. and governs the following infinitives (*monitum* [sc. *esse*] and *fuisse periturum*). For *si placet*, cf. on §28 (*inspiciamus, si placet*).

quae si suscipiamus . . . sternumenta erunt observanda: I.e., one will find oneself living the rules-bound life of the superstitious man depicted by Theophrastus (*Char.* 16). Pease ad loc. cites instances of such actions being taken as omens. **erunt observanda** "we shall have to pay great attention to, be mindful of" (*OLD* s.v. *observo* 6). A famous example was Caesar, who stumbled upon disembarking in Africa but quick-wittedly grabbed the earth and proclaimed, "I hold you, Africa," turning the incident into a good omen for the sake of his troops' morale (Suet. *Jul.* 59; Dio 42.58.3; a bit differently Front. *Strat.* 1.12.2; cf. Gelzer 1968, 265).

85–87a Lot-Divination

Quintus mentioned lot-divination in passing (1.34) and expressed disapproval of the itinerant *sortilegi* among other mercenary diviners (1.132; cf. Klingshirn 2006, 148–50). Evidently recalling the practice of lot-divination at the temple of Fortuna at Praeneste (mod. Palestrina), Cicero decided to explore it further. It thus becomes the only Italian divinatory practice discussed by Marcus that is centered on a specific site outside of Rome. The contents can be outlined as follows:

1. The nature of lot-divination and motives for its invention (85)
2. The founding and procedure of lot-divination at Praeneste
   a. Numerius Suffustius split a rock and discovered lots engraved on tablets of oak.
   b. Honey flowed from an olive tree from which a chest was made to hold the lots (86).
   c. A child shuffles and distributes them.
3. Criticism:

a. How were the lots produced?
b. The Stoic defense of them is superstitious.
c. Lot-divination has been marginalized except among the common people (87a).

85 Sortes restant et Chaldaei . . . et ad somnia: Assuming that augury has been dispatched, Marcus now turns to the remaining departments of technical divination, lot-divination and astrology (the latter at §§87b–99; for *Chaldaei* see ad loc.); for the general plan, cf. on §§28-99. Then (after an interlude: §§100–109) the two types of natural divination, inspired prophecy and dreams, will follow (at §§110–18 and §§119–47 respectively).

dicendum igitur putas de sortibus "You think, then, that we ought to discuss lots," perhaps an inference from 1.34 and §38 (not a question, as it is sometimes taken to be; see on §59 *init.*). However, one might consider reading *<quid> dicendum igitur putas de sortibus?* "What, then, do you think we ought to say about lots?"—an open-ended rhetorical question, but a reasonable one to start the discussion; cf., e.g., §136: *de nostris somniis quid habemus dicere?* To postpone *igitur* beyond the second position is not a problem; cf. *OLD* s.v. 2c.

quid enim sors est? . . . nec consilium valet: Marcus identifies lot-divination as essentially a game of chance, like *micare* (to play the game morra, that involves guessing "the total number of fingers held up by oneself and one's opponent": *OLD* s.v. *mico* 3) or one of the several types of dice-games played by the Romans (the *talus* being a cube marked on four sides, the *tessera* on all six; cf. *OLD* s.v. *tessera* 1). For the contrasting factors cf. *Marc.* 7: *numquam enim temeritas cum sapientia commiscetur nec ad consilium casus admittitur*; *Fam.* 5.2(2).8: *huius ego temeritati si . . . non restitissem, quis esset qui me in consulatu non casu potius existimaret quam consilio fortem fuisse?* For Cicero's disapproval of gaming and those who engage in it, cf. *Att.* 1.16(16).3 (of the jurors in the Bona Dea trial); *Off.* 1.150; *Phil.* 2.67, 3.35, 5.12, 8.26.

tota res est inventa . . . aut ad errorem: *inventio* was a topic Marcus had explored under haruspicy and augury (§§50b and 80). Here he emphasizes deceit (*fallaciis*) as the motive before he even names the inventor; this factor was highlighted at 1.132 and §83 and will be again at §97a. **ad quaestum** ("for gain") would apply to the *sortilegi* and other diviners denounced by Quintus at 1.132; Marcus does not, however, attempt to connect it specifically with the founder of Praenestine lot-divination, Numerius Suffustius.

atque ut in haruspicina . . . quae tradatur inventio: Marcus cross-refers to the story of Tages recounted at §50b. There is this difference, however: whereas Tages was supposed to have been the founder of *haruspicina* in general, Numerius Suffustius was the founder of lot-divination only at Praeneste, albeit it spread from there to Veii and Caere; cf. Riemann 1988, 62. The practice is also attested at Falerii, Patavium, etc. (cf. Latte 1960, 177n3; Champeaux 1990); hence Marcus qualifies this as the "discovery of the most distiguished lots" (*clarissumarum sortium . . . inventio*); cf. the prophecy reported at §86: *summa nobilitate illas sortis futuras.*

Numerium Suffustium . . . priscarum litterarum notis: *Numerium Suffustium* takes first position as the new topic. He is known from no other source (cf. Münzer, *RE* s.v. Suffustius). The *praenomen* "Numerius/Numesius" is attested in various Etruscan cities and has an Oscan variant *N(i)um(mp) si(o)s*; the earlier form *Numasius* appears on the Praenestine fibula (*CIL* XIV 4123, now again regarded as authentic [seventh century?]; cf. Maras 2012, reporting scientific research by E. Formigli and D. Farro); cf. Schulze 1904, 164, 198. The *nomen* "Suffustius" is otherwise unknown. That he was from a noble family (*honestum . . . et nobilem*) will have lent some credibility to his story. **Praenestinorum monumenta:** Perhaps priestly annals. Cicero's information is supplemented by excavations of the temple of Fortuna; cf. Fasolo and Gullini 1953; Kähler 1958; Hanson 1959, 33–36; Riemann 1988, who cites further literature. **somniis crebris, ad extremum etiam minacibus:** For a crescendo of threatening dreams, cf. the experience of the *rusticus Romanus* reported at 1.55. **perterritum visis** "frightened to death by the (dream-)visions." **inridentibus suis civibus** "though mocked by his fellow citizens." **sortis . . . in robore insculptas** "lots engraved on oak." Because of the perishable material, no lots are extant at Praeneste, but lots made of stone or metal have survived from other oracular sites; see further Champeaux 1990; Buchholz 2013. There is also a famous depiction of lot-divination on the engraved lid of a bronze box in the collection at the Villa Giulia (inv. no. 13133). The scene shows a child emerging from a cave and holding a tablet that he reads or presents to a pensive man beside him; other votaries are seen waiting their turn; cf. Brendel 1960, 45–46 with Figure 4; Klingshirn 2006, 144 and nn. 40–41. **priscarum litterarum notis** "with ancient lettering": *OLD* s.v. *nota* 6b; cf. *N.D.* 3.42: *Ioves quoque pluris in priscis Graecorum litteris invenimus*; Livy 7.3.5: *lex vetusta est, priscis litteris verbisque scripta*; Ov. *Fast.* 3.844: *et hoc signo littera prisca docet.* For the Praenestine inscriptions, including remarks on the early alphabet, cf. Vetter 1953, 333–56, esp. 334–35.

is est hodie locus . . . colitur a matribus: The place where the trove of sacred lots was discovered was fenced off (*saeptus*), as were the sites of other divine interventions (cf. 1.101 with Pease's n.). At the excavated site, this corresponds to a *puteal* of tufa with surrounding marble colonnade: Riemann 1988, 51. **propter Iovis pueri:** *propter* for *prope* ("near") is an archaism typical of Cicero's dialogues; cf. von Albrecht 2003, 87. Either a sacred precinct (*templum*) or a temple (*aedem*) could be supplied as the understood object of *propter*; the excavations show, however, that it was the former and was also the site of the foundation for a seated figure (the fill of the *puteal* brought the head of a goddess to light): Riemann 1988, 51–52. Cicero paints a picture of two cults at this site, one of *Iuppiter puer*, the other of Fortuna. This is very doubtful, however. A cult of *Iuppiter puer* is attested neither in votive inscriptions found at this site nor anywhere else (cf. Koch 1937, 47, emphasizing the uniqueness). Cicero's interpretation also creates the problem that at Praeneste Fortuna was both the "first-born child of Jupiter," as the votive inscriptions attest (*CIL* XIV 2863 and 2862), and the mother-figure nursing the infants Jupiter and Juno, as Cicero claims. In fact, the infants depicted being suckled by Fortuna or other goddesses are anonymous, and a suckling child is an *infans*, not a *puer*. Cicero's information could derive from popular misunderstanding of the iconography, learned guesswork, or priestly interpretation; cf. Riemann 1988, 51, 56, and 58. **lactens . . . in gremio sedens, mammam adpetens:** For *lactens* = "sucking, unweaned," cf. *OLD* s.v. *lacto* 1; similarly §47, *Romulus lactens*. *mammam adpetens* adds life and movement to what would otherwise have been a static picture. **castissime colitur a matribus:** I.e., this was a typical women's cult, as is also suggested by the oldest votive inscription at the site, dedicated by a matron thanking the goddess for successful childbirth (*CIL* I^2 60 with Schultz 2000, 53). Lot-divination at Praeneste was thus overlaid onto a preexisting cult of Fortuna: so Riemann 1988, 54. Cf. Champeaux 1982–87, 1:55, envisioning a different development, with the filiation "daughter of Jupiter" superimposed on the original wetnurse *Fortuna kourotrophos*. For a different view, doubting any special connection with mothers, cf. Miano 2018, 44.

86 eodemque tempore in eo loco . . . Fortunae monitu tolluntur: Honey flowing from an olive tree seems to be unparalleled, but in folklore honey is a widespread symbol of wealth (cf. on §66); hence the prophecy of the (surely local) haruspices; on the prosperity of the sanctuary see Carneades' comment (§87a). *arca* can denote any chest or box; there is no basis for assuming (as does Pease ad loc.) that the lots were merely stored in this box but drawn from some other container. For *tollo* used of "drawing" lots, cf. *OLD* s.v. 1b; it is varied by *ducuntur* in the next sentence.

quid igitur in his . . . cecidit, dolavit, inscripsit?: Upon the foundation narrative follows the critical deconstruction. For *quid . . . certi*, cf. on §8 *fin.* (*aliquid certi*). **in his:** Sc. *sortibus*, to which *istae* in the next sentence also refers back. Marcus takes up from §§15–18 the argument about the incompatibility of fortune with something that is fixed (and can therefore be predicted). Cicero tolerates repetitions (such as *Fortunae monitu*) in his less formal writing; cf. Dyck 1996, 616–17. **pueri manu:** Marcus takes this as a sign of the unreliability of the procedure (*quid . . . potest esse certi*), but in anthropological terms, the child is a "randomizing device," widely used even in modern times to help ensure that the process is not being manipulated by the administrators; cf. Maurizio 1995, 80–81. For deployment of children in lot-divination generally, cf. Grottanelli 1993, 41–52, and 2005, 132; in other forms of divination, Johnston 2001. A boy holding a tablet inscribed SORS appears on the reverse of a coin issued in the year 69 by M. Plaetorius Cestianus, who before his adoption was a native of Praeneste; cf. *RRC* 405/2. **in illo loco:** I.e., the place where in his dream Numerius Suffustius was commanded to cut the rock (§85). Marcus also wants to know who prepared the inscribed oak tablets and enumerates the stages of the process to emphasize the difficulty (*cecidit, dolavit, inscripsit*).

'Nihil est,' inquiunt . . . et miseria crederent!: Cf. §36a: *deorum . . . numini parere omnia*; *N.D.* 3.92: *vos* [sc. *Stoici*] *. . . ipsi dicere soletis nihil esse quod deus efficere non possit*; a similar point is attributed to the Stoics at *Luc.* 47. For the "wretchedness" resulting from the Stoic position, cf. §§149–50a as well as *N.D.* 3.14: *miserum est enim nihil proficientem angi nec habere ne spei quidem extremum et tamen commune solacium.*

86–87a sed hoc quidem genus divinationis . . . quam Praeneste vidisse Fortunam: *vita communis* "everyday life," as at 1.51. *explodo* is "to drive offstage by clapping, etc.," hence, as here, "reject": *OLD* s.v. 1 and 3. Cf. the similar dismissal at §148a: *explodatur* <*igitur*> *haec quoque somniorum divinatio*. Similarly of antiquated philosophical doctrines at *Off.* 1.6: *Aristonis, Pyrrhonis, Erilli iam pridem explosa sententia est.* Though Marcus has some respect for the *fani pulchritudo et vetustas* that preserves the fame (*nomen*) of the Praenestine lots (cf. 1.34: *ipsa sors contemnenda non est, si et auctoritatem habet vetustatis*), he quickly adds a restriction. **atque id in volgus** "and that among the common people." *in vulgus* is usually used with a verb such as *edo* indicating dissemination of information "to the general public" or "publicly": *OLD* s.v. *vulgus* 1b. In colloquial speech, the expression seems to have become a quasi adverb used where there is reference to knowledge or the lack of it; besides our passage, cf. *Att.* 9.5(171).2: *in vulgus ignotus* (rendered by Shackleton Bailey "generally unknown"); similarly *Agr.* 2.13: *lex in publicum proponitur*. From the fact that (Roman) magistrates and men of distinction do not consult them, it appears that centers of lot-divination currently have merely local significance. It was not always so, however. In the First Punic War, the senate intervened to thwart the plan of Q. Lutatius Cerco (cos. 241) to consult the Praenestine lots (V. Max. 1.3.2; cf. Ziolkowski 1987, but also Konrad 2015, arguing that V. Max. has confused two Lutatii and that Catulus [cos. 242] was meant)—the first attestation of the institution. But under the pressure of the Hannibalic War, the consul P. Sempronius Tuditanus vowed to build a temple of Fortuna Primigenia in the event of victory; cf. Livy 29.36.8 and 34.53.5; Wissowa 1912, 260 with n. 8; Orlin 1997, 64–65; Miano 2018, 105–7. But the cult seems not to have flourished at Rome, perhaps because the Romans distrusted the predictive power of lots; cf. Rosenstein 1995, esp. 48–50. **ceteris . . . in locis:** Cf. on §85 (*atque ut in haruspicina . . . quae traditur inventio*). **refrixerunt** "have cooled down, come to a halt": *OLD* s.v. *refrigesco* 2a. Cicero's report has been doubted on the ground that most of our information about lot-divination comes from this period: so Miano 2018, 40; cf. also Champeaux 1982–87, 1:81, finding Cicero's claim overstated. It is possible that Cicero put forward a tendentious claim to assist his polemic (see also Rüpke 2016, 27–28, criticizing Cicero for generally "failing to acknowledge the real level of religious pluralism"), but on the other hand, the earlier period will inevitably yield less evidence. If it is true that the centers of lot-divination were in decline at this time, this may be related to the fact that "independent diviners [i.e., the *sortilegi* of 1.132] had detached the sacred lots from such places and taken them on the road" (Klingshirn 2006, 149). **quod Carneadem . . . quam Praeneste vidisse Fortunam:** For Carneades and Clitomachus, cf. on §9. Perhaps the philosopher made a trip to Praeneste during his embassy to Rome in 155, on which see testimonies at Carneades T 7 Mette. **Praeneste** "at Praeneste" (the locative is homonymous with the nominative in neuter city-names ending in *-e*). Cicero was evidently struck by the play on words (which he renders *fortunatiorem . . . Fortunam*) and the justice of the comment (in view of the size and splendor of the temple).

87b–99 Astrology

It may have come as a surprise when Marcus mentioned at §85 that astrology (designated by the name of its practitioners, the *Chaldaei*) was to be treated. Though they were mentioned prominently in the proem (1.2), Quintus had referred to them only briefly in passing at 1.85 and 91; possibly this was because he took a dim view of the *de circo astrologi*, as he remarks at 1.132. In any event, the inclusion of astrology enables Cicero to comment on the horoscope of Rome recently prepared by Lucius Tarutius (§§98–99) and to conclude the treatment of technical divination with the strong point that the astrologers failed miserably to predict the manner in which Caesar, Pompey, and Crassus would meet their deaths (§99). On the "softer" position on astrology taken in *De fato* (§8), see Ioppolo 2002; on the explanation thereof by Green 2014, 86–93, see Dyck forthcoming.

Astrology was the most recent arrival of the forms of divination discussed in this work; it was imported from Babylon via Greece and received impetus from the new interest in the heavens fostered by Hellenistic astronomy. Astrology itself was not a unified discipline but had Babylonian, Greek, and Egyptian varieties; cf. Ripat 2011, 130. For collections of ancient (Greek) horoscopes, cf. Neugebauer and Van Hoesen 1959; Baccani 1992.

Astrologers are frequently called *Chaldaei* in our sources, a professional designation derived from an ethnic (= Babylonians; cf. *OLD* s.v. *Chaldaei* 1 vs. 2), but by the end of the Republic, astrologers "came from all over" (Ripat 2011, 129). They were well known at Rome by the second century: Cato forbids a steward to consult them (*Agr.* 5.4, quoted on §51 [*vetus autem illud Catonis*]), and they were banned from Rome and Italy by a praetor's edict in 139 (V. Max. 1.3; for such expulsions, which occurred repeatedly under the Empire, cf. in general Ripat 2011). Among the Stoics, Chrysippus appears to have accepted astrologers' predictions (*Fat.* 11b–16, 20 = *SVF* 2:954), whereas Diogenes of Babylon, a member of the "philosophers' embassy" to Rome in 155 (*SVF* 3 Diog. 6–10, 14), imposed some restrictions,and his pupil Panaetius of Rhodes rejected it altogther. Marcus' case is heavily dependent on the latter and may therefore not take account of more recent developments in astrological theory (see on §§92 *fin.* and 96). This section can be outlined as follows:

1. Eminent authorities in philosophy and astronomy reject astrology (87b).
2. The doctrine of astrology (89):
   a. A force permeating the heavens is variously affected by the stars and planets.
   b. The arrangement of heavenly bodies at one's birth determines a person's body, soul, and destiny.
3. Partial acceptance by Diogenes of Babylon (90):
   a. He allows that astrology can predict only general disposition and aptitudes.
   b. The case of the Spartan kings Procles and Eurysthenes.
4. Even this grants too much because (91)

a. Astronomical observations are unreliable, based upon evidence of the senses.
b. Mathematics teaches that the planets and stars are so distant that the posited influence can hardly exist.
c. Astrologers claim the same horoscope for all persons born anywhere on earth at the same time (92), but
   (1) Different constellations are visible above the horizon at different points on earth at the same time.
   (2) Weather conditions at birth might be expected to have an impact (94).
   (3) Astrology ignores the influence of parental seed on the child.
   (4) Empirical evidence shows people born at the same time have different characters (95).
   (5) The possibility of correction by surgery or training contradicts the theory of astral determinism (96).
   (6) Local variations in mind and body need to be taken into account.
   (7) The claim that the system is based on observations over 470,000 years is incredible (97).

5. Coda: further arguments supplied by Marcus:
   a. Those who died at Cannae all had the same fate, but hardly the same horoscope.
   b. Many are born simultaneously but with different fates.
   c. Under the theory, animals should also have horoscopes, but this is absurd (98).
   d. L. Tarutius' horoscope for the city of Rome is ridiculous.
   e. False prophecies were issued to Crassus, Pompey, and Caesar (99).

87b Ergo hoc divinationis genus . . . ad Chaldaeorum monstra veniamus: With *ergo . . . omittamus* Marcus draws a line under lot-divination. Marcus sets the tone for his refutation of astrology with *monstra* ("horrors"): the drastic expression is colloquial, to judge from its use in several of Cicero's letters: *venerat . . . Chaerippus, mera monstra* ["the most horrifying reports," tr. Shackleton Bailey] *nuntiarat* (*Att.* 4.7[77].1); *hunc igitur Catonem Lentulus a legibus removit et eos qui de Caesare monstra promulgarunt* (*Q.fr.* 2.5[9].3).

de quibus Eudoxus . . . minime esse credendum: Cicero begins his discussion of astrology by citing adverse judgments of experts, beginning with the eminent mathematician and astronomer Eudoxus of Cnidus (F 343 Lasserre), who might more accurately be called an associate than a pupil of Plato's (cf. also *Rep.* 1.22). On his contribution to astronomy, cf. Lloyd 1970, 86–94 and 97–98. The combination *facile princeps* is virtually Ciceronian property, six of seven attestations in classical Latin being his; cf., e.g., *Red. sen.* 5: *virtute gloria rebus gestis Cn. Pompeius . . . facile princeps.* It may seem odd that the man who is said to be *in astrologia . . . facile princeps* is opposed to what we would call "astrology." The reason is that the ancients made no clear distinction between *astronomia* and *astrologia* (cf. *OLD* s.v. the latter), the study of the stars per se and the study for predictive purposes. *notatio* here is "the action of defining or delimiting" (ibid. s.v. 5, where our passage is the sole citation); cf. §91: *cum . . . ea . . . animadvertant et notent sidera natalicia*; §146: *notandis rebus.*

88 nominat etiam Panaetius . . . praedicendi genus repudiavit: Panaetius doubted divination in general, as Cicero indicated at 1.6–7 = T 137 Alesse (cf. 1.12 = T 138 Alesse, where he is portrayed as the ally of Carneades); hence his rejection of astrology is no surprise. It is presumed that the general tenor of these sections (§§87b–97a *Panaetius dixerit*) derives from Panaetius (= T 140 Alesse, who, however, extends this to §98 *absurdius*), to which Cicero adds a coda with Roman examples and perhaps based at least in part on Carneades; see below. Long 2006, 132, suspects that Panaetius figures here as the major source because astrology was at most a minor topic in Carneades' refutation of Chrysippus. For Panaetius' position on astrology, see also Alesse 1994, 239–54. **nominat** is unusually construed with accusative and infinitive (*Anchialum et Cassandrum . . . non usos*), as if Cicero discovered in midsentence that he needed a verb of saying (translate: "identifies as not having used . . ."). In all, Panaetius cited the views of three astronomers who were his contemporaries and who all rejected astrology: the first two, Anchialus and Scylax, are otherwise uknown; Cassander may be the man who, according to Censorinus 18.11, estimated the length of the "great year." **idemque in regenda sua civitate princeps:** This fact lends him weight in Cicero's eyes; cf. *Off.* 1.19, where, after citing the studies of the astronomer C. Sulpicius and other theoreticians, he adds: *cuius studio a rebus gerendis abduci contra officium est* (he had, of course, argued the importance of political engagement in detail in the proem to *De republica*).

89 sed ut ratione utamur . . . natalia praedicta defendunt: At §27, Marcus had claimed that argumentation should have priority over witness-testimony; see ad loc. Since Quintus offered no case for astrology (cf. on §87b–99 *init.*), Marcus begins by setting out the basic doctrine before proceeding to a detailed refutation. **haec Chaldaeorum natalicia praedicta** "these astrologers' horosocopes," *hic* being used of what is familiar (and therefore possibly contemptible; cf. on §72 *haec sunt . . . internuntiae Iovis*).

vim quandam esse aiunt . . . quoque tempore "In the starry belt which the Greeks call the zodiac, they say there is a certain force of such a nature that every part of that belt affects and changes the heavens in a different way, according to the stars that are in this or in an adjoining locality at a given time" (tr. Falconer, slightly modified). **vim quandam** bears emphasis as the active agent, with *quidam* indicating that the *vis* is initially undefined (it is explained by the following *talem ut* . . .). **signifero in orbe:** As *signum* can be a "sign of the zodiac" (*OLD* s.v. 13b), so *signifer orbis* is used by Cicero of the zodiac itself; cf. *Arat.* 318 Soubiran; *N.D.* 2.53. Here Cicero chooses to clarify by adding the Greek term as well. **ut quaeque stellae in his finitumisque partibus sint:** By Cicero's day, it was known that the various signs of the zodiac are far distant, and the sun, moon, and planets are "in" them only by optical illusion; cf. §91; Bouché-Leclercq 1899, 574.

eamque vim varie moveri . . . et quadrata nominant) "This force is variously affected by the stars that are called 'wandering' stars when they have either come into that sign of the zodiac under which someone is born, or into a sign having some connection or accord [with the natal sign] (these they call 'triangles' or 'squares')" (tr. Falconer, modified). The lightly moving syllables of *vim varie moveri*, with vowels connected by glides, liquids, and nasals (*v*, *r*, *m*) and no obstruents, seem to mirror the agile force itself. Cicero leaves vague the respective contributions of the planets and the signs (of the zodiac) to the force he describes; see Bouché-Leclercq 1899, 181n1. **ab iis sideribus quae vocentur errantia:** *errantia* ("wandering") is a rendering of Greek πλάνητες; see further on §10. **cum aut[em] in eam ipsam partem . . . in qua . . . aut in eam quae:** The first *aut* is Thoresen's conjecture for the transmitted *autem*, a change surely needed to restore the proper relation of elements: one would expect that a clause joined with *autem* would be fully parallel to the preceding *vim quandam esse* etc., not merely a *cum*-clause. **coniunctum . . . consentiens:** For *coniunctum*, cf. Firm. Mat. *Math.* 2.23.1: *quaedam loca cum horoscopo diximus radiationis societate coniungi*; for *consentiens*, sch. Germ. *Arat.* p. 223.7–8 Breysig: *aspiciunt inter se stellae ex quinto signo, quod dicitur trigonum, et habent maximam consensionem*; see Pease ad loc. for further parallels. There is a problem, however, if these two terms, both favorable, are meant to refer respectively to the following *triangula* and *quadrata*, which are contrasting aspects. We may therefore have to burden Cicero with "a basic confusion" (Long 2006, 135). **(ea triangula illi et quadrata nominant):** *illi* are, of course, the astrologers. Cicero singles out the *triangula* and *quadrata* as the favorable and unfavorable aspects par excellence; they denote respectively distances of 120 and 90 degrees from one planet to the other; cf. Bouché-Leclercq 1899, 165–79; Pease 1920–23, 500.

etenim cum tempore anni . . . eventusque fingi: *etenim* introduces the explanation: "The fact is . . .": *OLD* s.v. a. Two causal *cum*-clauses provide the background. **tempore anni tempestatumque** "within the space of a year and of the seasons" (tr. Pease). **accessu stellarum et recessu** "as the stars approach and withdraw"; cf. §34a *accessus et recessus.* **ea vi solis efficiantur quae videmus:** *ea* is the subject of *efficiantur*. Cf. *N.D.* 2.49: *solis tum accessus modici tum recessus et frigoris et caloris modum temperant* with the following description of the resulting seasons. **non veri simile solum, sed etiam verum esse censent:** Cicero contrasts the dogmatist's assertion of truth with the probable, which the Skeptic aims at; cf. *N.D.* 3.95: *Velleio* [the Epicurean] *Cottae disputatio verior, mihi Balbi ad veritatis similitudinem videretur propensior.* **perinde utcumque temperatus sit aër . . . eventusque fingi:** Cicero cites examples at *Fat.* 7: *Athenis tenue caelum, ex quo etiam acutiores putantur Attici; crassum Thebis, itaque pingues Thebani et valentes*, on which see Sedley 1993, 321–31. **pueros orientis** "children at birth"; cf. *OLD* s.v. *orior* 6a. **animari atque formari** "are endowed with mental and physical characteristics." **actionem vitae** is the living of one's life (cf. §95 *ad agendam vitam*); cf. *Off.* 1.17: *ad eas res parandas tuendasque quibus actio vitae continetur.*

90 O delirationem incredibilem: For the exclamation involving a head noun and an evaluative adj., cf. Pinkster 2015, 363–64. *deliratio* is first attested at *Sen.* 36 (defined there as *senilis stultitia*); cf. §94 *tanta dementia*. Cicero exploits this sort of invective in speeches, such as *Pis.* or *Phil.* 2, but also in his more rhetorical *philosophica*; cf., e.g., *Parad.* 17 and 27. Long 2006, 133, notes that by the early Empire astrology had grown too strong to be dismissed so derisively.

non enim omnis error stultitia dicenda est: For the attraction of the verb to agree with the subject complement rather than the subject, cf. Pinkster 2015, 1261–62.

quibus etiam Diogenes Stoicus . . . fortunam plerumque disparem: Panaetius' teacher Diogenes of Babylon is the first Stoic known to have expressed reservations about the claims of astrology (*SVF* 3 Diog. 36). Long 2006, 132, explains that the Stoics grappled with astrology relatively late because horoscopic astrology was heavily dependent on developments in Hellenistic astronomy. Diogenes restricts astrology to being able "only" (*dumtaxat*) to predict a person's general nature (cf. on §95 *init.*) and aptitude and rejects any predictive power beyond that. As partial proof (*etenim*) he adduces twins, who may be similar in appearance (*forma*) but otherwise quite dissimilar; cf. Timpanaro 1988, 383, who thinks Diogenes may have taken over the argument about twins from Carneades (cf. *Luc.* 84–85). The topic was pursued by Augustine at *Civ.* 5.2–5, perhaps based on a lost passage of *Fat.* (cf. Kidd 1988 on Posid. F 111). For the reverberations of Augustine's treatment in the Middle Ages and Renaissance, cf. Pease ad loc.

Procles et Eurysthenes . . . rerum gestarum gloria praestitit: For the example introduced asyndetically, cf. on §56 *init.* These twin sons of Aristodemus, traditionally dated to the eleventh century, were the founders of the two royal lines at Sparta, as narrated by Herodotus (6.52) and Pausanias (3.1.7–9). *nec* coordinates with the following *-que. Procli* should be taken as gen. limiting *vita*; *is* refers to Procles as the nearer antecedent.

91 at ego id ipsum . . . animo videre debebant: *vir optimus* or *viri optimi* is often ironically applied to Epicurus and his followers when Cicero finds fault with them (cf. *Leg.* 1.21; *Tusc.* 1.6, 2.44, 3.50, etc.); similarly here with Diogenes. Marcus objects to the concession made *quasi quadam praevaricatione* ("as if collusively"), a litigator's term (*OLD* s.v. *praevaricatio*), hence the doubly apologetic *quasi quadam*; the reason is again introduced with *etenim*. **ortus nascentium:** A more compressed expression than *ortus eorum qui nascuntur* (cf. §89); cf. Laughton 1964, 79, arguing that the earliest substantivized participles were such masculine plurals. The moon is now given a prominence not foreshadowed by the general account of astrology at §89, albeit lunar influence was seen in the examples of the sympathetic bonds of the universe (§§33b–34). The influence of the moon is also emphasized, possibly after Posidonius, by the fourth century astronomical writer Cleomedes (2.3.179–80); cf. also Bouché-Leclercq 1899, 499–500 and 521n1; Kany-Turpin 2004, 24–25 n. 2, suspects that the older Chaldaean astrology is overlaid by a Stoicizing version. **animadvertant et notent:** These paired activities were invoked repeatedly by Quintus to give divination the aura of an objective science: 1.12, 25, 72; similarly 1.131 (*quae animadvertendo notarentur*); cf. also on §87b *fin.* (on *notatio*). **oculorum fallacissimo sensu iudicant:** Cicero assumes the critique of sense-based knowledge he put forward in the *Academici libri* (corresponding to *Luc.* 79–90). **quae ratione atque animo videre debebant:** Marcus explains in the sequel. For the sense of *videre*, cf. on §17 (*vident ex constantissimo motu lunae*); for an expression of obligation in indicative rather than subj., see on §71a (*parendum . . . religioni fuit*).

docet enim ratio mathematicorum . . . ultumum mundi est: *ratio mathematicorum* = the calculation of mathematicians (cf. *OLD* s.v. *ratio* 1; for *mathematici* cf. on §10). **quam istis notam esse oportebat:** A barbed comment: Sextus Empiricus reports that the astrologers put on airs by calling themselves *mathematici* (*M.* 5.2); cf. §98 of L. Tarutius Firmanus: *in primis Chaldaeicis rationibus eruditus. istis* carries a note of contempt (cf. on §59 [*nam si ista sequimur*]). In fact, the astrological system is based upon a naive picture of the universe that predates the mathematical calculations that revolutionized ancient astronomy (cf. on §10); cf. Bouché-Leclercq 1899, 572. *humilitas* is "lowness of position" (relative to earth); cf. *Tusc.* 5.69; *OLD* s.v. 2. The order of planets given here corresponds to that at *Rep.* 6.16 = 21 P. (except that there Mercury and Venus are said to revolve around the sun) but differs from that at *N.D.* 2.52–53, where the sun is omitted and Mercury and Venus are reversed. *N.D.* thus corresponds to Plato's order (*Rp.* 616d–e with Adam's note [where the moon and sun are added as the closest]; *Tim.* 38d [where the listing from near to far halts with Mercury]). Macrobius (*Somn. Scip. Comm.* 1.19.2) explains that Cicero follows Archimedes and the Chaldaeans, Plato the Egyptians. In any case, the more remote position of the sun reflects more recent and better astronomy. **cuius lumine conlustrari putatur:** Sc. *luna*; cf. on §10. **tria intervalla:** Actually four; perhaps Cicero (recalling *N.D.* 2.101?) decided to add the interval from Saturn to the heavens (*aether*), which is astrologically irrelevant, but forgot to alter the figure he found in his source. **quod extremum atque ultumum mundi est:** Similarly *N.D.* 2.101: *restat ultimus . . . caeli complexus, qui idem aether vocatur, extrema ora et determinatio mundi*; cf. *N.D.* 1.37.

92a quae potest igitur contagio . . . vel potius ad terram?: For *contagio* cf. on §33b (a different sense at §58). The astrologers countered that the moon and sun are likewise distant, but their influence is nonetheless conceded (cf. §33b). They supplemented that argument with the claim that where light penetrates, influence can also; cf. Bouché-Leclercq 1899, 572–74.

92b Quid, cum dicunt . . . caeli nosse appareat?: *id quod iis dicere necesse est*: Similar dictation at §21: *quod certe vobis ita dicendum est*; *N.D.* 1.84. **omnis omnium . . . in omni . . . omnibus:** The lumping together is heavily emphasized by polyptoton. **ortus** are the "risings," i.e., the planets appearing above the horizon (*OLD* s.v. 1). **quicumque <eodem tempore> gignantur:** In the transmitted form, the argument is incomplete (as the restatement of the argument in §93 shows); therefore *eodem tempore* is inserted between these two words, as proposed by Schäublin 1987, 185; a scribe's eye may have skipped from the *-e* of *quicumque* to that of *tempore.* **in omni terra quae incolatur:** The restriction is added advisedly; in his homily against earthly glory, the elder Africanus observed: *vides habitari in terra raris et angustis in locis . . . omnis . . . terra quae colitur* *a vobis* (*Rep.* 6.20–21 = 24–25 P.). **eademque . . . accidere necesse esse** "and the same accidents must occur to all," whereby "accident" has the sense "inessential qualities or properties"; cf. *condicio* at §93 *fin.*; Pease on *N.D.* 2.82 (*quaeque iis accidant*). **nonne eius modi <ea> sunt** "are they [i.e., the preceding claims of the astrologers] not such . . . ?" The insertion proposed by Timpanaro (1988, 384) seems to be required to complete the sense; otherwise the astrologers would have to be the subject of *sunt* as well as the subject of *nosse*. Marcus again guides the reader/interlocutor to the desired conclusion with a rhetorical question, this time with *nonne* signalling the expected (affirmative) response; cf. §9 on "railroading" *num.* **ut ne caeli quidem . . . nosse appareat?:** The irony is underlined by the repetition of *caeli*, the use of chiasmus, and by *ne . . . quidem*. As in §91 *(quam istis notam esse oportebat)*, *iste* carries an implication of contempt.

cum enim illi orbes . . . eodem tempore apud omnis: *(orbes) finientes* renders Greek ὁρίζοντες = horizons; cf. *OLD* s.v. *finio* 1c; cf. *finiens circulus* at Sen. *Nat.* 5.17.4; Chalcidius on *Tim.* 66 proposed instead *circulus finalis*. *aspectus* = "field of vision" (*OLD* s.v. 3a), not the astrological technical term "aspect." The variability of the horizon (the stars and planets appearing above which at the time of birth are decisive for the horoscope) vitiates the principle stated above: *omnis omnium ortus . . . eosdem esse*. But borrowing his critique from Panaetius, Cicero may not have adjusted to the current theory, since in the meantime the astrologers had developed the doctrine of the "ascensions" (ἀναφοραί) of the signs of the zodiac as a solution; cf. Bouché-Leclercq 1899, 580–81, with explanation of the system at 259–71; Long 2006, 138.

93 quodsi eorum vi . . . tanta sit dissimilitudo?: *eorum*: Sc. *siderum*. *modo hoc, modo illo modo* "now this way, now that"; cf. §24 with n. **qui potest** "how can . . . ?" (cf. on §17 *init.*). **vis . . . nascentium** "capacity of those who are born"; cf. *OLD* s.v. *vis* 14a; for the substantivized participle instead of a relative clause, cf. §91 with note. **caeli tanta . . . dissimilitudo:** Sc. because of the different phenomena visible above the horizon in various places.

in his locis quae nos incolimus . . . eadem condicione nasci: An illustrative example, in asyndeton (cf. on §56 *init.*). The Dog-Star or Sirius is designated in Latin in both poetry and prose as either *Canis* or *Canicula*. *Canis* is masculine in its earliest attestation (Cic. *Arat.* 138 Soubiran), and the variation in gender and the use of the diminutive have not been satisfactorily explained (for one attempt, cf. Hanssen 1952, 112–13). The rising of the Dog-Star at the latitude of Athens in 43 BCE would have occurred on July 29 (cf. Sharples 1991, 166), thus clearly "after the (summer) solstice." **et quidem**

aliquot diebus: Cf. on §68 (*et quidem subito*). **apud Trogodytas:** The Trogodytes were thought to live in the Eastern Desert of southern Egypt and Sudan (the spelling *Troglo-* is false as applied to this group; cf. *OCD* s.v.) and hence serve as an example of those in the extreme South. **ut scribitur:** Pease (ad loc.) suspects that Panaetius' source may have been Agatharchides of Cnidus, who is said to have written about the Trogodytes (*FGrH* 86 T 2 and 3). **si iam concedamus . . . pertinere:** *aliquid* should perhaps be taken as acc. of respect with *pertinere*; cf., e.g., *si quid forte ea res ad cogitationes tuas pertineret* (*Att.* 1.6[2].1). **confitendum sit illis:** *illi* are the astrologers; cf. §89 and below. **eodem tempore** but in different places. **in dissimilis incidere naturas** "enter into dissimilar natures": *OLD* s.v. *incido*[1] 6a, implying an inadvertent occurrence. **volunt enim illi . . . eadem condicione nasci:** On this "claim" of the astrologers (*volunt . . . illi*), see, however, on §92b *fin. condicio* is used in a broad sense "circumstance, situation" (*OLD* s.v. 6), covering both physical characteristics and course of life.

94–97a raise a series of further objections, still guided by Panaetius: (1) weather conditions at the time of birth might be thought more significant than astral influences; (2) the contribution of heredity (in Cicero's terms, "parental seed") should not be overlooked; (3) the theory makes no allowance for remedies via training or medical intervention; (4) climatic conditions must play some role.

94 Sed quae tanta dementia est . . . quae tempestas ubique sit?: Elliptical for *quae tanta dementia est, ut . . . nihil interesse existimetur* (Hottinger). Von Albrecht (2003, 28) notes Cicero's increasing preference for the more objective *dementia* over *amentia* in the course of his philosophical writing; cf. also on §114 (*demens*). For the charge of madness cf. on §90 *init.*

quarum rerum in proxumis locis . . . eveniat saepe tempestas: Tusculum was a city fifteen miles (twenty-four km) southeast of Rome (near mod. Frascati), the site of villas of many of the elite, including Cicero's, which is the scene of the present dialogue (1.8).

quod qui navigant . . . mutationes maxumas saepe sentiunt: Close as Rome and Tusculum are, a still more striking example of a sudden change in weather is provided by the experience of seafaring. Besides the basic meaning "bend," *flecto* can mean "round" a cape or turning-post; cf. *OLD* s.v. 2a; *Att.* 5.9(102).1: *Leucatam flectere molestum videbatur*. Pease ad loc. suspects that Cicero is stretching the semantic field of the Latin word on the analogy of Greek κάμπτειν.

haec igitur cum sit . . . ad puerorum ortus pertinere?: The long-range hyperbaton (*haec . . . serenitas . . . perturbatio*) supplies focus; cf. Powell 2010, 174–76 and 181. Marcus argues that the weather, albeit an obvious circumstance, is not held by astrologers to be relevant to a newborn, whereas astral forces, though imperceptible and scarcely comprehensible, are assigned influence. The contrasted ideas are presented in parallel: *hoc ad nascentium ortus pertinere non dicere . . . illud . . . dicere ad puerorum ortus pertinere* (for the *hoc . . . illud* structure cf. on §24 *si enim id quod eventurum . . . certa esse non possunt*). The problem here is the function of the transmitted clause *quod non certe pertinet*. In this passage Cicero is refuting with broad rhetorical strokes (*estne sanorum hominum* "is it the part of a sane person . . . ?"). The likely solution will therefore be Davies' simple deletion of *non*, which is in any case out of place, as Schütz saw, who placed it after *certe* (this fact suggests that *non* was not original but a later insertion). (The attempt of Pease to read an Academic equivocation into this highly rhetorical argument is unconvincing; and as Schäublin [1987, 186] points out, Pease fails to offer a parallel for his proposed interpretation of *non certe*.) Though the argument might have been more subtly formulated, the point is clear that such obvious factors as the weather at the time of birth are ignored by astrology (cf. §96, where climatic influences are discussed), whereas it claims importance for scarcely perceptible astral influences. This is, of course, merely an attempt to highlight a gap or inconsistency in astrological theory, not a seriously proposed alternative system. **nescio quid tenue** "that slight something-or-other": depreciatory; cf. on §79 (*fugit e proelio . . . et hospitem et regem*). **nullo modo:** Cf. on §24. **intelligi autem vix potest:** The claim of unintelligibility is raised repeatedly, e.g., by Velleius in his review of previous theories of the deity (*N.D.* 1.25, 27, 30, etc.) as well as by Cotta in his critique of Epicurean theology (ibid. 71, 74–75, 109). **quae a luna . . . caeli temperatio** "the moderating influence of the heavens that proceeds from the moon and the other stars" (*OLD* s.v. *temperatio* 3); the meaning is clarified by *N.D.* 2.92: *hi tanti ignes* [sc. the sun and the stars] *tamque multi non modo nihil nocent terris . . . sed ita prosunt ut si moti loco sint conflagrare terras necesse sit a tantis ardoribus moderatione et temperatione sublata.*

quid, quod non intellegunt . . . mediocris erroris est? "Is it a trivial error that they fail to recognize that the power of the seed . . . is wholly eliminated?" For *vis* as the power to produce some effect, cf. *OLD* s.v. 15. The *seminum vis* was a commonly accepted premise; cf. 1.128: *ut in seminibus vis inest earum rerum quae ex iis progignuntur*. For the ancient doctrine that both parents contribute both male and female seed to their offspring, cf. Potter 2012, Hippocrates, *On generation* §§7–8; for the background, Lesky 1950, 1305–7.

For the gen. of description as a subject complement, usually modified, as here (*mediocris erroris*), cf. Pinkster 2015, 775–77.

quis enim non videt . . . temperatio lunae caelique moderatio: *forma* ("appearance") was a point conceded to astrology by Diogenes of Babylon (see on §90) but is now claimed instead for heredity. For *formas effingere* cf. *N.D.* 2.81: *ita fingat* [sc. *natura*] . . . *ut* . . . *possint* . . . *ex sese similia sui gignere.* **status ac motus** are frequently combined as the aspects of one's self-presentation; cf. *Fin.* 3.56 and other passages cited by Pease ad loc. **effingere** is used of "reproducing, copying, imitating" (*OLD* s.v. *effingo* 3), Cicero making no clear distinction between inherited and learned. **gignentium** varies the preceding *parentes*; for the use of the substantivized participle cf. on §91 (*nascentium*). **temperatio lunae caelique moderatio:** An expansion of *caeli temperatio* above, with chiastic arrangement of the subjects and their adjuncts; the clausula is a variant of Cicero's third-favorite, the double cretic (with resolution of the second long).

95 quid, quod uno . . . nascendi tempus pertinere?: The precise simultaneity is emphasized by *uno et eodem temporis puncto.* **dissimilis et naturas et vitas et casus** "dissimilar natures, lives, and fortunes." In denying astrological control of the child's nature, i.e., general disposition (*OLD* s.v. *natura* 11a), Marcus contradicts another of Diogenes' concessions (§90). The *quod*-clause ("the fact that . . .") should serve as subject of the sentence; therefore Davies' *declarat* (for transmitted *declarant*, a confusion generated by the preceding *habent*) is needed. This is a development of the argument from twins; see §90 with note. **ad agendam vitam:** Cf. on §89 *fin.* (*actionem vitae*).

nisi forte putamus . . . talis fuit?: *nisi forte* is commonly used to introduced a far-fetched or absurd idea; cf. *OLD* s.v. *nisi* 2b. **conceptum et natum:** Only here in passing does Cicero touch on this distinction (which he had introduced apropos of "unnatural births" at §§49b–50a), which was in fact a major source of controversy among astrologers; cf. Bouché-Leclercq 1899, 373–83. **eodem tempore ipso . . . quo Africanum:** Cf. on §66 *fin.*

96a Quid, illudne dubium est . . . scalpello resectae liberarentur?: By *contra naturam* Cicero evidently means "contrary to the human norm"; for the restrictive definition of "normal" in Rome of the Republic, cf. Allély 2003, 155. *depravata* are crooked or distorted parts (*OLD* s.v. *depravo* 1); cf. Var. *L.* 9.11: *ut stulte faciant qui pueris in geniculis alligent serperastra* ["splints"], *ut eorum depravata corrigant crura. Natura* is clearly personified here (so Wopkens, cited by Pease ad loc.), not only because of the agent construction (cf. *N.D.* 2.133: *a Natura sustinentur* [sc. *arbores et herbae*]) but above all the following clause. *revoco* is to "recall to health or vigor": *OLD* s.v. 11a. **arte atque medicina:** *atque* can connect "a word . . . which strengthens or corrects the first term" (*OLD* s.v. 3): "and in fact." **ut quorum linguae . . . liberarentur:** Cicero describes the condition known as tongue-tie or ankyloglossia, in which the frenulum, the tissue by which the tongue is joined to the bottom of the mouth, is unusually short and thick, with the mobility of the tip of the tongue restricted and speech thereby impaired; as Cicero explains, surgery was a possible intervention (as it still is). See further Wikipedia s.v. Ankyloglossia. For Cicero's general account of vocal production, see *N.D.* 2.149. A *scalpellum* is a short knife (source of English "scalpel"), a rare word, but also found at *Sest.* 135 (cf. sch. Bob. 141.3 Stangl).

multi etiam naturae vitium . . . ut planissume diceret: *meditatione atque exercitatione* "practice and training" (*OLD* s.vv. *meditatio* 4, *exercitatio* 3). Perhaps the example of the speech impediment brought Demosthenes to mind (or vice versa). Cicero alludes to Demetrius of Phalerum fr. 168 We = 138 SOD, the source also of Q. Cicero (?), *Pet.* 3: *quae de Demosthenis studio et exercitatione scripsit Demetrius*; cf. also Phld. *Rhet.* 2.206 Sudhaus; D.H. *Dem.* 53; Plut. *Dem.* 11.1. On the articulation of rho in classical Greek, cf. Allen 1987, 41–45; for Demosthenes' difficulty with it, cf. *De orat.* 1.260; [Plut.] *Vit. X orat.* 8 = *mor.* 844e; and other passages cited by Pease ad loc. Though Cicero focuses here on physical defects alone, he supplements with a discussion of the overcoming of character flaws at *Fat.* 10–11.

quodsi haec astro . . . ea mutare posset: Marcus makes it explicit that these examples are fatal to the idea of an all-controlling astral influence. **nulla res** is a forceful (and more colloquial) equivalent for *nihil*; cf. Hofmann 2003, 208.

96b Quid, dissimilitudo locorum . . . dissimilitudoque sit: *hominum procreationes* are "products of human procreation," the plural lending concreteness; cf. *TLL* 10.2:1549.61. In order to account for such differences, astrologers developed, in fact, a doctrine according to which different parts of the inhabited world were under different signs. Certainly this was in place by the time of Manilius and probably in Cicero's day as well (though perhaps not yet when Panaetius wrote). See Bouché-Leclercq 1899, 327–47; Pease ad loc., with further references. The Indians and Persians tend to be juxtaposed as peoples of the East made familiar by Alexander's conquests; cf. Livy 9.19.5 and 10; Sen. *Dial.* 12.7.1; Lucan 10.33. Cicero could, of course, argue the similarity of all human beings with equal eloquence (*Leg.* 1.29–31).

97a ex quo intelligitur . . . ad nascendum valere "From this one realizes that location on earth has greater impact on one's birth than lunar influence." Cf. *OLD* s.v. *valeo* 7. *tactus* (cf. *OLD* s.v. 3) varies *contagio* (§33b and [of astral influences on moon and earth] §92); cf. also *temperatio lunae* (§94); similarly the *tactus* of the sun at *N.D.* 2.40.

nam quod aiunt . . . aut factum sciat: On *observatio diuturna* applied to astronomy/astrology, cf. on §28 (*persuaderi igitur cuiquam potest . . . unam omnium disciplinam*). Marcus quotes back to him the figure 470,000 years that Quintus cited at 1.36. Though the figure was in circulation in his day, Cicero is unable to name a source for it (*neminem . . . sciat*). It is presumed to go back to Berossus, a Babylonian who wrote a history of Babylonia in Greek ca. 200 (*FGrH* 680). The number varies in our sources, sometimes rising as high as 720,000 years (Epigenes *apud* Plin. *Nat.* 7.193); for details, see Pease on 1.36 and Bouché-Leclercq 1899, 39n1, who suspects that the variants result from different methods of calculating the "great year"; cf. *N.D.* 2.51. Favorinus (fr. 3 Barigazzi = Gel. 14.1) later took up the attack on the astrologers' claim to such antiquity. For *pono* followed by acc. + *in* + abl. in the sense "devote to," cf. *OLD* s.v. 14a. **fallunt** "they are practicing deceit." **si . . . esset factitatum** "if it had been done without interruption," *factito*, like *cantito*, being a rare so-called double frequentative; cf. Leumann 1977, 548.

videsne me . . . Panaetius dixerit?: *princeps Stoicorum*: Cicero likes to lend weight to his authorities by appending such complimentary descriptions; so already at 1.6: *princeps eius disciplinae* [sc. *Stoicae*] . . . *Panaetius*; cf. *Tim.* 2 (of Cratippus): *Peripateticorum . . . meo iudicio facile princeps*. The fact that Panaetius was a Stoic may not have made his views more palatable to Quintus, however, since he was no less skeptical of divination than Carneades, with whom Quintus pairs him at 1.12. These words presumably draw a line under Panaetius' contribution; cf. on §88 *init.*

97b Ego autem etiam haec . . . similis nemo Homeri: The battle of Cannae (fought in summer, 216) was the proverbial disaster of Roman history, at which "the Roman army perhaps suffered higher casualties in a single day's fighting than any other western army before or since" (J. F. Lazenby, *OCD* s.v. Cannae); for the sources, cf. *MRR* 1:247. If at §95 Marcus argued apropos of Africanus that others must also have been born under his star (but, implicitly, did not share his characteristics), here he reverses the case: the many who shared the fate of dying at Cannae would, if astrology were correct, have had to be born under the very same heavenly aspect. The argument recurs, stripped of the example of Cannae, in later authors (cf. Pease ad loc.), including the Skeptic Sextus Empiricus (*M.* 5.91–92); this fact may point to an underlying Carneadean argument; cf. Timpanaro 1988, 386. **uno astro:** Ablative of description: "(born) under a single star"; cf. Pinkster 2015, 782–83 and 1025–26. Marcus rings the changes on the "Africanus argument," restating it in generic terms (*qui ingenio atque animo singulares*), then with a specific culture hero (Homer) substituted for the military hero.

98 et, si ad rem pertinet . . . quid potest dici absurdius?: What might be called the "genus-and-species argument": if astrology applies to the *animal*, "living creature, animal" (*OLD* s.v. 1), then it should apply not only to human beings but also to the other species, "animals, wild beasts" (*bestiae*), an idea Marcus dismisses as absurd.

Lucius quidem Tarutius Firmanus . . . nec eius fata canere dubitabat: The extension of astrology beyond the casting of an individual's horoscope reaches a climax with this example. Little is known of Tarutius, whom Cicero identifies as hailing from Firmum in the Picene country. According to Plutarch (*Rom.* 12), he was a friend (ἑταῖρος) of Varro, who may have brokered Cicero's acquaintance with the man. It was Varro who requested that he cast a horoscope for Rome (ibid.). **quidem** (which need not be translated) should probably be classed as adversative, contrasting the horoscope of a city with the horoscopes of animals; cf. Solodow 1978, ch. 4.II. **in primis Chaldaeicis rationibus eruditus:** Cicero speaks of Tarutius himself with respect (similarly Solinus 1.18: *mathematicorum nobilissimus* [see on §91]; Plutarch [*Rom.* 12] calls him both a philosopher and an astrologer); it is the method, not the man, that he criticizes. **urbis etiam nostrae natalem diem . . . conditam accepimus:** Cicero speaks of Tarutius simply casting the horoscope for the traditional date of the founding of Rome, which was celebrated annually at the Parilia (April 21; cf. Scullard 1981, 103–5). In fact, however, Tarutius, evidently dissatisfied with the astrological configuration of the traditional date, calculated the foundation of Rome independently. The date given by Plutarch for Tarutius' horoscope corresponds to October 4, 754, which is confirmed by modern computation of the positions of the main heavenly bodies in his horoscope as reported by Solinus (1.18) and John Lydus (*Mens.* 1.14); see further Brind'Amour 1983, 246; Grafton and Swerdlow 1986, 150–52; Heilen 2007, 52–62. He will have been guided by several considerations. This was still within the third year of the sixth Olympiad (which would have extended approximately from July 754 to June 753; cf. R. D. Hicks in Whibley 1931, 71), Varro's date. Moreover, in comparison with the traditional date of founding, "the alignment chosen by Tarutius . . . is the most attractive for explaining in astrological terms the lasting military power of Rome and its just dominion of the world": Heilen 2007, 62; similarly Brind'Amour 1983, 246–47; for a different approach, cf. Abry 1996, 126–29. **in iugo cum esset luna** "when the moon was in Libra," i.e., the "arms" of Scorpio; cf. *OLD* s.v. *iugum* 7a. This is the sole astronomical phenomenon cited by Cicero; it was taken up by Manilius 4.773–75:

Hesperiam sua Libra tenet, qua condita Roma
orbis et imperium retinet discrimina rerum,
lancibus et positas gentes tollitque premitque.

("Italy belongs to the Balance, her rightful sign: beneath it Rome and her sovereignty of the world were founded, Rome, which controls the issue of events, exalting and depressing nations placed in the scales": tr. G. P. Goold). See Abry 1996, 129–35. **nec eius fata canere dubitabat:** I.e., he projected the duration of Rome, the length of life being the major point of astrological prediction; cf. Abry 1996, 135–39. For *cano* = prophesy, cf. 1.115; *Catil.* 3.18; *Cons.* F 10.32 Courtney; in general, *OLD* s.v. 8; for *fata canere*, *Sest.* 47: *non haec . . . a me tum* [sc. during his consulate] *tamquam fata in ipsa re gerenda canebantur?* For the implicit criticism of brazenness, cf. §31: *parum, credo, inpudenter, quod, cum factus es[se]t motus, dicere audent quae vis id effecerit.*

99 o vim maxumam erroris! . . . potuit valere?: *vis* appears here in two different senses: the exclamation involves "a large quantity or supply," usually of something concrete, as at Lucr. 1.1051: *infinita opus est vis undique materiai*, but here extended to the intellectual realm (cf. *OLD* s.v. 8b), whereas when limited by heavenly bodies it is the "power to produce some effect" (*OLD* s.v. 15); similarly *seminum vis* at §94. **ad . . . pertinebat** "came within the scope of": *OLD* s.v. *pertineo* 7. The imperfect is carried over from the preceding narrative of Tarutius' activities: *repetebat . . . dicebat . . . dubitabat*; at the same time, it serves to distance Cicero from the claim; cf. §76b (*differebat*); Pinkster 2015, 413–15. **fac** "suppose," making a concession for the sake of argument, as at §32 *init.*; similarly §106: *fac dare deos*; cf. *OLD* s.v. *facio* 20. **referre** "it makes a difference" (from the impersonal *refert*); *interesse* would also have been possible. **ex qua adfectione caeli** "beginning with what position of the heavenly bodies relative to each other": *OLD* s.v. *adfectio* 6a; similarly *Fat.* 8: *astrorum adfectio.* **num hoc in latere . . . potuit valere?:** *later* ("brick") and *caementum* ("rubble") are often juxtaposed as basic building materials: Cato *Agr.* 38.3; Livy 36.22.11; Vitr. 1.5.8, 6.8.9; Col. 8.14.1, 9.1.2, 9.7.2; Mart. 9.75.1–2. Cicero's question suggests that this is absurd, but under the empire horoscopes were drawn up for various cities (and even the world itself); cf. S. Weinstock in *CCAG* 9.2: 176–79.

sed quid plura? . . . re et eventis refelli: For *quid plura?* cf. §50b *init.* By ring composition, this passage begins and ends with the "daily" refutation of the astrologers' predictions. The anaphora of *quam multa*, each time accompanied by the name of one of the three so-called triumviri who dominated Roman politics during the 50s (Crassus, however, only to his death in 54), creates the impression of extensive evidence piling up against the astrologers. The astrologers' assurances to Pompey, Crassus, and Caesar appear to be unattested elsewhere. Did Tarutius perhaps supply Pompey's horoscope and hence form the link between the previous argument and this one (such a connection is suggested by Pompey's deep ties to the *ager Picenus*, on which cf. Badian 1958, ch. 11, esp. 267–68)? One also wonders whether such prophecies might have emboldened Pompey and Crassus to risk battles to which they were unequal; cf. §53 with note. **huic ipsi Caesari:** The adjs. lend focus to Caesar as the chief and most recent example. **permirum:** Cicero dominates the use of this word, four of six examples in Classical Latin being his. For the compound with *per-*, cf. on §48 (*permulta*). **re et eventis refelli:** This marks a fitting conclusion to the refutation of technical divination, Quintus having claimed that *eventa* ("outcomes") supported his case for divination; cf. 1.12 and 84; on §27 *fin.*

100–109 Intermezzo: Quintus' Recantation; Stoic and Peripatetic Arguments for Divination

Having concluded the case against technical divination, Marcus asks for permission to proceed to natural divination (inspired prophecy, dreams). Quintus not only consents to the plan but also, surprisingly, indicates his agreement with Marcus' argument against technical divination, with the remark that the Peripatetic view (accepting natural divination but rejecting technical divination) seemed to him preferable to the Stoic acceptance of all forms, which he brands as "too superstitious." Marcus takes this allusion to the philosophical schools as an opportunity to refute their general positions on divination (the Stoics at §§101–6, the Peripatetics at §§107–9).

100a Restant duo divinandi genera . . . si placet, disseramus: Deeming astrology to have been dispatched, Marcus politely (*si placet*; see on §28 [*Inspiciamus, si placet, exta primum*]) suggests that the conversation now turn to the two forms of natural divination, inspired prophecy and dreams.

100b 'Mihi vero,' inquit, 'placet . . . Stoicorum sententiam iudicabam: Quintus' consent to proceed is routine, but his next statement is a surprise: he now announces his agreement with Marcus' foregoing case against technical divination. Moreover, Marcus' argument, he says, has merely strengthened (*confirmavit*) the judgment he previously held on his own (*mea sponte*) that the Stoic view was too superstitious (*nimis superstitiosam*). Quintus' previous remarks contained no hint of these reservations. Indeed, he promised *quid ipse sentiam . . . exponam* (1.10). He seemed to speak as a convinced Stoic, citing Stoic authorities (e.g., 1.84: *hac ratione et Chrysippus et Diogenes et Antipater utitur*), wishing to sideline the Stoics' critics Carneades and Epicurus (1.12, 62, 87, and 109), and saying of the two natural forms of divination: *sint summa sane, modo ne sola* (1.113). Quintus' only comment on superstition was a defense of the Stoic doctrine of fate against the charge (1.126). Marcus' comment seemed apt: *adcurate tu quidem, Quinte, et Stoice Stoicorum sententiam defendisti* (§8). Though unusual, Quintus' move is not wholly unparalleled. Thus in *De oratore*, in Book 1 Antonius sets himself against Crassus' conception of the wide scope of the orator but then in Book 2 embraces it (2.33–38) and claims that he was previously merely trying to lure the younger participants, Sulpicius and Cotta, away from his rival's influence (2.40). In *De oratore*, the point was to provide in Book 1 some of the flavor of the forensic rivalry of the two great orators of the previous generation. In our dialogue, on the other hand, the move serves to clear technical divination from the table and raise the stakes for the following discussion of natural divination. At the same time, it gives a handle for Marcus' immediately following refutation of both Stoic and Peripatetic justifications for divination and makes the criticism of Cratippus' inconsistency at §109 apply to Quintus as well. Cf. also Woolf 2015, 81–82, who sees Quintus' partial recantation as "a device to move the discussion forward" but also perhaps to raise doubts about Quintus' judgment in general.

haec me Peripateticorum ratio . . . audire sane velim': The asyndeton of *haec me Peripateticorum ratio magis movebat* serves contrast. The pronominal adj. receives focus as host of *me* and from the hyperbaton (*haec . . . ratio*); cf. on §94 (*haec igitur cum sit* etc.). *ratio* is "explanation" (*OLD* s.v. 5); compare Quintus' repeated claim in Book 1 that an explanation of the causes of the phenomena he discussed was unnecessary (cf. on §27: *explicare nihil posses*). For *me . . . movebat*, cf. §9: *me movet illud*. The *Peripatetici* are divided between "old Dicaearchus" (late fourth century) and Cratippus, currently a leading representative of the school (cf. on §26b *init.*), who were paired in the author's preface (1.5 = F 14 We = 31A Mirhady) and by Quintus (1.113 = F 15 We = 31B Mirhady) as recognizing the two forms of natural divination alone. **oraclum:** See on §16 (*oraclis*). **si . . . aut somno relaxatus solute moveatur ac libere:** *solute . . . libere* "without restriction . . . freely," features of the generic description of natural divination at 1.4 (*cum . . . animi . . . motu ipsi suo soluto et libero incitarentur*) and 1.34 (*concitatione quadam animi aut soluto liberoque motu futura praesentiunt*); cf. Moraux 1973, 253. At 1.115 Quintus makes the mind/body dualism explicit: *viget enim animus in somnis liber ab sensibus omnique inpeditione curarum, iacente et mortuo paene corpore.* Our passage (which is Dicaearchus F 16 We = 31C Mirhady) raises several problems. First, it is hard to reconcile with a group of testimonies indicating that Dicaearchus denied the existence of the soul altogether. These are, however, deeply suspect (cf. Sharples 2001, 148–51): since Dicaearchus wrote about the soul in dialogue form (*Tusc.* 1.21 = F 7 We = 19 Mirhady), it may be that the argument of one of the interlocutors was mistaken for that of the author. The other problem is that Dicaearchus appears to be in agreement with the general Peripatetic tradition that rejects the idea that the soul is a substance separable from the body. Several different ways of reconciling our testimony with that general Peripatetic position have been explored; cf. Sharples 2001, 152–73, who concludes that Cicero attributes two irreconcilable positions to Dicaearchus. If, then, it appears that Cicero has assigned to Dicaearchus a generic conception of natural divination, was this perhaps because it was held by his fellow Peripatetic Cratippus? Subsequently he attributes the view to Cratippus alone; cf. Wehrli on Dicaearchus F 15–16.

101 Quae cum ille dixisset . . . probares: *quasi ab alio principio* "as if from another starting point," Quintus' concession having redrawn the terms of debate. For such a fresh onset, cf. *Leg.* 2.18 (*a capite*) with Dyck 2004b ad loc. Marcus graciously accepts his brother's claim and confirms that he "always" (*semper*) approved natural divination and doubted technical divination. **a libera mente:** See §100b *solute ac libere* with note.

dicam igitur de istis . . . quid valeat videro: A revised plan of procedure since §100a: Marcus will first test the validity (*quid valeat*) of the Stoic syllogism (§§101–6; cf. 1.82–83) and Cratippus' argument for divination (§§107–9; cf. 1.70–71), then give his opinion (*mihi quid videatur*) about the two natural forms of divination.

dixisti enim et Chrysippum . . . di significare possunt: This list of possible reasons why the gods, if they exist, might not provide humans with divinatory signs is repeated (with only trivial changes) from 1.84, where it is attributed to the same three Stoics (*SVF* 2:1192 [Chrysippus]; 3 Diog. 37 and Antip. 40): (1) they do not love human beings; (2) they do not know the future; (3)

they think it not in people's interests to know the future; (4) they think it incompatible with the divine grandeur to signal the future to human beings; (5) not even the gods themselves (*ne ipsi quidem di*) can send such signals.

102 at neque non diligunt . . . significant ergo: The Stoics now proceed to argue against the possible grounds for divine failure to send divinatory signs. The case concludes with a syllogism linking the existence of the gods with their signalling of the future. **neque non diligunt nos:** For the two negatives cancelling each other out, cf. Pinkster 2015, 724–26. **sunt enim benefici generique hominum amici:** The Stoic doctrine of divine care for the human race is set out in detail at *N.D.* 2.133–67. **ea quae ab ipsis constituta et designata sunt:** *ab ipsis* is emphatic. *constituta et designata* "put in place and planned," by hysteron proteron; for the latter, cf. *N.D.* 1.26: *Anaxagoras . . . omnium rerum discriptionem et motum mentis infinitae vi ac ratione designari et confici voluit*. The Stoics attributed the origin of the universe to the action of intelligent fire: L–S 46A–C. **erimus enim cautiores si sciemus:** Cf. §24 with n. **nihil . . . beneficentia praestantius** repeats 1.82; cf. *N.D.* 1.121: *quid enim melius aut quid praestantius bonitate et beneficentia?* **neque non . . . praenoscere** "and it is within their power to know the future"; for the negatives, see above. *praenosco* is often used with reference to divination, including Chrysippus' definition of its function at §130; cf. *TLL* 10.2:732.52. **non igitur di sunt nec significant nobis futura** "It is therefore not the case that there are gods and that they fail to signal the future to us." *non* negates the possibility that the two ideas can coexist.

et non, si significant futura . . . est igitur divinatio: Marcus now adds point (6): the gods would not provide such signals without also supplying the means for decoding them (*vias ad significationum scientiam*; the use of *ad* suggests that the original sense of *via*, "path," is still felt), since that would involve the gods in a vain activity (*frustra enim significarent*), an idea incompatible with divine intelligence; cf. §§44–45a. The existence of such methods thus establishes the existence of divination itself.

103 O acutos homines! . . . id quod dubitatur efficitur: Cicero likes to enliven his philosophical writings with such exclamations; cf. §41: *o mortalem beatum!* (Democritus); §99: *o vim maxumam erroris!*; *Parad.* 49: *o di immortales!* For Cicero's ironic use of *acutus homo*, cf., e.g., 1.48 (Hannibal), *Fin.* 1.19 (Epicurus) and 4.56 (Zeno), and *Phil.* 2.28 (Antony). **quam paucis verbis confectum negotium putant!:** For the notion that the Stoics used the syllogism when they were in a hurry, cf. §41 above with note. For *confectum negotium*, cf. *Fat.* 26. **conclusio autem . . . id quod dubitatur**

efficitur: Cicero advises the Stoics that a syllogism should proceed from reliable premises. He similarly criticizes Stoic syllogisms for failing to use generally conceded premises at *Fin.* 4.48b–52a and *N.D.* 3.21.

103–4 videsne Epicurum . . . pervenerit?: Epicurus was thought to despise or be ignorant of dialectic (cf. *Luc.* 97; *Fin.* 2.18; *N.D.* 1.89; however, Sedley 2019, argues that Epicurus rejected dialectic because of his ontological commitments); but he actually produced a model syllogism demonstrating the infinity of the universe (= fr. 297 Usener). **hebetem et rudem:** similarly *Luc.* 97: *isti* [sc. *Antiochus et Stoici*] *tardum* [sc. *Epicurum*] *putant*; cf. the attack on Epicurus' deficient philosophical education and unoriginality at *N.D.* 1.72–73a; similarly ibid. 2.74: *hominem sine arte, sine litteris . . . sine acumine* etc. At §116 *fin.* Marcus seems to accept the Stoics' disparagement of Epicurus' intelligence. **quod in natura rerum omne esse dicimus** "the universe" (*OLD* s.v. *omnis* 1b), taken up by *quod omne est* below. Latin at this period is just beginning to use such abstract concepts; hence the cumbersome paraphrase. Cicero used a different rendering for τὸ πᾶν in the title of the work that was to contain his translation from Plato's *Timaeus*: *De universitate* ("on the universe"); see further Sedley 2013b, 199. **'quod finitum est . . . infinitum sit necesse est':** The argument is reproduced from Epic. *Ep. Hdt.* 41 (cf. also Lucr. 1.958–64), each stage punctuated by an approving comment from Marcus; see Pease ad loc. for further testimonies.

104 hoc vos dialectici . . . nihilo magis efficiatur quod velitis: *hoc . . . non facitis* "This is precisely what you dialecticians fail to do," with *hoc* focalized as host of the following pronoun. **dialectici:** Ironic in this context. The Stoics were the dialecticians par excellence of the ancient world; Carneades himself had learned dialectic at the feet of the Stoic Diogenes (of Babylon): *Luc.* 98. **ea sumitis, quibus concessis, nihilo magis efficiatur quod velitis** "you adopt premises [*OLD* s.v. *sumo* 17] of such a kind that, even if granted, they still would not help your case"; cf. *Luc.* 116: *non quaero ex his illa initia mathematicorum, quibus non concessis digitum progredi non possunt*; for the participle cf. Laughton 1964, 111–12; for the subj. of tendency cf. on §19 (*nisi quod . . . rato tempore*).

primum enim hoc sumitis . . . quod dubium controversumque sit: Marcus now begins a point-by-point rebuttal of the Stoic claims. **quis hoc vobis dabit?:** Cotta voices similar criticism at *N.D.* 3.21: *videre oportet, Balbe, quid tibi concedatur, non te ipsum quod velis sumere.* **Epicurusne . . . nec sui:** It was a tried and true skeptical strategy to cite positions of other schools that did not share Stoic premises; cf. Striker 1980, 62. The first of Epicurus'

Key Doctrines states "that which is blessed and immortal neither has any trouble itself nor provides it to others; hence it is subject neither to anger nor favor; for any such feeling resides in a weak entity"; cf. the Latin version at *N.D.* 1.45; for the background, cf. Merlan 1967. **an noster Ennius . . . humanum genus?:** Cicero typically pairs a Greek example with a Roman one so as to stay in contact with the thought-world of his Roman readers (see further Dyck 1996 on *Off.* 2.26b), in this case, Ennius, *Telamo* vv. 270–71 J. = *TRF* F 117.6–7 = *FRL* F 117c. In these trochaic septenarii, Telamon is holding forth on the unreliability of seers. The attribution of indifference to the gods (*eos non curare opinor*) could be either cynical or Epicurean. Assuming the latter, Jocelyn ad loc. leaves open whether Ennius followed a model late enough to have been influenced by Epicureanism or added that element himself. **magno plausu . . . adsentiente populo:** This looks like a comment based upon viewing the play in performance. Though in his day mime dominated the stage, there were revivals of tragedies, albeit Cicero disliked the prevailing emphasis on spectacular productions; see further Goldberg 1996. **deum** is the archaic genitive plural, occurring four times in Ennius' tragedies (Jocelyn's vocabulary list s.v.). **et quidem . . . dicere quae sequuntur:** Cicero may possibly be alluding to v. 265 J. = *TRF* F 117.1 = *FRL* 117a = *N.D.* 3.79: *nam si curent, bene bonis sit, male malis; quod nunc abest.*

105 sequitur porro nihil deos ignorare . . . a dis inmortalibus constituta!: *quod omnia sint ab iis constituta*: This goes back to claim (2) *neque ignorant ea quae ab ipsis constituta et designata sunt* (§102). **negantium** is an example of Cicero's use of the present participle where in his earlier writing one would have expected a relative clause; cf. Laughton 1964, 45. **esse haec . . . constituta:** *haec* is sometimes used elliptically (cf. Dyck 2008 on *Catil.* 4.7.1–4), here with reference to the universe. The word order *esse . . . constituta* enables the double trochee. Epicurus, positing creation of the universe by collision of atoms, would, of course, be on the attack in this battle (cf. fr. 308 Usener; L–S 13F = Lucr. 5.156–234), perhaps also Democritus, some of the Peripatetics, and Carneades; cf. Timpanaro 1988, 389.

'at nostra interest . . . melius esse quam scire: This takes up (3) among the Stoic arguments (§102). **magnus Dicaearchi liber . . . quam scire:** *magnus* is emphasized so as to lend weight to the argument. The book's content is summarized without further ado in indirect discourse; in English supply "according to which" or the like. This is Dicaearchus F 17 We = 32 Mirhady; one wonders whether this may be identical with the work *On the Annihilation of Human Beings* cited at *Off.* 2.16–17 = F 24 We = 78 Mirhady.

Here Marcus allows this fact to stand as sufficient refutation (he had argued the point in detail at §§22–25). He could also have pursued an argument along the lines later developed by Favorinus (fr. 3 Barigazzi = Gel. 14.1.36).

negant id esse alienum . . . quid cuique conducat!: At §102 what was said to be "not at odds with the divine majesty" was simply *hoc*, i.e., transmitting signs of future events to mortals. Marcus reduces this to absurdity by imagining the gods peering into people's houses to determine their requirements. Carneades painted a similarly absurd picture of the consequences of augural doctrine: *omittat urguere Carneades . . . requirens Iuppiterne cornicem a laeva, corvum ab dextera canere iussisset*: 1.12. Cf. also *N.D.* 1.52 (where Velleius portrays the Stoic god *qui . . . terras et maria contemplans hominum commoda vitasque tueatur: ne ille est inplicatus molestis negotiis et operosis!*) with Bénatouïl 2009.

106 'neque non possunt . . . quid futurum sit: For the two negatives and *praenoscere*, see on §102 (*neque non diligunt nos*). **negant posse:** Sc. *deos futura praenoscere*. The deniers will be those, like Epicurus, who hold that events are not predetermined (cf. *Fat.* 18, 22–23, and 46–48). *fortuna* (implied by the Epicurean fortuitous collision of atoms) has already featured as an alternative explanation to fate at §§24, 36, 38, 66, and 75.

videsne igitur . . . certis atque concessis?: The opposite to the model Epicurean syllogism described at §§103–4 that proceeded *ad rem dubiam <a> concessis rebus*.

deinde contorquent . . . iam perfectum arbitrantur: *contorqueo* in philosophical contexts is to "twist, complicate"; cf. *Luc.* 75: *contorta et aculeata quaedam* σοφίσματα, with Reid 1885 ad loc.; similarly *Fat.* 17: *contortiones orationis*. **non igitur . . . significant futura:** Cf. on §102. *et* and *nec* coordinate (cf. on §90 apropos of *nec . . .-que*); *sunt* leading its clause has the strong existential sense; cf. Adams 1994a, 69–75; Devine and Stephens 2006, 150–53. **id enim iam perfectum arbitrantur** "They think that this has now been closed" (though the skeptical reservations invoked above show otherwise).

deinde adsumunt . . . et tamen esse di: *adsumo* is to adopt an additional (or minor) premise (cf. *OLD* s.v. 12); for the related noun *adsumptio*, cf. §§108 and 109. **quod ipsum non ab omnibus conceditur:** *quod ipsum* "this very point" or "even this": *OLD* s.v. *ipse* 8. Cicero offers specifics at *N.D.* 1.2, 62–63, and 117; on the relatively few attested ancient atheists, see Sedley

2013a and c; detailed study by Whitmarsh 2015. **'significant ergo':** This conclusion assumes points (1)–(5) stated at §102. **ne id quidem . . . et tamen esse di:** This denial is based upon the reservations voiced beginning in §104. Marcus anticipated this position at 1.10 (*ut sint di, potest fieri ut nulla ab iis divinatio generi humano tributa sit*) and §40 (*vester autem deus potest non inpertire, ut nihilo minus mundum regat et hominibus consulat*). He thus arrives at the gods-without-divination stand advocated at §41 and reaffirmed at §148 (*possunt enim . . . esse di*).

'nec si significent . . . quam Romanis darent?: Marcus now turns to point (6) from §102, the possibility that the gods might have withheld the means of decoding their signals. **non dant:** The conjecture *dant* (Lambin, 1565) is adopted here for the transmitted *dare*: surely the change was made under the influence of the preceding infinitives (*significare . . . esse*); the opposing position has been consistently quoted in syntactically independent *oratio recta*. Marcus' argument is a bit elliptical: he seems to mean that the gods may act arbitrarily in ways we cannot understand, e.g., by giving methods of divination to one people, but not another, whereby he takes the Etruscans and the Romans as his examples. The Romans, in fact, never mastered the *disciplina Etrusca*; therefore they consulted the Etruscan haruspices and made provision for their lore to be handed down from generation to generation (cf. 1.3: *omnem hanc ex Etruria scientiam adhibebant* [sc. *Romani*]; 1.92; *Leg.* 2.21; Rawson 1991, 300–302; Haack 2003, 41–42, suspecting that this occurred in the third century).

'nec, si dant . . . accipere non possumus?: A successful transmission requires both giving and receiving. Hence this last argument, the gods' bestowal of the means of decipherment (§102). **fac dare deos:** For the sake of argument, Marcus grudgingly grants the giving—he calls it *absurdum*—but not the receiving; for *fac*, see on §99.

extremum <est> . . . iacet igitur tota conclusio: For *extremum* as the conclusion of an argument, cf. *OLD* s.v. 3c. **sit extremum, effectum tamen non est** "Let us call it the conclusion, but it has not been proven." **ex falsis:** An intensification of the previous criticism *quae dubia sint* (§106; similarly §104 *fin.*). **ut ab ipsis didicimus** "as they have themselves taught us," i.e., the Stoics; cf. on §104 *init.*; perhaps Cicero has in mind his own Stoic teacher Diodotus (*N.D.* 1.6; *Brut.* 309). **iacet** "is overthrown, refuted": *OLD* s.v. *iaceo* 5a. **tota conclusio** effects the double cretic.

107 Veniamus nunc . . . Cratippum: Transition to the argument for divination put forward by the Peripatetic Cratippus and reported by Quintus at 1.70–71. Marcus refers to Cratippus as their friend, and the philosopher's contacts with the Tullii went back at least to the summer of 51; Marcus jr. was currently studying with him in Athens; see further Dyck 1996, 61–62. The following refutation (through §109) has been considered an independent philosophical argument of Cicero's; cf. Hoyer 1898, 61; Moraux 1973, 237n41.

'si sine oculis . . . vera cernentium: The matter in inverted commas is quoted with only slight variation from 1.71. This appears to be an adaptation of the argument developed regarding recollection at Pl. *Men.* 81d, viz., that once one has performed a single act of recollection, one will be able to discover everything; cf. Tarrant 2000, 71. *officium et munus* ("function and work") together render Greek ἔργον. **fungi suo munere** "perform their proper task"; cf. *Tusc.* 3.15: *oculus conturbatus non est probe adfectus ad suum munus fungendum.* **qui . . . is:** For the structure, with relative clause preceding main clause, cf. Dyck 2004b, 292 with literature. **vel semel** "even if only one time"; cf. *OLD* s.v. *vel* 6. **ut vera cerneret** "to see properly." *sensus* here is the "capacity" or "faculty": *OLD* s.v. 1 and 3; *sensus oculorum vera cernentium* is paraphrased in §108 as *vis videndi.*

item igitur si sine divinatione . . . confitendum est': *cum quis divinationem habeat* "when a person practices divination": *OLD* s.v. *habeo* 19a; *quis* substitutes for *aliquis* since this is part of the protasis; cf. Pinkster 2015, 1103–4. **errare . . . nec vera cernere:** Quintus himself had admitted the limited success of divination (*non semper*: 1.126) and made excuses for it (1.128); cf. also Marcus' remarks at §§52–53 and 99. **fortuito cecidisse:** Cf. §66 (*fortuito cecidisse potuerunt*); similarly §108: *fortuito accidisse.* **esse** is again marked as existential by its emphatic position; cf. on §106.

festive et breviter . . . nullo modo potest: *festive et breviter!*: Ironic praise. For *festive*, see on §35. Its very brevity can make a syllogism vulnerable; cf. *N.D.* 2.20: *cum . . . brevius angustiusque concluduntur, tum apertiora sunt ad reprendendum.* **bis sumpsit quod voluit:** I.e., he argued from arbitrary, not generally agreed premises; cf. §§103–4. The two premises (*sumptiones*: §108) are (1) that the person who has seen only once possesses sight and (2) that the person who has successfully practiced divination once possesses the power of divination. **faciles . . . ad concedendum** "amenable to making concessions." For *facilis* = "complaisant, indulgent, accommodating," cf. *OLD* s.v. 11a. **quod adsumit** "what he assumed in addition," i.e., the minor premise that there are innumerable cases of successful divination; the point is argued further at §109. For *nullo modo*, cf. on §24.

108 'si' inquit 'aliquando oculi peccent . . . vim divinandi': Marcus' summarizing paraphrase of Cratippus' foregoing analogy, but with substitution of *aliquando* for *semel.* Surely this is innocent variation, not, as Schäublin 1991 ad loc. suspects, a deliberate attempt to prepare the way for the following claim that the two cases are different. **aliquid . . . dixerit:** This appears to be a pregnant expression equivalent to "say something true"; cf. *Tusc.* 3.35: *diceres aliquid . . . si ea bona esse sentires quae essent homine dignissima*; similarly ibid. 4.46; *Fat.* 47; the opposite is *nihil dicere* (cf. on §139). No need for the insertion by Lambin (1565) of *vere* before *dixerit.* **in divinatione** substitutes for *cum quis divinationem habeat* (§107). **existumandus est** is restored here for transmitted *existumandus sit*; one expects indicative in the apodosis to match the construction of the analogue (*inest*); a scribe might have altered indicative to subjunctive to match preceding *peccet.*

vide, quaeso, Cratippe . . . id fortuito accidisse: Among Cicero's words for "please," *quaeso* is the most elegant and also the most frequent in his nonepistolary writings; cf. *Att.* 12.6a(243); Dickey 2015, 19–20. Marcus denies that the two cases are analogous and contrasts divination and sense perception, as he had at §9. **vel vaticinando vel somniando** "either by way of prophecy or dreams," abl. of the gerund functioning adverbially; this usage expands in Late Latin at the expense of the present participle; cf. H–S 380. Marcus again makes the fulfillment of the diviners' prophesies depend on chance (*fortuna atque casu*), as argued at §§13–18 and repeatedly invoked against technical divination (e.g., §47 *fin.*). For *nisi forte*, cf. on §95 (*nisi forte putamus . . . talis fuit?*). **qui somnia pro somniis habent:** I.e., and not messages from the gods; but this is also a pun, since *somnium* can be "fantasy, delusion, day-dream" (*OLD* s.v. 2; *N.D.* 1.39: *Chrysippus, qui Stoicorum somniorum vaferrumus habetur interpres*); on this reading, the meaning will be "those who hold nonsense to be nonsense." **verum evaserit** "came true": *OLD* s.v. *evado* 8a; cf. §109: '*multa vera . . . evadere*'; §146: *verum evasit.* **fortuito accidisse** varies *fortuito cecidisse* (§107).

108–9 sed demus tibi istas duas . . . non fortuitae': For the thought, cf. on §107 *fin.* In this work, unlike *Luc./Ac.* (cf., e.g., *Ac.* 1.40–41), Cicero does not usually emphasize his translations of Greek words, but here he makes an exception, evidently not expecting the dialectical terminology to be familiar, since he has not yet written on logic (cf. on §4b), albeit *adsumptio* had appeared at *Inv.* 1.67. *sumptio* and *adsumptio* ("premise" and "additional" or "minor premise") = λῆμμα and πρόσληψις respectively (for the latter, cf. Sext. Emp. *PH* 2.149); cf. also *adsumo* (§106).

109 'Sunt autem . . . nulla conclusio est: For *praesensio* cf. on §13. Marcus uses the same criticism he applied to the Stoics; cf. §104: *ea non sumitis ad concludendum quae ab omnibus concedantur*; §106: *iacet igitur tota conclusio.*

at impudentes sumus . . . esse docet?: *at impudentes sumus* paraphrases Cratippus' expected objection; cf. *Luc.* 115: *utrum igitur nos impudentes . . . an illi adrogantes qui sibi persuaserint scire se solos omnia?* For *perspicuus*, see above on §38 (*quid est tam perspicuum . . . qualis cuique obtigerit hostia?*). **multo plura falsa:** Marcus repeatedly emphasizes the fewness of the correct predictions; cf. §52: *quota enim quaeque res evenit praedicta ab istis* [sc. haruspices]; §99 of the many false predictions of peaceful deaths for the "triumviri," etc. **varietas, quae est propria fortunae:** *varietas* was originally "the quality of having two or more contrasting colors," hence "variety": *OLD* s.v. 1–2. Once again, *fortuna* and *natura* are the alternative explanations, with Marcus denying *natura* to divination because the results are unpredictable. Cf. §14: *haec ipsa fortuita sunt: plerumque enim, non semper eveniunt*; §146: *eadem et aliis aliter evadant et isdem non semper eodem modo*; *N.D.* 2.43: *fortunam, quae amica varietati constantiam respuit.*

deinde si tua ista conclusio . . . eadem illa possunt esse quae tollis: Marcus justly objects that the same syllogism could be used to defend technical divination, which Cratippus rejects. Was Cratippus really so incoherent, or was Quintus' presentaton of his argument incomplete? **(tecum enim mihi res est):** "I have to deal with you": *OLD* s.v. *res* 10c.; similarly *Fat.* 13: *tibi* [sc. *Chrysippo*] *. . . cum Diodoro certamen est.* Marcus chooses to direct his question to the author of the doctrine and relieve Quintus of the onus of defending it; similar substitution at §§35 and 69 above. **et haruspices . . . et Chaldaeos:** Cicero creates as long a list as possible with polysyndeton to emphasize that Cratippus has opened the door to all manner of diviners (and presumably fraud; cf. 1.132). There were special books containing lore about lightning strikes (*fulgurales . . . libri*: 1.72), and the specialist in this area, the *fulgurator*, was specifically mentioned beside the haruspex by Cato (*orat.* 102), but the differentiation is rare; see further Capdeville 1994, 68n81.

110–18 Inspired Prophecy

Under "inspired prophecy," Marcus focuses on particular examples cited by Quintus and seeks alternative explanations to supernatural influence. He begins with recent Roman material, then shifts to other places and earlier times. The argument can be outlined as follows:

1. The Sibylline Books (110)
   a. A rumor recently circulated that a passage would be cited in the senate in favor of naming Caesar as king.
   b. Their obscurity allows adaptation to various situations (111).
   c. The use of acrostics suggests poems based on artistry, not frenzy.
   d. The books should be closely held and used to eliminate, not create religious obstacles (112).
2. Cassandra and various Italian prophets are dismissed (113).
3. Coponius' oarsman in the civil war, driven out of his mind by terror, gave voice and prophetic form to what many were fearing (114).
4. Inspired prophecy at Delphi (115)
   a. The prophecy given to Croesus
   b. The prophecy given to Pyrrhus, according to Ennius, is unhistorical (116).
   c. Why have prophetic oracles ceased to be given at Delphi (117)?
   d. Demosthenes charged Delphi with accepting bribes (§118).

110 Quid vero habet auctoritatis . . . divinos adsecutos sit?: The very terms of the question prejudice the answer. **Quid . . . auctoritatis:** Cf. on §8 *fin.* (*aliquid certi*). **furor iste quem divinum vocatis:** *iste* adds a note of contempt; cf. on §59 (*nam si ista sequimur*). *furor divinus* was implied by Quintus at 1.66: *ea* [sc. *praesagitio*] *si exarsit acrius, furor appellatur, cum a corpore animus abstractus divino instinctu concitatur*; the phrase appears at §100 (but *furor* tout court at 1.5 etc.). Similarly, Plato spoke of natural divination as μανία (*mania*) at *Phaedr.* 244d–e (cf. 1.1). The plural *vocatis* makes this a general Stoic position. Both of the consequences sketched here stand the usual hierarchy on its head. The point was anticipated by Quintus at 1.85–86 (*quid deinde causae sit cur Cassandra furens futura prospiciat, Priamus sapiens hoc idem facere non queat*), where he goes on to say that this is not at issue but whether this and similar phenomena occur. *sapiens* is evidently used here as of Priam in the passage just quoted, i.e., not of the Stoic sage, on whom see on §61 *init.* Marcus uses a similar argument from hierarchies to discredit the example of the Rhodian oarsman at §114 *fin.* **ut . . . is qui humanos . . . divinos adsecutus sit?** "so that one who has lost a human mind has obtained a divine one," a reference to the divine possession supposedly experienced by inspired prophets; cf. Dodds 1951, 65–75. Cf. the similar contrast at §80: *placet igitur humanitatis expertis habere divinitatis auctores?*

Sibyllae versus observamus . . . fudisse dicitur: *observamus* "we regard as authoritative": *OLD* s.v. *observo* 6a; similarly §84 *pedis offensio . . . erunt observanda.* Février 2002, 839, underlines the irony of this sentence in view of the general Roman suspicion of inspired prophecy. A collection of Sibylline oracles in three books (in Greek) is said to have been kept at Rome and consulted for advice since monarchical times; when it was destroyed in a fire on the Capitol in 83, a three-man commission was appointed to gather oracles to replace it. See further *OCD* s.v. Sibyl; detailed study by Parke 1988; on procedures for consulting the archive, cf. Scheid 1998. **quos illa furens fudisse dicitur:** *furens* is the operative term, connecting with *furor iste* above, another example of the weight the participle can bear in the late Cicero. **fudisse:** See on §27 (*quasi fundi*) and for the perfect infinitive, §117. *dicitur* is used advisedly: Marcus will go on to undermine this picture.

quorum interpres nuper . . . si salvi esse vellemus: At the beginning and end (§112) of the discussion of the Sibylline verses, emphasis is placed on the recent rumor that L. Aurelius Cotta (cos. 65), a member of the *quindecimviri* who had charge of the Sibylline books (Rüpke 2008, §824; Radke, *RE* s.v. *Quindecimviri*) and who was related to Caesar on his mother's side, was about to propose in the senate that Caesar be given the title of king because the prophecies declared that Parthia could be defeated only by a king (albeit the proposal was forestalled by Caesar's assassination on the Ides of March); see Suet. *Jul.* 79.3; Plut. *Caes.* 60.2 and 64.3 (with Pelling 2011 ad locos); Plut. *Brut.* 10.3; App. *BC* 2.110/461; Dio 44.15.3–4. It thus appears that a preoccupation with politics is setting in and conflicting with Cicero's philosophical writing (*De officiis* provides further examples; cf. Dyck 1996, 392–93 and 495–96). **quorum interpres** "an interpreter of which [sc. the Sibylline verses]" describes Cotta as a member of the Board of Fifteen; see above. **falsa quadam hominum fama:** *falsa* is emphatic: "according to a false rumor." **eum quem re vera . . . appellandum quoque esse regem:** Sc. Caesar, whom Cicero called a *rex* in his private correspondence after the civil war and prior to the Ides of March (*Att.* 13.37[346].2; *Fam.* 6.19[262].2), but not publicly. The past tense here (*habebamus*) shows that these words were written after Caesar's assassination. **si salvi esse vellemus:** I.e., to avoid catastrophe in the Parthian War, attendant presumably on a rupture of the *pax deorum*; see above on §§24–25.

hoc si est in libris . . . definitione sublata: Upon the report of the rumor follows the critique. **hoc** focalizes the content just reported. Marcus leaves open the question of the oracle's authenticity (*si est in libris*). **in quem hominem et in quod tempus:** I.e., the oracle could not have been framed with reference to the recent situation, but may have been taken out of context; cf. Scheid 1998, 16. For this analysis, Cicero's rhetorical training proves useful, with its distinction between general questions (θέσεις, *proposita*) and questions with particulars attached (ὑποθέσεις, *causae*); cf. *Part.* 61; *Top.* 79–80; Quint. *Inst.* 3.5.5–18; Lausberg 1990, §§69–78. The Sibylline verses merely offered general propositions, to which the interpreter (*interpres*, in this case Cotta) attached particulars applying to the current situation. The orator's task is to reverse the process and strip away the particulars so as to focus on the underlying general point (cf. *De orat.* 2.133 and 3.120; *Orat.* 45), the procedure also followed here by Marcus as skeptical critic. **callide enim . . . definitione sublata:** The next segment of the argument centers on the characteristics of the author(s) of the Sibylline prophecies (*qui illa composuit*), the first being that he made them open-ended so that various events could be taken to have been predicted (a similar point is made at §§115–16 apropos of the oracle given to Croesus).

111 adhibuit etiam latebram . . . accommodari viderentur: for *latebra* ("subterfuge"), cf. on §46 (*sed te mirificam in latebram*). The other form of natural divination, dreams, will also be accused of *obscuritas* (§132); cf. also *Fam.* 6.6(234).8 (to Caecina) on the general obscurity of divinatory signs. **alias in aliam rem** "on one occasion to one thing, on another to another."

non esse autem . . . attenti animi quam furentis: *non esse . . . illud carmen furentis* "that is *not* the oracle of a raving madwoman," an emphatic denial; cf. *OLD* s.v. *carmen* 1c. The participle *furens* was substantivized at 1.4 and has been since *De orat.* 3.55; it may denote a temporary state (as opposed to *furiosus*); see below for the adjectival usage. **cum . . . tum** correlate the two halves of the proof, one based on the general tenor of the "poem itself," the other on the use of acrostics. **artis et diligentiae:** For artistry as a characteristic of poetry, cf. *Q.fr.* 2.10(14).3: *Lucreti poemata . . . ita sunt, multis luminibus ingeni, multae tamen artis*; for *diligentia*, cf. *De orat.* 3.184: *neque vero haec* [sc. the rhythms of prose] *tam acrem curam diligentiamque desiderant quam est illa poetarum.* **incitationis et motus** "excitement and passion" (cf. *OLD* s.v. *motus* 10). **ἀκροστιχίς** "acrostic." This is, according to the *TLG* database, the first attestation of the Greek word; hence Cicero introduces the term cautiously with *quae* ἀκροστιχίς *dicitur* and immediate explanation. **cum deinceps . . . conectitur** "when a continuous text is created from the first letters of each verse taken in turn," whereby Christ's *cuiusque* is adopted as necessary to complete the sense (so also Timpanaro, Schäublin). **'Q. Ennius fecit'** "Q. Ennius is the author" = *inc.* 53 Vahlen[2] = *FRL* 6. *fecit* is used in the sense of Greek ἐποίησεν ("composed, wrote"): LSJ s.v. ποιέω I.4; cf. *OLD* s.v. *facio* 5a. **id certe . . . quam furentis:** This comment on the use of acrostics matches the previous parenthetical insertion (*est enim magis . . . et motu*), so that the point is made explicit for both parts of the proof.

112a atque in Sibyllinis . . . non insani: "And indeed in the Sibylline books, the entire poem is bordered by first letters taken from the first verse of each oracle," i.e., the letters of the words of the first line provide the first letters of each subsequent line of the given oracle. This general sense, worked out by Diels (1890, 25–28), is accepted by recent translators (Timpanaro 1988; Schäublin 1991; Freyburger and Scheid 1992; Kany-Turpin 2004), though there is disagreement as to exactly how the Latin text should read. Here <*excerptis*> is inserted before *ex primo versu* (Dyck after the suggestion <*assumptis*> by Schäublin 1987, 189–90), and *illius sententiae* is deleted with Giomini (it is probably an alternative reading for *cuiusque sententiae* that crept into the text). Supposititious oracles were a problem in antiquity as early as ca. 500 (Onomacritus: Hdt. 7.6.3). Hence the acrostics served as a guarantee of authenticity. Dionysius of Halicarnassus (4.62.6) records that after the loss of the Sibylline books in the fire that destroyed the Capitol in 83, the acrostics aided the reconstruction of the collection; see further Santangelo 2013, 134–48 on the fire, the reconsititution of the Sibylline books, and their use as a political tool. **praetexitur** "is bordered": *OLD* s.v. *praetexo* 1. **hoc . . . non insani:** *hoc* summarizes and focalizes the procedure just described. First comes the general point that this is the method of a writer, since it involves arranging the text in a certain form on the page, not the effusions of a madperson (cf. §110 *quos illa furens fudisse dicitur*), then the characteristic *adhibentis diligentiam* as opposed to an insane person (cf. §111: *est enim . . . diligentiae*), where the substantivized forms, one a participle (with object), the other an adjective, are parallel, another example of Cicero's exploitation of the verbal properties of the present participle.

quam ob rem Sibyllam . . . ad suscipiendas religiones: A conclusion is drawn (*quam ob rem*) from the foregoing argument and applied to the recent case (§110). It takes the form of an exhortation (jussive *habeamus*); *Sibyllam* stands metonymically for the *Sibyllinos libros* or *versus*. *quidem* prepares for a contrast to follow, in this case between the Sibylline books and their keepers (adversative asyndeton prior to *cum antistitibus agamus*). **sepositam et conditam** "locked away and hidden." **id quod proditum est a maioribus** "as was handed down [*OLD* s.v. *prodo* 5] by our ancestors," an independent clause, hence set in dashes here, in apposition with the *ut*-clause. **iniussu senatus** "unless ordered by the senate": the point was to keep divinatory processes that might upset the political order firmly under the senate's control; similarly *Leg.* 2.20.5 (with Dyck 2004b, 303); D.H. 4.62.5; cf. Wissowa 1912,

538. **valeantque ad deponendas potius quam ad suscipiendas religiones** "and let them apply to clearing away rather than taking up religious obstacles." For the sense of *religio* here, cf. *OLD* s.v. 3a: "a state of impediment, etc., consequent on the violation or nonobservance of supernatural laws." The Sibylline books were ordinarily consulted upon occurrence of an event taken to be a prodigy; cf. Février 2002, 840. As North (1990, 54) notes, the Sibylline responses recorded by Livy consist almost exclusively of expiations prescribed for a previous breach of the *pax deorum*, as opposed to what Cicero wishes to avoid, viz., introducing new religious obstacles (such as the need for a king in order to defeat Parthia).

cum antistitibus agamus . . . nec homines esse patientur: *antistes* is a "priest" or "prophetic spokesman" (*OLD* s.v. 1b), used here for members of the Board of Fifteen, who counted as *publici sacerdotes* according to *Leg.* 2.20. **agamus** "let us plead" (*OLD* s.v. *ago* 42b), another exhortation, parallel to *habeamus*. **quem Romae . . . esse patientur:** *posthac*, i.e., after the experience of Caesar's "reign"; see on §110. Caesar, of course, did not take the title of king, but even the title "dictator," which he had assumed, was abolished at Rome on Antony's initiative; see further Ramsey 2003 on *Phil.* 1.28. Perhaps Cicero has that in mind as a basis for his assertion; cf. the view attributed to Scipio at Livy 27.19.4: *regium nomen alibi magnum, Romae intolerabile.*

112b 'At multi saepe . . . eheu videte!': An objection based upon the fact that there are true prophecies, as examples of which Quintus had cited these two speeches of Cassandra's from Ennius: 1. 67 = *Alexander* v. 43 J. = *TRF inc.* 151.12 = *FRL inc.* 151a12 and 114 = *Alexander* v. 47 J. = *TRF inc.* F 151.16 = *FRL inc.* 151b1. See Schultz 2014 ad locos.

113 num igitur me cogis . . . commenticiis rebus adiungere: Once again, Marcus claims a higher standard of truth for the current discussion (cf. §§27, 43b), mere myths (*fabulae*) being ruled out; cf. *N.D.* 3.77: *poetarum ista sunt, nos autem philosophi esse volumus, rerum auctores, non fabularum.* There is a similar drawing of boundaries, this time between poetic fiction on the one side and court testimony or historiography on the other, at *Leg.* 1.4–5. **quae delectationis habeant quantum voles** "however much pleasure they may furnish" (literally, "let them have as much pleasure as you wish"). The asyndeton after *adiuventur* creates a sharp contrast. *auctoritatem* is already emphatic by position but also reinforced by *quidem* (for adversative *quidem* see on §98) and powerfully negated by *nullam.* **commenticiis rebus** takes up the critique of *commenticia exempla* from §27.

eodemque modo . . . non modo prudenti probata sunt: Marcus dismisses three additional examples of successful prophecy cited by Quintus, Publicius (1.115; for *nescio cui*, cf. on §79 [*fugit e proelio . . . et hospitem et regem*]), the *carmina Marciana*, composed by a Marcius or possibly two brothers Marcii of noble birth, which were thought to have prophesied the disaster at Cannae (1.89 [see Schultz 2014 ad loc.] and 115; detailed study by Russo 2005), and Apollo (1.37–38), whose oracle at Delphi will, however, be discussed in detail at §§115–18. **Apollinis opertis** "the dark sayings of Apollo": *OLD* s.v. *opertum* 3; cf. *TLL* 9.2:680.19–20; similarly 1.115. **ficta aperte** is in implicit contrast with *operta*; Marcus cites evidence of fabrication at §118. **effutita** "blurted out, babbled," of reckless speech; cf. *OLD* s.v. *effut(t)io*. **numquam . . . probata sunt:** At §§87a-88 he similarly sought to undermine the credibility of astrology by citing the fact that it was rejected by expert astronomers,

114 'Quid,' inquies, 'remex ille . . . quae facta sunt?': An incident from the civil war, shortly before Pharsalus, cited by Quintus at 1.68 on the basis of Marcus' own account. C. Coponius was a friend of Cicero's and is mentioned at *Cael.* 24 as a young man dedicated to learning. As praetor during the crisis of 49, Coponius followed Pompey and together with C. Marcellus (cos. 49) held command of the Rhodian division of Pompey's fleet (*MRR* 2:276). In this capacity, Coponius paid a visit to the Pompeian camp at Dyrrachium and in the course of it reported to Cicero the prophecy of one of his oarsmen: within thirty days there would be a bloodbath in Greece, Dyrrachium would be plundered, and as they escaped by ship the defenders would see behind them a large-scale conflagration, but the Rhodian fleet would return home safe. On Coponius, who escaped the proscriptions thanks to his wife's intercession and is still found participating in debates in the senate as late as 32, cf. Münzer, *RE* s.v. Coponius 3.

ille vero, et ea . . . non aperte: *ille vero* "He did indeed." **et ea quidem:** see on §8 (*et iis quidem*). A remarkably candid admission for a Roman to make, given a state ideology strongly emphasizing martial valor. He goes on to explain the reasons for anxiety (*enim*). **castra enim . . . audiebamus** "we heard that they were camp against camp in Thessaly," where Pharsalus was located; cf. *OLD* s.v. *confero* 15a. Characteristics of the enemy contributed, defined as a surplus of *audacia* ("boldness"), usually with negative connotations (cf. Eisenhut 1973, 64 and n. 166), but perhaps an asset in a military context; cf. the remarks about Caesar early in the civil war: *multum vigilat, audet (Att.* 9.18[187].2). The explanation adds a dark shading: *quippe qui patriae bellum intulisset* (cf. *Att.* 7.11[134].1; *Phil.* 2.24). Another ominous characteristic is the Caesarians' possession of *robor* ("strength") *propter vetustatem*, i.e., Caesar's army had been forged into a powerful and cohesive instrument through the previous eight years of campaigning in Gaul; for these factors in combination, cf. *Agr.* 2.97: *si paululum adsumpserint vetustatis ac roboris, non continebuntur.* **quippe qui:** The addition of the particle *quippe* highlights the causal relation. The combination occurs fifteen times in Cicero's philosophical works, six times in his letters, but only twice in his speeches (*S.Rosc.* 52 , *Phil.* 3.4): PHI s.v. *quippe qui.* **casum . . . proeli** "the risk of battle": *OLD* s.v. *casus* 8b. **sed ita . . . non aperte:** For the consecutive clause with limiting force (usually marked with *sic* or, as here, *ita*), cf. G–L §552.R3. For the demands of *constantia* in such a situation, cf. *Off.* 1.80: *fortis vero animi et constantis est non perturbari in rebus asperis nec tumultuantem de gradu deici . . . sed praesenti animo uti et consilio nec a ratione discedere.* The described behavior also comes under *decorum*, maintaining a bearing appropriate to one's social role (*Off.* 1.93 ff.).

ille autem Graecus . . . perspicere potuisse?: In the Roman view, the Greeks tended to lose their nerve in military situations; cf. *Tusc.* 2.65: *Graeci . . . homines, non satis animosi . . . hostem aspicere non possunt.* **a mente atque a se ipse discessit:** I.e., he went mad (cf. *demens* in the sequel): *OLD* s.v. *discedo* 3e. **qua perturbatione animi . . . esse dicebat** "in this disturbed state of mind, he kept declaring in his madness that those things would happen which, when sane, he feared would come about." This ignores, however, the precise chronology (*minus XXX diebus*: 1.68) and the prophecy of the safe return of the Rhodian fleet. **qua perturbatione animi:** *perturbatio animi* is any mental disturbance (here of the rower's temporary insanity); it is also Cicero's regular rendering of πάθος ("emotion"); cf. *OLD* s.v. *perturbatio* 3–4. The causal ablative *qua perturbatione animi* is emphatic as the determiner of the change from normal behavior (cf. examples of causal ablative at Pinkster 2015, 903–4). **demens** is more objective than *amens* and twice as frequent in Cicero's *philosophica*; cf. on §94 *init.* **utrum tandem . . . consilia deorum inmortalium perspicere potuisse?:** The rhetorical question receives emphasis from the oath *per deos atque homines*; cf. on §53 (*di immortales*). Marcus raises here the same point that Quintus had made at 1.85: *quid . . . causae sit cur Cassandra furens futura prospiciat, Priamus sapiens hoc idem facere non queat*; similarly at §110: *ut quae sapiens non videat ea videat insanus*; see ad loc. An opponent might reply that there is no reason why prophetic gifts should be distributed according to the social hierarchy. —Dyrrachium was being held by Cato with fifteen cohorts; Cicero and the scholar M. Terentius Varro had remained behind there in ill health when the main Pompeian force, after breaking the siege, moved into Thessaly in pursuit of Caesar. Cf. Plut. *Cat. min.* 55.1; see further Fehrle 1983, 257–59. According to 1.68–69, word of the disaster at Pharsalus arrived a few days later, and the dénouement corresponded to the prophecy.

115 Sed iam ad te venio . . . evasit vox fera = fr. tr. inc. 19 R.[3], an iambic octonarius, followed by a trochaic septenarius; for the idea, cf. Eur. *Or.* 591–92. **umbilicum:** For Delphi as the "navel of the world," cf. Pease ad loc. This text incorporates Ursinus' substitution (from Var. *L.* 7.17) of *obtines* for *obsides*. **superstitiosa** "inspired, ecstatic," not pejorative ("superstitious") in archaic poetry; cf. *OLD* s.v. *superstitiosus* 1. On these verses, see further Timpanaro 1988, 395. For a verse-citation when launching a new topic in dialogue, cf. *Leg.* 2.7 (*a Iove Musarum primordia* [fr. 1 Soubiran = Arat. 1]). On inspired prophecy at Delphi and its background, cf. Burkert 1985, 116–17; Johnston 2008, 38–60.

tuis enim oraclis . . . ad dialecticum deferenda sint: For the form *oraclum*, see on §16 (*oraclis*); for Chrysippus on the Delphic oracle, cf. 1.37 as well as *SVF* 2:1214. Marcus' position is by now familiar: he objects that some are simply false, others true accidentally (*casu*), a frequent occurrence in the case of all utterances (*in omni oratione*), he adds (cf. his remarks at §§83b–84). Before *flexiloquis* one might wish to add *ita* to smooth the connection to the following consecutive clause. The compound *flexiloquus* ("expressed in tortuous language, riddling": *OLD* s.v.) looks like a poetic word but is first attested here (cf. *flexanimus* "having a disordered mind" [*OLD* s.v. 2] at Pacuv. F 251.1 Schierl; Bader 1962 §155); it is otherwise used twice by Ammianus Marcellinus (also in combination with *obscurus*): 18.5.6 and 31.2.11; cf. the strictures on obscurity at §§111 and 132–35a. **ut interpres egeat interprete** "hence the interpreter [i.e., the Pythia] requires an interpreter"; similarly Elias, *Proleg. Philos.* 4 (*CAG* 18.1, p. 7.4), speaks of the Pythia herself requiring a second Pythia. **ut . . . sors ipsa ad sortes referenda sit** "so that the oracle itself should be assigned to the lots" (an untranslatable pun), i.e., the meaning is so obscure that one might as well determine it at random; cf. §70 init. **quae ad dialecticum deferenda sint** "the kind that should be presented [for interpretation] to a dialectician," the dialecticians being the ancient world's leading experts in unravelling obscure language (cf. *Rhet. Her.* 2.16); for the subjunctive of tendency, cf. on §19 (*nisi quod . . . rato tempore*). *deferenda* (the reading of the corrector of V) is clearly required, referring back to *oraclis* (as indicated by the *partim . . . partim* structure), whereas the transmitted *deferendae* evidently resulted from the fact that *sortes* intervened, with scribal confusion entailed.

115–16 nam cum illa sors . . . verum oraclum fuisset: *nam* introduces an example of such ambiguity. *illa sors edita est* "that famous oracle was pronounced" (*OLD* s.v. *edo* 6; cf. §117: *Pythia . . . oracla ederet*). The Lydian king Croesus (*regn.* ca. 560–546) was told that if he crossed the Halys river he would destroy a great empire. Alluded to by Quintus at 1.37, the story was narrated by Herodotus (1.53–54) and no doubt figured in Chrysippus' collection (see above and §116 *fin.*). The Greek oracle is cited at Arist. *Rhet.* 1407a38 and elsewhere (cf. Pease ad loc.); Cicero offers his own Latin version (fr. 54 Bl.), whereby he borrows an Ennian hexameter-ending (*opum vim*: *An.* 151 Sk.). **hostium . . . suam:** the verse fails to specify the *vim* ("power") in question; the two possibilities frame this sentence with the verbs tucked away in the interior so as to form a chiastic contrast of delusion and reality. Because of this ambiguity, the oracle could not be proven false regardless of the outcome (similar criticism of the Sibylline books at §110 *fin.*).

116 cur autem hoc credam . . . de Pyrrho fingere Ennius?: Again Marcus supplements a Greek example with a Roman one from Ennius; cf. on §104 (*an noster Ennius . . . humanum genus*). **Herodotum cur veraciorem ducam Ennio?:** Cf. *Leg.* 1.5: *apud Herodotum, patrem historiae, . . . sunt innumerabiles fabulae* with Dyck 2004b, 69–70, citing recent skepticism of Herodotus' veracity, to which add Dunsch and Ruffing 2013. *verax* ("truthful"; cf. 1.38) is attested since Plautus, but its comparative is found only here in Classical Latin. *fingo* is to "engage in free invention" (cf. *OLD* s.v. 9).

quis enim est qui credat . . . ne Epicurum quidem: Marcus quotes *An.* v. 167 Sk., an oracle allegedly given to the Molossian king Pyrrhus of Epirus before he crossed to Italy in 280 to aid the Tarentines in their struggle against Rome; for orthography and scansion, cf. Skutsch 1985 ad loc. As Skutsch remarks (ibid.), Ennius may have used the Delphic response to Croesus as his model. Marcus raises four objections: (1) Apollo did not deliver his oracles in Latin, only Greek; (2) this oracle appears in no Greek source; (3) by Pyrrhus' time, the Pythia had ceased to give oracles in verse (cf. 1.37 *fin.*: *idem* [sc. Apollo] *iam diu non facit*; but Cicero exaggerates: though oracles in verse had disappeared by his day, they were still issued in Pyrrhus' time; oracles in prose continued to ca. 100 CE; cf. Parke and Wormell 1956, 1:247–48); (4) however stolid the Aeacidae (Achilles was the grandson of Aeacus, while Pyrrhus claimed descent from Achilles' son Pyrrhus/Neoptolemus) may have been (two verses from Ennius [*An.* 197–98 Sk.] are quoted to buttress the point), they could hardly have failed to see that ambiguity results from the fact that in *oratio obliqua* both subject and object are accusative. *amphibolia* ("ambiguity"), though a Greek word (first in Latin at *Rhet. Her.* 2.16), is sufficiently familiar that Cicero allows it to stand without translation or apology (cf. §11 apropos of *sorites*). **vel Chrysippum . . . ne Epicurum quidem:** Another strained antithesis (cf. on §71a [*Flaminius non paruit auspiciis*]), since the ambiguity of the two oracles is similar and in each case the error lies in leaping to an optimistic interpretation. Respect is shown for Chrysippus' intelligence (cf. 1.6 *acerrumo vir ingenio Chrysippus*), even though Marcus disagrees with him about divination (although he elicits some support from him at §61); for Epicurus, cf. on §§103–4 (*hebetem et rudem*).

117 Sed, quod caput est . . . nihil possit esse contemptius?: *caput* is the "chief point": *OLD* s.v. 15b. **isto modo** "in the manner you cite," with *iste* bringing Quintus back into the picture (cf. on §21 *fin.*). After *eduntur*, Schäublin (1991) restores a perspicuous structure by inserting *cur*, which can easily have dropped out after *-tur*. After *iam diu* the mss. offer the corrupt words *tantum modo iam*; the best solution so far offered is that of Schäublin (ibid.), *tam otiosa iacent* ("they lie so dormant"), which is adopted here. The decline of the oracles (admitted by Quintus at 1.37–38) was a marked phenomenon in the Hellenistic period; see in general Levin 1989. Plutarch entertained various explanations, including that they were controlled by demigods who were dying off (*Def. orac.* 16 ff. = *mor.* 418e ff.).

hoc loco cum urgentur . . . minus creduli esse coeperunt?: *hoc loco cum urgentur* "when they are pressed on this topic" (sc. the Stoics: *SVF* 2:1215). The explanation is the one Quintus gave (1.38), but again Marcus prefers to cite the originators of the theory (cf. on §35 *fin.*). The theory that mephitic gases (*anhelitus ille terrae*) caused the Pythia's trance was also considered by Plutarch (*Def. orac.* 44 and 50 = *mor.* 434b and 437c). Recent exploration has shown that two geological faults intersect beneath the *adyton* (sanctuary) where the Pythia experienced her trances, and the conclusion has been drawn that the Pythia's altered mental state was caused by ethylene intoxication, confirming Plutarch's account; cf. De Boer, Hale, and Chanton 2001 and Spiller, Hale, and De Boer 2002. This conclusion has been challenged: Foster and Lehoux 2007; Lehoux 2007; but see the reply of Spiller et al. 2008. The ethylene-intoxication theory seems to be currently accepted; see Johnston 2008, 47–50. **de vino . . . evanescunt vetustate:** Marcus cites the examples of wine or salted food, which may "lose strength, become weak" over time (*OLD* s.v. *evanesco* 2); for the former, cf. *Off.* 3.91 with Dyck 1996 ad loc. **de vi loci agitur . . . quae vim divinam conficere possit?:** Marcus argues that Quintus cannot have it both ways: if we are to follow traditional belief in the oracle, then the place itself is holy and endowed with the divine power (*vis divina*) that stimulates the Pythia's utterances. But then there is no possibility of connecting the oracle's decline with physical causes, as Quintus has done, since the general Greco-Roman assumption is that the gods and their powers are immortal, not subject to decay (but see above on the attribution to demigods). **quid tam divinum . . . numero versuque pronuntiet?:** Marcus enumerates the elements of the Pythia's performance, including the foreseeing of events and the formulation of metrical responses, in order to justify applying the epithet *divinus* to the vapor (*adflatus*). **an postquam homines minus creduli esse coeperunt?:** The cause lay perhaps not so much in the rise of skepticism, as Marcus suggests, but the fact "that other forms of religious reassurance were now available" (Dodds 1951, 75). These included deities of foreign (Persian, Egyptian) origin and magical practices; for an overview of trends in Hellenistic religion, see Mikalson 2006.

118 Demosthenes quidem . . . aliquid non sinceri fuisse: Cicero was a warm admirer of Demosthenes, whom he repeatedly holds up as a model of Attic eloquence (in opposition to Lysias, the stylistic ideal of the Atticists of his own day): *Orat.* 23, 29, etc.; cf. Bishop 2019: ch. 4. From the perspective of a patriotic Greek, Delphi had a bad record, "medizing" during the Persian Wars and "philippizing" during the confrontation with Philip of Macedon. Demosthenes does not use the verb φιλιππίζειν of the Pythia in his extant speeches, but Aeschines quotes him to that effect (3.130; see also Plut. *Dem.* 20), and Demosthenes complains of the favor Philip enjoys at Delphi (*Phil.* 3.32). For the administrative arrangements of 346 and 337 that strengthened Macedonian influence on the oracle, cf. Davies 1998, 3n17 and 13–14; on the relations of Philip and Alexander with the oracle in general, cf. Parke and Wormell 1956, 1:233–43. For bribery as a tactic used by Philip, cf. Cic. *Att.* 1.16(16).12: *neque auctoritate neque gratia pugnat* [sc. Clodius] *sed quibus Philippus omnia castella expugnari posse dicebat, in quae modo asellus onustus auro posset ascendere.* For a different view (sc. that Philip's "policy is wholly explicable without recourse to the hypothesis of bribery"), cf. Cawkwell 1978, 122–23. **cum Philippo facere**, Cicero's rendering of φιλιππίζειν = "take Philip's side": *OLD* s.v. *cum* 2. **quod licet . . . oraclis Delphicis:** *quod* is the relative pronoun, referring back to the previously described corruption and functioning as object of *existimare* (the following indirect statement is in apposition); no need for *quo* (a correction in mss. A and B). **aliquid non sinceri** "a corrupt element"; for the syntax, cf. on §8 *fin.*

sed nescio quo modo . . . quae non sunt credenda non credere: *nescio quo modo* "somehow or other" is parenthical and without influence on the syntax of the rest of the sentence. **isti philosophi** "those philosophers of yours." **superstitiosi et paene fanatici:** Cf. §86: *utinam sapientis* [sc.

deus] *Stoicos effecisset, ne omnia cum superstitiosa sollicitudine . . . crederent!* For superstition, cf. on §§19 and 76b; for Cicero on *superstitiosus*, cf. §136b with note. *fanaticus* underwent an interesting semantic development from "one associated with a temple" (*fanum*), sc. as a temple-servant or the like, to "one devoted to orgiastic rites," to "fanatic": *OLD* s.v. **quidvis malle . . . non ineptos** "prefer to cut any sort of figure at all except one that is not inept"; for Cicero's association of ineptness with the Greeks generally, cf. *De orat.* 2.17–18. In this case, the Stoics and Cratippus, along with Quintus (*mavultis*), prefer to hold a self-contradictory position (that something eternal can suffer extinction) rather than disbelieve an incredible phenomenon (the Pythia's divinatory power).

119–47 Divination from Dreams

Of the different divinatory arts, divination from dreams is second only to *haruspicina* in the length of Marcus' refutation, an indication that belief in it was deeply embedded (see on §128). This section concludes the argumentation and precedes the peroration. The argument can be outlined as follows:

1. General refutation of the idea that dreams contain messages from the gods (119):
   a. Philosophical theories of sleep and dreaming
      (1) Newer Stoic theory vs. Zeno's view
      (2) Theory of Pythagoras and Plato
      (3) Democritus (120)
   b. Dreamers take false things to be true.
   c. Similar interpretations could be offered of the fantasies of those who are delusional or drunk (121).
   d. No art, including medicine, can be imparted by dreams (122).
2. Threefold division of topics for refutation (124):
   a. Dreams are given by divine providence.
   b. Dream-interpretation is possible because of the συμπάθεια (*sympatheia*) of elements of the universe.
   c. Dream-interpretation is possible because of data collected by long-continued observation.
3. The hypothesis that dreams are sent by the gods (125):
   a. Dreams are an unsuitable medium for divine messages (126).
   b. How can one distinguish significant from meaningless dreams (127b)?
   c. An alternative explanation (by Aristotle) is based upon nature (128).

   d. Which explanation is more consistent with the divine nature (129)?
   e. Dreams are difficult to interpret because of their ambiguity (130).
   f. Various examples are considered, culminating in the brothers' own dreams (134).
      (1) Refutation of Democritus' theory of the origin of dreams (137)
      (2) The brothers' dreams can be interpreted in line with Aristotle's theory (139).
4. The hypothesis of *sympatheia* as a basis for dream-interpretation (142b):
   a. Example of a dream-cure with a natural cause: the man who expelled kidney stones (143)
   b. No such cause can be identified for Alcibiades' dream before his death.
   c. Dream-interpreters show off their cleverness rather than following a principle (144).
   d. Other arts, such as medicine or navigation, base predictions on physical signs (145).
5. Long-continued observation as a basis for dream-interpretation (146):
   a. How would this be possible, given the number and variety of dreams?
   b. Astronomy is an example of how numerous and varied phenomena can be reduced to a system.
   c. If one dream comes true, it should not be held to validate all other dreams.
6. Conclusion: the unreliability of dreams (147)

The three points listed under no. 2. above are not truly parallel; rather, a. is the basic thesis (the divine origin of dreams), whereas b. and c. are (not necessarily mutually exclusive) arguments for the possibility that dreams can be correctly interpreted. The three are linked in that if there can be no reliable interpretation of dreams, it becomes very doubtful that they have their origin in divine providence. Marcus takes the (by now expected) line that nature is a more plausible explanation for dreams than divine intervention and offers a theory of Aristotle's as an alternative (3.c.–d. and 4.a.).

119 Similis est error in somniis . . . quam longe est!: With these words Marcus effects the transition to the other form of natural divination, dreams. **in somniis** "in the case of dreams": *OLD* s.v. *in* 42. **quorum . . . defensio:** I.e., as predictive; cf. §150a: *somniorum patrocinium.* **repetita quam longe est!** "how far-fetched it is!": *OLD* s.v. *longe* 2d; cf., e.g., *De orat.* 3.160: *ingeni specimen est quoddam transilire ante pedes posita et alia longe repetita sumere*; Sen. *Con.* 1.1.3: *quid porro tam longe exempla repetis . . . ?*

divinos animos censent . . . cerni quae sint futura: *divinos . . . nostros* "They think that our minds are divine." Who is the subject? The doctrine that souls "have been drawn from outside" (*esse tractos extrinsecus*) is expressly assigned to Cratippus at 1.70; cf. on §26b. That point reappears at 1.110, with attribution to *doctissimi sapientissimique*, side by side with the content that follows in our passage (*animorumque . . . quae sint futura*). Prophecy as a result of contact with external divine souls has been claimed for Posidonius (Moraux 1973, 254; cf. 1.64 = F 108 E.–K.); cf. Struck 2016, 209–11; Brittain 2011 offers a reconstruction of Posidonius' theory of divinatory dreams. The factors are arranged chiastically so as to contrast *mentis et ipsius divinitate* with *coniunctione cum externis mentibus*.

contrahi autem animum Zeno . . . esse dormire = *SVF* 1:130. D.L. 7.158 adds detail: "Sleep occurs when the perceptual tension is relaxed round about the guiding part [τὸ ἡγεμονικόν, sc. of the soul]"; cf. Pohlenz 1978–80, 2:52; Repici 1991, 179; for further testimonies, Pease ad loc. This picture of the weakened soul contracting and falling into sleep is in contrast to the theory that the soul is vigorous (*viget*) and makes excursions while the body is asleep (1.63–64).

iam Pythagoras et Plato . . . ab aliquo philosophorum: Marcus takes up Quintus' report of the views of Pythagoras and Plato at 1.60–62. **locupletissimi auctores** "most reliable authorities," thus implicitly accepting Quintus' point *auctoritate . . . hos minutos philosophos* [sc. the Epicureans] *vincerent* [sc. Plato and Socrates] (1.62). *locuples* is originally "well endowed with land, wealthy"; a guarantor of such kind was therefore "reliable" (*OLD* s.v. 1 and 3). Quintus paraphrased Pl. *Rp.* 571c–572b, a description of a tyrant's immoderate dreams, and—citing the Pythagorean injunction against eating beans as a parallel—treated as a precept what in Plato had been descriptive. Though Quintus emphasized the Platonic/Socratic pedigree for rhetorical advantage (similarly *Tusc.* 5.34–36), the passage was probably cited (and reinterpreted as advice to those wishing to have prophetic dreams) by the Stoics; cf. Repici 1991, 178–79; and 1996, 57–58 and 63–66. In any case, Marcus, too, accepts this move (*quo in somnis certiora videamus* "in order for us to have clearer visions in our dreams"). **cultu atque victu** "regimen," a fairly frequent combination; cf. *OLD* s.v. *cultus* 8. **faba quidem Pythagorei utique abstinere:** Sc. *iubent*: "the Pythagoreans command that one abstain at all events (*utique*) from the bean" (~1.62). This interpretation appears to be found only in *Div.*; the Pythagorean prohibition of eating beans probably has other sources (resemblance to organs of procreation, impurity as a cause of gas); cf. Riedweg 2005, 69–71. In any case, it allows Marcus to launch a stinging riposte: *quasi vero eo cibo mens, non venter infletur!* **sed nescio quo modo . . . ab aliquo philosophorum:** Cf. §118 on philosophers appearing inept. Hence the philosophers now join the *physici* as objects of ridicule; cf. §30: *nugatur ut physicus*. For the subjunctive of tendency cf. on §19 (*nisi quod . . . rato tempore*). Var. *Men.* 122–23 Astbury makes a similar point: *postremo nemo aegrotus quicquam somniat / tam infandum quod non aliquis dicat philosophus*. One suspects that Cicero depends on Varro, the sneer at philosophers in general being expected in a satire; on the early date of the *Menippeae* (the latest datable reference is to the year 67; cf. also Cic. *Ac.* 1.8) and the work's tendency toward polemic, cf. Dahlmann, *RE* Suppl. 6:1268.4 and 1273.43. Cicero evidently did not foresee that this sneer could be turned against himself, as it was by Bolingbroke 1754, 1:279.

120 utrum igitur censemus . . . falsa pro veris: Marcus raises, but does not yet attempt to answer the question of how the soul forms dreams, whether on its own, as is assumed at *Luc.* 48 (*cum mens moveatur ipsa per sese, ut et ea declarant . . . quae vel dormientibus vel furiosis videntur*), or, as Democritus held (68 A 137 D-K; cf. B 166 = Sext. Emp. *M.* 9.19), in response to external stimuli. He offers his own account, based on Aristotle, according to which dreams are a residue of the soul's daytime activity, at §§128–29, and his refutation of Democritus' theory at §§137–39. **dormientium . . . somniantibus** "sleepers . . . dreamers": the substantivized participles instead of relative clauses aid conciseness; cf. also on §91 (*nascentium*). **sive enim sic est . . . falsa pro veris:** *sive . . . sic . . . sive illo modo*: cf. on §24: *vel hoc vel illo modo.* **permulta:** For the "urbane" prefix, cf. on §99 *fin.*

nam et navigantibus . . . ea quae stant: This is the first of three examples of false appearances that Marcus cites from the *Lucullus*, the first two optical illusions, the third the hallucinations of insane or drunk persons. Underlying are Carneades' polemics against Chrysippus' epistemology. Cf. *Luc.* 81: *videsne navem illam* [the dialogue takes place at Hortensius' seaside villa at Bauli]? *stare nobis videtur, at iis qui in nave sunt moveri haec villa* [sc. *videtur*]; cf. Lévy 1997, 333.

et quodam obtutu oculorum duo pro uno lucernae lumina "and by a certain fixed gaze of the eyes two lamplights appear instead of one." A bit vague: the experiment actually involved placing a finger beneath the eye and pressing it up or down; cf. Lucr. 4.447–52, where lamps are among the examples, as well as *Luc.* 80 with Reid 1885 ad loc.

quid dicam insanis, quid ebriis quam multa falsa videantur?: The point is argued and illustrated with quotations from tragedy at *Luc.* 88–89. The hallucinations of the insane will be further compared with dreams at §122a. Marcus concludes that dreams have no greater claim to credence than such phenomena.

120–21 nam tam licet . . . quae futura videantur: Marcus offers a kind of parody of the dream-interpreters' procedure, creating predictions for the aforementioned illusions by free association as if they had been dreams. Thus if stable things appear to move, an earthquake or a sudden flight (*repentinam aliquam fugam*) might be portended, whereas the double flame could be seen as a portent of civil strife/rebellion (*dissensionem ac seditionem*), as indeed the phenomenon of the double sun (i.e., sun dogs) was (implicitly) interpreted at *Rep.* 1.31. **iam ex insanorum . . . quae futura videantur:** By this method, infinite possibilities soon (*iam*) open up for extracting predictions of the future by *coniectura* from the visions (*ex . . . visis*) of those who are drunk or mad; cf. §145: *acumen hominum . . . coniecturam modo huc modo illuc ducentium*. Cf. the absurd portents Marcus invents at §59 *fin.*

121 quis est enim . . . non aliquando conliniet?: I.e., even such wild predictions may come true on occasion. The train of thought beginning here and continuing through *narrant qui somniaverunt?* in §122a could have been clearer, but there is no need to posit a lacuna before *quis est enim* (as is done by Christ and Pease); such rough patches are paralleled elsewhere in Cicero's late *philosophica* and are no doubt related to the haste with which he composed these works; see further Pease 1920–23, 28–29; Dyck 1996, 8–10. **qui . . . non aliquando conliniet** "who would fail to hit the mark in the end"; for the characterizing subjunctive, cf. G–L §631.2. This verb more frequently appears with an expressed object, e.g., *Fin.* 3.22: *si cui propositum sit conliniare hastam aliquo aut sagittam* ("If someone is set the task of driving a spear or arrow into some target").

totas noctes somniamus . . . id quod somniarimus evadere?: The first two statements might seem at first sight puzzling (Muretus proposed emending both verbs: *dormimus* for *somniamus* and *somniemus* for *dormiamus*; Falconer 1923a adopts these conjectures without signaling that they are such). But surely we should rather explain along these lines: "We dream whole nights through—and there is scarcely a night when we do not sleep—" etc.; cf. *Att.* 12.14(251).3: *totos dies scribo*. Marcus plunges in with the main point and then, as an aside, adds the general context; see above apropos of hasty composition. For *et indignantis*, cf. on §47 (*et tu scilicet mavis*). *somnio* may be intransitive or used with internal accusative, both illustrated in this sentence. *evado* can by itself mean "come true" (*OLD* s.v. 8b); for use in this sense with expressed predicate, cf. on §108 (*verum evaserit*). Woolf (2015, 83) relates this passage to what we would call "confirmation bias," i.e., the fact that we tend to remember the few successful predictions and forget the failures; Cicero restates the point in personal terms at §§141–42a.

quid est tam incertum . . . quam casu dicere?: In this example, casting the "Venus throw" substitutes for hitting the mark with a missile; again, repeated attempts are bound to bring ultimate success. Marcus gives no indication of having already used this example to discuss chance occurrences; see on §48. **Veneris . . . inpulsu** "at Venus' prompting"; similarly *Pis.* 46: *nolite . . . putare . . . homines consceleratos impulsu deorum terreri furialibus taedis ardentibus*; cf. §63, v. 12: *Iovis . . . pulsu.* Once again, divine causation and chance are the alternative interpretations; cf. on §§39 (*nam si casum . . . quam ista derideant*) and 55b.

quodsi ceteris temporibus . . . valeant falsa pro veris: Marcus refers to "false appearances" such as the examples discussed in §120. **non video . . . pro veris** "I fail to see what special property sleep has that in it the false should count as true." For the partitive *quid praecipui*, see on §67 above (*quid . . . admirationis*); for the consecutive relative clause, cf. G–L §630.

122a quodsi ita natura . . . efficerent motus somniantes: A hypothetical possibility is raised that does not relate to the prophetic quality of dreams but rather highlights their general outrageousness: *ut ea dormientes agerent quae somniarent* "that sleepers should act out the things that they dream"; cf. §§141b and 146 (*nihil tam praepostere . . . quod non possimus somniare*). Quintus had provided some examples of immoral dreams in his translation from Pl. *Rp.* 9.571c–d at 1.60; cf. also Artem. 1.78–80. **qui cubitum irent** "who go to bed": *OLD* s.v. *cubo* 2a. *motus*, emphasized by separation from *maiores*, are "disturbances, disorders": *OLD* s.v. 9a. In his apparatus ad loc., Schäublin (1991) proposes deleting *somniantes*, but he would thereby replace a double trochee with an unrhythmical clausula.

quodsi insanorum visis . . . narrant qui somniaverunt?: This is now the third sentence in a row beginning with *quodsi*, and there is another such sentence in §120. Sander (1908, 18–20) objected to this feature and to the repetitions of content (the first, second, and fourth examples say essentially the same thing). One suspects that the explanation may lie in lack of focus and haste to complete, not, as Sander supposed, that Cicero had left the work incomplete at his death so that it had to be edited and published by others (its publication is attested at *Fat.* 1b). There is a somewhat similar phenomenon at *Off.* 1.50–58; cf. Dyck 1996, 165–67. **insanorum visis . . . somniantium visis:** A *visum* is a thing seen; as our passage shows, it can apply to visions both of the insane and of dreamers, though in this section it will be regularly used of the latter (§§124, 126, 127, 128, 129a). **quae multo etiam perturbatiora sunt:** Cicero takes this as proven by the preceding hypothetical. **insani . . . non narrant, narrant qui somniaverunt:** The chiastic arrangement again achieves a nice contrast between the two subjects each governing the same verb, both juxtaposed at the center. For *coniector* cf. §62a *init. qui somniaverunt* varies *somniantes* and effects the cretic plus trochee.

122b Quaero etiam . . . praesens enim poena sit: Here Marcus reprises the Other Sciences argument of §§9–12, with dream-interpretation substituted for divination in general. **canere vel voce vel fidibus** "sing or play the lyre." **aut geometricum . . . explicare** "or explain some point of geometry, physics, or dialectic." The following *expedio* is synonymous with *explico*: "explain, expound" (*OLD* s.v. *expedio* 4). **ita gubernem ut somniaverim:** Marcus adds to the hypothetical case of §122a this illustration of the folly of transposing dream-behavior into the real world. For the ideal conditional, cf. G–L §596.

123 qui igitur convenit . . . gubernantibus non potest?: The older therapeutic method, still in competition with Hippocratic medicine in classical times, was that provided by traditional healers, sometimes based upon interpretation of the sufferer's dreams. For the arguments used to counter such traditional healers (not dissimilar to Marcus' arguments against divination), see Laskaris 2002, esp. 93–108. Some sanctuaries of Asclepius/Aesculapius (notably the one at Epidaurus) and other divinities provided dormitory-like facilities where votaries could spend the night so that upon awakening they could report their dreams to the priests and receive advice about treatment (*curatio*); see further Ehrenheim 2015, ch. 1.4; Renberg 2017, ch. 3. Aesculapius had a sanctuary at Rome (on the island in the Tiber) from 293 on; cf. Richardson 1992 and Degrassi, *LTUR* s.v. Aesculapius, Aedes; for the historical background, Orlin 1997, 106–8. Outside Egypt, Serapis is known to have had healing sanctuaries at Athens and Delos: Renberg 2017, 348–59; the god received cult (along with Isis) in a shrine in the Campus Martius from ca. mid-first century BCE; cf. Richardson 1992 s.v. Isis, Aedes (1); Coarelli, *LTUR* s.v. Iseum et Serapeum in Campo Martio, Isis Campensis. Marcus uses the previous argument about the ship's pilot as a basis for undermining the belief that cures could be disclosed in dreams. Since Neptune/Poseidon as a son of Saturn/Cronus was hierarchically superior to Aesculapius, a son of Apollo (to say nothing of Serapis, an Egyptian import), Marcus constructs an *a fortiori* argument: if the superior deity was incapable, how could the inferior . . . ? **qui . . . convenit** "How is it fitting?" *curatio valetudinis* appears twice in this section in the sense "treatment for disease" (*OLD* s.vv. *curatio* 2 and *valetudo* 1). *gubernationem* is supplied here prior to *gubernantibus*: it can easily have dropped out by saltation (i.e., a scribe's eye skipping from one similar item to another), and surely Neptune, like Aesculapius, Minerva, and the Muses, was associated with an appropriate named art.

et si sine medico . . . non dabunt?: This is a variant of the foregoing argument: if one divinity provides one type of benefit in dreams, why can another divinity/other divinities not provide a different type of benefit? Schäublin proposed deleting *si*, perhaps rightly. **medicinam dabit Minerva:** *medicina* and *curatio (valetudinis)* alternate in this section as the benefit provided by healing gods to their worshippers. Cicero clearly knew of Minerva as a healing divinity, like Aesculapius and Serapis. This seems to be confirmed by deposits of terra cotta healing votives that were discovered in Rome on the former Via Curva beginning in 1887 and are datable to the fourth to second centuries BCE. A temple of Minerva Medica is datable epigraphically to the imperial period (*CIL* VI 10133); see further Häuber 2014, 110–34 (esp. 120–23). **Musae scribendi . . . somniantibus non dabunt:** Possibly an allusion to Enn. *An.* 211–12 Sk.: *nec quisquam sophiam, sapientia quae perhibetur, / in somnis vidit prius quam sam* [= *eam*] *discere coepit*; cf. Timpanaro 1988, 400.

at si curatio daretur . . . auctoritas somniorum: Marcus uses the nonexistence of the postulated dream-benefits (instruction in navigation from Neptune and literacy and other arts from the Muses) to argue that the claimed benefit of medical advice from prophetic dreams is also nonexistent. Cf. §146 for similar reasoning in casting out the item that does not fit the general pattern. **qua sublata tollitur omnis auctoritas somniorum** "once this [sc. medical treatment disclosed by prophetic dreams] is eliminated, so too is any weight attached to dreams," i.e., belief in the prophetic power of dreams stems largely from this. Cf. the similar boast at §42a: *atque hac extispicum divinatione sublata, omnis haruspicina sublata est.*

124 Sed haec [quoque] . . . interiora videamus: Christ's deletion of *quoque* is adopted here; *pace* Pease, there is no clear term with which "these things" might be compared; surely *quoque* was inadvertently repeated from *haec quoque* in the previous sentence; cf. §148 *init.* for another reasonable example of *haec quoque*. In view of the sequel, one might have expected a contrasting *quidem*. **in promptu fuerint** "were perhaps obvious"; for the potential subj., see G–L §257. Marcus similarly downplays his initial argument at §26a (*haec fuerit nobis tamquam levis armaturae prima orationis excursio*). **interiora videamus** "let us penetrate more deeply": *OLD* s.v. *interior* 6a.

aut enim divina vis . . . quid sequi soleat: Marcus distinguishes three possible explanations for dream-divination: (1) divine providence creates meaningful dreams (the first of Posidonius' three explanations [1.125 = F 107 E.–K.]); (2) on the basis of a network of sympathetic connections (συμπάθεια) within the universe (cf.§33b), dream-interpreters understand what element from the dreams matches each thing (*quid . . . ex somniis*) and what follows each thing (i.e., the interpreters can connect the elements of the dream with the phenomena of the universe and because they know what follows the particular phenomenon, they can make a correct prophecy; cf. 1.126); or (3) observations have been made consistently and over a long span of time as to what is wont to follow when a given dream-vision has appeared. In that case, the distinction between technical and natural divination breaks down, since the prophecy is based, as in technical divination, upon a set of observations of similar phenomena, and the dreamer must rely upon a third-party interpreter; cf. 1.73; Woolf 2015, 69. **divina vis:** Cf. on § 29 (*vi divina*). **secundum quietem** ("in sleep") is not attested in previous Latin, but occurs six times in our work, besides our passage, 1.43, 48, §§126 (twice), 135. **quid evenire et quid sequi soleat:** The indirect questions depend upon *observatio*, its connection with *observare* being still strongly felt.

primum igitur intellegendum est . . . ut providere futura possemus: Marcus proceeds to refute explanation (1), divine causation. **nullam vim esse divinam effectricem somniorum** "there is no divine power that creates dreams"; similar sense at §147: *neque deus est effector somniorum. effectrix* is Ciceronian property, occurring in Classical Latin exclusively in his work: besides our passage, *Fin.* 1.67, 2.55, and *Tim.* 37. On Cicero's general fondness for such feminine agent nouns in his theoretical writings, cf. von Albrecht 2003, 29. **illud quidem perspicuum est:** For cataphoric or preparatory use of the demonstrative pronoun defined by a following clause or indirect statement, cf. Pinkster 2015, 1145–46; with *perspicuum* (on which cf. on §38): *Inv.* 1.66, *De orat.* 2.215, *Orat.* 74, *Luc.* 24 and 132, *Fin.* 1.56. **nostra enim causa di id facerent** "the gods would do this for our sake." The denial is based on this premise; the following argument will claim the futility of any such move.

125 quotus igitur est quisque . . . atque anilis putent?: Marcus' rhetorical questions oppose "the few" and "the many" but arrive at the same result, the marginalization of dreams. He begins with a tricolon containing responses to dreams that become increasingly feeble, ending with the mere recollection of them. **quotus . . . quisque:** Cf. on §52a. For *pareo* see on § 21 (*quodsi fatum fuit . . . idem eventurum fuisset*). **superstitionem . . . anilis:** Cf. on §19 (*anile sane et plenum superstitionis*).

quid est igitur . . . digna ducant?: *his hominibus*, i.e., people of the kind just described, who have such a view of dreams; the point will be further elaborated in the relative clause. *somniis* is emphatic: "by means of dreams" and not some other method.

nec enim ignorare . . . ab hominis constantia: One who holds this view must, Marcus argues, burden the gods either with ignorance or taking ineffective action, neither of which is in line with what is *dignum deo*, i.e., the traditional view of the divine nature; cf. §§44 *fin.*–45, 102; *N.D.* 2.77: *ignoratio rerum aliena naturae deorum est*; ibid. 3.76: *deus falli qui potuit?*; ibid. 3.90: *deo ne excusatio quidem est inscientiae.* **quod abhorret etiam ab hominis constantia** "since it is even at odds with the consistent behavior of a human being" (*OLD* s.v. *abhorreo* 5a), an implicit *a fortiori* argument. Good human behavior is again assumed as a standard for the gods (cf. §54).

ita si pleraque somnia . . . significari fatendum est: Restatement of the dilemma just posed to those who believe in prophetic dreams (*aut . . . aut*) and the resulting incompatibility with the divine nature; the emphatic and compulsory conclusion is then drawn (*nihil igitur . . .*). **somniorum significatione** "dream-signals"; for the defining gen., see on §19 (*fati nomen ipsum*). **at horum neutrum in deum cadit** "but neither of these applies to a god." *at* is needed for transmitted *et* to mark the contradiction (so already Ascensius 1521). Cf. *OLD* s.v. *cado* 22b; similarly §18 (*ut mihi ne in deum quidem cadere videatur*).

126 Illud etiam requiro . . . quam dormientibus: This argument was implicit in the preceding one (cf. on §125 [*quid est igitur . . . digna ducant?*] apropos of *somniis*). **ista visa** "those [dream-]visions you cite," perhaps also with a note of contempt. *nobis* can be taken both with *providere* ("provide for": *OLD* s.v. *provideo* 4b) and with *dare.* **vigilantibus . . . dormientibus:** Both are attributes of *nobis*; notable use of present participles for conciseness and to bear the main weight of the sentence.

sive enim externus . . . vigilantibus esse poterat: Whatever the cause of dreams—here Marcus reviews the possibilities, including Democritus' theory of external stimuli and the hypothesis that they result from the mind's own activity in sleep (cf. on §120)—the same cause would apply in the waking state. **poterat** "would be able": modal use of the indicative of this verb (cf. *NLS* §125).

idque si nostra causa . . . quam quae somniantibus: Here Marcus is able to invoke Chrysippus as an authority in favor of his argument (*SVF* 2:62); cf. on §61 *init*. As Marcus indicates, Chrysippus made this point in the course of refuting the Academics, i.e., his opponents probably cited the verisimilitude of dreams as an argument against the validity of the sense impressions to which the Stoics were, under certain conditions, prepared to give assent; see further *Luc*. 47, 75, 87, and 101; Cappello 2019, 289–90. Chrysippus replies that, in fact, the two sets of impressions are not so similar and that the impressions entertained in the waking state are "far clearer and more reliable" (*permulto clariora et certiora*). He gave them, in fact, different names, *phantasiai* for impressions received when awake and *phantasmata* for dream-impressions: D.L. 7.50 = *SVF* 2:55; cf. *Luc*. 52 (Antiochus' Stoicizing view); Cicero, however, uses *visum* for both.

fuit igitur divina beneficentia dignius . . . divina putanda non sunt: *fuit . . . dignius* "It would have been worthier," with indicative for subjunctive on the analogy of expressions of obligation; cf. *NLS* §123. *divina beneficentia dignius* varies *dignum deo* of §125. **cum consulerent nobis** "since they were taking thought for us," sc. *di*, easily supplied from the preceding *divina*, Marcus adopting the Stoic premise for the sake of argument. **per somnum** (*somnum* is Halm's generally accepted correction for transmitted *somnium*) substitutes for *somnianti* for variety's sake. The argument again concludes with an emphatic denial (*putanda non sunt*; cf. §125 *fin.*: *nihil . . . fatendum est*).

127a iam vero quid opus . . . quam dormienti daret?: For transitional *iam vero* (both here and in the next sentence), cf. on §55b. *quid opus circumitione et anfractu* "what need for a circuitous and winding course?" as opposed to the god proceeding *derecto* with the clear guidance *hoc facito, hoc ne feceris* given in the waking state rather than in sleep. As a result, we have recourse to *interpretes somniorum*, which varies *coniectores (sc. somniorum:*

§124), and thus the already discredited technical divination. **siquidem nobis consulebat:** The imperfect indicative represents the action as a pure supposition and does not commit to whether it is unreal or not; cf. K–S 2:389 and 391.

127b Iam vero quis dicere audeat . . . 'sed omnia non necesse est': Belief in the veracity of all dreams is seen as risky (*quis dicere audeat?*), and Ennius is cited as a representative of the *communis opinio* that holds some, but not all, to be true (v. 346 J. = *TrRF* op. inc. F 205 = *FRL* unidentified works F 7). Various emendations have been proposed in order to create a complete or partial trochaic septenarius, but the boundaries of the quotation are in doubt, and Cicero may simply be paraphrasing; see further on *TrRF* op. inc. F 205; Timpanaro 1988, 402.

quae est tandem . . . mendacibus visis concitare?: Marcus now examines the distinction between kinds of dreams more closely. **quae vera, quae falsa habet?** "What true and false things does it contain?" This in turn leads to the question of origins. Implicitly conceding that the true dreams may derive from god, Marcus wants to know if the false ones do also, and if so, the charge of acting inconsistently lies ready to hand. The charge of ignorance (*quid inscitius*) does not, however, fit the described action; cf. Schäublin 1989, 50–51. I have therefore substituted *quid insidiosius* ("what is more treacherous": *OLD* s.v. *insidiosus* 2a). **concitare** is to "excite, agitate"; cf. 1.38: *vis illa terrae quae mentem Pythiae divino adflatu concitabat*; *OLD* s.v. *concito* 2b.

sin vera visa divina sunt . . . necessario confitendum est: *quae est ista designandi licentia* "What is this unbridled indulgence in categorization?" *licentia* has, as usual, a negative connotation, implying a lack of proper discipline (cf. §150a; *Fat.* 15: *o licentiam iocularem!* and 38: *o admirabilem licentiam!*), with the sphere defined by the genitive *designandi* (cf. *OLD* s.vv. *licentia* 2b, *designo* 5) and further specified by the following *ut hoc deus, hoc natura fecerit*. The idea is that the boundary between the two causes, god and nature, is being drawn arbitrarily; cf. on §§29 and 55c. **quod quoniam illud negatis, hoc necessario confitendum est:** Marcus concludes this argument with a dilemma. *illud* is the former proposition, i.e., that god is responsible for all dreams, both true and false. Since you (i.e., the Stoics, in spite of Quintus' avowal at §100b; cf. §150a) deny that, you must necessarily admit the latter, i.e., that nature is the cause of all dreams. Again, the use of the gerundive (*confitendum est*) represents the conclusion as compulsory, this time reinforced by *necessario*. As often with Cicero's dilemmas, however, this one fails to capture all possibilities. For Democritus offered a theory of external stimulus without involvement of the gods (§120), which Cicero only addresses at §137. Cf. Kany-Turpin and Pellegrin 1989, 235.

128 naturam autem eam . . . existunt species somniorum: Here Marcus finally specifies what he means when he posits "nature" as an alternative to the gods as a source of dreams. **qua . . . potest** "that by which the soul can never, coming to a halt [*OLD* s.v. *insisto* 5a], be free of excitement and movement." **is cum . . . potest:** *is*, referring back to the soul (*animus*), is fronted as the focus; the background is provided in a *cum*-clause describing the state of sleep, first the general condition (*languore corporis* "on account of the body's sluggishness"), then the particulars (*nec . . . potest*). **incidit in visa varia et incerta** "happens upon various, indistinct visions": *OLD* s.v. *incido*[1] 4a. *incerta* accords with Chrysippus' comparison of visions in the sleeping and waking state (cf. on §126), but with the deity removed from the process, this ceases to be a problem. **ex reliquiis . . . inhaerentibus . . . cogitaverit** "from the clinging residue of things thought or done in the waking state." Cicero's information corresponds to three Aristotelian passages: *Insomn.* 461a17–19, 461b21–22, and *Div. per insomn.* 463a22–24. Though Cicero may have derived the doctrine from an intermediary source, there is no reason to deny that he read Aristotle himself; cf. van der Eijk 1993, 228–31, countering the skepticism of Kany-Turpin and Pellegrin 1989, 236–41 (similarly Kany-Turpin 2004, 49). For a summary and evaluation of Aristotle's contribution to the ancient discourse on dreams, cf. Harris 2009, 252–61, noting that he was "certainly far beyond what was generally believed in the wider culture," which still included fairly widespread belief in divinely sent dreams (260–61). Cicero had used the idea that dreams reflect the soul's previous waking activity to explain Scipio's dream at *Rep.* 6.10 = 14 P. Cf. also the thesis of Freud (1955, 165) that "in every dream it is possible to find a point of contact with the experiences of the previous day." **quarum perturbatione . . . species somniorum:** These "extraordinary images" (*mirabiles . . . species*) and their origin reflect Arist. *Insomn.* 461a21; cf. van der Eijk 1993, 228.

quae si alia falsa . . . sed haerebunt: With *quae si alia falsa, alia vera* Marcus returns to the problem raised at §127b init. For *nota* cf. on §17 *init.* For the Stoics, "the immediate cognitive objects of divinatory dreams are . . . actual, if distant, bodies" (Brittain 2011, 217). Therefore the question of whether there was a mark distinguishing true and false divinatory dreams is merely a subdivision of the larger debate between Stoics and Academics as to whether there was such a *nota* for impressions in general; cf. *Luc.* 40-44 with Brittain 2006 ad loc. and Frede 1983. The problem is not pursued here, however,

Marcus being content to establish that the dream-interpreters have no solution. **quid istos interpretes audiamus?** "why should we pay heed to those interpreters of yours?" (with a hint of contempt). **haerebunt** "they will be stuck" or "at a loss" (*OLD* s.v. *haereo* 9), the so-called "deductive" or "prophetic" future; cf. Pinkster 2015, 426.

129a venit enim iam in contentionem . . . an explicatione naturae?: Now that he has specified what he means by "nature," Marcus proceeds to define the contest between factors in such a way as to make the decision a foregone conclusion. **deos . . . immortalis . . . excellentis:** Such descriptions of the gods occur repeatedly in *N.D.* 2, e.g., 2.77: *nihil est . . . praestantius deo.* **concursare . . . verum etiam grabatos:** Cicero displays his gift for satire when he has Marcus undermine divinatory theory by drawing concrete pictures of the absurd things the gods would need to do if it were in fact true; cf. on §105 (*negant id esse alienum . . . quid cuique conducat*). *concurso* is to "run to visit" or "visit in turn" (*OLD* s.v. 3); one is reminded of Velleius' picture of the Stoics' *laboriosissimus deus* (*N.D.* 1.52; cf. Bénatouïl 2009). *grabatus*, a borrowing from Greek (κράβατ[τ]ος), previously used by Lucilius (284 W. = 256 K.), is a pallet, pauper's bed, or the like (*OLD* s.v.). **cum stertentem aliquem viderint** "when they see someone snoring"; again, the concrete description moves the picture into the realm of burlesque; cf. on §16 (*nondum dico quam haec signa nulla sint . . . nunc de universis*). **quae illi exterriti . . . deferant** "of such a kind that they, frightened out of sleep, report it in the morning to a dream-interpreter"; cf. *OLD* s.v. *exterreo.* Though *exterriti somnio* is the transmitted text, *exterriti somno* ("frightened out of sleep": A[1]) is preferable as an allusion to Ennius (*exterrita somno*: *An.* 35 Sk., quoted at 1.40); for confusion in the mss. between *somnium* and *somnus* cf. §§27 and 126. For the subjunctive of tendency, cf. on §19 (*nisi quod . . . rato tempore*). **quod vigilans viderit dormiens videre videatur** "seems to see in sleep what it saw when awake." The repetition of the verb with a change in the state carried by the participles (*vigilans, dormiens*) makes the process seem incontestably true. *dormiens*, flanked on both sides by pairs of words beginning with *vi-* plus obstruent, stands out. **philosophia dignius** varies what is "characteristic" or "worthy of a philosopher"; cf. on §§ 27, 46, 58. **sagarum superstitione . . . explicatione naturae:** The chiasmus sets the alternatives in stark opposition; for the former, cf. on §36a.

129b Ut, si iam fieri possit . . . divinum esse posse: *Ut* ("hence") introduces a consecutive clause with an embedded conditional (*si iam fieri possit . . .*). **eam:** Sc. *veram coniecturam*; this can be taken with both *profitentur* and *facere.* **ex levissimo . . . constant:** To judge by his strictures on *interpretes somniorum* at 1.132, Quintus does not disagree. **Stoici . . . divinum esse posse** = *SVF* 3:607 (see ibid. 605 for the Greek version); cf. Repici 1996, 49–55. With *Stoici . . . tui* Marcus continues to ignore Quintus' change of position; see on §127b *fin.* In Book 1 Quintus had invoked the diviners' fallibility to extenuate failures in divination: *male coniecta maleque interpretata falsa sunt non rerum vitio sed interpretum inscitia* (1.118; similarly 1.124). Possibly the relation of the sage to divination was a weak point or an unresolved issue within Stoicism (cf. *Off.* 3.91: *quasi controversa iura Stoicorum*); cf. Lévy 1997, 337.

130 Chrysippus quidem . . . significentur in somnis = *SVF* 2:1189. A general definition of divination moving within the conventional bounds of ancient cult from sign to interpretation to expiation, then a special application to dream-interpretation; it is invoked at this point to show the difficulty of the task set for dream-interpreters. Pease ad loc., following Hartfelder 1878, 19–20, speaks of "the failure of Cicero in this book to answer this definition," but in fact, the whole argument of the Book is directed at divination as so understood. **dei . . . significent** "what the gods' attitude toward human beings is and what they are signifying." For the anticipation of the subject of the indirect questions for emphasis, see on §63.2–3 (*fata queamus / scire*). *coniectio* varies *coniectura* in the sense "interpretation" (*OLD* s.vv. 2 and 3a respectively), its only use in this sense in Classical Latin (PHI).

quid ergo . . . cognovimus neminem: This repeats the essential idea of §129 *fin.* (*Stoici . . . esse posse*), the Stoic sage being a great rarity; cf. on §61 (*sapientem esse portentum est*). Alternatively, the theory could provide a self-corrective mechanism to compensate for flawed performance, but it does not; cf. Bobzien 1998, 170.

131a vide igitur ne . . . reperire possimus: The conclusion of the argument begun at §129b: even if divination is not thwarted in theory, it is in practice for want of a competent diviner. **vide ne:** See above on §12 (*vide igitur ne nulla sit divinatio*). **concessero:** Future perfect in the subordinate clause expresses time prior to another action (here *reperire possimus*); cf. Pinkster 2015, 465.

131b Qualis autem ista mens . . . loquerentur sine interprete: The concession made for the sake of argument in the previous sentence is now taken back. **Qualis . . . mens** "What purpose" (*OLD* s.v. *mens* 7), taken up by *quo pertinent* (§132). **quae ipsi per nos intellegamus** "such that we may understand them on our own," subj. of tendency, with *ipsi* strengthening *per nos*. The gods have closed off both possible paths of communication, direct or via interpreters. At this period, foreign ambassadors were typically admitted to address the senate in February (cf. Pina Polo 2011, 321); Cicero illustrates by comparing such behavior by the gods to ambassadors from Carthage or Spain addressing the senate in their native languages without an interpreter.

132 iam vero quo pertinent . . . nostra causa nos monerent: *iam vero* directs attention to the related topic of obscurity, which is now taken up: "Moreover." Greek *aenigma* is by now so thoroughly domesticated in Latin that Cicero feels no need for an explanation or an apologetic expression; cf. Hortensius' complaint during Verres' trial: *non intellego haec aenigmata* (*apud* Quint. *Inst.* 6.3.98). **di velle debebant** "the gods ought to have wanted": English places the action in the past, Latin the obligation; cf. on §71 (*parendum . . . religioni fuit*).

132–33 'Quid, poëta nemone . . . quid me igitur mones?: *poëta nemone* <*nemo*> is Timpanaro's correction for transmitted *poëta nemone*, here adopted (an easy saltation error). Obscurity was considered a stylistic fault (cf. *De orat.* 3.167), as Cicero's examples (Euphorion, Homer; Heraclitus, Democritus) and pointed questions (*uter . . . melior? . . . num . . . conferendi?*) imply. We have only relatively scanty remains of Euphorion, a scholar-poet of the third century (*CA* pp. 28–58; *SH* nos. 413–54), whose obscurity was also noted by Clement of Alexandria (*Strom.* 5.8.50.3); at *Tusc.* 3.45, after citing Ennius with approval, Cicero complains that that poet is despised by the *cantores Euphorionis*, by which he seems to mean "those who sing the praises of Euphorion" (*OLD* s.v. *cantor* 2; similarly *TLL* 3.1:292.24). For Heraclitus' obscurity, cf. Lucr. 1.638–39; *Fin.* 2.15 and *N.D.* 1.74; for praise of Democritus' style, cf. *De orat.* 1.49; *Orat.* 67. **me . . . mones:** Marcus apostrophizes the Stoic god.

133 ut si quis medicus . . . citharista, dicere?: The advice a physician gives to a patient is an obvious analogue for the messages the gods send to human beings for their benefit. But a benefit would hardly result if the doctor spoke in such riddles as the one cited by Cicero. **terrigenam . . . sanguine cassam** = fr. 56 Bl.: "earth-born, treading the grass, carrying its house, bloodless," Cicero's rendering of a riddling Greek verse describing a snail (for the medicinal use of which, cf. Pliny *Nat.* 30.44–46); a similar verse is cited by Athenaeus 2.63b: ὑλογενής, ἀνάκανθος, ἀναίματος, ὑγροκέλευθος ("born in the woods, spineless, bloodless, leaving a moist trail": tr. S. D. Olson, slightly modified). For *domiportam*, cf. Hes. *Op.* 571 (φερέοικος). **Pacuvianus**

Amphio: The indication of speaker identifies the play as the *Antiopa*, translated and adapted by Pacuvius from Euripides (no. 12 F 179–227 Kn.). **quadrupes . . . animali sono** = F 3 Schierl = 4–6 Warmington, who renders: "Four footed this, slow-stepping, haunting fields; / Low set and rude, and grim to gaze on, short / In head, snaky in neck, with gutted aspect, / Without breath, yet with breathing sound endowed," an allusion to the tortoise, whose shell provided the sounding board for the lyre; cf. the narrative of its invention by Hermes at *h.Hom.* 4.24–28. **capite brevi:** *brevi capite* (suggested by Ribbeck) would make a more metrically regular iambic senarius (and create alliteration). **tum Attici respondent:** Cicero seems to forget that this play, like its Euripidean model, was evidently set in Thebes, not Athens. However, Schierl (2006, 98) argues that the designation may be justified in view of Amphion's association with the mountain Aracynthus on the border between Boeotia and Attica. **non potueras . . . dicere?** "could you not have said?"; similar to expressions of obligation (on §132 [*di velle debebant*]). **citharista** identifies Amphion; the play famously staged a debate between Amphion and his brother Zethus on the merits of the political life (*vita activa*) vs. the *vita contemplativa*, a topic on which Cicero held firm views, expressed most famously in the proem to *Rep.* (hence perhaps the derisive address "lyre-player"); see further Luciani 2010: part 1, ch. 3.

134 defert ad coniectorem . . . reliquum argentum: An example of an obscure dream, introduced in asyndeton (cf. on §56 *init.*). Quintus might have been expected to narrate this among his examples of successful dream-divination at 1.39–59, many of them Greek and probably derived from Chrysippus (at §135b Marcus expresses surprise over an example omitted by his brother). **defert ad coniectorem:** Cf. §129a: *quae illi . . . ad coniectorem mane deferant.* The action itself is foregrounded and signals at once that we are still in the realm of dream-interpretation, the agent being either unknown or insignificant (hence *quidam* and below *hic nescio qui*). The narrative continues with the following stages also led by energetic verbs: *respondit . . . fodit, invenit . . . misit* (cf. on §79 *fugit e proelio*). **ex fascea lecti sui cubicularis:** A *fascia* or *fascea* is a strip of cloth, in this case "used to form the webbing of a bedstead": *OLD* s.v. *fascia* 1a. The Romans distinguished by function between the *lectus cubicularis* ("bed") and the *lectus tricliniaris* ("dining couch"): Var. *L.* 8.32. **in Chrysippi libro somnium** = *SVF* 2:1201. This work was already alluded to at 1.6 and 39; *somnium* is an archaic gen. pl. (cf. Enn. v. 57 J. = *TrRF* adesp. 76.8). **misit coniectori quantulum visum est de argento** "he sent the interpreter such little portion of the silver as he thought appropriate." This may have been either a fee agreed to when the interpretation was given or a gratuity expressing the client's satisfaction. **tum ille:** For *ille* used to change the subject, cf. on §74 (*ille renuntiat*). **'Nihilne . . . de vitello?'** "What? None of the yolk?" **id enim . . . aurum declarasse:** *id*, i.e., the *vitellum*.

134–35a nemone igitur umquam . . . consentanea maiestati deorum: Upon the report follows the critique (cf. on §§ 51 *init.* and 110 [*hoc si est in libris*]). Marcus objects on two grounds: (1) it is unjust for the gods to award treasure to this man but not to many other poor but deserving persons (*multi inopes digni praesidio deorum*); (2) the divine message was so obscure (*tam est obscure admonitus*; cf. §§131b–33). By now he need not say that chance is the alternative explanation. **hic nescio qui** "this nobody"; cf. on §79 (*fugit e proelio . . . et hospitem et regem*). **sicut aperte Simonides vetitus est navigare:** Sc. by the ghost of the man whose corpse the poet came upon and caused to be buried, a story told at 1.56; see further Schultz 2014 ad loc. **ergo obscura somnia . . . maiestati deorum:** Marcus thus resumes the criticism of dream-interpretation based on what is *dignum deo* (§§125–26) and draws a line under the criticism launched at §131b of the obscurity of the gods' supposed dream-messages.

135b Ad aperta et clara . . . eodem genere teli vulnerati: A second category of dreams contains ones that are clear and unambiguous, such as the dream of Simonides just cited. Another such dream narrated by Quintus involved two Arcadians who travelled to Megara, one of whom was killed by the keeper of the inn where they were lodging; there were two dreams, the first in which the victim begged his friend for help, the second asking him to recover his body and help avenge the crime (1.57 with Schultz 2014 ad loc.). A third example involves the wound from a poisoned arrow suffered by Ptolemy (the later founder of the dynasty that long ruled over Egypt), the remedy for which was revealed to Alexander in a dream. This was evidently a well-known anecdote; hence Marcus' surprise that his brother had failed to cite it (*quod a te praeteritum esse miror*). Cf. Diod. 17.103.3–8; Strabo 15.2.7 723C; Curt. 9.8.20–27; Justin 12.10.2–3; Oros. 3.19.11. Here Marcus simply narrates the anecdote; his comment is postponed to §141. **Ptolomaeus:** This (or *Ptolomeus*) is the regular spelling of the name in Latin mss. (instead of *Ptolem[a]eus*), an apparent example of progressive assimilation of vowels in adjacent syllables; cf. Volkmann, *RE* 23.2:1592.21–26; Leumann 1977, 100. **summo cum dolore** "in excruciating pain." Cf., e.g., *Tusc.* 2.44, where Epicurus is represented as arguing that Philoctetes, since afflicted only in his foot, *longe abest a summo dolore.* **Alexander adsidens:** *Alexander* is redundant in view of the preceding *de Alexandro . . . qui*, but may nonetheless be genuine (it was deleted by Kayser), Cicero sometimes using such anacolutha in his dialogues so that the important ideas emerge clearly (cf. H–S 730) and to imitate informal conversation; similarly, e.g., *De orat.* 2.276: *ut illud Nasicae, qui cum . . . Nasica sensit . . .* For *assideo* of "sitting beside, watching over" an invalid, cf. *OLD* s.v. 1c. **draco is quem mater Olympias alebat:** The determiner *is* is defined by the following relative clause (*OLD* s.v. 2a). Among our sources for the anecdote, the role of Olympias is mentioned only here. Cf. Plut. *Alex.* 2, claiming that Olympias raised and supplied tame snakes for orgiastic revels. *radicula* is a "root" used for medicinal purposes, probably here implying the whole plant; cf. *OLD* s.v. 2. Cf. 1.16, where an antidote for a snake's venom is said to have been revealed in a dream. In general, the association of snakes with healing is shown by the role of snakes in the iconography and cult of Asclepius and is also prominent in folklore; cf. Edelstein and Edelstein 1945, 2:226–31; Thompson 1955, B411.1. **quo . . . loci** "in what place"; cf. on §8 *fin.* **qui . . . quaererent:** For the final relative clause, cf. G–L §630. **eodem genere teli:** Sc. *telis venenatis*, as explained above.

136a multa etiam sunt . . . Caeciliae, Baliarici filiae, somnium: A list of the dreams Quintus cited from historical sources: Phalaris' mother (1.46); the Elder Cyrus (ibid.); the mother of Dionysius (1.39); Hamilcar (1.50); Hannibal (1.48–49); P. Decius (1.51); the dancer at the beginning of a religious procession (1.55); C. Gracchus (1.56); Caecilia, daughter of Baliaricus (1.4, 99). Cf. Schultz 2014 ad locos, and on Caecilia's dream see now Garofalo 2019, 46–48.

sed haec externa . . . quis enim auctor istorum?: Cicero operates here with a dichotomy between *externa* and *nostra*. He uses a similar argument in forensic cases to discard foreign witnesses en bloc on the ground that the things to which they testify are *ignota nobis* and therefore unreliable; cf. *Scaur.* 15–18 with Dyck 2012 ad loc. Here it turns out that *externa* is used in the different sense of "unconnected to us (personally)": *OLD* s.v. 2 vs. 3. **ficta:** Cf. §27: *commenticiorum exemplorum mirifica copia . . . testibus uti qui aut casu veri aut malitia falsi fictique esse possunt*; cf. §§31 *fin.*, 46 *fin.*, 66 (*quae tamen vel ipsa . . . fortuito cecidisse potuerunt*), 113. **quis enim auctor istorum?** "Who is the authority for those examples of yours?"

136b De nostris somniis . . . deduci iubente monumentum: *De nostris somniis* is fronted in asyndeton for contrast to *externa* and as the new topic. Marcus cross-refers to Quintus' reports of his own dream of Marcus and his horse disappearing into a river and reappearing on the riverbank (1.58; cf. on §67 for the similar dream of the disappearance and reappearance of

Dionysius' horse) and Marcus' dream of Marius with laureled fasces (a token borne by a general celebrating a triumph; cf. Marshall 1984, 132–33 and n. 47; Schäfer 1989, 201 and n. 38), ordering him to be brought to his own monument (1.59). The disappearance into a body of water of a horse or a man on horseback is widely attested in the ancient world, often associated with sacrifice or self-sacrifice; see the examples adduced by Versnel 1981, 152–56. **de emerso me . . . de Mario . . . iubente:** The participles, arranged chiastically with their related substantives, dominate these dream-pictures. **in suum . . . monumentum:** Sc. the temple of *Honos et Virtus* that Marius built from the spoils of his victory over the Teutones and Ambrones at Aquae Sextiae in 102; cf. Richardson 1992 s.v. Honos et Virtus (Mariana), Aedes 2; Palombi, *LTUR* s.v. Honos et Virtus, Aedes Mariana.

omnium somniorum, Quinte . . . depravatione superetur: The "single explanation for all dreams" that Marcus has in mind is the one already offered at §§128–29. But in order to establish its exclusivity, Marcus must refute the competing theory of Democritus (cf. §120), which he now proceeds to do. **per deos inmortalis:** For the use of the oath, cf. on §53 *init.*; similarly §114: *per deos atque homines.* **videamus ne . . . superetur** "Let us be on guard lest . . ."; cf. §12 *vide igitur ne nulla sit divinatio.* It is interesting that with *nostra* Marcus acknowledges that he, too, is subject to these all-too-human tendencies; cf. *Luc.* 66: *non . . . sum sapiens*; on §148b (*multum . . . profuturi videbamur*). **superstitione . . . superetur:** A play on words; cf. the (half-serious?) etymology of *superstitio* at *N.D.* 2.72: *nam qui totos dies precabantur et immolabant ut sibi sui liberi superstites essent superstitiosi sunt appellati.* On *superstitio* see on §19 (*anile sane et plenum superstitionis*). *depravatio* is "addiction to moral error, perversity"; cf. *Leg.* 1.29; *OLD* s.v. b.

137 quem enim tu . . . vult fluere imagines: Here Marcus begins to investigate the nature of the dream-vision more closely. **speciem . . . et imaginem** "his semblance and image" (*OLD* s.v. *species* 6a). *credo* ("I suppose") is ironic, as often. **unde profectam** "What is the source . . . ?" **a corporibus . . . solidis et a certis figuris:** Cicero expounds Democritus' theory of the different types of atoms at *N.D.* 1.66: *esse corpuscula quaedam, levia alia, alia aspera, rotunda alia, partim autem angulata et hamata, curvata quaedam et quasi adunca* (Lucretius 2.333–477 offers further detail). The basic doctrine is that objects give off effluents that meet a cone-shaped radiation that is projected from the eyes toward the object; the two then condense the intervening air in such a way as to form an image (Cicero's *imago*, *eidolon* in Greek) that somehow reaches and is processed by the eye; see further Furley 1987, 131–35; detailed account by Sassi 1978, 96–109.

The Epicurean Velleius uses the same essential theory to explain how human beings receive their picture of the gods (*N.D.* 1.49); similarly ibid. 1.109 and 114; cf. Essler 2011, 67–147.

quod igitur Mari corpus . . . nisi pulsu imaginum: *igitur* "in that case" (*OLD* s.v. 2), i.e., in view of the response *a corporibus.* **ista igitur . . . persequebatur?** "Was *that*, then, the image of Marius that pursued me to the plain of Atina?" *ista* is at once contemptuous and emphatic; cf. §72: *haec sunt igitur aves internuntiae Iovis!* The reference is to a plain on the Via Popilia about twenty-five miles south of Nares Lucanae, on the route that Cicero followed as he went into exile (cf. *Att.* 3.2[48], written from Nares Lucanae on March 27, 58). **'Plena sunt . . . pulsu imaginum':** Here Christ's transposition is adopted (as also by Pease, Timpanaro, and others): the words *plena sunt imaginum omnia* are transmitted after *quod fuerat* but function better as a response to the local query *ista igitur me imago Mari in campum Atinatem persequebatur?* Then the following *nulla enim species cogitari potest nisi pulsu imaginum* can function as confirmation/explanation (as the connection with *enim* suggests). For the doctrine of omnipresent images (coexisting, uneasily, with a doctrine of omnipresent *daimones*), cf. Democ. 68 A 78 D.–K. *nulla* is emphatic. **pulsu imaginum:** Cf. *N.D.* 1.107: *fac imagines esse quibus pulsentur animi.*

138–39 quid ergo, istae imagines . . . me aliqua pellit?: *quid ergo . . . accurrant?*: "Tell me, then, are those images of yours so obedient to us as to come running as soon as we wish?" Cf. Lucr. 4.781–82: *anne voluntatem nostram simulacra tuentur / et simul ac volumus nobis occurrit imago . . . ?* Cicero launched a similar criticism of the Epicurean theory of images at *Fam.* 15.16(215).1–2 (to Cassius, January 10, 45; cf. Griffin 1995, 343); cf. also the half-facetious remarks on the subject at *Att.* 2.3(23).2 (end of the year 60). **etiamne earum rerum quae nullae sunt?:** This was a problem for the Epicureans as well as Democritus; Lucretius promised to clarify it (1.127–35) but failed to do so. Cotta raises a similar objection to the Epicurean gods at *N.D.* 1.105: *quid interest utrum de hippocentauro an de deo cogitemus? omnem talem conformationem animi ceteri philosophi motum inanem vocant* with Essler 2011, 111–12. Marcus goes on to cite things that are nonexistent now because they are past (Babylon, Homer), whereas at *N.D.* 1.107–8 Cotta instances Homer and other figures of the past but also pure products of the imagination, such as the Scylla or chimaera. **invisitata** = "strange" or "novel": *OLD* s.v. *invisitatus* 2. **quam non sibi ipse fingere animus possit:** Cf. the way Cicero introduces the "thought-experiment" at *Mil.* 79: *fingite animis—liberae sunt enim nostrae cogitationes et quae volunt sic intuentur ut* *ea cernamus quae non videmus.* For *ipse* reinforcing the reflexive pronoun, cf. on §83b (*Atque his superstitionibus . . .*'); for the consecutive relative clause, on §121 *fin.* **oppidorum situs, hominum figuras:** The walls of Babylon, famously described by Herodotus (1.178–79) and counted as one of the seven wonders of the world, serve to exemplify the former, Homer the latter. For "railroading" *num*, cf. on §9. Marcus' skeptical queries replace an argument: in the sequel the point is taken as proven (*omnia igitur . . . nullae ergo imagines* etc.). **imago illorum me aliqua pellit:** As the theory would dictate; cf. above *nulla enim species . . . nisi pulsu imaginum* (§137).

139 omnia igitur quae volumus . . . nihil diceret: *omnia igitur . . . cogitare nequeamus*: I.e., we do not need the hypothesis that external images can be summoned instantaneously (§138). **nullae ergo imagines . . . nec omnino fluunt ullae:** Emphatic denials that such external images enter the mind of sleepers or exist at all. **nec . . . fluunt** responds to *vult fluere* (sc. Democritus) at §137. **nec cognovi . . . nihil diceret:** So far Marcus has shown respect for Democritus, as when he cites his view about the character of available feed determining the appearance of the entrails of sacrificial animals (§30: *non inscite*, albeit critical remarks follow) or his explantion of why cocks crow before dawn (§57: *optumis verbis*); Quintus cited him as anticipating a view of Plato's (1.80); and he is called a *gravis auctor* in the author's preface (1.5); cf. also *Fin.* 1.21, where Democritus is said to be praised *a ceteris* but reviled by Epicurus. Hence his great *auctoritas*, in sharp contrast with the precipitous drop in his credibility. *nihil dicere* ("talk nonsense") is perhaps a Grecism based upon οὐδὲν λέγειν; cf. LSJ s.v. λέγω III.6; *Tusc.* 1.14: *aut nihil dicis omnino*; *Fat.* 32; on §108 (*aliquid . . . dixerit*); Chiarini 2019; cf. also colloquial *nihil agis*: Hofmann 2003, 276 and 354.

animorum est ea vis . . . multa dici videntur: *ea vis eaque natura*: For *is* functioning like *talis* in prompting a consecutive clause, cf. *OLD* s.v. 3. **vigeant:** Cf. 1.63: *viget autem et vivit animus.* **nullo adventicio pulsu:** In contrast to Democritus' theory, as described at §120: *externa et adventicia visione pulsari*; §126: *externus et adventicius pulsus;* §137 *pulsu imaginum* **suo motu:** Cicero regarded the doctrine of the soul as a self-mover as so important as to warrant a precise rendering from Pl. *Phaedr.* 245c at *Rep.* 6.27–28 (= 31–32 P., repeated at *Tusc.* 1.53–54); cf. Zetzel 1995, 251–52 for details. Here it is invoked not to argue for the soul's immortality, but to combat the Democritean idea that an external push (*externus pulsus*) causes the soul to dream. The idea of a constant and autonomous movement of the soul is, however, alien to Aristotle (cf. *De an.* 408a29–b18). This seems, therefore, to be Cicero's own development of the doctrine; cf. Kany-Turpin and Pellegrin 1989, 238–39; Kany-Turpin 2004, 48 and n. 3. **hi cum sustinentur . . . cernunt, cogitant, sentiunt:** Marcus picks up from §126 Chrysippus' point about superior perception in the waking state; see ad loc. Here he explains why the waking images are clearer and more reliable: they are supported by the senses; cf. Kany-Turpin and Pellegrin 1989, 236. **cum autem . . . ipse per sese:** Cf. 1.63, 70, 115, and §128 as well as *suo motu* just above. **itaque in eo . . . multa dici videntur:** I.e., dreams occur. **versantur** "are constantly present": *OLD* s.v. *verso* 11b.

140 haec scilicet . . . de illo somniandi fuisse: *in inbecillo remissoque animo*: Cf. Zeno's picture of sleep quoted at §119. *remissus* = relaxed; cf. *OLD* s.v. 3. **omnibus modis** "completely" is probably, like *nullo modo* (cf. on §24 *init.*), colloquial (four times in Plautus); cf. also *Ac.* 1.27: *omnibusque modis mutari.* **maxumeque reliquiae . . . aut egimus:** Aristotle's theory; cf. on §128. **egimus** = *quae egimus* ("which we occupied ourselves with": *OLD* s.v. *ago* 22a; cf. §148: *id maxime egimus*), with relative supplied from the previous *de quibus.* **ut mihi temporibus illis . . . constanti tulisset:** Sulla's march on Rome at the head of an army in 88 caught his enemy C. Marius by surprise, and he had to flee hastily and in risky circumstances. He ultimately found refuge with a colony of his veterans at Cercina in Africa. After Sulla's departure to fight Mithridates in Asia, Marius returned to Rome at the head of his own army of veterans the following year (Plut. *Mar.* 35–44; Carney 1961, chs. 10–12; Santangelo 2016a, ch. 4; Weynand, *RE* Suppl. 6:1141.14 ff.). At *Red. sen.* 38 and *Red. pop.* 19–21, Cicero refers to Marius' exile and return and compares it to his own experience; cf. van der Blom 2010, 204–5. Cicero's poem, the *Marius*, may have been written around this time; cf. Courtney 2003, 177–78; Dyck 2004b, 57–58. Our passage, together with the poem and the cited passages from the speeches, suggests that Cicero took his fellow Arpinate as a model of how to handle the situation of exile. **hanc credo causam de illo somniandi fuisse:** The constituents of the topic *hanc . . . causam* are split by the verb (nonironic *credo*), which takes second place; cf. Devine and Stephens 2006, 178 (for similar pattern with weak pronoun, cf. on §62a [*hoc ille responso*]). **de illo:** I.e., *de Mario.* The dream of Marius is thus explicable on the Aristotelian theory that dreams contain a residue of daytime mental activity. Näf (2004, 85) points out that this is the earliest example of analysis of a dream of one's own with reference to a theory of dream-interpretation.

tibi autem de me . . . demersus rursus apparuit: *tibi autem de me cum sollicitudine cogitanti*: Turning to Quintus' dream (*autem*), Marcus first establishes the context as his brother's concerned thoughts when, as governor of Asia (*MRR* 2:198), he learned of Marcus' sudden departure for exile. **inerant . . . vestigia** "There were in both of our minds traces of our waking thoughts," a confirmation of Aristotle; see above. **at quaedam adiuncta sunt** "but certain elements were added." If the *at* is felt to mark too sharp a contrast, Timpanaro (1988, 407) suggests *a<d quae> quaedam*. Marcus specifies these elements as Marius' monument (in his own dream), i.e., the temple of *Honos et Virtus* (see above on §136b), where, at the end of May 57, the senate took the first effective steps toward Cicero's recall from exile (cf. *Red. sen.* 24, *Dom.* 85, *Sest.* 128, *Pis.* 34; Stein 1930, 32), and the horse on which his brother was seen riding (in Quintus' dream).

141a an tu censes . . . temere concurrerent?: This question concludes the discussion of the brothers' dreams. For the *anus*, cf. on §19 (*anile sane et plenum superstitionis*). Marcus cannot dismiss these dreams as apocryphal, nor does he deny that they can be taken as prophetic, as he had previously said his dream was (1.59 *fin.*; cf. Näf 2004, 84). Therefore, he falls back on chance (*casus*) as the explanation for their fulfillment. **concurrerent** "be in agreement, harmonize," sc. with reality; cf. *OLD* s.v. *concurro* 6a.

141b Alexandro draco loqui . . . magnum somnianti: Turning back to *externa* (i.e., others' dreams: §136a), Marcus now adds his commentary on the anecdote narrated at §135. **ut verum sit** "even if one grants that it is true" (sc. for the sake of argument): Pohlenz's correction for *utrum sit*; for the concessive *ut*-clause, cf. §33b; *OLD* s.v. *ut* 35. **non est mirabile:** This is Davies' correction for *non esse mirabile* (there is a similar substitution of *dare* for *dant* at §106); Plasberg's insertion of *vides* (after *sed*) and retention of *esse* is also conceivable. **non . . . audivit . . . sed est visus audire:** If he had heard a serpent speaking, it would have been miraculous, but he merely dreamed it. For the folktale motif of the speaking snake, cf. Thompson 1955, B211.6.1. **quo maius sit . . . locutus est:** A further violation of verisimilitude, mocked as *maius* than the talking serpent. **nihil est magnum somnianti:** I.e., anything is possible in dreams; cf. §§122a and 146.

quaero autem cur Alexandro . . . nec multa ceteris: The rarity itself can give rise to suspicion. Strabo 15.2.7 723C is even more skeptical, suspecting that Alexander received word of the antidote from a native informant and that the dream-story was invented to flatter the king. **alias** "on another occasion." **nec multa:** Sc. *inlustria somnia*.

mihi quidem . . . tam longa in aetate!: *hoc Marianum*: Cf. on §136. **nihil sane** "absolutely nothing": *OLD* s.v. *sane* 4b. **frustra igitur**

consumptae . . . in aetate!: Cf. §121: *totas noctes somniamus—neque ulla est fere qua non dormiamus* with note. Another dream is ascribed to Cicero, however: he is alleged to have seen a boy whom he did not know at the time lowered from heaven by a golden chain and deposited at the door of the Capitol, where Jupiter handed him a whip; he later recognized the boy as Octavius (Augustus); cf. Suet. *Aug.* 94.9; Plut. *Cic.* 44.5–7; Tertull. *De an.* 46.2; Dio 45.2.2. **tam longa in aetate:** Born January 6, 106, Cicero would have been sixty-two at the time he wrote these words. The average life expectancy of members of the senatorial class around this time has been estimated at twenty-five to thirty years at birth; cf. Hopkins 1983, 146–59; Scheidel 1999, 266. Hence even as consul, aged forty-three, Cicero could say *neque turpis mors forti viro potest accidere neque immatura consulari* (*Catil.* 4.3); later this year he would assert: *mihi fere satis est quod vixi vel ad aetatem vel ad gloriam* (*Phil.* 1.38; similarly ibid. 2.119).

142a nunc quidem . . . tantis praesertim de rebus: *propter intermissionem forensis operae*: After the civil war, Cicero no longer participated in the regular work of the courts, though he did speak in several quasi-judicial processes before Caesar (*Lig.*, *Deiot.*); see further Bringmann 1986. **et lucubrationes detraxi et meridiationes addidi** "I have stopped burning the midnight oil and have introduced siestas" (*OLD* s.vv. *detraho* 9a, *meridiatio*), two parallel strategies (*et . . . et*) for counteracting fatigue. **nec tam multum . . . sum admonitus** "and even though I was sleeping so much, no dream warned me." **tantis praesertim de rebus** is rather vague. From our perspective, it seems natural to think of Caesar's assassination (cf. Timpanaro 1988, LXX). But this period saw a series of developments shocking to republican sensibilities, such as Caesar's dictatorship for life, his creation at the end of 46 of the *praefectura urbis* to handle during his absence functions traditionally exercised by the urban quaestors and praetors, the election of C. Caninius Rebilus as suffect consul for the last day of 45, or Mark Antony's offer of a diadem to Caesar at the Lupercalia (February 15, 44). Cicero could, of course, also have added the words *tantis praesertim de rebus* in revising after the Ides of March; see above 30–31. For a different contextualization, cf. Boes 1981, 174–75.

nec mihi magis . . . somniare "I think that I am never dreaming more than when I see the magistrates in the Forum or the senate in the senate-house," i.e., they are mere phantoms, preserving the form but not the substance; cf. §71: *simulacra . . . auspiciorum*; the suggestion of Jacobs 2010, 323–24 n. 28, that *somniare* should be deleted is misguided. This detachment reflects Cicero's feeling of "inner exile" under Caesar's dictatorship; cf. *Att.*

12.21(260).5 and *Fam.* 4.6(249).2; cf. Herescu 1961, 143–46; Edwards 2018, 185–86; Dyck (forthcoming). There may already be a hint of this feeling in Cicero's letters to Caelius from Cilicia; cf. Rühl 2019, 62.

142b Etenim . . . ex ovo intellegi debeat?: *Etenim* ("And indeed") introduces a rhetorical question (*OLD* s.v. b). **ex divisione hoc secundum est:** I.e., of the explanations of divination from dreams; cf. §124. **continuatio coniunctioque naturae:** Cicero experiments with various Latin equivalents for συμπάθεια; cf. on §33b, *coniunctio* occurring at §§34a, 119, and 124, *continuatio* ("interconnexion": *OLD* s.v. 4) only here; cf. also *N.D.* 2.19: *consentiens conspirans continuata cognatio.* Cicero returns to the egg in the dream that was taken to be prophetic of hidden treasure (§134) and asks what *coniunctio* could account for it. Similarly, at §34a Marcus wondered what *sympatheia* could connect a mark on the liver of a sacrificial animal with his profit.

nam medici ex quibusdam rebus . . . intelligi posse dicunt: There is a similar contrast of the signs used by astronomers and diviners at §§17–18. **ex quibusdam rebus** "from certain symptoms." **advenientis . . . crescentis:** The participles add vividness, perhaps a Grecism in place of expected infinitives after *intellego* (cf. *OLD* s.v. 1b), though such Latin constructions as *medicus morbum ingravescentem . . . providet* (§16) may have facilitated the change. **ut hoc ipsum** "for instance, this very point." **pleni enectine simus** "whether we are full or dying [sc. of hunger]": cf. §73: *inclusa in cavea et fame enecta* [sc. *avis*]; *OLD* s.v. *eneco* c. Cf. Pease ad loc., citing the relevant medical literature.

thesaurus vero . . . naturali cognatione iunguntur?: In contrast (*vero*) to the purely physical connections just mentioned are the enhancements in wealth or prestige often predicted by divination. Marcus would like to know "by what natural kinship they are connected with dreams."

143 dicitur quidam . . . non opinio [erroris] effecerit: The example is introduced in asyndeton, as usual. **cum in somnis complexu Venerio iungeretur** "when engaged in sexual intercourse in his dream"; cf. *OLD* s.v. *somnus* 1c. **calculos eiecisse** "expelled kidney stones" (*OLD* s.v. *calculus* 2). **video sympathian** "I see the sympathetic connection," i.e., between the dream and the cure, with the ironic implication that such a connection, though claimed by the Stoa, is usually murky. **visum est . . . tale obiectum dormienti** "such a dream-vision was presented to the sleeper"; cf. *Luc.* 49: *si tale visum obiectum est a deo dormienti; Fat.* 43: *visum obiectum.* **ut id . . .**

effecerit "that the force of nature, not opinion, produced the result," i.e., this was a therapeutic dream based on purely physical causes, without a diviner's interpretation (*opinio*) intervening between the dream and the therapy. Contrast §147: *ii qui interpretantur coniecturam adhibeant, non naturam.* (This passage has been oddly misunderstood as indicating that "the dream was the effect and not the cause" of the expulsion of stones: so Falconer [1923a, 530n1]; similarly Hottinger and Timpanaro [1988, 408]; but *cum in somnis . . . iungeretur* is clearly a framing condition for the incident.) A similar dream is recorded at Asclepius' sanctuary at Epidaurus: "A man with a stone in his member. He saw a dream. It seemed to him that he was lying with a fair boy and when he had a seminal discharge he ejected the stone and picked it up and walked out holding it in his hands" (Edelstein and Edelstein 1945, 1:232 no. 14; their translation, slightly modified). The transmitted text stretches the possibilities of a genitival limitation for *opinio* to the breaking point: it should be a "belief in," "mental picture of," or "reputation for" something: *OLD* s.v. *opinio*. In fact, *erroris* is not wanted (see above); it may have been added by a reader who thought *opinio* needed clarification. With or without *erroris*, the clausula is a double cretic (with elision if *erroris* is removed).

quae igitur natura . . . ut eveniret casus effecit?: *quae . . . natura* is short for *quae . . . sympathia naturae*. For Simonides' dream, cf. on §134 *fin.* With this question, Marcus implicitly doubts that any such physical force can be identified as the cause of that dream. Like Alexander's dream (§135), Alcibiades' dream was not narrated by Quintus. In the year 404, Alcibiades took refuge with the Persian satrap Pharnabazus, who, however, at Lysander's bidding, turned against him and ordered him to be killed. V. Max. 1.7 ext. 6 follows Cicero's account; the anecdote also appears in Greek sources (Plut. *Alcib.* 39; *Suda* s.v. *Alkibiades*). **quid naturae copulatum** "what connection to nature" (for *copulatus* with dative, cf. *OLD* s.v. 1a). **paulo ante interitum:** For the belief that persons near death have special divinatory powers, cf. 1.64 = Posidonius F 108 E.–K. and implicitly the example of Callanus at 1.47. **amicae esse amictus amiculo** "was covered with his mistress's cloak," a notable example of assonance, on the use of which in Latin, cf. Coleman 1999, 49. Plutarch (*Alcib.* 39) identifies the mistress as a certain Timandra. Anaphoric *is* is placed before its clause for focus; see above on §63, vv. 2–3. **proiectus inhumatus . . . desertus:** Cf. *Tusc.* 1.104 (of Diogenes the Cynic): *proici se iussit inhumatum*; *Phil.* 14.34: *eosque nec inhumatos esse nec desertos*; cf. also Caesar *trucidatus ita iaceret ut ad eius corpus non modo amicorum sed ne servorum quidem quisquam accederet* (§23). **suo pallio:** The *pallium* was, in the eyes of the Romans, a characteristically Greek garment; cf. *OLD* s.v. 1b. **ergo hoc inerat . . . ut eveniret casus effecit?**

"Was this, then, inherent in future events and did it have natural causes, or did chance cause both the vision and the outcome?" The former is the Stoic explanation, which Cicero will explore further in *De fato* (cf. §§3 and 19), the latter, of course, the solution Marcus has been promoting.

144 Quid, ipsorum interpretum . . . consensumque naturae?: As he did with Zeno (§119) and Chrysippus (§126) and sometimes in his forensic speeches (*Caec.* 24–30, *Mil.* 46), Marcus now proposes to elicit evidence from the other side, in this case, the professional dream-interpreters themselves (*ipsorum interpretum*, *ipse* emphasizing identity: *OLD* s.v. 8). The claim will be, as suggested in this "railroading" question (*nonne*), that their inferences (*coniecturae*) put their own talents (*ingenia*) on display rather than any sort of natural harmony of the elements of the universe. The following anecdotes provide another example of Cicero's concise but pointed narrative style (cf. on §79). For contested dream-interpretation in antiquity, see also Van Hove 2019, esp. 424–31.

cursor ad Olympia . . . et vis equorum': As usual, the example is introduced asyndetically. **ad Olympia . . . cogitans** "planning to depart for the Olympic games" sets the context. **visus est . . . vehi** "in his dream saw himself riding in a four-horse chariot." **mane ad coniectorem:** By now this elliptical narrative suffices; cf. §129: *quae illi . . . ad coniectorem mane deferant*; he becomes even more laconic in §145 (*rettulit*). For *ille* used to change the subject, see on §74 (*ille renuntiat*).

post idem ad Antiphontem . . . ante te cucurrisse?': The response of Antiphon the sophist (87 B 80 D-K = *Onirocritici* p. 46, fr. 7 del Corno; it is disputed whether he should be identified with Antiphon the orator), already cited as an acute dream-interpreter by Quintus (1.39). **'Vincare . . . necesse est** "Your defeat is inevitable." The first interpreter, with his flattering inference, no doubt hoped for a gratuity from a pleased client (cf. §134), whereas Antiphon may have reckoned that the odds were in favor of his prophecy. Antiphon's dream-book may already have juxtaposed the two interpretations; cf. Pendrick 2002, 425–26. In any case, Marcus makes his point that there are no fixed principles of interpretation, merely a competition in cleverness between diviners.

ecce alius cursor . . . nulla vehementius': *ecce* adds liveliness to an enumeraton: "Lo and behold!" Cf. *Tusc.* 1.106: *ecce alius exoritur e terra, qui matrem dormire non sinat*; *OLD* s.v. 4–5. The parenthetical insertion is typical of Cicero's dialogues, as he aims to reproduce the relaxed tone of conversation among the upper class at leisure. As Quintus already indicated, both Chrysippus and Antipater collected examples of dream-interpretation (1.39; *SVF* 2:1206 and 3 Antip. 42). **vehementius** "more energetically" or "powerfully."

huic eidem Antipho . . . ipsa postrema est': This second example makes essentially the same point as the first, Antiphon matching his competitor's optimistic prediction with a cynical one. **Baro** is a derisive form of address: "fool," "blockhead," or the like (*OLD* s.v., positing an Etruscan origin); it appears to be unrelated to (though sometimes confused with) Germanic *baro*, which is in turn connected with English *baron*; see further E.–M. s.v. **ista enim avis . . . ipsa postrema est'** "that bird, chasing and harassing the other birds, is always last." A similar anecdote involving Antiphon's interpretation of a runner's dream about an eagle occurs at Diogenes of Oenoanda NF 122 Smith, possibly derived from the Stoic source used by Cicero; see further Pendrick 2002, 216–21 and 426–28.

145 parere quaedam matrona . . . obsignari nihil solere: Again, two opposite interpretations are offered by competing diviners. The anecdote is elsewhere told of Olympias, mother of Alexander (Plut. *Alex.* 2; Tertull. *De an.* 46.5); Augustine also alludes to it (*Contra Julianum op. imperf.* 5.17 = *PL* 45.1450). **obsignatam habere naturam** "that her womb was sealed": *OLD* s.v. *natura* 15. *natura* is also used for the penis (*N.D.* 3.56), Cicero's usage suggesting that the word "had a polite tone," as Adams 1982, 59, notes. **inane obsignare nihil solere:** Its position lends focus to *inane*, and the hyperbaton emphasizes *nihil.* Quintus once told Tiro that his mother used to seal up empty bottles so that she would know that any that were empty but unsealed had been drained on the sly (*Fam.* 16.26[351].2); hence the telling of this anecdote may be a kind of private joke between the brothers (so with a query Kany-Turpin 2004, 50n2).

quae est ars coniectoris . . . modo illuc ducentium?: *eludo* is "play tricks, mock": *OLD* s.v. 1 and 4; cf. *Luc.* 123: *et vos* [sc. *Stoici*] *ab illo* [sc. *Epicuro*] *inridemini et ipsi illum vicissim eluditis.* **quae conlecta habent Stoici** "which the Stoics have gathered"; such combinations of *habeo* + perfect participle, not uncommon in Cicero, are the origin of the perfect system in the Romance languages; cf. Pinkster 2015, 478–81; Pieroni 2016. **acumen** ("acuteness") was already used of dream-interpreters by Quintus (1.39). **ex similitudine aliqua** "based on some resemblance." **coniecturam modo huc modo illuc ducentium** "guiding the inference now this way, now that," i.e., with no underlying principle and hence not an art (*ars*). Cf. §24: *si enim id quod eventurum est vel hoc vel illo modo potest evenire, fortuna valet plurimum*; §55b: *coniectura . . . ingeniis hominum in multas aut diversas aut etiam contrarias partis saepe diducitur.*

medici signa quaedam habent . . . nullo modo: Marcus returns to the analogy of the physician or the ship's pilot, representatives of recognized arts; cf. §§14, 16, and 142b. Both follow specific physical signs in making their predictions about a patient's health or the weather, in one case the veins and the breath, in the other the behavior of squid (*lolligines*) or dolphins. **haec** summarizes and lends focus to the phenomena used as indicators by physicians or pilots. **ad naturam revocari facile possunt** "can easily be connected with nature": *OLD* s.v. *revoco* 14; cf. §66: *ad coniecturam aliqua interpretatione revocantur.* **ea vero quae paulo ante dixi:** I.e., the dreams used as indicators by diviners. **nullo modo:** See on §24.

146 'At enim observatio . . . fecit artem': *At* signals a contradiction, *enim* that an explanation will now follow: "But the fact is . . ." To salvage dream-interpretation as an art, Quintus now falls back on the third explanation, long-continued observation; cf. §124. **notandis rebus:** Cf. on §§ 87b *fin.* (on *notatio*) and 91 (*animadvertant et notent*).

ain tandem? . . . observando notare possumus?: *ain tandem?* is colloquial, implying doubt: "Really?" (similarly §68 *itane?*). Cf. *Leg.* 3.14; *OLD* s.v. *aio* 2; Hofmann 2003, 157 and 362. **'Somnia observari possunt'** is probably best taken as an assertion by Quintus, rather than a question; similarly §37 *fin.* ('*Haruspices dicunt*'); cf. on §59 *init.* **nihil tam praepostere . . . quod non possimus somniare:** An explanation in asyndeton and therefore punctuated with a preceding colon. For the idea, cf. §122a with note. For the consecutive relative clause, see on §121 *fin.* This is the unique occurrence of *monstruose* in Classical Latin. **observando notare** picks up *observatio . . . notandis rebus* in the dogmatist's assertion.

astrologi motus errantium . . . quae concursatio somniorum: *astrologi*: For the lack of a clear distinction between *astronomia* and *astrologia*, cf. on §87b (*de quibus Eudoxus . . . minime esse credendum*). Astronomy provides the prime example of long-continued observation of many phenomena leading to a systematic body of knowledge; cf. on §28 (*persuaderi igitur cuiquam potest . . . unam omnium disciplinam*). **cedo** "describe to me" or "explain to me": *OLD* s.v. *cedo*[2] 2a; it is an old imperative related to the deictic local adv. *-ce*; cf. Leumann 1977, 468. **concursatio** "grouping" or "conjunction," on the analogy of the behavior of the stars and planets in astronomy; cf. *Tim.* 29:

ea concursatione quam inter se habent Lucifer, Mercurius, sol (this text follows the suggestion at *TLL* 4.1:113.82–84).

quo modo autem . . . non semper eodem modo?: Marcus returns to the point raised at §128: *si alia falsa, alia vera, qua nota internoscantur scire sane velim.* **cum eadem . . . eodem modo** "since the same (dreams) turn out differently for different people and not always the same way for the same people."

ut mihi mirum videatur . . . ex uno innumerabilia confirment: Marcus finds the complete failure of skepticism on this point strange (*mirum*): though a liar would be disbelieved even if he once told the truth, how is it that those Stoics of yours (*isti*) do just the opposite in the case of dreams, regarding a single success as a confirmation of countless other predictions, rather than withholding belief in the one in view of all the others? This argument would, of course, also apply to Cratippus' attempt to justify both forms of natural divination (§§107–9). **verum evasit:** Cf. on §108 (*verum evaserit*). **uni fidem derogent** "deny credibility to the one"; cf. *Flac.* 9: *non quo nationi huic* [sc. the Greeks] *ego unus maxime fidem derogem.*

147 Si igitur neque deus . . . somniis tribuendum sit: Marcus draws the conclusion from his arguments against each of the three explanations for dream-divination listed at §124. The rejection of god as an *effector somniorum* takes up the point *intellegendum est nullam vim esse divinam effectricem somniorum* (§124). **neque naturae societas . . . inveniri potuit scientia:** A summary of the findings since §144: dream-interpretation is based neither on a connection with nature nor systematic observation. **nihil prorsus somniis tribuendum sit** "no weight at all should be assigned to dreams." For *nihil prorsus* cf. on §12 *init.*; similarly *nihil sane* at §141.

praesertim cum illi ipsi . . . in somniorum visis effecerit: Marcus raises three further arguments against dream-divination: (1) the dreamers themselves (*illi ipsi qui ea vident*) do not engage in divination (cf. §54: *quid . . . volunt di inmortales . . . ea significantes quae sine interpretibus non possimus intellegere*); but as Altman (2008, 111) points out, in Plato's account (*Rp.* 571c3–e2) dreamers who have healthy and temperate souls need no interpreters for their dreams, and Cicero interpreted his own dream of Marius (according to 1.59); (2) the interpreters use *coniectura* ("inference" or "guesswork") as their basis, not nature (in implicit contrast to the physician or ship's pilot, who relies on natural signs [§145]; cf. also on §143: *opinio*); (3) chance is a plausible explanation for the successes in dream-divination, which are a small subset of chance outcomes in the course of the ages.

neque coniectura . . . quicquam sit incertius: The sheer malleability of *coniectura* makes it unreliable (and, implicitly, no suitable basis for an art). **quae in varias partis duci possit, non numquam etiam in contrarias:** Cf. §145 on the *acumen hominum ex similitudine aliqua coniecturam modo huc, modo illuc ducentium* as well as the examples cited at §§144–45.

148a explodatur <igitur> . . . pariter cum ceteris: Marcus thus draws a line under the second of the two forms of natural divination. *igitur*, added in the margin of Lambin's 1583 edition, can easily have dropped by saltation after *-tur.* For *explodo*, cf. on §§86–87a *init.; for somniorum divinatio*, on §42a (*extispicum divinatio*). **pariter cum ceteris** "together with the others."

148b Nam ut vere loquamur . . . inbecillitatem occupavit: Here begins the peroration, a homily against superstition. It is hard not to believe that "the voice of Marcus and the voice of Cicero coincide" in this passage (Santangelo 2013, 13); see above 26–30. **fusa per gentis:** Cicero began the proem by noting the wide diffusion of divination throughout the known world (1.1–2). Here that fact takes on a malign aspect; see also §81; *N.D.* 1.55, where Velleius connects divination with superstition. **oppressit omnium fere animos** "has overwhelmed almost everyone's thinking." Cf. *Ver.* 2.5.14: *quis dubitet quin servorum animos summa formidine oppresserit*; ibid. 139: *istius effrenatum animum . . . tanta oppressit amentia.* **hominum inbecillitatem occupavit** "it took advantage of human weakness." Cf. *Leg.* 1.29: *si opinionum vanitas non imbecillitatem animorum torqueret et flecteret.*

quod et in iis libris . . . si eam funditus sustulissemus: For criticism of superstition in *N.D.* from an Epicurean, a Skeptical, and a Stoic point of view, cf. 1.55 and 117, 2.63 and 70–71; for such crticism in our work, see above 29. **id maxume egimus** "this was what I worked at most of all": *OLD* s.v. *ago* 22a. **multum . . . profuturi videbamur:** Cicero already made it clear that he aimed to benefit his fellow citizens by this writing (§1: *quanam re possem prodesse quam plurimis*; §7: *ut . . . prodessemus civibus nostris*), but one might not have thought that he would directly benefit. He evidently includes himself among "almost all people" whose minds have been affected (just above); more specifically, he drew comfort from his dream of Marius on his way into exile (cf. 1.59 and §136b). Cf. *Tusc.* 5.2–4, where Cicero confesses that he was not actually so firmly convinced of the Stoic position as he previously gave out and that the healing he was dispensing was meant for himself as well. So the possibility that this work was meant, in part, to strengthen his own resolve should be kept in mind.

nec vero . . . cogit confiteri: Cotta complained that the Epicureans, in fact, eliminated religion along with superstition (*N.D.* 1.117). Marcus, like Cotta in *N.D.*, has avowed his respect for and commitment to the traditional religious rites that were closely bound up with the Roman state; cf. *N.D.* 3.5; §28; cf. also *Har.* 18–19; Goar 1972, 109–11. **sacris caerimoniisque:** A frequent combination (*Dom.* 33, 104, 109; *Har.* 8; *Mil.* 83; *Leg.* 2.20; *N.D.* 3.5; Livy 27.8; V. Max. 1.1.10, etc.), one suspects because the trochaic rhythm of the latter word lends weight. For *caerimonia*, used in pl. of "religious rites," see *OLD* s.v. 3; Roloff 1953. **esse praestantem aliquam . . . cogit confiteri:** For existential *esse*, cf. on §106 (*non igitur . . . significant futura*). *praestans natura* is a standing periphrasis for the deity in *N.D.*: 1.45, 47, 56, 96, 100, 116, 121, 2.46. Cicero thus arrives at a kind of synthesis of Epicurean and Stoic elements with an admixture of Roman patriotism: he acknowledges the *praestans natura* posited by both Epicureans and Stoics; he accepts, as the Stoics hold, that this is responsible for the design of the universe and is therefore worthy of admiration (cf. Cicero's [carefully hedged] verdict at *N.D.* 3.95); he rejects, however, Epicurean atomism and the Stoic defense of divination and holds that one should engage in worship for sociopolitical reasons (*rei publicae causa*), i.e., worship is decoupled from metaphysics.

149 quam ob rem . . . stirpes omnes eligendae: *religio . . . quae est iuncta cum cognitione naturae*, i.e., as he has just described, in contrast to *superstitio*, which cannot be reconciled with the laws of nature, as Marcus has repeatedly argued; cf. on §19 (*anile sane et plenum superstitionis*). Cf. Lehoux 2012, 39, emphasizing that "*religio* emerges from the learned and careful contemplation of nature, and it is from this knowledge that the *sapiens* gains his political and moral authority"; cf. *Leg.* 1.58–61. **eligendae** "must be extracted" or "uprooted" (*OLD* s.v. *eligo* 1), Gruter's generally accepted emendation for transmitted *eiciendae*; cf. *Tusc.* 3.83: *stirpes . . . aegritudinis . . . omnes eligendae sunt*; Oakley 1997–2005, 2:369–70 (on 7.39.6). For Toland's approving citation of this passage, see above 37n121.

instat enim et urget . . . quieta mente consistere: The initial placement of the verbs mirrors the aggressive actions; cf. on §79 (*fugit e proelio . . . et hospitem et regem*). Cf. the similar but shorter list at §83b *fin.* **quo te cumque verteris persequitur** "it is on your heels at every turn." For the interrogative as host of the unstressed pronoun, cf. §37 (*quis hoc physicus*); in this case, the result is the tmesis of *quocumque*. In the sequel, he enumerates the various areas where one can fall into superstitious thinking. **omen** here has the technical sense of an omen contained in a chance remark; cf. on §83b above. **si Chaldaeum, si haruspicem videris:** Apparently the mere sight of an astrologer or diviner might trigger a reflexive tendency to credit their activities; contrast the attitude of the Elder Cato (§51 *fin.*). **si tactum aliquid erit de caelo** "if something is struck by lightning": *OLD* s.v. *tango* 4c. **ostenti simile** "something like a portent," worded so as to avoid recognizing the supernatural; cf. on §26b (*ostentis*). **ut numquam liceat quieta mente consistere:** *consisto* is to "be at rest" (*OLD* s.v. 5a); cf. §83b with note.

150a perfugium videtur . . . et perfecti putantur: *perfugium*, a favorite word of Cicero's, appeared already in his first speech in a criminal case (*S.Rosc.* 150: *unum perfugium . . . una spes reliqua est Sex. Roscio*), but died out soon after him, being replaced by *refugium*. **at ex eo ipso** "but even from this," *ipse* identifying an extreme case (*OLD* s.v. 9a). **qui quidem ipsi per sese** "on their own, these . . ." (ibid. 2). **somniorum patrocinium** "the defense of dreams," i.e., as containing prophetic messages from the gods; cf. §119 *quorum* [sc. *somniorum*]. . . *defensio*. **nec ii quidem contemptissimi . . . perfecti putantur:** An explanation of why it was necessary to refute the Stoics at such length. Cf. *N.D.* 3.3–4, where Cotta shows much greater respect for the Stoic than the Epicurean position, as well as Cicero's judgment at 3.95 (cited on §89 [*non veri simile . . . verum esse censent*]); cf. also on §116 *fin.* **nec ii quidem:** This is the negative equivalent of *et is quidem*, a common way of adding an emphatic attribute: "—and they not utterly contemptible, but . . ."; cf. *OLD* s.v. *is* B7; on §8 (*et iis quidem*). **sed in primis acuti:** Cicero often calls Stoics, collectively or individually, "acute" (*acuti*), e.g., *Fin.* 4.67; cf. §116 *fin.* apropos of Chrysippus. **consequentia et repugnantia videntes:** For the Stoics as the dialecticians par excellence, cf. on §104 *init.* **qui prope iam absoluti et perfecti putantur:** Presumably because of their self-consistent theory, which Cicero elsewhere praises (*Fin.* 3.74, 4.53, 5.79 *fin.*); see further Inwood 2012.

quorum licentiae nisi Carneades . . . prudentissimeque defendere: Carneades turned their own dialectical weapons on the Stoics (cf. on §104 *init.*) and caused them to reformulate their positions. It was not the case, however, as Cicero's words might seem to imply, that the Skeptical Academy gained ground at the expense of the Stoics. *N.D.* 1.11 suggests, rather, that the former has by now been completely marginalized. In this passage, where he seeks to build up the Stoics, Cicero ignores the Epicureans, who were the Stoics' most formidable opponents (cf. on §81). **cum quibus omnis fere nobis . . . contentio . . . est:** Similarly *Fin.* 2.68: *omnis est enim de virtutis dignitate contentio.* **non quod . . . contemnamus, sed quod videntur . . . :** The first explanation is theoretical (and invalid) and therefore subj.; cf. G–L

§541.2. **acutissime . . . prudentissimeque:** The combination *prudenter et acute* or the like recurs at *Brut.* 108, *Tusc.* 4.48, *Amic.* 6; cf. also §12 *acutius . . . prudentius.*

150b Cum autem proprium . . . integrum ac liberum: A description of the general Academic procedure, paralleled in several prefaces: *Luc.* 7: *neque nostrae disputationes quicquam aliud agunt nisi ut in utramque partem dicendo et audiendo eliciant et tamquam exprimant aliquid quod aut verum sit aut ad id quam proxime accedat*; *Tusc.* 1.8: *haec est . . . vetus et Socratica ratio contra alterius opinionem disserendi. nam ita facillime quid veri simillimum esset invenire posse Socrates arbitrabatur.* The addition of this point here (rather than at the beginning of the work, as in the passages just quoted) "appears somewhat forced," as Fox 2007, 226, acknowledges, even though he wants to lend weight to this passage as a "quasi-sphragis," i.e., an author's seal of authenticity (ibid. 228). The point surely is to recognize the value of the debate per se and to allow the interlocutors to part on a note of agreement. **iudicium suum nullum interponere:** *nullum* is a more emphatic equivalent for *non*; cf. *N.D.* 1.10: *qui autem requirunt quid quaque de re ipsi sentiamus curiosius id faciunt quam necesse est; non enim tam auctoritatis in disputando quam rationis momenta quaerenda sunt* etc. **nulla adhibita sua auctoritate:** Cf. the strictures on the Pythagorean *ipse dixit* at *N.D.* 1.10 (following the words cited above).

tenebimus hanc consuetudinem . . . surreximus: *tenebimus hanc consuetudinem* "we shall abide by, hold to this custom"; cf., e.g., *Phil.* 1.27: *sin consuetudinem meam . . . tenuero.* **Quinte frater:** For the form of address, cf. on §8. This seems to point to a plan for further dialogues between these interlocutors, which was, however, no more to be realized than the plan for future dedications to his son at *Off.* 1.4: *sed cum statuissem scribere ad te* [sc. Marcus jr.] *aliquid hoc tempore, multa posthac . . .* Possibly the original plan was for *De fato* also to be conducted as a two-person dialogue between Quintus and Marcus; cf. 1.127; *Fat.* 1b; Weidemann 2019, 165. **quam saepissime utemur:** Cf. *Fam.* 9.8(254).2 (to Varro): *sed haec coram et saepius.* **'Mihi vero' . . . 'nihil potest esse iucundius':** Unlike Cato in *Fin.* (4.80) or Balbus in *N.D.* (3.94), Quintus does not offer to return later with arguments to meet the refutation. **surreximus:** Some such action typically ends the dialogues, e.g., *Luc.* 148: *nos ad naviculas nostras descendimus*; *Fin.* 5.96: *in oppidum ad Pomponium perreximus omnes*; *N.D.* 3.95: *discessimus.*

Editions Cited

Editio princeps. 1471. Rome.
Ascensius, I. B. 1521. 2nd ed. Paris.
Lambin, D. 1565, 1573, 1581. Paris.
Wilhelm, J., and J. Gruter. 1618-19. Hamburg.
Davies, J. 1730. 2nd ed. Cambridge.
Hottinger, J. J. 1793. Leipzig.
Christ, W. 1862 (in ed. of Orelli-Baiter-Halm, 1845–62). Zurich.
Baiter, J. G., and C. L. Kayser. 1863. Leipzig.
Thoresen, V. 1894. Copenhagen.
Mueller, C. F. W. 1910. Leipzig.
Pease, A. S. 1920–23. Urbana.
Falconer, W. H. 1923. London.
Ax, W. 1938. Leipzig.
Timpanaro, S. 1988. Milan.
Schäublin, C. 1991. Munich.
Kany-Turpin, J. 2004. Paris.
Schultz, C. E. 2014. Ann Arbor (Book 1 only).
Older conjectures, atheteses, and the like are cited from Ax's edition.

Bibliography

Abry, J.-H. 1996. "L'horoscope de Rome (Cicéron, *Div.*, II, 98–99)." In *Les Astres: Actes du colloque international de Montpellier 23–25 Mars 1995*, 2:121–40. Montpellier.

Adam, J., ed., comm. 1963. *The Republic of Plato*. 2 vols. Cambridge.

Adams, J. N. 1982. *The Latin Sexual Vocabulary*. London.

Adams, J. N. 1994a. *Wackernagel's Law and the Placement of the Copula 'esse' in Classical Latin*. Cambridge.

Adams, J. N. 1994b. "Wackernagel's Law and the Position of Unstressed Personal Pronouns in Classical Latin." *Transactions of the Philological Society* 92.2: 103–78.

Adams, J. N. 2013. *Social Variations and the Latin Language*. Cambridge.

Adams, J. N. 2016. *An Anthology of Informal Latin, 200 BC–AD 900: Fifty Texts with Translations and Linguistic Commentary*. Cambridge.

Albrecht, M. von. 1989. *Masters of Roman Prose from Cato to Apuleius*. Tr. N. Adkin. Leeds.

Albrecht, M. von. 2003. *Cicero's Style: A Synopsis Followed by Selected Analytic Studies*. Leiden.

Alesse, F. 1994. *Panezio di Rodi e la tradizione stoica*. Naples.

Allély, A. 2003. "Les enfants malformés et considérés comme *prodigia* à Rome et en Italie sous la République." *Revue des Études Anciennes* 105: 127–56.

Allen, J. 2001. *Inference from Signs: Ancient Debates about the Nature of Evidence*. Oxford.

Allen, J. 2014. "Why Are There Ends Both of Goods and Evils in Ancient Ethical Theory?" In Lee, 231–54.

Allen, W. S. 1987. *Vox Graeca: A Guide to the Pronunciation of Classical Greek*. 3rd ed. Cambridge.

Altman, W. H. F. 2008. "How to Interpret Cicero's Dialogue on Divination." *Interpretation* 35: 105–21.

Altman, W. H. F. 2016. *The Revival of Platonism in Cicero's Late Philosophy:* Platonis aemulus *and the Invention of Cicero*. Lanham, MD.

André, J. 1951. "Les adjectifs et adverbes à valeur intensive en *per-* et *prae-*." *Revue des Études Latines* 29: 121–54.

Arata, F. P. 2010. "Osservazioni sulla topografia sacra dell'*arx* Capitolina." *Mélanges de l'École française de Rome, Antiquité* 122: 117–46.

Arnold, M. 1905. *On Translating Homer*. New ed. by W. H. D. Rouse. London.

Arweiler, A. 2003. *Cicero Rhetor: Die* Partitiones oratoriae *und das Konzept des gelehrten Politikers*. Berlin.

Baccani, D. 1992. *Oroscopi greci: Documentazione papirologica*. Messina.

Bader, F. 1962. *La formation des composés nominaux du latin*. Paris.

Badian, E. 1958. *Foreign Clientelae (264–70 B.C.)*. Oxford (corr. repr. 1984).

Bakker, F. A. 2016. *Epicurean Meteorology: Sources, Method, Scope and Organization*. Leiden.

Balsdon, J. P. V. D. 1958. "The Ides of March." *Historia* 7: 80–94.

Baraz, Y. 2012. *A Written Republic: Cicero's Philosophical Politics*. Princeton.

Beard, M. 1986. "Cicero and Divination: The Formation of a Latin Discourse." *Journal of Roman Studies* 76: 33–46.

Beard, M. 2007. *The Roman Triumph*. Cambridge, MA.

Beard, M. 2012. "Cicero's 'Response of the *haruspices*' and the Voice of the Gods." *Journal of Roman Studies* 102: 20–39.

Beard, M., J. North, and S. Price. 1998. *Religions of Rome*. 2 vols. Cambridge.

Beck, H. 2005. *Karriere und Hierarchie: Die römische Aristokratie und die Anfänge des cursus honorum in der mittleren Republik*. Berlin.

Begemann, E. 2012. *Schicksal als Argument: Ciceros Rede vom* fatum *in der späten Republik*. Stuttgart.

Begemann, E. 2015. "Damaged Go(o)ds: Cicero's Theological Triad in the Wake of German Historicism." In W. H. F. Altman, ed., *Brill's Companion to the Reception of Cicero*, 247–80. Leiden.

Bénatouïl, T. 2009. "How Industrious Can Zeus Be? The Extent and Objects of Divine Activity in Stoicism." In R. Salles, ed., *God and Cosmos in Stoicism*, 23–45. Oxford.

Bénatouïl, T., ed. 2019. *Dialectic after Plato and Aristotle*. Cambridge.

Berry, D. H. 1996. "The Value of Prose Rhythm in Questions of Authenticity: The Case of *De optimo genere oratorum* Attributed to Cicero." *Papers of the Leeds International Latin Seminar* 9: 47–74.

Berry, D. H. 2012. "Cicero and Greek Art." *Papers of the Langford Latin Seminar* 15: 223–41.

Berthelet, Y. 2015. *Gouverner avec les dieux: Autorité, auspices et pouvoir, sous la République romaine et sous Auguste*. Paris.

Bett, R. 1989. "Carneades' *pithanon*: A Reappraisal of Its Role and Status." *Oxford Studies in Ancient Philosophy* 7: 59-94

Bett, R. 1990. "Carneades' Distinction between Assent and Approval." *The Monist* 73: 3–20.

Bishop, C. 2019. *Cicero, Greek Learning and the Making of a Roman Classic*. Oxford.

Bivar, A. D. H. 1983. "The Political History of Iran under the Arsacids." In E. Yarshater, ed., *The Cambridge History of Iran*, 3.1: 21–99. Cambridge.

Blank, D. L., tr., comm. 1998. Sextus Empiricus. *Against the Grammarians (Adversus Mathematicos I)*. Oxford.

Blänsdorf, J. 1991. "Augurenlächeln: Ciceros Kritik an der römischen Mantik." In H. Wissmann, ed., *Zur Erschliessung von Zukunft in den Religionen: Zukunftshoffnung und Gegenwartsbewältigung in der Religionsgeschichte*, 45–65. Würzburg.

Blecher, G. 1905. *De extispicio capita tria*. Giessen.

Bleckmann, B. 2002. *Die römische Nobilität im Ersten Punischen Krieg: Untersuchungen zur aristokratischen Konkurrenz in der Republik*. Berlin.

Bleicken, J. 2015. *Augustus: The Biography*. Tr. A. Bell. London.

Bobzien, S. 1998. *Determinism and Freedom in Stoic Philosophy*. Oxford.

Boes, J. 1981. "À propos du *De divinatione*, ironie de Cicéron sur le *nomen* et l'*omen* de Brutus." *Revue des Études Latines* 59: 164–76.

Bolingbroke, H. St. J., viscount. 1754. *Philosophical Works*. 5 vols. London.

Bonitz, H. 1870. *Index Aristotelicus*. Berlin (repr. Graz, 1955).

Bornecque, H. 1907. *Les clausules métriques latines*. Lille.

Bouché-Leclercq, A. 1899. *L'astrologie grecque*. Paris.

Braun, M. 2003. "Stabilisierung und Destabilisierung sozialer Werte in Ciceros Reden." In Haltenhoff, Heil, and Mutschler, 71–91.

Brendel, O. J. 1960. "Two Fortunae, Antium and Praeneste." *American Journal of Archaeology* 64: 41–47.

Brind'Amour, P. 1983. *Le Calendrier romain: Recherches chronologiques*. Ottawa.

Bringmann, K. 1986. "Der Diktator Caesar als Richter? Zu Ciceros Reden 'Pro Ligario' und 'Pro Rege Deiotaro.'" *Hermes* 141: 72–88.

Briquel, D. 1986. "Art augural et *Etrusca disciplina*: Le débat sur l'origine de l'augurat romain." In *La divination dans le monde étrusco-italique*. Caesarodunum. Supplement 56, 68–100. Tours.

Briquel, D. 1991. *L'origine Lydienne des Étrusques: Histoire de la doctrine dans l'Antiquité*. Rome.

Briquel, D. 1993. "Les voix oraculaires." In *Les bois sacrés: Actes du colloque international organisé par le Centre Jean Bérard et l'École Pratique des Hautes Études (Ve Section), Naples, 23-25 novembre 1989*, 77–90. Naples.

Briquel, D. 2014. "*Etrusca disciplina* and Roman Religion: From Initial Hesitation to a Privileged Place." In D. Engels and P. van Nuffelen, eds., *Religion and Competition in Antiquity*, 112–32. Brussels.

Brisson, L. 2002. *Sexual Ambivalence: Androgeny and Hermaphroditism in Graeco-Roman Antiquity*. Tr. J. Lloyd. Berkeley.

Brittain, C. 2001. *Philo of Larissa: The Last of the Academic Sceptics*. Oxford.

Brittain, C., ed., tr., comm. 2006. *Cicero: On Academic Scepticism*. Indianapolis.

Brittain, C. 2011. "Posidonius' Theory of Predictive Dreams." *Oxford Studies in Ancient Philosophy* 40: 213–36.

Brittain, C. 2016. "Cicero's Sceptical Methods: The Example of *De finibus*." In J. Annas and G. Betegh, eds., *Cicero's* De finibus: *Philosophical Approaches*, 12–40. Cambridge.

Buchholz, L. 2013. "Identifying the Oracular *sortes* of Italy." In M. Kajava, ed., *Studies in Ancient Oracles and Divination*, 111–44. Rome.

Burckhardt, L. A. 1988. *Politische Strategien der Optimaten in der späten römischen Republik*. Stuttgart.

Burkert, W. 1985. *Greek Religion, Archaic and Classical.* Tr. J. Raffan. Oxford.

Burnyeat, M. 1982. "Gods and Heaps." In M. Schofield and M. C. Nussbaum, eds., *Language and Logos: Studies in Ancient Philosophy Presented to G. E. L. Owen*, 315–38. Cambridge.

Butler, S. 2002. *The Hand of Cicero.* London.

Capdeville, G. 1989. "Les dieux fulgurants dans la doctrine étrusque." In *Atti [del] Secondo Congresso Internazionale Etrusco* 3: 1171–90. Rome.

Capdeville, G. 1994. "Le vocabulaire technique dans les traités d'*Etrusca disciplina* en langue latine." *Revue de Philologie, de Littérature et d'Histoire Anciennes* 68: 51–75.

Cappello, O. 2016. "Everything You Wanted to Know about Atticus (But Were Afraid to Ask Cicero): Looking for Atticus in Cicero's *ad Atticum*." *Arethusa* 49: 463–87.

Cappello, O. 2019. T*he School of Doubt: Skepticism, History and Politics in Cicero's Academica*. Leiden.

Carlà-Uhink, F. 2017. "*Alteram loci patriam, alteram iuris*: 'Double Fatherlands' and the Role of Italy in Cicero's Political Discourse." In L. Cecchet and A. Busetto, eds., *Citizens in the Graeco-Roman World: Aspects of Citizenship from the Archaic Period to AD 212*, 259–82. Leiden.

Carney, T. F. 1961. *A Biography of C. Marius*. Assen, Netherlands.

Carruba, A. M., and L. De Masi. 2006. *La Lupa Capitolina: Un bronzo medievale.* Rome.

Castner, C. J. 1988. *Prosopography of Roman Epicureans from the Second Century B.C. to the Second Century A.D.* Frankfurt am Main.

Cawkwell, G. 1978. *Philip of Macedon*. London.

Champeaux, J. 1982–87. *Fortuna: Recherches sur le culte de la Fortune à Rome et dans le monde romain des origines à la mort de César.* 2 vols. Rome.

Champeaux, J. 1990. "Sors oraculi: Les oracles en Italie sous la République et l'Empire." *Mélanges de l'École française de Rome, Antiquité* 102: 271–302.

Champion, C. B. 2017. *The Peace of the Gods: Elite Religious Practices in the Middle Roman Republic.* Princeton.

Chiarini, S. 2019. "Οὐδὲν λέγειν/*nihil dicere*: A Lexical and Semantic Survey." *Mnemosyne* 72: 114–49.

Chinnici, V. 2000. *Cicerone interprete di Omero*. Naples.

Ciafardone, G. 2017. "Cicerone e l'esistenza divina: Qualche appunto su *de divinatione* 2.41." *Prometheus* 43: 97–111.

Cimma, M. R. 1976. *Reges socii et amici populi Romani.* Milan.

Citroni, M. 2003. "I proemi delle Tusculanae e la costruzione di un'immagine della tradizione letteraria romana." In M. Citroni, ed., *Memoria e identità: La cultura romana costruisce la sua immagine*, 149–84. Florence.

Clark, A. C. 1918. *The Descent of Manuscripts.* Oxford.

Coarelli, F. 1991. "Gli emissari dei laghi laziali: Tra mito e storia." In M. Bergamini, ed., *Gli Etruschi maestri di idraulica*, 35–41. Perugia.

Coleman, R. G. G. 1999. "Poetic Diction, Poetic Discourse and the Poetic Register." In J. N. Adams and R. G. Mayer, eds., *Aspects of the Language of Latin Poetry*. Proceedings of the British Academy 93, 21–93. Oxford.

Collins, A. 1713. *A Discourse of Free-Thinking*. London.

Combès, R. 1966. *Imperator: Recherches sur l'emploi et la signification du titre d'imperator dans la Rome républicaine.* Paris.

Corbeill, A. 2012. "Cicero and the Etruscan *haruspices*." *Papers of the Langford Latin Seminar* 15: 243–66.

Courtney, E., ed., comm. 2003. *The Fragmentary Latin Poets*. Paperback ed. with addenda. Oxford (orig. 1993).

Craig, C. P. 1993. *Form as Argument in Cicero's Speeches: A Study of Dilemma.* Atlanta.

Cristofani, M. 1985. "Il cosidetto specchio di Tarchon: Un recupero e una nuova lettura." *Prospettiva* 41: 4–20.

Cusset, C., ed. 2003. *La Météorologie dans l'Antiquité entre science et croyance.* Saint-Étienne.

Darab, A. 1995. "Cicero bei Plinius dem Älteren." *Acta Classica Universitatis Debreceniensis* 31: 33–41.

Davies, J. K. 1998. "Finance, Administration and *Realpolitik*: The Case of Fourth-Century Delphi." *Bulletin of the Institute of Classical Studies.* Supplement 71, *Modus Operandi: Essays in Honour of Geoffrey Rickman*, 1–14. London.

De Boer, J. Z., J. R. Hale, and J. Chanton. 2001. "New Evidence for the Geological Origins of the Ancient Delphic Oracle." *Geology* 29: 707–10.

Dench, E. 2005. *Romulus' Asylum: Roman Identities from the Age of Alexander to the Age of Hadrian*. Oxford.

Denyer, N. 1985. "The Case against Divination: An Examination of Cicero's *De divinatione*." *Proceedings of the Cambridge Philological Society* 31: 1–10.

Devine, A. M., and L. D. Stephens. 2006. *Latin Word Order: Structured Meaning and Information*. Oxford.

Dickey, E. 1997. "*Me autem nomine appellabat*—Avoidance of Cicero's Name in His Dialogues." *Classical Quarterly* 47: 584–88.

Dickey, E. 2002. *Latin Forms of Address from Plautus to Apuleius*. Oxford.

Dickey, E. 2015. "How to Say 'Please' in Post-Classical Latin: Fronto and the Importance of Archaism." *Journal of Latin Linguistics* 14: 17–31.

Diderot, D. 1875. *Oeuvres complètes*. Ed. J. Assézat. Vol. 1. Paris (repr. Nendeln, Liechtenstein, 1966).

Diels, H. 1890. *Sibyllinische Blätter.* Berlin.

Dieu, E. 2009. "Les formes de gradation vieil-anglaises *sēlra* 'meilleur,' *sēlest* 'le meilleur' et le superlatif latin *sōlistimus / sollistimus* 'très favorable.'" *Historische Sprachforschung* 122: 31–38.

Dodds, E. R. 1951. *The Greeks and the Irrational.* Berkeley.

Dorandi, T. 1994. "Cratippos de Pergame." In R. Goulet, ed., *Dictionnaire des philosophes antiques,* 2:501–3. Paris.

Driediger-Murphy, L. G. 2018. "Falsifying the Auspices in Republican Politics." In H. van der Blom, C. Gray, and C. Steel, eds., *Institutions and Ideology in Republican Rome: Speech, Audience and Decision,* 183–202. Cambridge.

Driediger-Murphy, L. G. 2019. *Roman Republican Augury: Freedom and Control.* Oxford.

Drogula, F. K. 2019. *Cato the Younger: Life and Death at the End of the Roman Republic.* New York.

Dubourdieu, A. 2003. "Divinités de la parole, divinités du silence dans la Rome antique." *Revue de l'histoire des religions* 220: 259–82.

Dugan, J. 2012. "*Scriptum* and *voluntas* in Cicero's *Brutus.*" In M. Citroni, ed., *Letteratura e civitas: Transizioni della Repubblica all' Impero; In ricordo di Emanuele Narducci,* 117–28. Pisa.

Dumézil, G. 1966. *La Religion romaine archaïque.* Paris.

Dumézil, G. 1970. *Archaic Roman Religion.* Vol. 1. Tr. P. Krapp. Chicago.

Dunsch, B., and K. Ruffing, eds. 2013. *Herodots Quellen—Die Quellen Herodots.* Wiesbaden.

Durand, R. 1903. "La date du 'De divinatione.'" In *Mélanges Boissier,* 173–83. Paris.

Düring, I. 1961. *Aristotle's* Protrepticus*: An Attempt at Reconstruction.* Gothenburg.

Düring, I. 1966. *Aristoteles: Darstellung und Interpretation seines Denkens.* Heidelberg.

Dyck, A. R. 1996. *A Commentary on Cicero,* De officiis. Ann Arbor.

Dyck, A. R., ed., comm. 2003. Cicero, *De natura deorum, Book 1.* Cambridge.

Dyck, A. R. 2004a. "Cicero's *devotio*: The Roles of *dux* and Scapegoat in His *post reditum* Rhetoric." *Harvard Studies in Classical Philology* 102: 299–314.

Dyck, A. R. 2004b. *A Commentary on Cicero,* De legibus. Ann Arbor.

Dyck, A. R., ed., comm. 2008. Cicero, *Catilinarians.* Cambridge.

Dyck, A. R., ed., comm. 2010. Cicero, *Pro Sexto Roscio.* Cambridge.

Dyck, A. R., tr., comm. 2012. M. Tullius Cicero, *Speeches on Behalf of Marcus Fonteius and Marcus Aemilius Scaurus.* Oxford.

Dyck, A. R. Forthcoming. *Cicero: The Man and His Works.*

Earl, D. C. 1961. *The Political Thought of Sallust.* Cambridge.

Edelstein, E. J., and L. Edelstein. 1945. *Asclepius: A Collection and Interpretation of the Testimonies.* 2 vols. Baltimore.

Edwards, C. 2018. "On Not Being in Rome: Exile and Displacement in Seneca's Prose." In W. Fitzgerald and E. Spentzou, eds., *The Production of Space in Latin Literature*, 169–94. Oxford.

Ehrenheim, H. von. 2015. *Greek Incubation Rituals in Classical and Hellenistic Times*. Liège.

Eisenhut, W. 1973. *Virtus Romana: Ihre Stellung im römischen Wertsystem*. Munich.

Elder, J. P., W. C. Greene, R. M. Gummere, D. T. W. McCord, and M. Hammond. 1965. "Faculty Minute on Arthur Stanley Pease, 1881–1964." *Harvard Studies in Classical Philology* 69: ix–xi.

Engels, D. 2007. *Das römische Vorzeichenwesen (753–27 v. Chr.): Quellen, Terminologie, Kommentar, historische Entwicklung*. Stuttgart.

Essler, H. 2011. *Glückselig und unsterblich: Epikureische Theologie bei Cicero und Philodem*. Basel.

Evans, J. 1998. *The History and Practice of Ancient Astronomy*. New York.

Eyben, E. 1993. *Restless Youth in Ancient Rome*. Tr. P. Daly. London.

Falconer, W. A., ed., tr. 1923a. Cicero, *De senectute, De amicitia, De divinatione*. London.

Falconer, W. A. 1923b. "A Review of M. Durand's 'La date du *De divinatione*.'" *Classical Philology* 18: 310–27.

Fantham, E. 2002. "Orator and/*et* actor." In P. Easterling and E. Hall, eds., *Greek and Roman Actors: Aspects of an Ancient Profession*, 362–76. Cambridge.

Fantham, E., ed., tr. 2017. Francesco Petrarca, *Selected Letters*. 2 vols. Cambridge, MA.

Fasolo, F., and G. Gullini. 1953. *Il santuario della Fortuna primigenia a Palestrina*. Rome.

Fehrle, R. 1983. *Cato Uticensis*. Darmstadt.

Feig Vishnia, R. 2012. *Roman Elections in the Age of Cicero: Society, Government, and Voting*. New York.

Février, C. 2002. "De l'usage des Livres: Le décemvir, prêtre ou *uates*?" *Latomus* 61: 821–41.

Fezzi, L. 2008. *Il tribuno Clodio*. Rome.

Flower, H. 2010. *Roman Republics*. Princeton.

Flower, H. 2017. *The Dancing Lares and the Serpent in the Garden: Religion at the Roman Street Corner*. Princeton.

Flower, M. A. 2008. *The Seer in Ancient Greece*. Berkeley.

Fortenbaugh, W. W., and P. Steinmetz, eds. 1989. *Cicero's Knowledge of the Peripatos*. New Brunswick, NJ.

Foster, J., and D. Lehoux. 2007. "The Delphic Oracle and the Ethylene-Intoxication Hypothesis." *Clinical Toxicology* 45.1: 85–89.

Foti, G. 2011. "Funzioni e caratteri del 'pullarius' in età repubblicana e imperiale." *Acme* 64: 89–121.

Fox, M. 2007. *Cicero's Philosophy of History*. Oxford.

Frank, H. 1992. Ratio *bei Cicero*. Frankfurt am Main.

Frede, M. 1983. "Stoics and Skeptics on Clear and Distinct Impressions." In M. Burnyeat, ed., *The Skeptical Tradition*, 64–93. Berkeley.

Freud, S. 1955. *The Interpretation of Dreams*. Tr. J. Strachey. New York.

Freund, S. 2013. "Verres als Frauenschänder: Tyrannentopik und Voyeurismus in Ciceros Rhetorik." *Gymnasium* 120: 413–37.

Freyburger, G., and J. Scheid, tr., comm. 1992. *Cicéron: De la divination*. Pref. by A. Maalouf. Paris.

Frier, B. 1985. *The Rise of the Roman Jurists*. Princeton.

Fuhrmann, M. 2000. "Cicero im 19. Jahrhundert." In M. C. Ferrari, ed., *Gegen Unwissenheit und Finsternis: Johann Caspar von Orelli (1787–1849) und die Kultur seiner Zeit*, 101–17. Zurich.

Furley, D. 1987. *The Greek Cosmologists*. Vol. 1, *The Formation of the Atomic Theory and Its Earliest Critics*. Cambridge.

Garbarino, I., ed. 2003. *Philosophorum Romanorum fragmenta usque ad L. Annaei Senecae aetatem*. Bologna.

Garcea, A. 2005. *Cicerone in esilio: L'epistolario e le passioni*. Hildesheim.

García Hernández, B. 1992. "*Summanus*. II. Su identidad divina." *Emerita* 60: 205–15.

Garofalo, P. 2019. "Sulla, i Caecilii Metelli e Lanuvium." *Hermes* 147: 42–52.

Gärtner, H. A. 2003. "Ciceros *De officiis* und die römischen Institutionen." In Haltenhoff, Heil, and Mutschler, 245–58.

Gatti Lo Guzzo, L. 1978. *Il deposito votivo dell' Esquilino detto di Minerva Medica*. Florence.

Gawlick, G. 1963. "Cicero and the Enlightenment." *Studies in Voltaire and the Eighteenth Century* 25: 657–82.

Gelzer, M. 1968. *Caesar: Politician and Statesman*. Tr. P. Needham. Cambridge, MA.

Gelzer, M. 1969. *Cicero: Ein biographischer Versuch*. Wiesbaden.

Ghirotto, S., F. Tassi, E. Fumagalli, V. Colonna, A. Sandionigi, M. Lari, S. Vai, E. Petiti, G. Corti, E. Rizzi, G. De Bellis, D. Caramelli, and G. Barbujani. 2013. "Origins and Evolution of the Etruscans' mtDNA." *PLOS One* 8.2: 1–11.

Gildenhard, I. 2006. "Reckoning with Tyranny: Greek Thoughts on Caesar in Cicero's *Letters to Atticus* in Early 49." In S. Lewis, ed., *Ancient Tyranny*, 197–209. Edinburgh.

Gildenhard, I. 2007. *Paideia Romana: Cicero's* Tusculan Disputations. Cambridge.

Glucker, J. 2012. "Cicero's Remarks on Translating Philosophical Terms: Some General Problems." In J. Glucker and C. Burnett, eds., *Greek into Latin from Antiquity until the Nineteenth Century*. Warburg Institute Colloquia 18, 37–96. London.

Goar, R. J. 1972. *Cicero and the State Religion*. Amsterdam.

Goldberg, S. M. 1995. *Epic in Republican Rome*. New York.

Goldberg, S. M. 1996. "The Fall and Rise of Roman Tragedy." *Transactions of the American Philological Association* 126: 265–86.

Gordon, R. 2008. "*Superstitio*, Superstition and Religious Repression in the Late Roman Republic and Principate (100 BCE–300 CE)." In S. A. Smith and A. Knight, eds., *The Religion of Fools? Superstition Past and Present. Past and Present.* Supplement 3, 72–94. Oxford.

Görler, W. 1974. *Untersuchungen zu Ciceros Philosophie*. Heidelberg.

Görler, W. 1989. "Cicero und die 'Schule des Aristoteles.'" In Fortenbaugh and Steinmetz, 246–63.

Görler, W. 1997. "Cicero's Philosophical Stance in the *Lucullus*." In Inwood and Mansfeld, 36–57.

Görler, W. 2017. "Roman Philosophy? A Ciceronian Ambition." In Y. Z. Liebersohn, I. Ludlam, and A. Edelheit, eds., *For a Skeptical Peripatetic: Festschrift in Honour of John Glucker*, 220–32. Sankt Augustin.

Gottschalk, H. B. 1987. "Aristotelian Philosophy in the Roman World." *Aufstieg und Niedergang der römischen Welt*. II 36.2, 1079–1174.

Gourinat, J.-B. 2005. "Prediction of the Future and Co-fatedness: Two Aspects of Stoic Determinism." In C. Natali and S. Maso, eds., *La catena delle cause. Determinismo e antideterminismo nel pensiero antico e in quello contemporaneo*, 215–40. Amsterdam.

Grafton, A. T., and N. M. Swerdlow. 1986. "The Horoscope of the Foundation of Rome." *Classical Philology* 81: 148–53.

Green, S. J. 2014. *Disclosure and Discretion in Roman Astrology: Manilius and His Augustan Contemporaries*. Oxford.

Greene, W. C. 1944. *Moira: Fate, Good, and Evil in Greek Thought*. Cambridge, MA.

Grice, H. P. 1957. "Meaning." *Philosophical Review* 66: 377–88.

Griffin, M. T. 1995. "Philosophical Badinage in Cicero's Letters to His Friends." In Powell 1995b, 325–46.

Griffin, M. T. 1997. "The Composition of the *Academica*: Motives and Versions." In Inwood and Mansfeld, 1–35.

Grodzynski, D. 1974. "Superstitio." *Revue des Études Anciennes* 76: 36–60.

Grottanelli, C. 1993. "Bambini e divinazione." In O. Niccoli, ed., *Infanzie: Funzioni di un gruppo liminale dal mondo classico all'età moderna*, 23–72. Florence.

Grottanelli, C. 2005. "*Sorte unica pro casibus pluribus enotata*: Literary Texts and Lot Inscriptions as Sources for Ancient Kleromancy." In S. I. Johnston and P. T. Struck, eds., *Mantikê: Studies in Ancient Divination*, 129–46. Leiden.

Guillaumont, F. 1984. *Philosophe et augur: Recherches sur la théorie cicéronienne de la divination*. Brussels.

Guillaumont, F. 1986. "Cicéron et les techniques de l'haruspicine." In D. Briquel and C. Guittard, eds., *La divination dans le monde étrusco-italique*. Vol. 2, 121–35. Tours.

Guillaumont, F. 1996. "La nature et les prodiges dans la religion et la philosophie romaines." In C. Lévy, ed., *Le Concept de nature à Rome*, 43–64. Paris.

Guillaumont, F. 2006. *Le* De diuinatione *de Cicéron et les théories antiques de la divination*. Brussels.

Guittard, C. 2003. "Les calendriers brontoscopiques dans le monde étrusco-romain." In Cusset, 455–66.

Haack, M-L. 2003. *Les haruspices dans le monde romain*. Bordeaux.

Hadas-Lebel, J. 2012. "Enquête sur le nom latin des Grecs et de la Grèce." *Revue de Philologie, de Littérature et d'Histoire Anciennes* 86: 53–75.

Hagendahl, H. 1967. *Augustine and the Latin Classics*. Studia Graeca et Latina Gothoburgensia 20, vols. 1–2. Gothenburg.

Hahm, D. E. 1977. *The Origins of Stoic Cosmology*. Columbus.

Haltenhoff, A., A. Heil, and F.-H. Mutschler, eds. 2003. *O tempora, o mores! Römische Werte und römische Literatur in den letzten Jahrzehnten der Republik*. Munich.

Hankinson, R. J. 1988. "Stoicism, Science and Divination." *Apeiron* 21.2: 123–60.

Hanson, J. A. 1959. *Roman Theater-Temples*. Princeton.

Hanssen, J. S. T. 1952. *Latin Diminutives: A Semantic Study*. Bergen.

Harris, W. V. 1971. *Rome in Etruria and Umbria*. Oxford.

Harris, W. V. 2009. *Dreams and Experience in Classical Antiquity*. Cambridge, MA.

Hartfelder, K. 1878. *Die Quellen der zwei Bücher von Ciceros De divinatione*. Progr. Freiburg i.B.

Häuber, C. 2014. *The Eastern Part of the* Mons Oppius *in Rome: The Sanctuary of* Isis et Serapis *in* Regio III, *the Temples of* Minerva Medica, Fortuna Virgo *and* Dea Syria, *and the* Horti *of Maecenas*. Rome.

Haury, A. 1995. *L'Ironie et l'humour chez Cicéron*. Leiden.

Heilen, S. 2007. "Ancient Scholars on the Horoscope of Rome." *Culture and Cosmos* 11: 43–68.

Herescu, N. 1961. "Les trois exils de Cicéron." *Atti del I Congresso Internazionale di Studi Ciceroniani* 1:137–56. Rome.

Hobbes, T. 2012. *Leviathan*. Ed. N. Malcolm. 3 vols. Oxford.

Hofmann, J. B. 2003. *La lingua d'uso latina*. 3rd ed. Ed. L. Ricotilli. Bologna.

Hohti, P. 1975. "Aulus Caecina the Volaterran: Romanization of an Etruscan." In *Studies in the Romanization of Etruria*. Acta Instituti Romani Finlandiae 5, 405–33. Rome.

Homeyer, H. 1964. *Die antiken Berichte über den Tod Ciceros und die Quellen*. Baden-Baden.

Hopkins, K. 1983. *Death and Renewal: Sociological Studies in Roman History*. Vol. 2. Cambridge.

Houston, G. W. 2014. *Inside Roman Libraries*. Chapel Hill.

Hoyer, R. 1898. "Quellenstudien zu Ciceros Büchern de natura deorum, de divinatione, de fato." *Rheinisches Museum* 53: 37–95.

Humpert, C. 2001. *Wege zur Männlichkeit im Rom der Späten Republik: Cicero und die* adulescentes. Halle.

Inwood, B. 1990. "*Rhetorica disputatio*: The Strategy of *de Finibus II*." *Apeiron* 23: 143–64.

Inwood, B. 2012. "How Unified Is Stoicism Anyway?" In R. Kamtekar, ed., *Virtue and Happiness: Essays in Honour of Julia Annas*. Oxford Studies in Ancient Philosophy. Supplementary volume, 223–44. Oxford.

Inwood, B., and J. Mansfeld, eds. 1997. *Studies in Cicero's* Academic Books. Leiden.

Ioppolo, A. M. 2002. "L'astrologia nel *De fato* di Cicerone." In A. Pérez Jiménez and R. Caballero, eds., *Homo mathematicus: Actas del Congreso Internacional sobre Astrólogos Griegos y Romanos, Benalmádena, 2001*, 224–48. Málaga.

Jacobs, J. 2010. "Traces of the Omen Series *šumma izbu* in Cicero, *De divinatione*." In A. Annus, ed., *Divination and Interpretation of Signs in the Ancient World*, 317–39. Chicago.

Jehne, M. 2000. "Wirkungsweise und Bedeutung der centuria praerogativa." *Chiron* 30: 661–78.

Jocelyn, H. D., ed. comm. 1967. *The Tragedies of Ennius: The Fragments*. Cambridge.

Jocelyn, H. D. 1973. "Greek Poetry in Cicero's Prose Writing." *Yale Classical Studies* 23: 61–112.

Joffre, M.-D. 2010. "Cohérence textuelle et deixis: Le jeu *hic / ille* dans la prose latine." In P. Anreiter and M. Kienpointner, eds., *Latin Linguistics Today: Akten des 15. Internationalen Kolloquiums zur Lateinischen Linguistik, Innsbruck, 4.-9. April 2009*, 561–74. Innsbruck.

Johnston, S. I. 2001. "Charming Children: The Use of the Child in Ancient Divination." *Arethusa* 34: 97–118.

Johnston, S. I. 2008. *Ancient Greek Divination*. Malden, MA.

Jordan, B. 2017. "The Consular *provinciae* of 44 BCE and the Collapse of the Restored Republic." *Hermes* 145: 174–94.

Judson, S., and A. Kahane. 1963. "Underground Drainageways in Southern Etruria and Northern Latium." *Papers of the British School at Rome* 31: 74–99.

Kähler, H. 1958. Review of Fasolo and Gullini 1953. *Gnomon* 30: 366–83.

Kany-Turpin, J. 2003. "Météorologie et signes divinatoires dans le *De divinatione* de Cicéron." In Cusset, 367–78.

Kany-Turpin, J., ed., tr., comm. 2004. *Cicéron, De la divination. De divinatione*. Paris.

Kany-Turpin, J., and P. Pellegrin. 1989. "Cicero and the Aristotelian Theory of Divination by Dreams." In Fortenbaugh and Steinmetz, 220–45.

Kaster, R. A. 2005. *Emotion, Restraint, and Community in Ancient Rome*. Oxford.

Keaveney, A. 1983. "Sulla and the Gods." *Studies in Latin Literature and Roman History* 3: 44–79.

Keaveney, A. 2005. *Sulla: The Last Republican*. 2nd ed. London.

Kidd, I. G. 1988. *Posidonius II: The Commentary*. 2 vols. Cambridge.
Kinsey, T. E. 1969. "Cicero and *perspicuus*." In J. Bibauw and M. Renard, eds., *Hommages à Marcel Renard*, 501–5. Brussels.
Klingshirn, W. E. 2006. "Inventing the *sortilegus*: Lot-Divination and Cultural Identity in Italy, Rome, and the Provinces." In C. E. Schultz and P. B. Harvey, eds., *Religion in Republican Italy = Yale Classical Studies* 33: 137–61.
Koch, C. 1937. *Der römische Juppiter*. Frankfurt am Main (repr. Darmstadt, 1968).
Konrad, C. F. 2004. "Signa vellere." In C. F. Konrad, ed., *Augusta auguria: Rerum humanarum et divinarum commentationes in honorem Jerzy Linderski*, 169–203. Stuttgart.
Konrad, C. F. 2015. "Lutatius and the *sortes Praenestinae*." *Hermes* 143: 153–71.
Konrad, C. F. 2016. "Polybius and the Consulship of Iunius Pullus." *Hermes* 144: 178–93.
Kroon, C. 1995. *Discourse Particles in Latin: A Study of* nam, enim, autem, vero, *and* at. Amsterdam.
Krostenko, B. A. 2000. "Beyond (Dis)belief: Rhetorical Form and Religious Symbol in Cicero's *de Divinatione*." *Transactions of the American Philological Association* 130: 353–91.
Krostenko, B. A. 2001. *Cicero, Catullus and the Language of Social Performance*. Chicago.
Kunkel, W., and R. Wittmann. 1995. *Staatsordnung und Staatspraxis der römischen Republik*. Vol. 2, *Die Magistratur*. Munich.
Ladewig, M. 2014. *Rom—die antike Seerepublik: Untersuchungen zur Thalassokratie der res publica populi romani von den Anfängen bis zur Begründung des Principat*. Stuttgart.
Langlands, R. 2018. *Exemplary Ethics in Ancient Rome*. Cambridge.
Laskaris, J. 2002. *The Art Is Long:* On the Sacred Disease *and the Scientific Tradition*. Leiden.
Latte, K. 1960. *Römische Religionsgeschichte*. Munich.
Laughton, E. 1964. *The Participle in Cicero*. London.
Laurand, L. 1911. "Les fins d'hexamètre dans les discours de Cicéron." *Revue de Philologie* 35: 75–88.
Lausberg, H. 1990. *Handbuch der literarischen Rhetorik*. 3rd ed. Stuttgart = *Handbook of Literary Rhetoric: A Foundation for Literary Study*. Tr. M. T. Bliss, A. Jansen, and D. E. Orton; ed. D. E. Orton and R. D. Anderson. Leiden, 1998.
Lebek, W. D. 1970. *Verba prisca: Die Anfänge des Archaisierens in der lateinischen Beredsamkeit und Geschichtsschreibung*. Göttingen.
Lebek, W. D. 1996. "Moneymaking on the Roman Stage." In W. J. Slater, ed., *Roman Theater and Society*. E. Togo Salmon Papers 1:29–48. Ann Arbor.
Lee, M.-K., ed. 2014. *Strategies of Argument: Essays in Ancient Ethics, Epistemology, and Logic*. Oxford.
Lehoux, D. 2007. "Drugs and the Delphic Oracle." *Classical World* 101.1: 41–56.

Lehoux, D. 2012. *What Did the Romans Know? An Inquiry into Science and Worldmaking*. Chicago.

Leighton, R. 2004. *Tarquinia: An Etruscan City*. London.

Lesky, E. 1950. *Die Zeugungs- und Vererbungslehren der Antike und ihr Nachwirken*. Akademie der Wissenschaften und Literatur, geistes- und sozialwissenschaftliche Klasse 1950 no. 19. Mainz.

Letzner, W. 2000. *Lucius Cornelius Sulla: Versuch einer Biographie*. Münster.

Leumann, M. 1977. *Lateinische Laut- und Formenlehre*. Munich.

Levin, S. 1989. "The Old Greek Oracles in Decline." *Aufstieg und Niedergang der römischen Welt* II.18.2: 1599–1649.

Levine, P. 1957. "The Original Design and the Publication of the *De natura deorum*." *Harvard Studies in Classical Philology* 62: 7–36.

Lévy, C. 1995. "Le mythe de la naissance de la civilisation chez Cicéron." In S. Cerasuolo, ed., *Mathesis e philia: Studi in onore di Marcello Gigante*, 155–68. Naples.

Lévy, C. 1997. "De Chrysippe à Posidonius: Variations sur le thème de la divination." In J.-G. Heintz, ed., *Oracles et prophéties dans l'antiquité*, 321–43. Paris.

Lévy, C. 2012. "Philosophical Life versus Political Life: An Impossible Choice for Cicero?" In W. Nicgorski, ed., *Cicero's Practical Philosophy*, 58–78. Notre Dame, IN.

Lévy, C. 2018. "De la rhétorique à la philosophie: Le rôle de la *temeritas* dans la pensée et l'oeuvre de Cicéron." In G. M. Müller and F. Mariani Zini, eds., *Philosophie in Rom—Römische Philosophie?: Kultur–, Literatur– und philosophiegeschichtliche Perspktiven*, 283–303. Berlin.

de Libero, L. 1992. *Obstruktion: Politische Praktiken im Senat und in der Volksversammlung der ausgehenden römischen Republik (70–49 v. Chr.)*. Stuttgart.

Liebeschuetz, J. H. W. G. 1979. *Continuity and Change in Roman Religion*. Oxford.

Linderski, J. 1972. "The Aedileship of Favonius, Curio the Younger, and Cicero's Election to the Augurate." *Harvard Studies in Classical Philology* 76: 181–200.

Linderski, J. 1982. "Cicero and Roman Divination." *Parola del Passato* 37: 12–38.

Linderski, J. 1986. "The Augural Law." *Aufstieg und Niedergang der Römischen Welt*. II 16.3: 2146–2312.

Linderski, J. 1995. *Roman Questions: Selected Papers*. Vol. 1. Stuttgart.

Lintott, A. 1999. *The Constitution of the Roman Republic*. Oxford.

Liuzzi, D., ed. 1983. *Nigidio figulo "astrologo e mago": Testimonianze e frammenti*. Lecce.

Lloyd, G. E. R. 1970. *Early Greek Science, Thales to Aristotle*. London.

Long, A. A. 2006. "Astrology: Arguments Pro and Contra." In A. A. Long, *From Epicurus to Epictetus: Studies in Greek and Roman Philosophy*, 128–54. Oxford.

Long, A. G. 2015. "Academic Eloquence and the End of Cicero's *De finibus*." *Ancient Philosophy* 35: 183–98.

Luciani, S. 2010. *Temps et éternité dans l'oeuvre philosophique de Cicéron*. Paris.

Luck, G. 1978. "On Cicero, *De fato* 5 and Related Passages." *American Journal of Philology* 99: 155–58.

MacBain, B. 1982. *Prodigy and Expiation: A Study in Religion and Politics in Republican Rome*. Brussels.

MacKendrick, P. 1989. *The Philosophical Books of Cicero*. New York.

Magnaldi, G. 1995. "Note in margine al *De divinatione* di Cicerone." *Quaderni del Dipartimento di filologia, linguistica e tradizione classica* 4: 59–73.

Mahy, T. 2013. "Antonius, Triumvir and Orator: Career, Style, and Effectiveness." In Steel and van der Blom, 329–44.

Manuwald, G., ed., tr., comm. 2007. Cicero, *Philippics* 3–9. 2 vols. Berlin.

Manuwald, G. 2016. Review of Ott 2013. *Klio* 77: 773–77.

Manuwald, G., ed., tr., comm. 2018. Cicero, *Agrarian Speeches*. Oxford.

Maras, D. F. 2012. "Scientists Declare the Fibula Praenestina and Its Inscription to Be Genuine 'beyond Reasonable Doubt.'" *Etruscan News* 14.

Margel, S. 2006. "Religio/Superstitio: La crise des institutions de Cicéron à Augustin." *Revue de Théologie et de Philosophie* 3rd ser. 138: 193–207.

Marouzeau, J. 1938. *L'ordre des mots dans la phrase latine*. Vol. 2, *Le verbe*. Paris.

Marshall, A. J. 1984. "Symbols and Showmanship in Roman Public Life: The *fasces*." *Phoenix* 38: 120–41.

Martin, P. M. 2014. "Entre prosopographie et politique: La figure et l'ascendance de Brutus dans le *Brutus*." In S. Aubert-Baillot and C. Guérin, eds., *Le* Brutus *de Cicéron: Rhétorique, politique et histoire culturelle*, 215–35. Leiden.

Matijevič, K. 2006. *Marcus Antonius: Consul—Proconsul—Staatsfeind; Die Politik der Jahre 44 und 43 v. Chr.* Rahden.

Maurizio, L. 1995. "Anthropology and Spirit Possession: A Reconsideration of the Pythia's Role at Delphi." *Journal of Hellenic Studies* 115: 69–86.

Meier, C. 1966. *Res publica amissa: Eine Studie zu Verfassung und Geschichte der späten römischen Republik*. Wiesbaden.

Melchior, A. 2008. "Twinned Fortunes and the Publication of Cicero's *Pro Milone*." *Classical Philology* 103: 282–97.

Merguet, H. 1887–94. *Lexikon zu den philosophischen Schriften Ciceros*. 3 vols. Jena.

Merlan, P. 1967. "Aristoteles' und Epikurs müssige Götter." *Zeitschrift für philosophische Forschung* 21: 485–98 = *Kleine philosophische Schriften*, ed. F. Merlan, 289–302. Hildesheim, 1976.

Miano, D. 2018. *Fortuna: Deity and Concept in Archaic and Republican Italy*. Oxford.

Mikalson, J. D. 2006. "Greek Religion: Continuity and Change in the Hellenistic Period." In G. R. Bugh, ed., *The Cambridge Companion to the Hellenistic World*, 208–22. Cambridge.

Mitchell, T. N. 1979. *Cicero: The Ascending Years*. New Haven.

Mommsen, T. 1887–88. *Römisches Staatsrecht.* 3 vols. in 5. Berlin.
Montero, S. 2006. *Augusto y las aves: Las aves en la Roma del Principado; prodigio, exhibición y consumo.* Barcelona.
Moraux, P. 1973. *Der Aristotelismus bei den Griechen von Andronikos bis Alexander von Aphrodisias.* Vol. 1. Berlin.
Moreau, P. 1982. *Clodiana religio: Un procès politique en 61 avant J.C.* Paris.
Morrell, K. 2017. *Pompey, Cato, and the Governance of the Roman Empire.* Oxford.
Mouritsen, H. 1998. *Italian Unification: A Study in Ancient and Modern Historiography.* London.
Mueller, H.-F. 2002. *Rome and Religion in Valerius Maximus.* London.
Mueller-Goldingen, C. 2003. "Wertewandel, Werteverfall und Wertestabilität in Ciceros *De re publica*." In Haltenhoff, Heil, and Mutschler, 119–36.
Mutschler, F.-H. 2003. "Geschichtsbetrachtung und Werteorientierung bei Nepos und Sallust." In Haltenhoff, Heil, and Mutschler, 259–85.
Näf, B. 2004. *Traum und Traumdeutung im Altertum.* Darmstadt.
Nagy, A. A. 2002. "*Superstitio et coniuratio.*" *Numen* 49: 178–92.
Nelsestuen, G. A. 2019. "A Matter of *Prudentia*: Atticus and His Friends in Nepos and Cicero." *TAPA* 149: 353–93.
Neugebauer, O., and H. B. Van Hoesen. 1959. *Greek Horoscopes.* Memoirs of the American Philosophical Society 48. Philadelphia.
Nisbet, R. G. M. 1992. "The Orator and the Reader: Manipulation and Response in Cicero's *Fifth Verrine*." In T. Woodman and J. Powell, eds., *Author and Audience in Latin Literature*, 1–17. Cambridge.
Noble, F. M. 2014. "Sulla and the Gods: Religion, Politics and Propaganda in the *Autobiography* of L. Cornelius Sulla." Diss. Newcastle.
North, J. 1990. "Diviners and Divination at Rome." In M. Beard and J. North, eds., *Pagan Priests: Religion and Power in the Ancient World*, 49–71. London.
Nougayrol, J. 1955. "Les rapports des haruspicines étrusque et assyro-babylonienne, et la foie d'argile de *Falerii Veteres* (Villa Giulia 3786)." *Comptes Rendus des Séances de l'Académie des Inscriptions et Belles-Lettres* 99: 509–19.
Oakley, S. P. 1997–2005. *A Commentary on Livy Books VI–X.* 4 vols. Oxford.
Ogilvie, R. M. 1965. *A Commentary on Livy Books 1–5.* Oxford.
Oksala, P. 1953. *Die griechischen Lehnwörter in den Prosaschriften Ciceros.* Helsinki.
Orlin, E. M. 1997. *Temples, Religion and Politics in the Roman Republic.* Leiden.
Osorio, P. 2019. Review of Cappello 2019. *Bryn Mawr Classical Review.* 2019.12.06.
Ott, F.-T. 2013. *Die zweite Philippica als Flugschrift in der späten Republik.* Berlin.
Otto, W. F. 1909. "Römische Sondergötter." *Rheinisches Museum* 64: 449–68.
Parke, H. W. 1988. *Sibyls and Sibylline Prophecy in Classical Antiquity.* Ed. B. C. McGing. London.
Parke, H. W., and D. E. W. Wormell. 1956. *The Delphic Oracle.* 2 vols. Oxford.

Paschall, D. 1936. "The Origin and Semantic Development of Latin *vitium*." *Transactions of the American Philological Association* 67: 219–31.

Pavis d'Escurac, H. 1981. "La pratique augurale romaine à la fin de la République: Scepticisme, tradition." In *Religion et culture dans la cité italienne de l'Antiquité à nos jours. Actes du colloque*, 27–39. Strasbourg.

Pease, A. S., ed., comm. 1920–23. *M. Tulli Ciceronis De divinatione libri duo.* Urbana (repr. Darmstadt, 1963).

Pelling, C., tr., comm. 2011. Plutarch, *Caesar*. Oxford.

Pendrick, G. J., ed., comm. 2002. *Antiphon the Sophist: The Fragments.* Cambridge.

Perlwitz, O. 1992. *Titus Pomponius Atticus: Untersuchungen zur Person eines einflussreichen Ritters in der ausgehenden Republik.* Stuttgart.

Pfeffer, F. 1976. *Studien zur Mantik in der Philosophie der Antike.* Meisenheim am Glan.

Piccaluga, G. 1976. "I Marsi e gli Hirpi." In *Magia: Studi di storia delle religioni in memoria di Raffaela Garosi*, 207–31. Rome.

Pieroni, S. 2016. "'Habeo' plus Perfect Participle in Cicero." *Pallas* 102: 127–35.

Pina Polo, F. 2011. *Consul at Rome: The Civil Functions of the Consuls in the Roman Republic.* Cambridge.

Pina Polo, F. 2016. "I, Cicero: Reflexions on Myself." In F. M. Simón, F. Pina Polo, J. M. Rodríguez, eds., *Autorretratos. La creación de la imagen personal en la antigüedad*, 101–14. Barcelona.

Pinkernell-Kreidt, S. 1997. "Das Erkennen des καιρός in Ciceros dritter Philippischer Rede." In B. Czapla, T. Lehmann, and S. Liell, eds., *Vir bonus dicendi peritus: Festschrift für Alfons Weische zum 65. Geburtstag*, 331–44. Wiesbaden.

Pinkster, H. 2015. *The Oxford Latin Syntax.* Vol. 1, *The Simple Sentence.* Oxford.

Pohlenz, M. 1978–80. *Die Stoa: Geschichte einer geistigen Bewegung.* 5th ed. 2 vols. Göttingen.

Potter, P., ed., tr. 2012. Hippocrates, *Generation, Nature of the Child, Diseases 4, Nature of Women, and Barrenness.* Cambridge, MA.

Poulle, B. 2010. "Remarques sur la voix prophétique de Junon Moneta." In D. Briquel, C. Février, and C. Guittard, eds., *Varietates fortunae: Religion et mythologie à Rome; Hommage à Jacqueline Champeaux*, 147–58. Paris.

Powell, J. G. F., ed., comm. 1988. Cicero, *Cato maior de senectute.* Cambridge.

Powell, J. G. F. 1995a. "Cicero's Translations from Greek." In Powell 1995b, 273–300.

Powell, J. G. F., ed. 1995b. *Cicero the Philosopher.* Oxford.

Powell, J. G. F. 2010. "Hyperbaton and Register in Cicero." In E. Dickey and A. Chahoud, eds., *Colloquial and Literary Latin*, 163–85. Cambridge.

Purcell, N. 1995. "Literate Games: Roman Urban Society and the Game of *alea*." *Past and Present* 147: 3–37.

Ramelli, I. 2003. *Cultura e religione etrusca nel mondo romano: La cultura etrusca dalla fine dall'indipendenza.* Alessandria.

Ramsey, J. T., ed., comm. 2003. Cicero, *Philippics I–II*. Cambridge.

Ramsey, J. T. Forthcoming. Asconius, *Commentaries on Speeches of Cicero*. Tr., comm. R. G Lewis, rev. J. T. Ramsey.

Ramsey, J. T., and K. Raaflaub. 2017. "Chronological Tables for Caesar's Wars (58–45 BCE)." *Histos* 11: 162–217.

Rasmussen, S. W. 2000. "Cicero's Stand on Prodigies: A Non-Existent Dilemma?" In R. L. Wildfang and J. Isager, eds., *Divination and Portents in the Roman World*, 9–24. Odense.

Rawson, E. 1985. *Intellectual Life in the Late Roman Republic*. London.

Rawson, E. 1991. *Roman Culture and Society: Collected Papers*. Oxford.

Regell, P. 1878. "De augurum publicorum libris, I." Diss. University of Frankfurt (Oder). Bratislava (repr. in P. Regell and C. Thulin, *Roman Augury and Etruscan Divination* [New York, 1975]).

Regell, P. 1882. *Fragmenta auguralia*. Progr. Hirschberg (repr. in P. Regell and C. Thulin, *Roman Augury and Etruscan Divination* [New York, 1975]).

Regell, P. 1893. *Commentarii in librorum auguralium fragmenta specimen*. Progr. Hirschberg (repr. in P. Regell and C. Thulin, *Roman Augury and Etruscan Divination* [New York, 1975]).

Reid, J. S., ed., comm. 1885. *M. Tulli Ciceronis Academica*. London.

Rein, E. 1919. *Die Schlangenhöhle von Lanuvium*. Helsinki.

Reinhold, M. 1970. *History of Purple as a Status Symbol in Antiquity*. Brussels.

Renberg, G. H. 2017. *Where Dreams May Come: Incubation Sanctuaries in the Greco-Roman World*. 2 vols. Leiden.

Repici, L. 1991. "Aristotele, gli stoici e il libro dei sogni nel *de divinatione* di Cicerone." *Métis: Anthropologie des mondes grecs anciens* 6: 167–203.

Repici, L. 1995. "Gli stoici e la divinazione secondo Cicerone." *Hermes* 123: 175–92.

Repici, L. 1996. "Il sapiente stoico, la divinazione, la città." *Quaderni di Storia* 44: 41–69.

Reynolds, L. D., ed. 1983. *Texts and Transmission: A Survey of the Latin Classics*. Oxford.

Richardson, L., Jr. 1992. *A New Topographical Dictionary of Ancient Rome*. Baltimore.

Riedweg, C. 2005. *Pythagoras: His Life, Teaching and Influence*. Tr. S. Rendall. Ithaca (orig. 2002).

Riemann, H. 1988. "*Praenestinae sorores*." *Mitteilungen des Deutschen Archaeologischen Instituts, Römische Abteilung* 95: 41–73.

Riginos, A. S. 1976. *Platonica: Anecdotes Concerning the Life and Writings of Plato*. Leiden.

Ripat, P. 2011. "Expelling Misconceptions: Astrologers at Rome." *Classical Philology* 106: 115–54.

Rising, T. 2015. "Caesar's Offer, Cicero's Rebuff, and the Two Land Commissions of 59 B.C." *Historia* 64: 419–27.

Roller, L. E. 1983. "The Legend of Midas." *Classical Antiquity* 2: 299–313.

Roller, M. B. 2018. *Models from the Roman Past: A World of Exempla*. Cambridge.

Roloff, K.-H. 1953. "Caerimonia." *Glotta* 32: 101–38.

Ronconi, F. 1998. "*De optimo genere oratorum*: Storia di un abbozzo." In *Appunti romani di filologia: Raccolta di studi e communicazioni di filologia, linguistica e letteratura greca e latina, prefazione di A. Masaracchia*, 43–68. Rome.

Rosenberger, V. 1992. *Bella et expeditiones: Die antike Terminologie der Kriege Roms*. Stuttgart.

Rosenberger, V. 1998. *Gezähmte Götter: Das Prodigienwesen der römischen Republik*. Stuttgart.

Rosenberger, V. 2007. "Republican *nobiles*: Controlling the *res publica*." In J. Rüpke, ed., *A Companion to Roman Religion*, 292–303. Malden, MA.

Rosenstein, N. S. 1990. *Imperatores victi: Military Defeat and Aristocratic Competition in the Middle and Late Republic*. Berkeley.

Rosenstein, N. S. 1995. "Sorting Out the Lot in Republican Rome." *American Journal of Philology* 116: 43–75.

Ruch, M. 1958. *Le préambule dans les œuvres philosophiques de Cicéron: Essai sur la genèse et l'art du dialogue*. Paris.

Rühl, M. 2019. *Ciceros Korrespondenz als Medium literarischen und gesellschaftlichen Handelns*. Leiden.

Rüpke, J. 1990. *Domi militiae: Die religiöse Konstruktion des Krieges in Rom*. Stuttgart.

Rüpke, J. 2008. *Fasti sacerdotum: A Prosopography of Pagan, Jewish and Christian Religious Officials in the City of Rome, 300 B.C. to A.D. 499*. Tr. D. M. B. Richardson. Oxford.

Rüpke, J. 2016. *Religious Deviance in the Roman World: Superstition or Individuality?* Tr. D. M. B. Richardson. Cambridge.

Rüpke, J., and N. Belayche. 2004–6. "Divination romaine." *Thesaurus cultus et rituum antiquorum*. 7 vols. + index. 3:79–104. Los Angeles.

Russo, F. 2005. "I carmina Marciana e le tradizioni sui Marcii." *Parola del Passato* 60: 5–32.

Sachot, M. 1991. "'Religio/superstitio.' Historique d'une subversion et d'un retournement." *Revue de L'Histoire des Religions* 208: 355–94.

Sambursky, S. 1956. "On the Possible and the Probable in Ancient Greece." *Osiris* 12: 35–48.

Sander, G. 1908. "Quaestiones de Ciceronis libris quos scripsit De divinatione." Diss. Göttingen.

Santangelo, F. 2011. "Pax deorum and Pontiffs." In J. H. Richardson and F. Santangelo, eds., *Priests and State in the Roman World*, 161–86. Stuttgart.

Santangelo, F. 2012. "Law and Divination in the Late Roman Republic." In O. Tellegen-Couperus, ed., *Law and Religion in the Roman Republic*, 31–54. Leiden.

Santangelo, F. 2013. *Divination, Prediction and the End of the Roman Republic.* Cambridge.

Santangelo, F. 2016a. *Marius*. London.

Santangelo, F. 2016b. Review of Schultz 2014. *Exemplaria Classica* 20: 309–14.

Santoro, M., ed., tr., comm. 2000. [Demetrio Lacone], *[La forma del dio] (PHerc. 1055)*. Naples.

Sassi, M. M. 1978. *Le teorie della percezione in Democrito*. Florence.

Satterfield, S. 2015. "Prodigies, the *pax deum* and the *ira deum*." *Classical Journal* 110: 431–45.

Sauer, J. 2007. *Argumentations- und Darstellungsformen im ersten Buch von Ciceros Schrift* De legibus. Heidelberg.

Schäfer, T. 1989. *Imperii insignia: Sella curulus und fasces; Zur Repräsentation römischer Magistrate.* Mitteilungen des Deutschen Archaeologischen Instituts, Römische Abteilung 29. Ergänzungsheft. Mainz.

Schallenberg, M. 2008. *Freiheit und Determinismus. Ein philosophischer Kommentar zu Ciceros Schrift* De fato. Berlin.

Schäublin, C. 1987. "Kritische und exegetische Bemerkungen zu Cicero, De divination II." *Museum Helveticum* 44: 181–90.

Schäublin, C. 1988. "Ciceros demosthenische Redezyklen: Ein Nachtrag." *Museum Helveticum* 45: 60–61.

Schäublin, C. 1989. "Weitere Bemerkungen zu Cicero, De divinatione." *Museum Helveticum* 46: 42–51.

Schäublin, C., ed., tr., comm. 1991. M. T. Cicero, *Über die Wahrsagung*. Munich.

Scheid, J. 1987–89. "La parole des dieux: L'originalité du dialogue des Romains avec leurs dieux." *Opus* 6: 125–36.

Scheid, J. 1998. "Les Livres Sibyllins et les archives des Quindécemvirs." In C. Moatti, ed., *La mémoire perdue: Recherches sur l'administration romaine*, 11–26. Rome.

Scheid, J. 2003. *An Introduction to Roman Religion*. Tr. J. Lloyd. Edinburgh (orig. 1998).

Scheid, J. 2007. "Les sens des rites: L'exemple romain." In J. Scheid, ed., *Rites et croyances dans les religions du monde romain*, 39–63. Vandoeuvres.

Scheid, J. 2012a. "Le rite des auspices à Rome: Quelle évolution? Réflexions sur la transformation de la divination publique des Romains entre le IIIe e le Ier siècle avant notre ère." In S. Georgoudi, R. K. Piettre, and F. Schmidt, eds., *La raison des signes: Présages, rites, destin dans les sociétés de la Mediterranée ancienne*, 109–28. Leiden.

Scheid, J. 2012b. "Roman Animal Sacrifice and the System of Being." In C. A. Faraone and F. S. Naiden, eds., *Greek and Roman Animal Sacrifice: Ancient Visions, Modern Observers*, 84–95. Cambridge.

Scheidel, W. 1999. "Emperors, Aristocrats, and the Grim Reaper: Towards a Demographic Profile of the Roman Élite." *Classical Quarterly* 49: 254–81.

Scheuermann, E. S. 2015. *Cicero und das Geld.* Frankfurt am Main.

Schierl, P., ed., comm. 2006. *Die Tragödien des Pacuvius.* Berlin.

Schilling, R. 1962. "À propos des 'exta': L'extispicine étrusque et la 'litatio' romaine." In M. Renard, ed., *Hommages à Albert Grenier*, 3:1371–78. Brussels.

Schneider, M. 2004. *Cicero "haruspex": Political Prognostication and the Viscera of a Diseased Body Politic.* Piscataway, NJ.

Schofield, M. 1983. "The Syllogisms of Zeno of Citium." *Phronesis* 28: 31–58.

Schofield, M. 1986. "Cicero for and against Divination." *Journal of Roman Studies* 76: 47–65.

Schofield, M. 1999. "Academic Epistemology." In K. Algra, J. Barnes, J. Mansfeld, and M. Schofield, eds., *The Cambridge History of Hellenistic Philosophy*, 323–50. Cambridge.

Schofield, M. 2002. "Academic Therapy: Philo of Larissa and Cicero's Project in the *Tusculans*." In G. Clark and T. Rajak, eds., *Philosophy and Power in the Graeco-Roman World: Essays in Honour of Miriam Griffin*, 92–107. Oxford.

Schofield, M. 2008. "Ciceronian Dialogue." In S. Goldhill, ed., *The End of Dialogue in Antiquity*, 63–84. Cambridge.

Scholz, P. 2011. *Den Vätern folgen: Sozialisation und Erziehung der republikanischen Senatsaristokratie.* Berlin.

Schultz, C. E. 2000. *Women's Religious Activity in the Roman Republic.* Chapel Hill.

Schultz, C. E. 2009. "Argument and Anecdote in Cicero's *De Divinatione*." In P. B. Harvey Jr. and C. Conybeare, eds., *Maxima debetur magistro reverentia: Essays on Rome and the Roman Tradtion in Honor of Russell T. Scott*, 193–206. Como.

Schultz, C. E. 2014. *Commentary on Cicero,* De Divinatione I. Ann Arbor.

Schulze, W. 1904. *Zur Geschichte lateinischer Eigennamen.* Berlin.

Scullard, H. H. 1981. *Festivals and Ceremonies of the Roman Republic.* London.

Seager, R. 1973. "Iusta Catilinae." *Historia* 22: 240–48.

Seager, R. 2002. *Pompey the Great: A Political Biography.* 2nd ed. Oxford.

Sedley, D. N. 1993. "Chrysippus on Psychophysical Causality." In J. Brunschwig and M. C. Nussbaum, eds., *Passions and Perceptions: Studies in Hellenistic Philosophy of Mind*, 313–31. Cambridge.

Sedley, D. N. 1997. "The Ethics of Brutus and Cassius." *Journal of Roman Studies* 87: 41–53.

Sedley, D. N. 2007. *Creationism and Its Critics in Antiquity.* Berkeley.

Sedley, D. N. 2013a. "The Atheist Underground." In V. Harte and M. Lane, eds., Politeia *in Greek and Roman Philosophy*, 329–48. Cambridge.

Sedley, D. N. 2013b. "Cicero and the *Timaeus*." In M. Schofield, ed., *Aristotle, Plato and Pythagoreanism in the First Century B.C.*, 187–205. Cambridge.

Sedley, D. N. 2013c. "From the Pre-Socratics to the Hellenistic Age." In S. Bullivant and M. Ruse, eds., *The Oxford Handbook of Atheism*, 139–51. Oxford.

Sedley, D. N. 2019. "Epicurus on Dialectic." In Bénatouïl, 82–113.

Seppänen, M., and A. Lampinen. 2019. "'Interpreters of Interpreters': Oracular and Grammatical Hermeneutics." *Mnemosyne* 72: 883–907.

Shackleton Bailey, D. R., ed., tr., comm. 1965–70. *Cicero's Letters to Atticus*. 7 vols. Cambridge.

Shackleton Bailey, D. R. 1971. *Cicero*. London.

Sharples, R. W., ed., tr., comm. 1991. *Cicero: On Fate* (De fato) *and Boethius: The Consolation of Philosophy* (Philosophiae consolationis) *IV.5–7, V*. Warminster.

Sharples, R. W. 1996. *Stoics, Epicureans and Sceptics: An Introduction to Hellenistic Philosophy*. London.

Sharples, R. W. 2001. "Dicaearchus on the Soul and on Divination." In W. W. Fortenbaugh and E. Schütrumpf, eds., *Dicaearchus of Messana: Text, Translation, and Discussion*, 143–73. New Brunswick, NJ.

Skutsch., O., ed., comm. 1985. *The* Annals *of Q. Ennius*. Oxford.

Solmsen, F. 1960. *Aristotle's System of the Physical World*. Ithaca.

Solodow, J. B. 1978. *The Latin Particle* quidem. Boulder.

Spahlinger, L. 2005. *Tulliana simplicitas: Zu Form und Funktion des Zitats in den philosophischen Dialogen Ciceros*. Göttingen.

Spiller, H., J. Hale, and J. De Boer. 2002. "The Delphic Oracle: A Multidisciplinary Defense of the Gaseous Vent Theory." *Clinical Toxicology* 40: 189–96.

Spiller, H., J. De Boer, J. Hale, and J. Chanton. 2008. "Gaseous Emissions at the Site of the Delphic Oracle: Assessing the Ancient Evidence." *Clinical Toxicology* 45: 487–88.

Staveley, E. S. 1972. *Greek and Roman Voting and Elections*. London.

Steel, C.. 2005. *Reading Cicero*. London.

Steel, C. 2012. "Cicero's Autobiography: Narratives of Success in the Pre-Consular Orations." *Cahiers Glotz* 23: 251–66.

Steel, C., and H. van der Blom, eds. 2013. *Community and Communication: Oratory and Politics in Republican Rome*. Oxford.

Stein, P. 1930. "Die Senatssitzungen der Ciceronischen Zeit." Diss. Münster.

Stevenson, T. 2009. "Antony as 'Tyrant' in Cicero's First Philippic." *Ramus* 38: 174–86.

Stok, F. 1981. *Omnes stultos insanire*. Pisa.

Strasburger, H. 1990. *Ciceros philosophisches Spätwerk als Aufruf gegen die Herrschaft Caesars*. Ed. G. Strasburger. Hildesheim.

Striker, G. 1980. "Sceptical Strategies." In M. Schofield, M. Burnyeat, and J. Barnes, eds., *Doubt and Dogmatism: Studies in Hellenistic Epistemology*, 54–83. Oxford.

Stroh, W. 1983. "Ciceros demosthenische Redezyklen." *Museum Helveticum* 40: 35–50.

Stroup, S. C. 2010. *Catullus, Cicero, and a Society of Patrons: The Generation of the Text*. Cambridge.

Struck, P. 2016. *Divination and Human Nature: A Cognitive History of Intuition in Classical Antiquity*. Princeton.

Stucchi, S. 2013. "Notazioni sul concetto di *elegantia* in Cicerone." *Latomus* 72: 642–59.

Sullivan, R. D. 1990. *Near Eastern Royalty and Rome, 100–30 BC*. Toronto.

Sutton, D. 1981. "Critias and Atheism." *Classical Quarterly* 31: 33–38.

Syme, R. 1939. *The Roman Revolution*. Oxford (corr. repr. 1952).

Talanga, J. 1986. *Zukunftsurteile und Fatum: Eine Untersuchung über Aristoteles'* De interpretatione *9 und Ciceros* De fato, *mit einem Überblick über die spätantiken Heimarmene-Lehren*. Bonn.

Tarrant, H. 2000. "Recollection and Prophecy in the *De divinatione*." *Phronesis* 45: 64–76.

Tatum, W. J. 1999. *The Patrician Tribune P. Clodius Pulcher*. Chapel Hill.

Thompson, S. 1955. *Motif-Index of Folk Literature*. 6 vols. Bloomington.

Thorsrud, H. 2010. "Arcesilaus and Carneades." In R. Bett, ed., *The Cambridge Companion to Ancient Skepticism*, 58–80. Cambridge.

Thulin, C. O. 1905–9. *Die etruskische Disciplin*. 3 vols. Gothenburg (repr. Darmstadt, 1968).

Thulin, C. O. 1906. *Scriptorum disciplinae Etruscae fragmenta*. Berlin (repr. in P. Regell and C. Thulin, *Roman Augury and Etruscan Divination* [New York, 1975]).

Timpanaro, S., ed., tr., comm. 1988. *Cicerone: Della divinazione*. Milan.

Timpanaro, S. 1994. "Alcuni fraintendimenti del *De divinatione*." In S. Timpanaro, *Nuovi contributi di filologia e storia della lingua latina*, 241–64. Bologna.

Toland, J. 1726. *A Collection of Several Pieces*. London.

Treggiari, S. 2007. *Terentia, Tullia and Publilia: The Women of Cicero's Family*. London.

Tucci, P. L. 2005. "'Where High Moneta Leads Her Steps Sublime.' The 'Tabularium' and the Temple of Juno Moneta." *Journal of Roman Archaeology* 18: 6–33.

Tucci, P. L. 2014. "A New Look at the *Tabularium* and the Capitoline Hill." *Atti della Pontificia Accademia Romana di Archeologia, Rendiconti* 86: 43–123.

Turfa, J. M. 2012. *Divining the Etruscan World: The* Brontoscopic Calendar *and Religious Practice*. Cambridge.

Usher, S. 2010. "Cicero's *First Philippic* and the Fall of the Republic." *Bulletin of the Institute of Classical Studies* 53: 129–36.

van der Blom, H. 2010. *Cicero's Role Models: The Political Strategy of a Newcomer*. Oxford.

van der Blom, H. 2016. *Oratory and Political Career in the Late Roman Republic*. Cambridge.

van der Eijk, P. 1993. "Aristotelian Elements in Cicero's 'De divinatione.'" *Philologus* 137: 223–31.

van der Meer, L. B. 1987. *The Bronze Liver of Piacenza: Analysis of a Polytheistic Structure.* Amsterdam.

Van Hove, R. 2019. "A Dream on Trial: The Contest of Oracular Interpretations and Authorities in Hyperides' *In Defence of Euxenippus.*" *Mnemosyne* 72: 405–36.

Versnel, H. R. 1981. "Self-Sacrifice, Compensation, and the Anonymous Gods." In O. Reverdin and J. Rudhardt, eds., *Le Sacrifice dans l'Antiquité*, 135–85. Vandoeuvres.

Versnel, H. R. 1990–93. *Inconsistencies in Greek and Roman Religion.* 2 vols. Leiden.

Vetter, E. 1953. *Handbuch der italischen Dialekte.* Heidelberg.

Voltaire. 1968–2018. *The Complete Works of Voltaire.* Ed. T. Besterman, W. H. Barber, U. Kölving, A. Mason, and N. Cronk. 144 vols. Geneva.

Ward, A. M. 1977. *Marcus Crassus and the Late Roman Republic.* Columbia, MO.

Wardle, D., tr., comm. 2006. Cicero, *On Divination Book 1.* Oxford.

Weidemann, H., ed., tr., comm. 2019. Cicero, *Über das Schicksal.* Berlin.

Weinstock, S. 1950. "C. Fonteius Capito and the Libri Tagetici." *Papers of the British School at Rome* 18: 44–49.

Weinstock, S. 1951. "Libri fulgurales." *Papers of the British School at Rome* 19: 122–53.

Weiss, M. 2009. *Outline of the Historical and Comparative Grammar of Latin.* Ann Arbor.

Welch, K. 1996. "T. Pomponius Atticus: A Banker in Politics?" *Historia* 45: 450–71.

Whibley, L. 1931. *A Companion to Greek Studies.* Cambridge (repr. New York, 1963).

Whitmarsh, T. 2015. *Battling the Gods: Atheism in the Ancient World.* New York.

Wilkins, J. 1710. *Of Principles and Duties of Natural Religion.* 6th ed. London.

Wilkinson, L. P. 1963. *Golden Latin Artistry.* Cambridge.

Wiseman, T. P. 1995. *Remus: A Roman Myth.* Cambridge.

Wissowa, G. 1904. "Echte und falsche 'Sondergötter' in der römischen Religion." In *Gesammelte Abhandlungen zur römischen Religions- und Stadtgeschichte*, 304–26. Munich (repr. New York, 1975).

Wissowa, G. 1912. *Religion und Kultus der Römer.* 2nd ed. Munich (repr. 1971).

Wistrand, M. 1979. Cicero imperator: *Studies in Cicero's Correspondence 51–47 B.C.* Gothenburg.

Wood, J. R. 1980. "The Myth of Tages." *Latomus* 39: 325–44.

Woolf, R. 2015. *Cicero: The Philosophy of a Roman Sceptic.* London.

Wright, A. 2001. "The Death of Cicero: Forming a Tradition; The Contamination of History." *Historia* 50: 436–52.

Wülker, L. 1903. *Die geschichtliche Entwicklung des Prodigienwesens bei den Römern: Studien zur Geschichte und Überlieferung der Staatsprodigien.* Leipzig.

Wynne, J. P. F. 2014. "Learned and Wise: Cotta the Sceptic in Cicero's *On the Nature of the Gods*." *Oxford Studies in Ancient Philosophy* 47: 245–73.

Wynne, J. P. F. 2019. *Cicero on the Philosophy of Religion*: On the Nature of the Gods *and* On Divination. Cambridge.

Zellmer, E. 1976. *Die lateinischen Wörter auf -ura.* 2nd ed. Frankfurt am Main.

Zetzel, J. E. G., ed., comm. 1995. Cicero, *De re publica: Selections.* Cambridge.

Zielinski, T. 1929. *Cicero im Wandel der Jahrhunderte.* 4th ed. Leipzig (repr. Stuttgart, 1967).

Zillinger, W. 1911. *Cicero und die altrömischen Dichter*. Würzburg.

Ziolkowski, A. 1987. "Q. Lutatius Cerco cos. 241 and the 'sortes Fortunae Primigeniae.'" *Civiltà Classica e Cristiana* 8: 319–32.

Index of Greek Words and Phrases

Index of Latin Words and Phrases

Index of Topics

Index of Proper Names

Dialogue-characters are generally not included, though their real-life counterparts are.